EXPLORING THE LAND OF OOO

EXPLORING THE LAND OF OOO

An Unofficial Overview and Production History
of Cartoon Network's *Adventure Time*

PAUL A. THOMAS

UNIVERSITY PRESS OF MISSISSIPPI / JACKSON

The University Press of Mississippi is the scholarly publishing agency of the Mississippi Institutions of Higher Learning: Alcorn State University, Delta State University, Jackson State University, Mississippi State University, Mississippi University for Women, Mississippi Valley State University, University of Mississippi, and University of Southern Mississippi.

www.upress.state.ms.us

The University Press of Mississippi is a member of the Association of University Presses.

Copyright © 2023 by University Press of Mississippi
All rights reserved

First printing 2023

∞

Library of Congress Cataloging-in-Publication Data

Names: Thomas, Paul A., 1992– author.
Title: Exploring the land of Ooo : an unofficial overview and production history of Cartoon Network's "Adventure time" / Paul A. Thomas.
Description: Jackson : University Press of Mississippi, 2023. | Includes bibliographical references and index.
Identifiers: LCCN 2023006030 (print) | LCCN 2023006031 (ebook) | ISBN 9781496846686 (hardback) | ISBN 9781496846693 (trade paperback) | ISBN 9781496846709 (epub) | ISBN 9781496846716 (epub) | ISBN 9781496846723 (pdf) | ISBN 9781496846730 (pdf)
Subjects: LCSH: Adventure time (Television program)—History and criticism. | Children's television programs—United States—History and criticism. | Cartoon characters—United States. | Animated television programs—United States—History and criticism.
Classification: LCC PN1992.77.A29 T466 2023 (print) | LCC PN1992.77.A29 (ebook) | DDC 791.45/72—dc23/eng/20230419
LC record available at https://lccn.loc.gov/2023006030
LC ebook record available at https://lccn.loc.gov/2023006031

British Library Cataloging-in-Publication Data available

To Trina—thanks for being the Marceline to my Bubblegum

CONTENTS

Acknowledgments ix
Introduction: "C'mon, Grab Your Friends . . .". 3

Part I: Who's Who in the Land of Ooo? Character Profiles

1. Two Rad Bros: Finn the Human and Jake the Dog. 15
2. Sugar and Spice: Princess Bubblegum and Marceline the
   Vampire Queen. 30
3. "Best Friends [and Foes] in the World": The Ensemble Characters. . . . 53
4. The "C-Listers": Other Characters of Note 76

Part II: Come Along with Me: A Production History of *Adventure Time*

5. Behind the Easel: How an Episode Was Made 97
6. The Fun Begins: The Pilot and Season 1. 105
7. From Cult Favorite to Mainstream Hit: Seasons 2–5 123
8. Coming of Age in Ooo: Seasons 6 and Beyond 148
9. Good Jubies: The Guest-Animated Episodes. 174

Part III: The Wider World of *Adventure Time*

10. The Institute of So Und: The Music of *Adventure Time* 199
11. The Ancillary Adventures of Finn and Jake:
    Comics, Video Games, and More. 232
12. Utter Finndemonium! The Ins and Outs of the
    Adventure Time Fandom 251
Conclusion: The Fun Will Never End 275

Notes. 277
Index. 317

ACKNOWLEDGMENTS

There are numerous individuals who helped to make this book a reality. Special thanks go to all the crew members, series affiliates, and fans who have shared their valuable insights with me over the last few years. I would also like to thank Jack Mullin, Ryan Witt, Asia Martusia, Cynthia Zhang, and several anonymous peer reviewers for reading through chapter drafts and offering me suggestions. Your comments and support have made this work a better book; let's be stupid forever!

EXPLORING THE LAND OF OOO

Introduction

"C'MON, GRAB YOUR FRIENDS..."

When I was a child growing up in the nineties, I watched a lot of cartoons. I had a soft spot for Nickelodeon shows like *Hey, Arnold!*, *Doug*, and *Rugrats*, and the CBS program *Garfield and Friends*, but the truth is that I would watch pretty much anything animated if given the chance. I liked media that had silly set pieces, wacky dialogue, and zany action. Most cartoons scratched that itch. My love for animation was so intense that in elementary school, I tried my hand at cartooning, and I even toyed around with the idea of one day entering the cartoon industry.

Unfortunately, as I grew older and "matured" (read: began to internalize many of my interests so as to not appear too "weird" to my judgmental peers), my love of cartoons fell to the wayside. (It was childish, I told myself. I needed to leave it in the past and "grow up.") Instead, I began preoccupying myself with other hobbies, like reading fantasy literature, playing computer games, and performing music. By the time I graduated from high school and entered into the "adult world," my interest in cartoons was a thing of the past.

Or so I thought...

Things started to change when I went to university in 2011. I roomed in a dorm with fifty other students, several of whom were art majors with eclectic tastes in popular culture. This meant I often found myself engrossed in conversations about the merits or defects of contemporary animation. During one discussion in particular, a friend of mine suggested that I watch a silly cartoon called *Adventure Time* about a boy named Finn and a magic dog named Jake. At the time, I had only seen a few snippets of the show, which, to be honest, had not impressed me that much; this disinterest was largely due to my ignorance, as I erroneously assumed that *Adventure Time* was some sort of hyperactive nonsense factory, grounded solely on "random" humor and gross-out comedy. (Oh, how naive I was...)

My limited understanding of the show persisted until the start of the fall 2012 semester. During the afternoon on a day in late August, I was chatting with my hall-mates in our communal TV room when I noticed the friend who had earlier recommended *Adventure Time* sitting in the corner. He was looking at something on his computer and laughing. Always in the mood for something funny, I meandered over and saw that he was watching one of the newest episodes of *Adventure Time* (specifically Season 4's "Sons of Mars," in which the main characters journey to Mars and meet Abraham Lincoln). What I saw on that computer screen was captivating. The show was overflowing with the lushest of colors, it had a magnificent handle on made-up language, and its humor was versatile.

Perhaps it is corny to say, but I felt something deep within me. It was a sort of pure, unmediated joy—the kind I remembered feeling as a child when I would wake up early to watch Saturday morning cartoons or when I would draw a comic strip that usually made only myself laugh. That night, I queued up the first episode of *Adventure Time*, "Slumber Party Panic," and took the deep dive into the Land of Ooo; I binged the rest of the series soon thereafter, and by Christmas of that year, I was hooked.

When 2013 rolled around, I was purchasing merchandise and joining online fan communities made up of people who were just as passionate about the show as I was. Then, in the summer of 2014, I took my interest to the next level by starting a Tumblr blog titled GunterFan1992, on which I posted my thoughts about individual episodes. I also used this site to reblog production updates and share artwork made by the show's crew members. Hardly anyone paid me attention when I made my first few posts, but in time, more and more people were dropping by. Within a few months, I had somehow amassed several thousand followers.

As my readership continued to grow, I decided to mix things up a bit, so, in July of 2015, I reached out to some of the folks who had worked on the show, hoping to conduct "mini-interviews" about the show's production via email. At the time, I firmly believed that only one or two artists would bother to respond, so consider my surprise when almost every single person whom I messaged agreed to my request. Within no time, I was chatting with the writers and producers of one of my favorite television programs, learning the behind-the-scenes details which fans are so often eager to hear about. After posting transcripts of these interviews on my Tumblr, I gained even more followers, and at one point, Adam Muto (the *Adventure Time* showrunner during Seasons 5–10) was even following my blog!

In September 2018, just after the *Adventure Time* finale aired, I decided to write a few paragraphs about what made the show special as a sort of mourning exercise: I wrote about Marceline and Bubblegum, I began explicating the show's complex mythology, and I delved into the Ice King's tragic backstory. In only a handful of days, a few paragraphs had grown into a few pages, which in turn grew into a few dozen essays. Several weeks later, I reached out to the writers and storyboard artists with whom I had previously corresponded, inquiring if they were once again interested in discussing their work. These informal email chats soon evolved into bona fide online interviews, and in time I had a nice little trove of production secrets about the show's creation. During the latter part of 2018, I started collating my personal musings with the information provided to me by my contacts, and soon I had an embryonic manuscript focused on all things *Adventure Time*.

After months of fine-tuning, the first edition of this book was published on July 7, 2020, by the University of Kansas Libraries. Feedback was immediate and overwhelmingly positive, with fans from across the globe reaching out to share their thoughts about the book. Several members of the *Adventure Time* production staff also had nice things to say, and I even exchanged emails with Adam Muto, who thanked me for taking the time and effort to do an in-depth look at the show's history. But while the book was well-received by those whose opinions I cared the most about, for some reason, I could not help but feel that it was unfinished; after all, there was so much information about the show that still needed to be documented!

I thus continued to collect bits and pieces of production information, and in only a few months' time, I had assembled dozens of pages of unreleased interview write-ups, recently unearthed production secrets, and other assorted facts about the show's creation. I then began integrating this new material into my original manuscript—a task that quickly spiraled into a total rewrite of the original. At the end of 2020, I reached out to the University Press of Mississippi—a scholarly publisher that has released several fascinating works on animation, such as Tim Lawson and Alisa Persons's *The Magic Behind the Voices: A Who's Who of Cartoon Voice Actors* (2004), Timothy S. Susanin's *Walt before Mickey: Disney's Early Years, 1919–1928* (2014), and Ross Anderson's *Pulling a Rabbit out of a Hat: The Making of "Roger Rabbit"* (2019)—and I inquired if they were interested in publishing a revised and substantially expanded edition of my book. Their answer? An enthusiastic yes!

Now, after almost four years of thinking, interviewing, writing, editing, publishing, rewriting, re-editing, and republishing, here we are. It is not hyperbole to say that I poured my heart into the writing of this book, and consequently it functions as both an overview of and a love letter to a series about which I care deeply.

...

This book is an overview and production history of *Adventure Time*, the exuberant cartoon series created by Pendleton Ward that aired from 2010–18 on

Cartoon Network. Like most cartoons, *Adventure Time* was written primarily for children, but unlike many others, it managed to also amass a fan following of teenagers and young adults, almost all of whom were drawn to the series because of its distinct sense of humor, bold aesthetic choices, and memorable characters. The show was also a critical darling, and during its original run, it netted three Annie Awards, eight Emmys, and a coveted Peabody—all while earning accolades from publications like the *New Yorker* and the *Los Angeles Times*. Although the series finished its original run in 2018, the program still has legions of fans and is credited by many in the animation world as the catalyst that ushered in a new golden age of animation.

In the mid-2010s, it seemed like *Adventure Time* was everywhere—from t-shirts sold in malls to Macy's Day Parade balloons. But while it is undeniable that *Adventure Time* grew into something of a pop culture phenomenon, only a few books and journal articles have looked at the show through a scholarly lens. What is more, most of the research about the show was published roughly half a decade ago, during the middle of the show's run. This book (which I began writing just after the *Adventure Time* series finale "Come Along with Me" aired in 2018 and which I finished in 2022, after the release of the *Distant Lands* specials) is my attempt to present an overview of the show that is both holistic and up to date.

Chances are that the person reading this book has a basic understanding of *Adventure Time*, but just to be safe, let me recap the premise of the series: set in the fantastical Land of Ooo, *Adventure Time* follows the colorful escapades of two brothers: Finn the Human and Jake the Dog. While Finn is just a normal human teenager, Jake is a talking canine with an ability to shapeshift that he and his brother often use (and occasionally abuse) to solve life's problems. The two live in a rustic tree fort with their friend, the sentient video game console BMO.

When they are not kicking back or off exploring, Finn and Jake serve as the *de facto* knights of the Candy Kingdom, a city-state ruled by the benevolent but uber-utilitarian Princess Bubblegum, who, as her name suggests, is made from chewing gum. Finn and Jake also spend time with their many friends, including Marceline the Vampire Queen (a vampiric rocker chick whose tough and apathetic exterior hides a kind, tortured soul), Lumpy Space Princess (a spoiled and obnoxious drama queen who hails from an alien dimension known as "Lumpy Space"), and Flame Princess (the sweet but short-tempered princess of the Fire Kingdom). At other times, Finn and Jake find themselves trying to foil the plans of the misguided Ice King (a lonely wizard whose insanity is matched in intensity only by his social ineptitude) or their arch-nemesis, the Lich (a primordial entity whose driving purpose is to extinguish all life in the multiverse).

Finn and Jake's Ooo is a dreamlike realm, inhabited by unusual characters and whimsical creatures, but this cheerful exterior belies a darkness, for Ooo is actually the shattered remnants of Earth—*our* Earth—one thousand years in the future, following a calamitous thermonuclear conflict known as the "Mushroom War." This war is never discussed directly in the series, but clues scattered across various episodes suggest that it occurred sometime during the early twenty-first century, killing billions and leaving the planet in shambles; so thorough was this destruction that for most of the series, Finn believes that he is the only human left in existence. But while this nuclear holocaust was undeniably horrific, it did have one positive effect: It reintroduced into the world magic—a fundamental aspect of creation that had for the most part been dormant on Earth for millions of years. This means that the Ooo inhabited by Finn and Jake is something of a contradiction, being both a radioactive wasteland full of monsters as well as an enchanted paradise abounding in effervescent magic.

"WHAT THE CABBAGE!?": EXPLAINING THE POPULARITY

People who watch the series for the first time—especially after hearing people go on about how good it is—can sometimes be put off by its tone. This is understandable, as the earliest seasons are defined by a certain, shall we say, juvenility (for frame of reference, the show's first episode, "Slumber Party Panic," ends with a fart joke non sequitur). But as with many great works of pop culture, *Adventure Time* matured as it went along, meaning that while early episodes are often predicated on standard cartoon hijinks and "childish" humor, latter-series episodes often weave together topics as heavy as sexuality, depression, existentialism, and even the inevitability of death.

Much of this evolution was the result of the series' interest in character growth, which is perhaps most obvious when considering the show's main character, Finn. At the beginning of the series, he is a wide-eyed child of twelve, but by the time of *Adventure Time*'s tenth-season finale, he is seventeen and on the cusp of manhood. In the intervening episodes, we the audience journey with Finn as he discovers the joys of life (e.g., video games, ice cream waffles) and its pitfalls (e.g., heart break, abandonment).[1] But it is not just Finn who grows; in fact, many of the show's more outwardly flamboyant characters—like Princess Bubblegum, Marceline the Vampire Queen, and even the villainous Ice King—start off as one-dimensional archetypes before metamorphosing into multifaceted individuals with rich inner lives. It is this sort of character development that led James Poniewozik of the *New York Times* to conclude that "material of great drama . . . lies . . . under [the show's] confectionery surface" and that, ultimately, the show is a "wonderland of broken, misfit toys learning to fix one another."[2]

All this talk about *Adventure Time* "maturing" may give a reader the impression that over its ten-season run, the show became "serious" and lost its goofy sense of humor. This is incorrect, and even at its most pensive, *Adventure Time* was able to find laughter in almost any situation—be it the mundane, the absurd, or the flatulent.

It is also worth noting that *Adventure Time*'s sense of humor was always a bit different in that it was fundamentally kind. Characters are not usually jerkasses to one another, and if they are, it is in service to a larger point and not just for cheap laughs. This is in stark contrast to the many shows that encourage viewers to laugh *at* the main characters, rather than *with* them.

And contrary to the popular understanding of the show's humor as "random" or "just for stoners,"[3] most of the show's jokes are clever, working on different levels. This is not to say that "you have to have a very high IQ to understand" *Adventure Time*—simply that the series is versatile and can be enjoyed by diverse audiences, including everyone from preliterate school children to graduate students.[4]

This last point has generated much discussion: It is understandable why a cartoon might gain popularity with children, but why did a show like *Adventure Time* become so popular with the teen and college sets? Many commentators invoke what I call the "nostalgia theory" to answer this question. A textbook example of this can be found in a 2012 video essay published by the PBS Idea Channel, in which host Mike Rugnetta argues that watching "*Adventure Time* is like remembering your childhood . . . [and] ach[ing] for a time passed that you can't recreate."[5] A year later, Jennifer Luxton would write something similar when she snarked: "In a time when nostalgia reigns supreme . . . it's understandable why adults may want to revisit their childhood through a cartoon for grown-ups. . . . *Adventure Time* jumps in with infantile innocence and the right amount of twisted humor to lure in even the most discretionary man-child."[6]

While critical theorist Grzegorz Czemiel concedes that *Adventure Time* has nostalgic aspects—in that it "offer[s] a trip down memory lane to the world of 8-bit consoles, classic role-playing games, bouts of gorging on candy, and agonizing over how to speak to girls'"[7]—he attributes the show's popularity not simply to a yearning for the "good old days," but rather to its fundamentally "cute" aesthetic. Citing the writings of critical theorist Sianne Ngai, Czemiel contends that cuteness as an aesthetic category is deeply ambiguous, being "the site of a surprisingly complex power struggle" that functions as both "a form of resistance and a capitalist pacification."[8] Czemiel argues that

Adventure Time explicitly reflects this ambiguity in its cuteness by "moving freely between the childish and the mature,"[9] thereby subverting expectations of "proper" adulthood.

For late millennials and early zoomers—two demographic cohorts slated to inherit a world demarcated by late capitalism's many failings (e.g., global warming, debt crises, housing problems)—this "cute" aesthetic is appealing; given that it was the so-called "proper adults" who caused many of the problems that plague the world now, why would millennials or zoomers want to emulate their predecessors' "proper adult" behavior? Czemiel thus concludes that young adults are drawn to *Adventure Time* because its cuteness offers a way to make "new subjectivities . . . [and] ontologies" that will allow humans to overcome future obstacles.[10]

A synthesis of the nostalgia theory and Czemiel's argument can arguably be found in a 2016 article on the *kawaii* culture of Japan by design theorist Hui-Ying Kerr, who writes:

> Looking at the adult landscape, with its pressures of debt, competition and responsibility, it is no wonder that people want to escape into the infinite time, space and promise of childhood. Cute becomes a way of resisting the adult world. It's not just a means of escape and denial, but also a way to fight back against the curtailment of possibility. . . . In the West, cute becomes a foil for millennials against the diminishing of privileges that mark the end of the late-20th century as a Golden Age. . . . Childhood means the luxury of not growing up, but also denial of adulthood and the refusal of responsibility. But while *kawaii* may seem like a closing of one door, held in its small furled fist is a key that opens another. To be simultaneously adult and child means to straddle both worlds, a symbol of resistance and boundless possibility.[11]

On one hand, Kerr's assertion recalls the nostalgia theory's focus on the yearning to "escape" into the idyllic past that is childhood. On the other hand, it recalls Czemiel's argument that cuteness—and thus, by extension, the cuteness of *Adventure Time*—is an aesthetic category that, while commercially exploited, can be used to push back against a cold capitalist world. Applying Kerr's full argument to *Adventure Time*, I think it is reasonable to conclude that the show's sizable teen and adult following can be at least partially attributed to its nostalgic *and* cute aesthetic, which simultaneously reminds viewers of their childhood while offering them a new, radical approach to adulthood.

(Also, the show has fart jokes!)

THEORETICAL FIGHTONOMICS: BOOK OUTLINE

To make this book easier to navigate, I have organized it into three sections. The first, entitled "Who's Who in the Land of Ooo," is composed of chapters that survey the show's characters. In addition to detailing behind-the-scenes information about how Finn, Jake, and their many friends came to be, this part of the book also discusses how the characters developed over the course of the show's run and how they were received by fans and critics.

Part 2, "Come Along with Me," documents the production of the show. In the first chapter, "Behind the Easel," I explicate the process by which an average *Adventure Time* episode was storyboarded and animated. In the second chapter, "The Fun Begins," I dive into the history of the show by detailing how the *Adventure Time* pilot and the show's first season were produced. The following chapter, "From Cult Favorite to Mainstream Hit" tracks *Adventure Time*'s continued development during Seasons 2–5 (a time in which the series experienced a meteoric rise in popularity). The next chapter, "Coming of Age in Ooo," covers the show's final few seasons, its finale, and the *Distant Lands* specials; this chapter also discusses the show's growing thematic depth and its interest in the miniseries format. This section of the book closes with "Good Jubies," which serves as a production guide to the show's unique guest-directed episodes.

Part 3 of the book, entitled "The Wider World of *Adventure Time*," considers different aspects of the show and its legacy. In the first chapter, "The Institute of So Und," I focus on the show's music. This chapter opens with a discussion of series composers Casey James Basichis and Tim Kiefer, placing particular emphasis on the styles of music that inspired them and how they created the show's distinct soundtrack. The chapter then outlines the show's most notable songs. In the subsequent chapter, "The Ancillary Adventures of Finn and Jake," I survey the main *Adventure Time* comic book line issued by BOOM!, the five major *Adventure Time* video games, and the theatrical movie that was rumored to be in production in 2015. The book's final chapter, "Utter Fandemonium," focuses on the show's fandom. Based in part on interviews that I conducted with dozens of *Adventure Time* fans from across the world, this chapter explores the many behaviors endemic to the show's following while also detailing several key websites that served as bastions for fandom during the show's run.

Most of this book is rooted in the historical and journalistic traditions, which necessitated that I scour through hundreds of books, journal articles, blog posts, Tweets, Formspring/Ask.fm answers, Wikia articles, and Archive.org pages to reconstruct past events. To supplement these findings, I also interviewed many of the artists who worked on *Adventure Time*, asking them about their unique experiences as part of the show's crew. The historical sections of this work are thus complex amalgamations of oral history and primary source analysis. If any mistakes have been made in reconstructing the past, they are mine and mine alone.

Now, with that out of the way, it is time to grab your friends—and maybe a few bacon pancakes while you are at it. We're going to very distant lands . . .

Part I

WHO'S WHO IN THE LAND OF OOO? CHARACTER PROFILES

1.

TWO RAD BROS

Finn the Human and Jake the Dog

Given its narrative and thematic complexities, articulating the essence of *Adventure Time* in just a few short words is a task far trickier than one might initially assume it to be. But if the series must be defined as only one thing, then I would argue it is best viewed as the story of two brothers: Finn the Human and Jake the Dog. In this chapter, I will explore this dynamic duo in detail, considering how Finn and Jake first emerged in the mind of Pendleton Ward, which actors provided their iconic voices, and how their characterization evolved as the series progressed.

FINN THE HUMAN

Finn the Human (full name: Finn Mertens) is the main protagonist of *Adventure Time*. As his seemingly redundant epithet makes clear, Finn is a human boy who, for much of the show, believes himself to be the last scion of humanity left in the postapocalyptic Land of Ooo. Finn is set apart from the show's many characters by his distinctive white bear hat, his eccentric weapons (like a cursed grass saber or a blade made out of an alternate-universe version of himself), and the quirky vernacular sprinkled into his dialogue (e.g., "Shmowzow!," "Mathematical!"). Finn shares a close, mutualistic relationship with his adoptive brother, Jake: Jake often functions as a mentor, giving Finn sage advice. Finn, in turn, counteracts his brother's lazier tendencies and serves as a moral compass for the somewhat hedonistic Jake.

Finn is, at the onset of the series, an excitable twelve-year-old who serves Princess Bubblegum, the ruler of the Candy Kingdom, as one of her knights. In these early episodes, Finn sees the world in strict terms of "good" and "evil," often failing to recognize moral nuance and shades of grey. This, in turn, leads him to sometimes rush head-long into problems. By the time the series ends,

Jeremy Shada provided the voice of Finn the Human. His older brother, Zack, had voiced the character in the pilot short. Photo courtesy of Joel Feria.

however, Finn's varied life experiences have molded him into a mature young adult, one whose adventuring skills are surpassed perhaps only by his newfound awareness of life's many complexities. This maturation is best seen when a viewer considers how Finn approaches conflict: in the first few seasons, he operates on "a punch first, ask questions later" basis, but by series' end, he is more willing to diffuse problems with discourse before resorting to violence.

The exact story of how Ward came up with Finn's character is somewhat unclear, although it is probable that the hero of Ooo's look was inspired by an earlier Ward creation known as "Bueno the Bear." This odd little critter—a white bear with noodle limbs, small bumps for ears, and no visible nose[1]—was dreamt up by Ward when he was a student at the California Institute of the Arts

(CalArts), and the character starred in several of Ward's student films and web comics.[2] While Ward has never confirmed a connection between Bueno and Finn, it seems unlikely that the similarities are a coincidence.

The earliest incarnation of Finn proper can be traced back to 2005, when Ward drew a doodle of a kid wearing a white hat, whom he dubbed "Pen the Human." This character was initially just a rough sketch—a doodle that Ward has emphasized carried no deeper meaning[3]—but Ward decided to work him into a minute-long video short that he pitched to Nickelodeon Studios.[4] While Nickelodeon passed on the concept, Ward successfully pitched it to the executives of the production company Frederator sometime later, leading him to write and storyboard his first professional animated project, the seven-minute film entitled *Adventure Time*.[5] In this short, Pen (voiced at the time by Zack Shada) is introduced as an energetic kid wearing a distinctive "awesome" hat who teams up with his dog, Jake, to rescue Princess Bubblegum from the evil Ice King.

The *Adventure Time* short first aired on the Nicktoons Network in early 2007, and against all odds, it became a viral success. Recognizing that they might have a hit on their hands, Frederator and Ward began working to convert *Adventure Time* into a full-fledged television series. It was during this period of reworking that Ward made a few tweaks to Pen's character—most notably, renaming him "Finn." As to why he made this name change, Ward told the audience of a 2009 Comic-Con panel: "Pen is my name and I didn't want to see my name on the back of sweatpants . . . So I changed it to Finn."[6] The now-familiar look of the character was eventually finalized by Phil Rynda, the show's lead character and prop designer. While reminiscing about the character in a 2021 interview, Rynda told me: "I love how flexible Finn's design is and how far we [could] push his face to have an incredible range of expressions."[7]

After Cartoon Network agreed to produce a full *Adventure Time* series, Ward also decided to recast the character's voice actor. One of the dozens of children who auditioned for the part was Jeremy Shada, the younger brother of Zack. In an interview with Brendon Connelly of Bleeding Cool, Jeremy Shada relayed the following:

> We got a breakdown [of the *Adventure Time* series] from my agent . . . and they had the characters and the lines all in there. And then Zack was like, "I just did that pilot like three years ago!" I'm like, "Oh really?" And so we listened to it and . . . my voice sounded amazingly like his. So then I kind of even tweaked it a little bit to really match [his voice]. Then I went in and auditioned; they had me back a couple times. And then I booked it and nobody except the creator of the show actually knew that I was [Zack's] brother until the first day of recording. They just thought I sounded a ton like him![8]

Jeremy has emphasized on numerous occasions that despite his "taking" the job from his brother, there is no animosity between the two and that Zack was quite happy that they were "keeping [the role] in the family."[9]

While Ward based Finn's sometimes-naïve scrupulousness on a younger version of himself,[10] much of Finn's characterization was based on Mike Roth, an animator who worked alongside Ward on the Cartoon Network series *The Marvelous Misadventures of Flapjack*; when asked about this at a 2014 ArcadeCon talk, Ward explained that he was drawn to Roth because of Roth's seeming incongruity: "He's a really sweet guy, but he's also really tough . . . [I found that] really funny and interesting."[11] Ward modeled other aspects of Finn on Jean-Luc Picard, the captain of the USS *Enterprise* in the popular science fiction series *Star Trek: The Next Generation* (1987–94), played by Patrick Stewart. In an interview included on the DVD set for *Adventure Time*'s third season, Ward explained, "Even when he is not fully confident, [Picard] still makes a decision. He still moves forward on something. He doesn't waiver, [and] he's always on the ball." The same can be said of Finn.[12]

A Hero's Journey: The Growth and Development of Finn the Human

Unlike many animated characters, Finn ages throughout the show's run. This was in large part necessitated by Shada's real-life development, specifically the voice changes that accompanied Shada's passage through puberty. In an interview with Skwigly, Shada noted: "Luckily for me they've aged the character throughout the show . . . [I]f you go back and listen to [the voice of] season one Finn and season eight Finn, it's definitely different."[13] In retrospect, this decision to age Finn in real time was a masterstroke as it foregrounded the character's journey through the snares of adolescence into adulthood. This forced the show's producers to explore real-life issues that many teenagers face as they grow up, such as youthful romances and bouts of depression. These topics are explored casually in early episodes, many of which feature Finn's fruitless pining for Princess Bubblegum. Alas, after almost constant rejection, Finn finally realizes in the third-season finale "Incendium" that he and Bubblegum will never be together, leading him to experience his first real depressive spell. But much to *Adventure Time*'s credit, the show has Finn get over his obsession with Bubblegum in a way that allows the two to maintain a close, healthy, and decidedly platonic friendship.

In Season 4, Finn begins dating the heir to the Fire Kingdom: Flame Princess. The romance between Finn and his new beau is more "real" than anything he experienced with Bubblegum, resulting in the show's more romance-focused episodes becoming increasingly mature as their relationship evolves. This maturation reaches a fever pitch in the fifth-season episode "Frost and Fire," in which Finn begins to dream of Flame Princess pleasurably shooting fire at his groin. The visuals in this dream, while somewhat abstract, are recognizable allusions to nocturnal emissions and, more broadly, sexual dreams—experiences that many adolescents may experience without any explanation from the adults in their lives.

Unfortunately, Finn lies and manipulates Flame Princess so that he can experience more of these dreams. When Flame Princess learns of Finn's betrayal, she breaks off their relationship. "Frost and Fire" ends with Flame Princess walking away from Finn, sending a clear message to the audience that relationships are based on trust and consent, not lies and manipulation. While Finn tries to smooth things over with Flame Princess in subsequent episodes like "Earth & Water" and "The Red Throne," it is clear that his actions are driven largely by selfishness, and needless to say, he fails in getting back together with his ex. This development makes one thing clear: Flame Princess is a *person*, not just some prize to be won.

During Season 6, Finn's sadness about his romantic failings is compounded when he both loses his right arm and is rejected by his biological father, Martin, resulting in our hero falling into a deep, season-long depression. Finn tries a whole slew of techniques to make himself feel better—including plotting revenge ("The Tower") and going on a promiscuous kissing spree ("Breezy")—before accepting in the sixth-season finale "The Comet" that he and his father are simply different people, and he will never mold Martin into the dad that he wants.

Finn's epiphany in "The Comet" is a watershed moment for the character—one in which he comes to a larger realization about life itself. Life is not just a string of fun adventures in which we always win or get what we want. Sure, sometimes we go on fun adventures. But sometimes our significant other dumps us, or we learn that our father is a jerk. These low points hurt, but they also give us meaning, allowing us to determine and enjoy what is good; in other words, if we reject the bad, we also reject the good because the two can only exist as a duad. In "The Comet," Finn is given the explicit option to transcend this duality, but instead of bailing, Finn decides to stay in "this meat reality" and "see it through." In doing so, Finn embraces the good/bad binary and learns from it. Recognizing that he cannot change his father, Finn forgives Martin. Recognizing how much he hurt her, Finn apologizes to Flame Princess. Recognizing that life is both bad *and* good, he overcomes his existential funk.

Some fans reacted negatively to the show's portrayal of Finn in Seasons 5 and 6, with many arguing that Finn's romantic mishaps and his overall depression deflated his character's appeal and took the "adventure" out of *Adventure Time*. To be blunt, these are rather shallow complaints, and what really seems to have perturbed these fans was the realization that their fictional hero could stumble like a real person. But arguably it is this stumbling that makes Finn such a unique character. By portraying Finn as an individual who struggles with romance, depression, and existential angst, *Adventure Time* stresses the humanity of the character. The show emphatically declares that even so-called heroes can struggle on this journey that we call life! No one has *all* the answers, and that is okay. This is an important message to send to viewers (especially pre/pubescent viewers!) who might feel as if their particular struggles are unprecedented. You are not an outlier, the show asserts. You are a human—just like Finn.

Memories of Boom Boom Mountain: The Origin Story of Finn

Like all good monomythic heroes, Finn has an elaborate origin story, but in the show's earliest episodes, this story is a glaring mystery. During the first season, for instance, the only snippet of Finn's genesis that is privy to the audience is that when he was an infant, he was discovered crying in the woods by the sentient dogs Joshua and Margaret. The two adopted Finn, raising him alongside their other sons, Jake and Jermaine.

While alluded to here and there, the mystery of Finn's parentage is largely ignored until the fifth-season finale, "Billy's Bucket List," in which Finn learns that his human father is still alive and is trapped somewhere known as "The Citadel." In the Season 6 premiere, "Wake Up"/"Escape from the Citadel," Finn and Jake journey to this mysterious location and come face to face with the former's biological dad, Martin Mertens (voiced by Stephen Root). Finn—expecting his father to be some intergalactic hero of renown—is crushed to learn that Martin is a smooth-talking conman. Martin attempts to flee the scene, and in the ensuing chaos, Finn loses his arm. During the remainder of the sixth season, Finn attempts to bond with his father and understand his behavior, all to no avail. By the time that the season finale "The Comet" rolls around, Finn has come to terms with the fact that "there ain't no changing" his dad.[14]

But Finn's father is only one side of the biological coin; what about Finn's mother? The mystery of her identity is not resolved until the eighth-season miniseries *Islands*. At the onset of this event series, Finn discovers information suggesting that a colony of humans is extant on a small islet known as "Founders Island," so he—with the help of Jake, Susan Strong, and a stowaway BMO—journeys out to sea, along the way learning the truth about his genesis.

Years prior, Martin was a simple conman living on Founders Island. After breaking his leg attempting to scam a group of "Hiders" (that is, humans seeking to leave the safety of Founders Island), Martin was sent to the hospital, where he met a lovely "helper" (that is, a medical doctor) named Minerva Campbell[15] (voiced by Sharon Horgan). Soon thereafter, the two fell in love, and in time, Minerva gave birth to a son, whom she and Martin named Finn.

While Martin abandoned his life of petty crime to take care of his new family, his past misdeeds would soon catch up to him; one night, while he and Finn were alone at home, Martin was ambushed by the Hiders whom Martin had previously attempted to scam. Martin and Finn escaped the surprise attack by jumping onto a raft, but they were separated at sea, with Finn eventually being marooned in the Land of Ooo. This separation would leave Finn with a subconscious fear of the ocean; as for Martin, it is implied that the emotional toll of losing both his son and his partner caused him to have a mental breakdown, thereby explaining his borderline sociopathic tendencies in the show's sixth season.

Minerva, too, was grief stricken by the loss of her entire family, but instead of collapsing inward, she became fixated on helping the inhabitants of Founders Island. In time, a horrible plague ravaged the island, and to maximize her effectiveness as a helper, Minerva uploaded her consciousness into a computer program, which allowed her to aid those around her without fear of dying from their deadly illnesses. (Unfortunately, this also meant that she forever severed most of her ties with the physical world.)

At the conclusion of *Islands*, Finn and Minerva are reunited, and the latter is overjoyed to see the former alive and all grown up. While Minerva initially tries to force her son to stay on Founders Island, Finn decides to return to his home and follow in his mother's footsteps by helping those in need. Just before Finn sets sail for Ooo, he and his mother share a touching goodbye with the help of virtual reality equipment.

Given this backstory's relative cohesiveness, a viewer would be forgiven if they thought it had been planned from the start. In reality, the writers developed this backstory as they went along. That said, during the second season, creative director Patrick McHale attempted to draft out a rough skeleton of a backstory for Finn. According to McHale:

> Our decision to make Finn afraid of water in the first season episode "Ocean of Fear" was sort of arbitrary, so to make sense of it, my idea was that Finn and Susan Strong were [siblings] . . . [When he was a baby] Finn's family was on a boat at sea and [they were] hit by storm. . . . Finn and Susan washed ashore in Ooo in different places. Susan was discovered by mutated [hyoomans] and was raised by them . . . Meanwhile, Finn tossed and turned on the ocean, separated from his family ([thereby explaining his] fear of the ocean, but not of water in general) until he ended up in Ooo and was discovered by Jake's family.[16]

Although McHale undoubtedly put immense energy into connecting all these dots, this take on Finn's backstory never fully clicked with the other writers.

Finn's origin story was consequently shelved until early 2012, when the show's writers and storyboard artists were working on the fourth-season finale, "The Lich." In the episode's original storyboard, artist Skyler Page blocked out a scene in which Finn learns that his father is a great hero who has been locked away in a dimension known as the "Citadel." But because Ward felt that this scene "threw everyone" and "didn't reveal as much as you wanted it to," he cut it from the episode.[17]

The idea that Finn's father was trapped in some space prison was then revived in 2013, when the writers started outlining the fifth-season finale "Billy's Bucket List." However, when breaking the story, the writers soon found themselves faced with a decision. "We knew [Martin] was trapped in a kind of space prison," Jack Pendarvis told me in an interview, "so the question [became], 'Is he being held unfairly, or did he do something bad?' The second option is more dramatic [and] a flawed character is always more interesting to explore."[18] Ultimately, it was the second option that prevailed, as the writers chose to portray Martin not as a champion of righteousness, but rather as a sleazy "bozo" (to quote Tom Herpich).[19] This decision in turn inspired the writers years later to depict Minerva as something of Martin's opposite, with Pendarvis telling me, "Certainly it's interesting to see a character like Martin in love with a character who is not like Martin, and vice versa."[20]

...

In addition to Finn's biological backstory, there is also the question of his spiritual origin (after all, in the Oooniverse,[21] souls are real and persist after death). The first episode to arguably look into this topic is the third-season spookfest "The Creeps," in which Finn finds himself haunted by the eerie specter of a smiling woman. After cameoing in Season 4's "King Worm" and Season 5's "Sky Witch," the specter gained substantial attention from the fandom, and many began to speculate that this ghost was that of Finn's mother, who had yet to be introduced. However, this hypothesis was later quashed in the fifth-season episode "The Vault," wherein it is revealed that this mysterious spirit is actually that of Shoko, one of Finn's many past lives.

Hundreds of years prior to the start of the series, Shoko was a one-armed bandit who roamed the land of Ooo with a tiger friend, taking odd jobs for various crime bosses. One day, Shoko was tasked with stealing a powerful amulet owned by Princess Bubblegum, who at the time had just begun constructing the central fortress of the future Candy Kingdom citadel. Shoko infiltrated the kingdom, but she and Bubblegum developed a friendship, with Bubblegum even constructing for Shoko a prosthetic arm. Shoko was conflicted about her assignment, given the princess's kindness, but in the end, she stole the amulet from Bubblegum anyway. Unfortunately, while fleeing from the kingdom, Shoko fell into a pool of radioactive sludge, dying over the tree that would one day grow into Finn and Jake's beloved tree fort.

While the logistics of Finn haunting himself are never quite explained, the reincarnation storyline added a spiritual depth to the series that would be explored further to great effect in the sixth-season finale "The Comet." At the end of this episode, Finn learns in a discussion with the titular entity that he has been repeatedly reborn and that in his earliest incarnation, he happened to be a catalyst comet that hit Earth and brought along with it a new cycle of change and renewal.

This revelation engendered much discussion—and considerable confusion—among fans, many of whom erroneously believed that the episode was painting Finn as some sort of demigod who had been delivered unto Ooo by means of the comet to "save" it from evil. Storyboard artist Jesse Moynihan, who played a large role in developing the episodes detailing Finn's past lives, later rebutted this interpretation with a 2015 Reddit post:

> I've noticed a recurring misunderstanding of Finn-as-cosmic-god variation. I guess I blame myself for not being clearer, at the same time the focus of my writing in [Season 6] was to not be clear all the time. If it helps at all, as a personal footnote—Finn is not a cosmic god or whatever. He's just a normal human. His soul was delivered to Earth by a comet, but it should be understood that Earth is as cosmic as the comet. We all derive from the same source material.[22]

Later the following year, on his personal website, Moynihan expounded on this final point:

> Finn's soul arrived on Earth by way of a mysterious living comet. But all of our souls arrived on Earth by way of a creative explosion that sent us hurtling through the void. Earth itself is a living, cosmic being, and the souls that inhabit it derived from the same material that formed stars and planets billions of light years away. The theme of reincarnation was used to imply the specialness/non-specialness of Finn as his soul migrates through time in different identities and meets other incarnations of other souls. Finn is "special" not because in another life he was [some supernatural deity or powerful entity] . . . but because he decided to be great in this moment.[23]

In other words, Finn is not extraordinary because he was some sort of cosmic "god-baby"[24]; instead, "[He] is special because we're all special."[25]

JAKE THE DOG

Jake the Dog is a talking canine and Finn's older, adoptive brother. Affirming the aphorism that heroes come in all shapes and sizes, Jake possesses the fantastic ability to morph his body into almost any form. While his superpowers make him an intimidating foe in battle, Jake is more often than not a creature of comfort who yields to his lazier impulses—often to the chagrin of the more energetic Finn.

Jake is usually portrayed as a champion of Ooo, but unlike Finn, he is not as obsessed with following the letter of the law, and in an early part of his life, he was even the leader of an infamous gang that committed numerous robberies—a "seedy past"[26] of which he is not proud but that is alluded to nonetheless across several episodes. And unlike Finn, who by the show's end sees violence as an option of last resort, Jake is more than willing to use his strength as a means to an end. Because Jake's moral alignment can vacillate between the twin poles of "lawful" and "chaotic," Ward has argued that Jake is best understood in *Dungeons & Dragons* terms as a "neutral good" character.[27] Luckily, most of Jake's more irresponsible character traits are mitigated by Finn's fealty to virtue.

Finn and Jake usually function as a comedic double act, and while both characters can play the "funny-man" role, Jake is often the source of the comedy, thanks in large part to his magical powers (which allow him to morph into countless humorous shapes) and his carefree attitude (which often leads him to be blunt about what he is thinking). But as with all brothers, the two can also occasionally turn on one another, with each serving as the other's foil. In the fourth-season episode "Who Would Win," for instance, Finn and Jake get into a violent fight, with each trying to best the other in direct combat. A lighter (albeit still violent) example of this sort of brotherly contention comes to us in the fifth-season episode "Jake Suit," in which the brothers make a bet as to who can tolerate the most pain. This leads to Jake taking over Finn's body and subjecting him to "all kinds of pain"[28]—ranging from physical to emotional punishment. But regardless of squabbles like these, at the end of the day, Finn and Jake almost always find a way to overcome their differences and reaffirm their close relationship.

In terms of design, Jake is a pudgy bulldog,[29] with orange-amber fur, prominent eyes, and large drooping jowls. Series creator Pendleton Ward whipped up the initial design that would evolve into Jake sometime around 2005, when he doodled "a kid with a bear hat and his bulldog riding on a boat."[30] Ward found

Jake the Dog was voiced by veteran voice actor John DiMaggio. When he first started, DiMaggio was confused by the show's bizarre dialogue and its wacky outlines. Photo courtesy of Gage Skidmore via Creative Commons (CC) Attribution-ShareAlike 2.0 Generic (CC BY-SA 2.0) license, https://flic.kr/p/czELL3.

the drawing "fun-looking and cool,"[31] and in time, it became the basis for the original *Adventure Time* short (2007).

Ward based much of Jake's personality on Bill Murray's character Tripper Harrison from the 1979 comedy classic *Meatballs*. In the film, Tripper is a counselor at a summer camp made up of misfits. While he is fond of mischief and lewd jokes, Tripper is also well meaning and capable of providing solid advice when the need arises. Tripper's influence on Jake is made most explicit in the series' pitch bible:

> [Jake's] relationship with Finn is similar to Bill Murray's character relating to [the child camper] Rudy in the movie *Meatballs*. Like Murray, Jake is very jokey, everything can be poked fun at until it gets serious. And when it's serious, like when Finn is feeling low or sad, Jake is good at listening and knowing the most thoughtful things to say.[32]

Jake thus serves in a variety of archetypical roles. Sometimes Jake plays the role of the "wise old man" who uses his life experience to train the hero,[33] and other times, Jake is the "comic mentor" who gives often ridiculous advice about life, growth, and love.[34]

Jake was voiced by veteran voice actor John DiMaggio, who prior to working on *Adventure Time* was perhaps best known for playing the crude robot Bender on the Fox/Comedy Central animated comedy *Futurama* (1999–2003, 2008–13). DiMaggio secured the role of Jake during production of the pilot and was the only original voice actor retained when the series was picked up by Cartoon Network.[35] During the recording of the first few seasons, DiMaggio found the show's dialogue confusing, and he often struggled with understanding its appeal. While speaking with io9 in 2013, DiMaggio explained:

> I was trying to figure out from the beginning what the big deal was. I was like, "I'm not sure I understand what's going on here." . . . You just had these lines that said whatever, and it was like, "I don't get it." I said to Tom Kenny once, I was like, "Dude, I don't get this show at all. I have no idea." And he was like, "Listen, man. Just trust me. This is this generation's *Yellow Submarine*. Just leave it at that." And he was right. The art direction on the show, the whole world is great—the Land of Ooo is just weird. . . . It's just a weird thing, you know. I love doing the show. It's fun as hell.[36]

The specific voice that DiMaggio uses when playing Jake, while a bit gruff, still manages to reflect the warm nature of the character, and in a 2015 episode of the *Conversation Parade* podcast, DiMaggio contended that Jake's voice is really just "[his] natural voice with a little bit of a hug on it."[37]

A Postnuclear Family: Jake the Son and Jake the Dad

As mentioned at the start of this section, Jake is perhaps most notable for his "stretchy powers"—that is, his fantastic ability to morph, alter, or twist his body into practically any shape. Jake claims in the first-season episode "The Witch's Garden" that he received his powers after rolling around in a magical mud puddle as a pup. This whimsical origin story, however, is later retconned in the sixth-season episode "Joshua and Margaret Investigations," wherein the audience learns that the character is actually the graftling of a shapeshifting alien creature named "Warren Ampersand"[38] (voiced by Dave Foley), who at one point implanted a parasitic "egg" into Joshua the Dog's head. Jake—like some sort of extraterrestrial Athena—was subsequently born from Joshua's head wound, making him half dog and half shapeshifter.

Joshua and Margaret decided to adopt Jake (despite his being the scion of a parasite) and raise him alongside their biological son, Jermaine, and their other adopted son, Finn. Many years later, in the tenth-season episode "Jake the Starchild," Ampersand would return to Ooo and abduct Jake in the hopes of stealing his son's powers, thereby extending his own life. Jake, however, is nott one who is easily outsmarted, and by episode's end, Jake tricks his "rube" of a father and pitches him into a black hole. (Talk about daddy issues!)

By making Jake's bio-dad an alien from some mysterious planet, the *Adventure Time* writers were able to explicitly dabble in the tropes of science fiction, despite the show ostensibly being predicated on the trappings of fantasy. Sometimes, this sci-fi experimentation was successful (e.g., Season 6's "Joshua & Margaret Investigations," which easily merges sci-fi horror with the intrigue of the mystery genre); other times, it was not (e.g., Season 10's "Jake the Starchild," which resolves the mystery of Jake's parentage in a rather abbreviated and underwhelming eleven minutes). Regardless, when viewed as a thematic unit, the episodes focusing on Jake's sci-fi genesis do a nice job painting the character as a truly enigmatic "other"—and in a land full of talking candies and vampire bassists, this is saying something.

...

Despite the complicated relationship with his immediate family (both biological and adoptive), Jake has a much more straightforward relationship with his long-term romantic partner, Lady Rainicorn, and in the fifth-season episode "Jake the Dad," the two welcome five "pups" to the world, all of whom have various superpowers like their parents. The pups include the following:

Charlie, who is able to lower the density of her being, thereby allowing her to grow to a huge size while retaining a consistent body mass. Charlie lives in a crumbling Egyptian pyramid and is a skilled occultist quite adept at reading tarot cards. Charlie was designed by Steve Wolfhard and named by Tom Herpich.[39] The character was voiced by Alia Shawkat, perhaps best known for her starring role as Maeby Fünke in the Fox cult comedy *Arrested Development*.

Jake Jr., who can shapeshift using her hair in a way similar to her father. Living up to her namesake, Jake Jr. reunites her father's old gang in Season 5's "One Last Job" and steals the Baker's Shard—an action that earns her a strong talking-to from Jake. Jake Jr. was designed by Herpich and Wolfhard (the former of whom proposed that the character not have a standard face), and named by Wolfhard.[40] Jake Jr. was voiced by Kristen Schaal, whose distinctive voice can also be heard in several other animated shows, like *Gravity Falls* (Disney) and *Bob's Burgers* (Fox).

Kim Kil Whan, who possesses the ability to teleport and colorize objects. Kim Kil Whan is a no-nonsense realtor who is often exasperated by his father's childlike antics. (The character also has a rebellious daughter named Bronwyn, voice by Rae Gray, who bonds with her grandfather over their mutual love of skateboarding.) Kim Kil Whan was designed by Wolfhard and named after the founder of SAEROM animation studio, Kim Gilhwan.[41] The character was voiced by comedian and improv actor Marc Evan Jackson.

- **T.V.**, who is capable of teleportation and colorizing objects. A stereotypical "basement dweller," T.V. often gets lost in elaborate daydreams, and by series' end, he sets up a detective agency. T.V. was designed and named by Wolfhard[42] and voiced by Dan Mintz, who costars alongside Schaal in *Bob's Burgers*.
- **Viola**, who possesses the powers of teleportation. One of the more mature pups, Viola has dreams of becoming a famous stage actress, which leads her to take part in Lumpy Space Princess's play *Summer Showers*. Viola was designed and named by Wolfhard[43] and voiced by Paget Brewster, perhaps best known for her role as Special Agent Emily Prentiss in the CBS series *Criminal Minds*.

(After mingling with and marrying other magical creatures, the offspring of Lady and Jake's children will develop into a separate species called "pups," and one thousand years after the time of Finn and Jake, the "Pup Kingdom" will be a hegemonic city-state, ruled by President Gibbon, the nigh-immortal son of Charlie.)[44]

It was first revealed to the audience that Jake and Lady would have children in the fourth-season episode "Lady & Peebles," and when this announcement was made, many fans were excited, as they assumed the introduction of Jake-lettes would force Jake into a newer, more mature role. Alas, these hopes were dashed when it is revealed that Rainicorn-Dog hybrids grow at an accelerated rate; in fact, by the time "Jake the Dad" ends, Jake's children are all grown up and no longer require Jake's constant attention. This decision to "age up" the characters was met with a mixed response from fans and critics, with some applauding the clever way *Adventure Time* returned to the original status quo, and others lambasting the show for introducing a major development and then dumping it at the last minute to "play it safe."

Perhaps in response to some fans' disdain for the "overnight age-up"[45] of the pups, the show's writers and producers began exploring Jake's rather distant relationship with his grown-up children in the later part of the show's run. In some episodes, such as the Season 6 installment "Ocarina," Jake is clearly shown goofing off, much to the chagrin (and occasional detriment) of his children. In others, such as Season 7's "Summer Showers," he is more self-aware, bemoaning the fact that he was only able to be a "good dad" to his pups for just a few days. All of these episodes, when taken together, create a nuanced depiction of

Jake as a father who loves his children but who is not a great caretaker. This is diametrically opposed to the stereotypical "bad" parent often seen in popular media, who is portrayed as hyperbolically cruel or evil. Jake is far from evil; he is just a touch irresponsible.

"A BOY AND HIS DOG": FINAL THOUGHTS

The third *Distant Lands* special *Together Again* is something of a doozy, given that it revolves around Finn and Jake's quest to reunite in the afterlife. A veritable rollercoaster of emotion, the special jumps from heavy theme to heavy theme, but perhaps the most poignant moment comes at the very end. After defeating the Lich one final time, Finn and Jake are each given the choice of settling into the Dead Worlds or being reincarnated back on Ooo. Finn opts for the latter option and plunges into the transmigratory river of souls. Jake, on the other hand, chooses to return to the paradisaical Fiftieth Dead World. But as he floats away to nirvana, Jake abruptly changes his mind and follows after Finn. The two subsequently meet up in the bright river of souls, where Jake happily declares: "I'm just coming back for fun. Because it's great being alive with you!" The two then fist-bump a split second before they are reincarnated, and the special ends with a simple card reading: "Finn and Jake are Together Again."

This tearjerker of a scene—the literal culmination of Finn and Jake's life stories—is a beautiful summary of the brothers' relationship. They are best friends who might not always see eye to eye but who nevertheless care deeply for one another. Finn and Jake are the heart and soul of *Adventure Time*, and over the course of the series' run, the audience is given the opportunity to see them grow as individuals while simultaneously reaffirming their brotherly bond—in both life and in death! In the world of animation, Finn and Jake are thus special, set apart from other famed cartoon characters like SpongeBob SquarePants, Bart Simpson, or Bugs Bunny, who, while funny, are often missing some key emotional core. Finn and Jake are best friends who thrive off their brotherly love, and this emotional connection makes them worthy additions to the pantheon of cartoon protagonists.

2.

SUGAR AND SPICE

Princess Bubblegum and Marceline the Vampire Queen

Finn and Jake are the stars of *Adventure Time*, but they are far from the only characters that matter. Two other players of immense importance are the show's major female characters: Princess Bubblegum of the Candy Kingdom and Marceline the Vampire Queen. Although both were introduced in Season 1 as simplistic ciphers who do little more than inaugurate episode plots, Bubblegum and Marceline quickly grew into two of the show's most interesting characters. In this chapter, I will explore the characters' origins, their development, and their complex relationship with one another—a relationship that began as a simple rivalry and bloomed into one of the most famous queer romances in the world of animation.

PRINCESS BUBBLEGUM

Princess Bubblegum (full name: Bonnibel Bubblegum; often called "PB" and occasionally "Bonnie") is the brilliant ruler of the "Candy Kingdom," a polity that looms large as one of Ooo's few true superpowers. In the show's earliest seasons, Finn and the audience believe that Princess Bubblegum is only eighteen years old, but in the fifth-season episode, "The Vault," it is revealed that she is effectively a biologically immortal creature that has lived for well over eight centuries. Bubblegum is also the current incarnation of the Candy Elemental, making her the sentient manifestation of one of the four primordial elements that constitute the known Oooniverse (the others being ice, fire, and slime, naturally).

For the show's first three or so seasons, Bubblegum serves as both a mentor to young Finn and the object of his affection; in fact, many early episodes focus on his often hair-brained quests to woo the princess. Unfortunately for young Finn, Bubblegum rejects him at almost every turn. Part of her disinterest is due to the age gap separating the two: at the start of the show, Finn is twelve years old, whereas Bubblegum is over eight hundred. But another reason Bubblegum scorns Finn's advances is that throughout the series, it is implied (and eventually confirmed) that Bubblegum is in love with her oldest friend, Marceline. After several seasons in which the two behave prickly around one another, Bubblegum and Marceline (re)admit their feelings for one another and become an official couple in the series finale "Come Along with Me."

Much like Ice King and Marceline the Vampire Queen, Bubblegum has a complicated backstory, and it is only after seasons of buildup and teasing that the audience learns that centuries prior to the start of the series, Bubblegum was "birthed" from a sentient mass of radioactive chewing gum known as the "Mothergum." Because Bubblegum had no other family members except for her socially anxious brother, Neddy (voiced by Andres Salaff), she decided to create her own family: an uncle named Gumbald, an aunt named Lolly, and a cousin named Chicle. Gumbald, however, grew jealous of Bubblegum's controlling tendencies and, with the help of Lolly and Chicle, attempted to overthrow his niece. While their *coup d'état* failed (and Gumbald and his familial stooges were accidentally turned into simple-minded candy people in the process), Bubblegum was nevertheless shaken, and so when she began building up her kingdom, she decided to create candy subjects who were relative simpletons, thereby ensuring that they would not rise up against her like her family had. After several centuries, her kingdom became a hegemonic city-state, and in time she befriended Finn the Human and his brother, Jake the Dog, enlisting the two to serve as her knights.

Princess Bubblegum was one of the first *Adventure Time* characters that Pendleton Ward created, and she appeared in the 2005 short that preceded the production of the show's pilot, which Ward had mocked up when trying to pitch the series to Nickelodeon.[1] Ward had wanted to name the character "Bettie," likely after his mother, but when *Adventure Time* went into production at Cartoon Network, he decided to instead christen the monarch "Bonnibel."[2]

In terms of her aesthetic, Bubblegum is a "pretty pink princess" in the style of other fictitious royals like Peach or Zelda. The earliest designs for Bubblegum are simplistic, with the character resembling an elongated, pink gumdrop. Animator Robertryan Cory, who worked for a few months as the show's first *de facto* lead character designer, tweaked this initial look by giving the character a "more hour-glass figure" and by adding the "upside down heart" design onto her dress sleeves.[3] Bubblegum's look was finalized by character designer Phil Rynda during production of the show's first season.

In the Nicktoons short, Bubblegum was voiced by Paige Moss (an actress who notably played Veruca, the lascivious werewolf in the WB series *Buffy the Vampire Slayer*),[4] but when the show was picked up by Cartoon Network, the producers decided to recast the role.[5] One of those who auditioned for the part was actress Hynden Walch, who at that time was perhaps best known for

Hynden Walch—the voice actress of Princess Bubblegum—believed that *Adventure Time* would be a "huge" success before she even landed a role on the show. Photo courtesy of Isabella Vosmikova.

voicing the heroic alien Starfire on the Cartoon Network series *Teen Titans*. When discussing her audition, Walch told me:

> I was one of just a few who went in to Cartoon Network to read for [Bubblegum]. . . . I remember that I loved the short with Abraham Lincoln. I thought it was funny and amazing. I knew the show would be huge (really, I did!) And I felt like I really got the humor, so I thought to myself, "Of all the things I'm up for right now, *this* is the one I want. *This* one." . . . The scene [with which I auditioned] was a made-up scene with Ricardio breaking up with [Bubblegum] or something. And I just

really went for it. I remember the script said, "[Bubblegum] cries" and I cried and whinnied and wailed for a good (uncomfortably) long time.

I remember I didn't hear that I'd gotten the part for awhile. . . . I'm not sure how long it actually was between audition and casting. My agent at the time called me and said I'd gotten "Adventure Land." I said, "Adventure Land?" Then totally disinterested, she said, "Yeah, I guess you read for a commercial for [a] theme park or something." Wow! My own agency didn't know I was just cast in the most genius animated show of the century? Suffice it to say, that agency didn't represent me for long.[6]

When discussing how her approach to Bubblegum evolved over the seasons, Walch told me that the "character was always there in [her]," but that early on, there was a minor disagreement between her and a voice director about how the character should be played:

> We had a series of different voice directors on [*Adventure Time* over the course of ten seasons]. What I bet a lot of people don't know is [that] we don't have free reign playing a character. . . . No, there are a lot of people telling us what to do. And depending on where the show is (Is it at the beginning? Is it super successful? Are we in season 2 or 3 or infinity?) there are more people telling us how to do what we do. So in the case of [Bubblegum], one of our [first] voice director's perception of her was "Disney Princess," which was something I never agreed with. So, for a while there it was a little bit of a tug of war between what I felt was right for the character (multi-dimensional, interesting, super smart, and a little dark) and what I was being directed to do (16 year old sweet, candy princess.) Then when [Bubblegum] showed up in the script upending tables and shouting in German, I was like, yep, see. This is where I thought we were going with this. Not too far into the series the writers and artists started directing us themselves, which worked out very favorably for the show, I think.[7]

Walch does not cartoonishly inflect her voice when playing the character—an inspired decision, given that the pleasantness of Walch's everyday voice contrasts with the character's darker, more complex personal history. The irony of this clash is delightful.

"Mystical Hoo-Doo": Bubblegum and the Supremacy of Science

Princess Bubblegum begins the series looking like a "pretty pink princess," but from the get-go her character also bucks gendered stereotypes by being portrayed as a scientific wunderkind who has pushed genetics to its limit in a quest to create candy life. (Case in point: The show's first episode, "Slumber Party Panic," opens with Bubblegum working on a potion to revive the deceased).[8] Bubblegum's experiments are at first portrayed in a wacky light, but as the show goes on, her research grows increasingly unprincipled. This is most manifest in episodes like "You Made Me!" and "Goliad," in which her actions paint her as an archetypical mad scientist, whose "intellectual ambitions scorn traditional morality and challenge the prerogatives of God[9] himself."[10] While this macabre change in Bubblegum's characterization certainly made her more interesting from a story standpoint—after all, what do morals even mean to a nigh-immortal elemental?—it also led to some fans online growing disgusted with her antics, with some even comparing her to Nazi medical doctors. (It certainly did not help matters that Bubblegum has a penchant for shouting angrily in German!)

Bubblegum's adoration of science, logic, and all things rational also leads her to espouse a controversial view: the fantastical magic that permeates the Land of Ooo is nothing more than complex natural phenomena that can be explained in reasonable terms using the scientific method. This radical scientism puts her in direct conflict with those who view magic as a fundamentally mysterious facet of reality. Further compounding the issue is Bubblegum's assertion that those who believe in magic are mere "dupes,"[11] uncritically accepting what is comfortable rather than what is true. This science-vs.-magic debate reaches a fever pitch in the fifth-season episode, "Wizards Only, Fools." After sneaking into Wizard City with Finn and Jake, Bubblegum is arrested, but the Grand Wizard in charge of the city cuts her and her friends a deal: If she simply acknowledges that "wizards rule," she and her friends can go, scot-free. The request is fairly minor—simply requiring Bubblegum to acknowledge the authority of wizards on their own turf—but Bubblegum refuses. The princess believes that she alone is right and is unwilling to even acknowledge that other worldviews exist. Unfortunately, Bubblegum's bullheadedness results in her and her friends getting thrown into wizard jail.

In many ways, Bubblegum's radically scientific beliefs can be read as a parody of the views held by "new atheist" zealots like that of evolutionary biologist Richard Dawkins, the cognitive scientist Daniel Dennett, the neuroscientist Sam Harris, and the late writer Christopher Hitchens. For many philosophers of religion (both religious and not), these skeptics have become so wrapped up in their ultra-naturalistic worldview that they have lapsed into an uncritical system of personal faith, much like those which they decry. This too is Bubblegum's problem. Certain that Ooo is governed by natural laws, Bubblegum refuses to entertain the idea of magic. The problem here is that in Ooo, magic objectively exists; in fact, it is baked into the very nature of reality! By denying this, Bubblegum ironically embraces an obstinate sort of fundamentalism like the zealous wizards whom she openly criticizes. Thankfully, following the events of "Wizards Only, Fools," Bubblegum keeps her antimagic views mostly to herself. This suggests that she has come to see that different people hold different worldviews, and that forcing hers—regardless if it is "right" or not—onto others is abrasive and intolerant.

A Candy-Coated Fascist? The Governing Philosophy of Princess Bubblegum

Bubblegum does her best to appear outwardly "sweet," but countless episodes suggest that she is an iron-fisted ruler with a fixation on control—controlling her citizens, controlling her allies, and even controlling her friends—all in the name of "protecting" them. This is first made apparent in the fourth-season episode "Goliad," in which Bubblegum reveals that her near-death experience in the Season 2 finale "Mortal Folly"/"Mortal Recoil" triggered an existential crisis about who might lead her kingdom were she to die. She consequently creates a candy sphinx (the titular Goliad) from her own DNA, who becomes focused on negating the free will of her candy subjects. Bubblegum manages to defuse the situation by episode's end, but the audience is still left with a lingering unease about Bubblegum's oft-guarded psyche. Is it not ominous that the literal offspring of Bubblegum almost immediately turned into a mind-controlling dictator?

Over the next few seasons, Bubblegum's controlling nature leads her down the road of radical utilitarianism, and she begins to do whatever it takes to keep her kingdom "safe." This results in her establishing what is effectively an autocratic surveillance state. She hides cameras everywhere and closely monitors her citizens, routinely spies on her political enemies, and increasingly takes a "Candy Kingdom *über alles*" mentality when it comes to the geopolitics of Ooo. Bubblegum's political unscrupulousness reaches an explosive apex in the Season 6 episode "The Cooler" when she attempts to disarm the Fire Kingdom via blatant sabotage. It is only after an intense fight with Flame Princess that Bubblegum realizes her desire for control in the name of safety has turned her into a candy-coated fascist. The episode ends with Bubblegum unplugging her kingdom-wide system of security cameras—a visual indication that she wants to become a better, more trusting, and less totalitarian leader.

But Bubblegum's past sins would soon catch up to her, and in "Hot Diggity Doom" (the first part of the sixth-season finale), the King of Ooo dupes the citizenry into electing him their new princess. This political rejection at the hands of the citizens about whom she had invested so much attention is such a wake-up call for Bubblegum that she abandons the throne in shock and anger.

After journeying to her uncle's derelict cabin in the middle of nowhere and establishing a realm in exile, Bubblegum initially tries to make the best of her situation, but she finally breaks down in the seventh-season episode "Varmints," admitting to Marceline through tears that instead of protecting those close to her, her desire for control only pushed them away. It is not hyperbole to call "Varmints" a watershed moment for Bubblegum for by the episode's end, she admits to both Marceline and herself that she is tired of micromanaging everything. It is this admission that opens the door for her radical character growth in the following seasons.

Near the end of the *Stakes* miniseries, Bubblegum's former citizens recognize the error of their ways. They thus depose the King of Ooo and reinstall Bubblegum as their "One True Princess." Thereafter, Bubblegum is noticeably more down to earth, and it seems her time in exile caused her to develop a greater sense of empathy not only for her close circle of friends, but also her candy subjects. This is best showcased in a short, oft-overlooked scene from the series finale, "Come Along with Me." Following the materialization of the malevolent deity GOLB, Bubblegum recognizes the potential disaster that the demon has in store for her army. She consequently climbs to the top of a large boulder and begins addressing her troops. Given the circumstances at hand and the monarchical register that the princess uses at the start of her address (beginning with the sobering order "Banana guards! Obey my command!"), it is heavily implied that Bubblegum is about to ask her loyal servants to sacrifice themselves for the Greater Good. However, these expectations are immediately subverted when the princess demands that her citizens abandon her and "flee for their lives."[12] Greater Good be damned!

Because it is a complex lamination of various plot points, Bubblegum's character arc can be read a variety of different ways. On one level, it is a meditation on ideal governance. Echoing the ideas of Aristotle, the show uses Bubblegum's story to put forth the idea that the best sort of ruler is a monarch—but only if that monarch embodies justice, truth, equality, and above all else virtue. If an impious leader (e.g., the King of Ooo) seizes the throne through usurpation or direct election, however, then the whole system collapses into tyranny—the worst form of government. (The belief that both tyrannical monarchies *and* direct democracies are a great evil is one that we see echoed time and time again throughout *Adventure Time*, most notably in episodes like Season 2's "The Silent King" and Season 6's "The Pajama War.")

On another level, Bubblegum's arc can be seen as an allegorical condemnation of the systems of mass surveillance that emerged in the United States following the 9/11 terrorist attacks, specifically those promoted by DARPA's Information Awareness Office or engendered by the passage of the PATRIOT Act. The parallels here are striking, with perhaps the most obvious being that both Bubblegum and the United States began encroaching upon the civil liberties of their citizens not necessarily out of a baseless yearning to usurp power, but rather out of a desire to "protect" and promote "safety." Alas, in both cases, this need for "total information awareness" spiraled into something far more sinister. When read this way, Bubblegum's development is decidedly political, castigating governmental overreach that needlessly (if not maliciously) infringes upon the civil liberties of innocent people.

The good news is that while Princess Bubblegum's character arc is one marked by bouts of darkness, exile, and despair, it is ultimately a story of political redemption, and by series' end, Bubblegum has managed to abandon many of her questionable ways, conquer her dictatorial yearnings, and become a truly virtuous leader.

MARCELINE THE VAMPIRE QUEEN

Marceline the Vampire Queen (full name: Marceline "Marcy" Abadeer)[13] is an immortal human-demon hybrid and the monarch of vampires—of which she is the only one left. She is also the heir apparent to the devilish dimension of utter bedlam known as the Nightosphere, which is ruled by her demonic father, Hunson Abadeer. Despite vampires being among the most feared creatures in Ooo—after all, the usually indomitable Finn and Jake are reduced to hysterics when Marceline first drops by their house in her debut episode "Evicted!"—Marceline subverts expectations by donning the appearance of a cool punk rocker who feasts not on the blood of her hapless victims but rather on red pigment itself.

Marceline is an immensely powerful being who can shapeshift into almost any form and effortlessly heal herself when injured. But far from being an unrelenting monster, Marceline is for the most part a laid-back loner who enjoys hanging out with friends and focusing on her greatest hobby: music. An accomplished bassist, her preferred instrument is a guitar that she retrofitted out of a large, double-bitted battle axe that previously belonged to her father. Marceline is also a gifted vocalist who expresses her complex emotions through catchy tunes.

Ward came up with Marceline when he was putting together the series' pitch bible, intending for the character both to serve "as a sort of antithesis to Bubblegum,"[14] and "to make [the show] a little more scary when [the writers] needed it."[15] Ward wanted Marceline to be "rad"—the sort of character that "weirdo little kids" would have a crush on[16]—and so he gave her a chic emo-goth aesthetic. As for the character's unique appellation, Ward took it from the middle name of his childhood friend, Marie,[17] who had a fondness for dark clothing and classic horror movies, such as Alfred Hitchcock's 1960 film *Psycho*.[18] The name (which only saw modest popularity at the tail end of the 1920s) has an old-timey ring to it, which is fitting, given the character's extreme age.

Marceline's black hair and pale skin evoke the aesthetic of traditional vampires, but the character is set apart from the rest of her coven-mates thanks to her casual attire and her iconic red boots. Although Marceline was Ward's creation, the character's unique look was finalized by Phil Rynda, the show's lead character and prop designer. When I asked Rynda what exactly inspired Marceline's appearance, he explained:

> When I was designing Marceline, I was looking at a lot of rock stars and super models for inspiration, but my sketches didn't quite feel like a character I cared about. Pen had done some early drawings of her but I needed to finish her up. I ended up scrolling through my Facebook friends and realized that there was a friend from middle school and high school that had some Marceline-esque qualities. So parts of Marceline were inspired by her.[19]

Rynda also mentioned that of the many characters that he designed for the show, Marceline is among his favorites because he could manipulate the look of her hair to "enhance her emotions."[20] "In *our* reality," he explained to me via email, "hair is a passive element [but] Marceline [has] hair that can move/react to [her] emotions.... I think it's a great cartooning tool, and [it is] something I just really like drawing."[21]

The casting process for Marceline was exacting, as Ward was determined to find someone who could effortlessly convey her "darker" nature. One day, he caught an episode of the Disney cartoon *Phineas and Ferb* featuring the character Vanessa Doofenshmirtz. Ward had no idea who played the character, but the actress's "angsty teenager thing" was exactly what he was looking for.[22] Ward subsequently reached out to his friend and colleague Martin Olson—a writer, musician, and comedian who served as the lead storyline writer for the first season of *Phineas and Ferb*—and asked him if he knew the actress in question. To Ward's great surprise, Martin told Ward that the actress was none other than his seventeen-year-old daughter, Olivia.[23]

Ward was delighted by the coincidence and brought Olivia in for an audition, at which she tried out for both Princess Bubblegum and Marceline. While Ward and the casting directors felt that Olson's style of delivery and vocal timbre were not a good match for Bubblegum,[24] they agreed that she was a natural fit for the more cynical Marceline, and soon thereafter she was cast in that role. Fortuitously for the show, Olson was also a gifted vocalist (who first gained recognition in 2003, when at the age of thirteen she performed a

Marceline the Vampire Queen was voiced by Olivia Olson, a talented actress and singer, who first gained notice for singing "All I Want for Christmas Is You" in the 2003 holiday classic *Love Actually*. Photo courtesy of Joel Feria.

spectacular rendition of Mariah Carey's hit song "All I Want for Christmas Is You" for the cult classic *Love Actually*), and the show made good use of her talents during its run by giving her character several songs. Years after Olson's casting, Ward emphatically declared that "her voice is incredible!" and mused that "having Olivia in episodes is inspiration enough to write a song for her to sing."[25]

The Shapeshifter: Marceline's Evolving Role

It is interesting to note, given the major role she would play in later seasons, that when Marceline is introduced in the first-season episode "Evicted," she serves not as an ally, but as the antagonist who steals our heroic duo's beloved Tree

Fort! Marceline is therefore similar to other Season 1 baddies in that she tests Finn and Jake's patience before engaging them in direct combat, but Marceline is set apart from other foes in how Finn and Jake defeat her—namely, that they do not. Indeed, during the episode's climactic fight sequence, Marceline almost effortlessly gains the upper hand. She neutralizes Jake by biting him, and after turning into a giant bat, she nearly kills Finn. It is only after Finn successfully lands a punch that she lets Finn and Jake win. She even gives them back the Tree Fort as a "gift."

Marceline lets our heroes go simply because she thinks they are fun. This is the first hint that there is something more to her character than her just being an "evil vampire"—a hint that is ultimately confirmed in the follow-up first-season episode "Henchman." This episode sees Finn slowly learn that Marceline's evil exterior is an elaborate facade and that she is, as Finn puts it, "a radical dame who likes to play games."[26] This exclamation in particular has led most fans and critics to read Marceline as a classic trickster character.[27] However, Marceline is a multifaceted character who is not so easily defined. In her initial appearances, for instance, she also displays elements of the "shapeshifter" archetype, who "change[s] appearance or mood, and [is] difficult for the hero and the audience to pin down. [She] may mislead the hero or keep [him] guessing, and [her] loyalty or sincerity is often in question."[28] Both Marceline's ability to change physical form and her penchant for pranking Finn clearly index her shapeshifter qualities. Marceline can also be viewed as an archetypical "wild woman" who is playful in general but fierce when provoked; free to do as she likes but loyal to her friends; and well-meaning but sadly "hounded, harassed, and falsely imputed to be devouring and devious."[29]

Although the pitch bible implies that Marceline was intended as a romantic interest for Finn,[30] refreshingly, this never comes to pass. Instead, Marceline comes to function more like Finn and Jake's affable (if at times mercurial) older sister, often coming to their aid when they need it the most. Considering that Marceline was introduced as a simplistic bully, this is quite the character development! Much of this evolution can arguably be attributed to the influence of storyboard artist Rebecca Sugar, who related deeply to the character. Sugar used this connection to flesh out the more emotional elements of Marceline's story, which in turn led naturally to Marceline becoming one of the show's more complex characters.[31]

Fangs for the Memories: Popularity and Backstory

Despite technically playing second fiddle to Finn and Jake, Marceline is one of the show's most popular characters (if the myriad bass-wielding cosplayers often spotted at fan conventions mean anything), and she is easily one of the show's breakout stars. Marceline's fandom dates all the way back to early 2010, before the debut of the first season! At the time, promotional shots of Marceline engendered an embryonic following for the character on forums like ToonZone—a following that exploded into a bona fide fan base after a preview of "Evicted!" aired on March 18, 2010.[32] With every new season, fans were demanding more and more Marceline, and when the producers began working on their first miniseries, they decided to focus it entirely around her. Even today, in online rankings of the show's best characters, Marceline almost always places in the top three, and she is beloved by the creators of both fanart and fanfiction alike. Part of Marceline's allure is almost certainly due to her undeniably "cool" characterization: she is a powerful she-demon who also happens to be a stylish bassist that enjoys having a good time with her friends.

But another factor that almost certainly helped catapult the character onto the collective fandom's "best of" list is Marceline's enigmatic backstory, which was teased out slowly over the show's run. While a few story clues were sprinkled into the show's first season, it is not until the second-season premiere, "It Came from the Nightosphere," that her personal history starts coming to the fore. In this episode, the audience is introduced to Marceline's demonic father, Hunson Abadeer (voiced by Olivia Olson's actual father, Martin), who we learn is not a great dad. The next piece of the puzzle comes in the third-season episode "Memory of a Memory," in which we learn that Marceline was a child during the Great Mushroom War. (The postfinale special "Obsidian" would later expand on this piece of the character's history, detailing how in the aftermath of the war Marceline's mother died presumably from radiation sickness, forcing Marceline to fend for herself in a postapocalyptic hellscape).

Marceline's backstory is then blown wide open in the penultimate episode of Season 4, "I Remember You," and the follow-up fifth-season episode "Simon and Marcy." Over the course of these two episodes, we learn that following the Mushroom War, Marceline was discovered by a still-sane Simon Petrikov, who had managed to survive the mutagenic horrors of the conflict thanks to the power of his ice crown. Simon took little Marceline—whom he affectionately called "Marcy"—under his wing and began raising her like his own daughter. Unfortunately, while Simon was at first able to resist the magic of the crown, it eventually consumed his mind, causing him to forget both himself and poor Marceline. In one of his last lucid acts, Simon abandoned a preteen Marceline to spare her from his increasingly dangerous psychosis. (When "I Remember You" and "Simon and Marcy" debuted, they were both lauded for substantially deepening Marceline and Ice King's characterization, and today, many fans consider them to be the series' best episodes.)

The audience finally learns the last key pieces of Marceline's backstory over the course of the eight-episode miniseries *Stakes*, which aired in late 2015 during the show's seventh season. This event series reveals that when a then-mortal Marceline was about eighteen years of age, she came into conflict with gangs of murderous vampires who had recently awakened after centuries of hibernation deep within the earth. Marceline quickly grew tired of these bloodsucking foes, and so she devoted herself to eradicating the vampiric threat; to aid in her task, she began using her demonic powers to absorb the souls—and consequently, the abilities—of those vampires that she slew. As she eliminated the alpha vampires, she grew ever stronger in the process. From a vampire named the Fool, she took the power of flight; from another named the Empress, the power of invisibility; from the Hierophant, the power to shape shift; and from the Moon, the power to self-heal. Marceline eventually confronted and killed the Vampire King himself. Alas, it was something of a Pyrrhic victory, for in that climactic fight, Marceline herself was bitten, ironically turning into the very abomination that she so deeply despised.

While the flashback sequences in *Stakes* can be read as broad considerations of trauma, they are arguably best understood as sobering meditations on the horror of physical/sexual abuse, in particular. This is exemplified in one of the show's darkest sequences: Marceline's turning. In this scene, Marceline is shown pinned to the ground by the hulking, masculine Vampire King. While Marceline struggles in vain to free herself, the King penetrates her neck with his fangs, and when his teeth pierce her skin, Marceline lets out a terror-filled scream that is neither cartoony nor comedic. It does not take a Freudian to see the obvious visual and aural parallels in the scene. The Vampire King's actions are the equivalent of rape.

So distressing was her turning that roughly a millennium later, Marceline tells Princess Bubblegum, "When I became a vampire, I was just a messed-up kid. Now it's 1,000 years later, and I'm *still* messed up!"[33] The show could not be clearer. Poor Marceline needs therapy! As it just so happens, the events of *Stakes* play out like psychotherapeutic trauma recovery: First, Marceline faces down her old vampiric foes, thereby "confront[ing] the horrors of the past."[34] Then, by remembering the events leading up to her turning, she is given the chance to "mourn the old self that the trauma destroyed."[35] At the miniseries' climax Marceline fully "sheds her victim identity"[36] by flying into the heart of the Vampire King's essence, determined to bring it down. By consuming the essence, Marceline knows she will again become the vampire queen, but this does not matter, for now *she* is the agent of change. *Stakes* concludes with a revampirized Marceline expressing her contentedness, noting that the events of the miniseries have allowed her to "reclaim the present and the future"[37] and thereby "grow up."[38]

Suffice it to say, episodes like "I Remember You" or the flashbacks in *Stakes* paint Marceline as a strong-willed survivor of abuse: a victim of war, who was pulled from her mother, abandoned by her biological father, forgotten by her adoptive father, and then graphically assaulted. It is more than fair to say that Marceline has lived "through many lifetimes of trauma," to quote Olivia Olson.[39] But the character's strength in the face of so much adversity is also admirable, and many fans who have been dealt a bad hand empathize with the character, finding solace in her triumphs. Marceline is far from perfect, but over the course of the show's ten seasons, she nevertheless shows a willingness to learn from her flaws and make peace with her troubled past. In this way, she is arguably one of the show's richest, most human characters (which is ironic, given that she is an immortal vampire demon).

THE SAGA OF "BUBBLINE"

As was briefly discussed earlier in this chapter, throughout the series, it is heavily suggested—and eventually confirmed in the series finale—that Princess Bubblegum and Marceline have feelings for one another. While this pairing of the show's leading ladies may be one of the more famous queer[40] relationships in the history of Western animated television, only a few sources have considered the topic in-depth,[41] and hardly any detail the behind-the-scenes drama that the pairing engendered. What follows is thus an attempt to fill the hole in the literature by providing a detailed history of "Bubbline" (the shipping portmanteau of "*Bubb*legum" and "Marce*line*").

The Story Begins

Despite what some people believe, the romantic relationship between the two characters was never planned from the start.[42] In fact, the series pitch bible describes Marceline and Bubblegum as being "friendly rivals," with the implication that both were to eventually be love interests for Finn.[43] In a 2012 interview with io9, Pendleton Ward explained that this early approach to Bubblegum and Marceline was inspired largely by the *Archie Comics*, specifically the characters Betty Cooper and Veronica Lodge; in the long-running comic series, Betty and Veronica—despite being best friends—are constantly competing against one another for the attention of title character Archie Andrew. According to Ward: "That was the cliché that I was interested in, and I liked that there were these two girls that liked messing with Finn's head, and he's totally true of heart. . . . I liked that relationship."[44]

This Betty-and-Veronica approach to Bubblegum and Marceline is perhaps best illustrated in the second-season episode "Go with Me." In this installment, Finn hopes to get Bubblegum to go with him to the movies on couples' night,

Storyboard artist Rebecca Sugar (pictured here at a Comic-Con panel for her own show, *Steven Universe*) is seen by most in the *Adventure Time* fandom as the principal architect of "Bubbline." Photo courtesy of Sue Lukenbaugh via CC Attribution-ShareAlike 2.0 Generic (CC BY-SA 2.0) license, https://flic.kr/p/fkiBpS.

so he and Marceline flirt in an attempt to make the princess jealous. When Bubblegum first acknowledges Marceline, the former is noticeably irritated by the latter's presence, almost as if the vampire queen has long annoyed her with her careless antics. Marceline, on the other hand, seems delighted to both be bothering the princess and messing with Finn.

It would not be until the third-season episode "What Was Missing" that the two would once again interact, but this time the nature of their relationship would be deepened substantially. In this episode, Finn, Jake, Marceline, Bubblegum, and BMO chase down a "doorlord" who has stolen a prized possession from each of them. The doorlord soon hides behind a magical entryway that will only open to "music from a genuine band." Marceline, being a natural musician, grabs her ax bass and kicks things off with an emotive song entitled "I'm Just Your Problem," the lyrics of which are not-so-subtly directed at Princess Bubblegum. The song suggests that in the past Bubblegum pushed Marceline away, seemingly for not being "serious" enough. The lyrics also express Marceline's frustration that, despite feeling as if she has done nothing wrong, she wants to make up with the princess regardless.

Based on many of the plot points in "What Was Missing"—such as the lyrics to "I'm Just Your Problem," or the fact that Bubblegum's prize possession is a shirt that Marceline gave her—it is abundantly clear that Marceline and Bubblegum share a complicated past. But what exactly was the nature of that past? According to "What Was Missing" storyboard artist Rebecca Sugar, with whom I corresponded via email in February 2020:

Before ["What Was Missing"] Marceline and Bubblegum had interacted once [in "Go with Me"], an exchange Tom Herpich had written, where Marceline snidely referred to Bubblegum [as] "Bonnibel." It was clear they had history . . . so [when I got the outline for "What Was Missing"] I pitched that they had been in a romantic relationship in the past, but Bubblegum's priorities shifted to her kingdom, and Marceline took it hard. I had a ton of theories about their dynamic, that Bubblegum had admired Marceline's powerful, evil exterior only to find out she was secretly very vulnerable, and that Marceline had once looked to Bubblegum for affection and validation, before watching her assume her role as a mad-scientist dictator. They were perfect opposites, both pulled in by the other's surface persona and pushed away by what was going on underneath. They complemented each other! I pitched this to Adam first and we wrote that into "What Was Missing," which we presented to Pen and the show team.[45]

Unfortunately, due to the prejudices of the time, Sugar and Muto had to be strategic in how they worked this romantic angle into their storyboard:

Back in the early 2010s . . . we couldn't be direct [about their relationship]. To put this into context, for the entire first year I was working on *Adventure Time*, "Don't Ask Don't Tell" was still in effect, and same-sex marriage wouldn't be legal in the US for another half a decade. There was a national conversation about how, if we were to legalize same-sex marriage, children would no longer be "protected" from LGBTQIA+ awareness, and may even get the impression that it's "ok to be gay" (which, of course, it absolutely is).[46]

These sociocultural barriers meant that, in the final episode, the nature of Marceline and Bubblegum's relationship is a bit more subtextual than it perhaps would have been had Sugar and Muto been given free rein by the network.

Despite this roadblock, Sugar and Muto were confident that the show's fans would get what they were going for, and indeed, when "What Was Missing" aired on September 26, 2011, a sizeable portion of the fanbase immediately recognized the queer subtext in the episode for what it was. However, there were those who protested any romantic interpretation of the episode, arguing that Marceline and Bubblegum were your standard "frenemies" who had simply had a falling out. Soon, a full-on debate had erupted within the fandom.

It was around this time that the Frederator-sanctioned recap series "Mathematical!" accidentally added further fuel to the fire by referencing the topic in one of their video summations, wherein a voice-over speculates that Marceline "might like Princess Bubblegum a little more than she'd like to admit. Maybe a little more than Finn."[47] The producers of the recap series also chose to complement this voice-over with select drawings (some by character designer Natasha Allegri), which depicted Marceline and Bubblegum in loving embrace.

Because the "Mathematical!" series was produced by Frederator, many interpreted the video as explicit confirmation that Marceline and Bubblegum had in fact been a couple. This, in turn, engendered pushback from some fans, who were worried that the show was trying to "force a narrative" on them. This growing controversy resulted in Frederator axing the "Mathematical!" series altogether; Fred Seibert himself even issued the following apology:

> Well, I completely screwed up.
>
> There's been chatter on the internet recently about our latest *Adventure Time* "Mathematical!" video recap that we created, posted, and removed here at Frederator. I figure it's time to clear up the matter.
>
> In trying to get the show's audience involved we got wrapped up by both fan conjecture and spicy fanart and went a little too far. . . . I let us goof in a staggering way and I'm deeply sorry it's become such a distraction for so many people.[48]

Many in the fandom were livid, with this anger perhaps best expressed by Kjerstin Johnson of *Bitch* magazine: "It's hard not to see Seibert's language as pretty coded: By 'spicy' [fanart], I think he was referring to the depictions of Bubblegum and Marceline being more than just friends (though the images in the video are, at most, PG-13)."[49] Was queerness in a kid's show really *that* much of a taboo?

Soon after, many of those involved with the show tried to distance themselves from the controversy: Pendleton Ward called it "a big hullaballoo" and decided not to take a stand one way or the other because "there were [already] so many extreme positions taken on it all over the Internet."[50] Adam Muto, the costoryboarder of "What Was Missing," channeled his inner Barthes by arguing that Marceline and Bubblegum's relationship was best left up to the viewer's interpretation.[51] While these "impartial" comments were meant to prevent any further controversy, they only served to further foment strong feelings in the fanbase. In this way, what had started out as a seemingly fringe pairing had become one of the fandom's most famous "ships." Bubbline had officially set sail.[52]

The Tide Begins to Turn

It seems that the controversy generated by "What Was Missing" was so volatile that the show held off on producing episodes that costarred Marceline and

Bubblegum for years. This dearth of episodes, sometimes sardonically called the "Great Bubbline Drought" by fans, finally ended with the fifth-season episode "Sky Witch," which aired on July 29, 2013, and features Marceline and Bubblegum teaming up to take down a "sky witch" named Maja. With the airing of "Sky Witch," many in the fandom wondered if the show's writers and producers were finally ready to embrace rather than avoid the elephant in the room.

The answer, unfortunately, was "not yet."

After the airing of "Sky Witch," months went by without any other Marceline/Bubblegum episodes. By mid-2014, hope for Bubbline seemed lost, but then, at a question-and-answer panel with fans on August 7, 2014, Olivia Olson dropped the following bombshell:

> I was at the recording studio [the other day] and Pen was actually there because he was recording for Lumpy Space Princess. And I . . . wanted to pick Pen's brain a little bit [about Marceline and Bubblegum's relationship]. And he said, "Oh, you know they dated, right?" And I said, "That's what I figured from all the creepy fanart." . . . I said, "Are they going to [date] on the show at all? Or can we say anything about it in the [*The Enchiridion & Marcy's Super Secret Scrapbook*]?" And he's like, "I don't know about the book, but in some countries where the show airs [queer relationships are] illegal." So that's why they're not putting it in the show.[53]

Olson's revelation was met with jubilant hoots and hollers from the audience, but part of this joy was later undercut when Olson surreptitiously tweeted that she "like[s] to make things up at panels" and that fans "take [her] stories way too seriously."[54] While Olson never addressed which "stories" she was referring to, many fans assumed she was talking about the Bubbline reveal.

But why, some fans asked, would Olson have dropped such an explosive fib? After all, Olson was not known for spreading major rumors during panel presentations. This discrepancy led many fans to suspect that the tweet was not so much a recantation as it was Olson's attempt to back-peddle—possibly on behest of an unhappy network that had been indirectly shamed for its practices. As it turns out, this is exactly what happened, and in a 2020 interview on *The Ship-It Show*, Olson confirmed that indeed, she was chastised by the higher-ups at Cartoon Network after spilling the secret about Bubbline, prompting her aforementioned "retraction."[55]

Luckily for Bubbline shippers, good news was right around the corner for while all this drama was unfolding, the writers had just started to work on the show's seventh season. Realizing that they had not placed as much attention on Marceline and Bubblegum in the past, the producers decided it was time to once again shine the spotlight on their leading ladies. This refocusing is immediately noticeable in the second episode of the season, "Varmints," which aired on November 3, 2015. In this episode, Marceline and Bubblegum team up to hunt the titular monsters, and in the process, they begin to discuss their past. In a scene about midway through the episode, Bubblegum, in a rare moment of vulnerability, breaks down into tears, apologizing to Marceline for the way she pushed her away. In an equally rare display of tenderness, Marceline comforts Bubblegum and assures her that she has nothing to apologize for. The two then finish off the varmints and call it a night. The episode ends with Bubblegum falling asleep on Marceline's shoulder while the two, for lack of a better word, snuggle on Bubblegum's porch.

Things are then kicked up a few more notches in the miniseries *Stakes*, in which five fearsome vampires return from the dead, forcing Bubblegum and a devampirized Marceline (along with Finn, Jake, and Peppermint Butler) to stop them. For many who had up to this point remained Bubbline skeptics, *Stakes* is what caused their dam of doubt to break. Indeed, to call *Stakes* queer is an understatement. Across the miniseries' eight episodes, Marceline and Bubblegum engage in a whole slew of quasiromantic behavior, such as cradling one another lovingly, talking about living together, and dreaming about growing old. In one of the more direct scenes, Marceline, while training with Bubblegum, even mistakes long-forgotten human feeling (in this case, hunger) for "love."

Stakes was in many ways a catalyst for the Bubbline movement, and after the miniseries' debut, episodes featuring Marceline and Bubblegum became much more frequent, which each new episode providing more and more subtext than the last: soon, the two were "meeting the parents" ("Broke His Crown," "Marcy & Hunson"), going on "dates" ("Broke His Crown," "Wheels"), and even holding hands in public ("Seventeen").

The Kiss Seen 'round the World

By the time the show's final season rolled around, the idea that Bubbline was just a "fan theory" seemed ludicrous to many, given the voluminous subtext that had piled up. That said, the show had yet to explicitly foreground the romantic element of Marceline and Bubblegum's close relationship, instead choosing to veil it slightly or to hide it in the background.

This all changed in the series finale, "Come Along with Me": in the episode, Bubblegum is battling a chaos beast when she is nearly killed. For a moment, Marceline believes that Bubblegum has died and flies into a blind rage, unleashing her full vampiric power, which allows her to effortlessly defeat the creature that (apparently) felled her friend. Once Marceline realizes that the creature did not kill Bubblegum, she flies into the princess's arms and, through tears of happiness and regret, tells her: "Even when we weren't talking, I was so afraid something bad would happen to you and I wouldn't be there to protect you . . . I don't want to lose you again."[56] After Bubblegum assures Marceline that she will not be going anywhere, the two lovingly embrace, and then—to the delight of shippers the world over—they kiss.

The scene was met with near-universal acclaim from critics and fans alike, but what many might not know is that it nearly did not make it into the final episode. According to Muto:

> [The kiss] actually wasn't in the outline when it was submitted. It didn't say that they kiss. It just said they "have a moment." . . . It was really up to Hanna K. [Nyström], the storyboard artist who got that scene, to decide what her take on it was going to be. . . . When Hanna boarded that, there was a little note in the margin that said "Come on!" with a big exclamation point. That was the only note. I can't argue with that.[57]

Part of this hesitation was because Muto and some of the other producers feared that too heavy a focus on Bubblegum and Marceline's romance could be misinterpreted by the audience as crass fetishization of queer sexuality, rather than an earnest depiction of normal behavior that has been unfairly marginalized for centuries.[58] Having said that, were the show to have not addressed the romance at all, or down-played the queer subtext, the show would have likely been accused of queerbaiting its audience. It was a tightrope act, but in the end, the show stuck the landing.

But while the overt queerness on display in "Come Along with Me" was widely celebrated, some fans and critics were also frustrated that this all came at the eleventh hour. ("It's unfortunate that *Adventure Time* has to play catch-up with these characters so late in the game," Eric Kohn of IndieWire opined in an otherwise positive review of the finale.[59] Similarly, in a book chapter on queerbaiting, the media scholars Bridget Blodgett and Anastasia Salter wrote, "It is notable that . . . it is only the queer-coded relationship that remains unlabeled until the final moments of the show, when commercial viability is no longer at risk."[60]) If only the show could have devoted more time to the couple! Imagine how satisfying an in-depth look at their relationship could have been!

It seems that the writers had similar thoughts, for when Cartoon Network Studios ordered the *Distant Lands* specials, an in-depth look at Bubbline was a top priority. "We all knew we wanted to tell a [Bubbline] story early on," Nyström told me via Instagram. "I definitely pushed for [a story] to explore why their relationship would work this time around."[61] The result was the forty-four-minute "Obsidian," released exclusively though HBO Max in late 2020. This special builds off the Bubbline kiss in "Come Along with Me," juxtaposing the details of the couple's infamous breakup (long ago alluded to in "What Was Missing") with their happy, postfinale life as a couple. "Obsidian" is a strong special that sidesteps easy fan service and instead places its focus on the emotional strides Marceline and Bubblegum have made as romantic partners. Gone are the ambiguities, and gone are the coded lines of dialogue. If "Come Along with Me" was a strategic win for the queer community, "Obsidian" is nothing short of a decisive victory that proudly and emphatically celebrates the queerness of Bubbline in a definitive way.

Why Bubbline Matters

In February 2020, while finishing my initial draft of this chapter, I emailed Rebecca Sugar (rightfully considered by most the principal architect of Bubbline) and asked for her take on, as I put it, "the 'canonization' of Bubbline in the finale." Sugar was gracious enough to respond, emphasizing first and foremost that from her perspective as the writer of "What Was Missing," Bubbline had long been canon:

> It's critical to see LGBTQIA+ characters love and kiss and have happy futures ahead of them, especially in media for kids—but the idea that the queerness of Marceline and Bubblegum was "canonized" in the finale misses the fact that they were always written as queer individuals, even when they weren't actively dating.[62]

Then, in a moment of vulnerability that I was not expecting, Sugar explained to me just how deeply personal the characters and their relationship were to her own identity:

> I felt particularly attached to Marceline. As a bisexual person I'd never written for a bisexual character [like her] before, [who is] struggling with the anxieties I'd struggled with and putting up a front like I had....
>
> Being out in the workplace, while creating content for children based on one's own queer experiences, was not acceptable [when I first started storyboarding] and continues to be difficult now. But I was able to speak through the characters. Before I could say "I'm bisexual" I could say, "I put a lot of myself into Marceline," and people would understand. I'd had no access to community, because I'd been "protected" from everyone I could have related to and learned from. But suddenly, because of the show, I found people who recognized me as a queer individual, based not just on the relationships I'd been in but also on my relationship with myself, my work, and my hopes and dreams.

Writing those characters was the first step I took toward finding community, coming out to myself, my family and my partner, and ultimately, my bosses, which then allowed me to fully voice why I felt it was so important to include queer content in kids' media. The years we spent speaking code in order to find each other were part of a specifically queer experience that many of us are still living daily, which is why it's so impactful to finally see [Marceline and Bubblegum] kiss . . . in the finale.[63]

Sugar's comments here underscore why Bubbline is so important. This is not just the tale of an unlikely romance, or of passionate shippers "winning out in the end": rather, it is the story of increased representation and the increasing acceptance of queer identities in modern society.

On June 10, 2022, Cartoon Network posted a short video celebrating Pride Month in which Princess Bubblegum and Marceline (voiced by Walch and Olson) stress the acceptance of all sexual and gender minorities. ("People get built different," Bubblegum casually tells us in the video. "We don't need to figure it out; we just need to respect it—whether people are gay, they, trans or any part of the queer spectrum.")[64] The fact that Cartoon Network—the company that for years tried hard to stamp out the flames of Bubbline—produced this is astounding, and it serves as a testament to how things changed since 2010. There is still much work to be done before queer identities are normalized in the media that we consume, but thanks to artists like Rebecca Sugar, Hanna K. Nyström, and the many other artists who pushed to make Bubbline a reality, progress is being made.

COMPLEX LEADING LADIES:
FINAL THOUGHTS ON BUBBLEGUM AND MARCELINE

While in this chapter I have attempted to eschew preferentialism in favor of impartiality, I normally make no secret that Princess Bubblegum and Marceline are my favorite *Adventure Time* characters. There are numerous factors that I could cite to defend this position (both subvert gender stereotypes without rejecting femininity wholesale, both have intriguing backstories situated in the broader mythology of the series, both have colorful and creative character designs), but I think the most important factor is the characters' complexity.

It is true that Marceline is a vampire—a rather "traditional" fantasy monster—but she is also a sensitive soul, a loyal friend, and a talented musician whose emo tunes are certified earworms. Likewise, while Bubblegum might be a princess in pink, she is also a scientific wunderkind whose governing philosophy makes Machiavelli look like Abe Lincoln. Bubblegum and Marceline are thus more than your friendly neighborhood monster girls; they are characters with an astonishing amount of depth, which allows them to transcend easy understandings of what it means to be a "vampire" or a "princess." Marceline and Bubblegum are fundamentally *interesting*, and if that is not the sign of a great character, then I do not know what is.

3.

"BEST FRIENDS [AND FOES] IN THE WORLD"

The Ensemble Characters

Every good hero needs sidekicks, and every good hero needs a villain; as the undisputed champions of Ooo, Finn and Jake have both in spades. In this chapter, I will explore a few of our heroes' more important allies, as well as a few of their more formidable foes.

BMO

BMO (in some sources stylized as "B-MO" or spelled out phonetically as "Beemo") is a small robot who lives with Finn and Jake in their grassland tree fort. Gregarious and relatively carefree, BMO treats Finn and Jake at times like its parents and at other times like its peers.

According to Patrick McHale, BMO was inspired by a robotic character named Raye that he had mocked up in the late 2000s for his own personal pilot project: "a quirky cosmic opera with deeper philosophical themes" entitled *Space Planet*.[1] After *Adventure Time* entered into production and McHale was hired on as a creative director, Ward asked him if Raye could be dropped into the budding Land of Ooo: "At some point Pen [asked me] if he could put Raye into *Adventure Time* because I think he just liked the idea of a little computer person," McHale revealed to me via email. "Then we started riffing on the character by doing goofy Speak & Spell–style computer voices. Somehow we landed on the name BMO. . . . I think the name came from the idea that people would ask BMO stupid questions, and he would respond, 'You need to be more smart' (which sounded like 'You need to B MO smart' in my Speak & Spell voice)."[2]

In terms of an aesthetic design, the character is best described as a cross between a Nintendo Game Boy and an old Macintosh Classic II.[3] But under the mundane facade of late twentieth-century technology, BMO is a technologically advanced multitool, capable of performing a bevy of futuristic tasks (e.g., projecting holograms, downloading human consciousness into its "main game brain frame") alongside more humdrum functions (e.g., printing readouts on continuous stationery, playing old VHS tapes, functioning as a flashbulb camera).

BMO is voiced by Niki Yang, a writer and animator from South Korea who worked on the first season of *Adventure Time* as a storyboard artist and who also provided the voice of Lady Rainicorn. Yang, who speaks English with a Korean accent, got the part of BMO almost accidentally, as she revealed in an interview with Sweety High:

> [The producers] were . . . having a hard time finding BMO's voice. At first they tried really low, tough voices, but at the end of the day, Pen asked me if I wanted to give it a try, so I did. I'm not an actor, so to me my BMO voice sounds really immature and I think with my [Korean] accent it sounds childish, but that's what they liked about it, and I got the role.[4]

When looking back on her audition, Yang told me:

> I auditioned for the role without knowing how successful the show would be and how iconic [the] character . . . would turn out. And no one else did. So it was a fairly quick process of hiring. I was excited but super nervous especially when you record with veteran actors like Tom Kenny and John DiMaggio in the same room.[5]

Later, in a 2020 email exchange with the author, Yang joked: "Who would know having an accent opens a door of golden opportunity!"[6]

At the start of the show, BMO appeared mostly in the background and usually only had a handful of lines every few episodes. But as the show's fanbase grew, and many began highlighting the robot as their favorite character, BMO began finding itself in the spotlight more and more. This eventually led to the fourth-season episode "BMO Noire," which stars BMO as a hard-boiled detective attempting to solve a case. "BMO Noire" marked the first time that Yang had to carry an episode almost entirely by herself, and when it came time to do the voice recording for the episode, she worried that she would not be able to do the storyboard justice.[7] Despite her uncertainty, Yang did an excellent job, and "BMO Noire" is often cited by fans as a stand-out episode of the show's fourth season. The success of this episode arguably led to the writers penning a number of BMO-heavy episodes thereafter, and as a result BMO readily became part of the show's group of main characters.

BMO.init(backstory): A Robotic Origin Story

For the first half of the series, the characters remain oblivious to BMO's origins. This all changes in the fifth-season episode "Be More," in which Finn, Jake, and the audience learn that BMO was constructed by an eccentric transhuman inventor named Moseph "Moe" Mastro Giovanni. Moe initially wanted BMO to be playful and affectionate, and so he specifically designed the robot to "be more" than the average android. Later, in the two-part Season 7 episode "The More You Moe, the Moe You Know," the audience learns that Moe also created a robot named AMO, who functioned effectively as BMO's older sibling. While BMO was designed to give love, AMO was designed to receive it; alas, this turned AMO into a needy monster who grew jealous of all the attention given to BMO. At the end of the episode, AMO and BMO confront one another, and in the fray, AMO "dies" after accidentally falling off a cliff.

The genesis for this elaborate backstory can be traced back to the show's third season, when storyboard artists Adam Muto and Rebecca Sugar pitched an episode about BMO's origin.[8] The original outline developed at this time focused on Finn, Jake, and BMO's epic journey "to find the giant AMO, which [was] . . . buried under the ground,"[9] but for unclear reasons, this episode was pushed off until the production of Season 5, whereupon it was transmuted by storyboard artists Tom Herpich and Steve Wolfhard into the episode "Be More." Herpich and Wolfhard's approach to the story differed substantially from Muto and Sugar's initial pitch. ("I changed the original Moe design," Wolfhard told me in an interview. "He had been frightening like the Borg queen from *Star Trek: First Contact*. I [also] added the breakroom scene, the cart sequence, and the AMO mystery.")[10] Nevertheless, when I asked Sugar how the finished episode compared to her initial pitch, she was emphatic that Herpich and Wolfhard's version was the best possible approach to BMO's origin story.[11]

Wolfhard would later take the ideas he had worked into "Be More" and extrapolate them into the seventh-season holiday two-parter "The More You Moe, the Moe You Know." While the finished special is easily the season's moodiest entry, Wolfhard's initial idea for the episode was originally much darker:

> The original pitch for this was for an episode I wanted to do that would have been called "Be Mourn." My idea was that BMO had died. I love party episodes, and I thought a funeral episode could be really fun to have everyone in the treehouse talking about BMO. He would be in a little glass casket, like Snow White. And there would be a tandem story of BMO in the Dead World, talking with Moe, who was also in the Dead World. BMO would be watching his own funeral and see AMO show up as Moe, and [he would] come back to life and fight AMO.[12]

(Although the idea of a robot afterlife is wonderfully inventive, it is not hard to see why the show's producers steered Wolfhard away from the funeral angle.)

In the epilogue of the series' finale, it is revealed that BMO not only has an important connection to Ooo's past, but that the robot also plays a major role in its future: One thousand years after Finn and Jake's time, BMO is still "alive," living in a small house atop Mount Cragdor (the same mountain that had housed the *Enchiridion* prior to Finn's acquisition of the book). Believed by most to be nothing more than a folklore legend, BMO is known at this time simply as the "King of Ooo"—having presumably usurped at some point the title from the character of the same name. It is "King" BMO who narrates the story of the Great Gum War to Shermy and Beth, and it is BMO who inspires the two to find the Finn-Sword embedded in the trunk of the Fern-Tree. In this way, BMO is something of a constant in a universe built on change, uniting the past, present, and future of Ooo all as one.

A Roleplaying, Genderfluid Robot

Whether intentional on the part of the show's writers or not, BMO's characterization subverts many of the tropes and clichés associated with sentient robots in modern media. For instance, while many robots—like the Terminator in the movie series of the same name, or the Machines from *The Matrix* franchise—are depicted as conscienceless killers who think only in terms of mass slaughter, BMO is depicted as childlike, yearning not for destruction, but rather play. BMO also manages to eschew the "uncreative robot" trope often found in pop culture by being arguably the most imaginative member of *Adventure Time*'s main cast. In fact, so creative is BMO that the robot regularly engages in elaborate role plays or pretends to be a "living boy" or a "real baby girl." This side of BMO is best showcased in episodes like Season 4's "Five Short Graybles," wherein the character talks to itself in the bathroom mirror, believing that its reflection is really a doppelganger named "Football" who lives in a parallel mirror world; in several subsequent episodes, BMO and Football discuss their separate lives, express their affection for one another, and even switch places for a day!

Another fascinating aspect of BMO's characterization is that the robot has no clearly assigned gender, instead "appear[ing] inherently fluid," as theorists Christopher Olson and CarrieLynn Reinhard put it.[13] Because of this fluidity, BMO can, at a moment's notice, "adopt any identity or inhabit any gender it wishes."[14] The fourth-season standout "BMO Noire" provides a fascinating case study to consider this fluidity. In this episode—which overtly lampoons black-and-white noir films from the early half of the twentieth century—BMO dons the role of a hard-boiled detective, attempting to solve the case of Finn's missing sock. Throughout the episode, BMO interacts with a variety of "suspects," all of whom are given a uniquely inflected voice by the robot; included in this motley group of suspects is the episode's *poule fatale*, Lorraine the chicken. When playing the detective role in "BMO Noire," BMO copies the behavior of stereotypical masculine private eyes (like Sam Spade or Philip Marlowe) by talking in a gruff voice, threatening violence to get answers, and making cynical observations about the world. Conversely, when giving voice to Lorraine, BMO mimics the stereotypical behavior of femme fatales, such as using flirtatious dialog in an attempt to manipulate the detective.

In this episode, BMO is on one level consciously choosing to role play as both a male detective and a femme fatale; on another level, however, the specific behaviors that BMO chooses to imitate are predicated on "sociocultural codes that categorize individuals as man [or] woman"[15]—codes that BMO passively assumes are "correct." In other words, BMO's gendered behavior can be both intentional and unintentional—sometimes in interlocking ways. "BMO Noire" is thus an excellent example of both Erving Goffman's understanding of gender as a "performance" (i.e., that gender is actively and consciously enacted by subjects to convey information to others), as well as Judith Butler's understanding of "gender performativity" (i.e., that gender is unconsciously enacted, cited, and replicated by subjects).[16] For Olson and Reinhard, *Adventure Time* thus uses BMO as a clear example that gender is "fluid and subject to change at either a conscious or unconscious level."[17]

Given BMO's penchant for shifting genders depending on the situations at hand, characters routinely address the robot with whatever titles or pronouns seem most appropriate. What is more, in the show, there is never any obsession with this fluidity, and characters do not express anxiety about getting BMO's gender "correct." The same cannot be said about fans of the show online; in fact, a simple Google search for "BMO's gender" will return hundreds of forum posts in which fans debate whether BMO is a "he," "she," "it," "they," or some other gender. In all fairness, some confusion may stem from the fact that BMO is voiced by a female actress, while being depicted partaking in stereotypically "boy" activities (e.g., skateboarding, playing video games).[18] At the same time, the show's producers have time and time again declared that BMO is genderfluid.

Because of this genderfluidity, BMO is a radically political character—one who emphasizes the socially constructed (and thus arbitrary) nature of gender and gender norms. For those fighting for transgender and nonbinary rights, BMO is thus something of an unlikely ally, capable of illustrating how a world without the shackles of gender is not some meaningless dystopia, but rather a freeing space of endless possibilities!

...

Due to its idiosyncratic behavior and humorous lines of dialog, BMO is beloved by many fans of the show and is often heralded as one of its greatest characters. (The robot has even wired its way into the hearts of both Ward and Muto, who at different points have cited the character as one of their favorites.)[19] When I asked Yang if she thought her voice acting played a part in BMO's popularity, she responded with modesty:

> I know BMO is very popular, but I'm not sure if my voice has anything to do with that. BMO is a great character with an irresistible personality created by great writers, storyboard artists, designers, and of course the creator. I did my best to bring all the charms and love that they poured into [the character]. I'm only the transmitter of those creative minds behind it. I'm deeply grateful for being the [voice of the] tiny robot who carries their vision.[20]

LUMPY SPACE PRINCESS

Lumpy Space Princess (often referred to simply as "LSP") is a self-absorbed princess made up of "irradiated stardust"[21] from a dimension known as "Lumpy Space." A hyperbolic caricature of a contemporary teenage girl, Lumpy Space Princess is vain, self-centered, dramatic, boy-crazy, and obsessed with being fashionable. She is also frequently depicted rebelling against her parents, which generally takes the form of her running away from home; in fact, for much of the series, she lives as a veritable hobo in the woods of Ooo. But despite this litany of negatives, the character is nevertheless a close friend to Finn and Jake.

As one of Ooo's more unusual inhabitants, it is only appropriate that Lumpy Space Princess should have an equally unusual production backstory. According to Patrick McHale:

> [During the production of Season 1] I remember . . . Pen and myself staying up really late working on the storyboards for "Prisoners of Love." I went in to Pen's office to see how he was doing on his section, and he was passed out at his desk, and he was still holding his pencil, which was still touching the paper. He was basically storyboarding in his sleep. I picked up the paper and looked at it, and it was really just a bunch of scribbles and blobs with faces, along with some impossible-to-read dialog that Pen wrote in some half-dream state. I woke him up and he pitched the board in sleepy mumbles, explaining that it was Lumpy Space Princess . . . That's how I remember it.[22]

Lumpy Space Princess speaks with an exaggerated Valley Girl accent, making heavy use of the quotative "like," vocal fry, and hip "swears" (e.g., "Lump off!" "What the stuff?" "Oh my Glob!"). In contemporary Western culture, it has long been (erroneously) assumed that the Valley Girl accent indexes a sort of vapid stupidity, and by giving Lumpy Space Princess this accent, the show coded her as shallow, unintelligent, and vain. But it would be a mistake to write Lumpy Space Princess off entirely, for as Ward noted, "She has some heart and soul to her."[23] (Unfortunately, this side of the character is usually covered by a thick layer of narcissism.)

Lumpy Space Princess is voiced by none other than Pendleton Ward himself, whose vocal performance is overtly comedic, shrill, and nasal. At the 2011 Toronto Comic Arts Festival, Ward revealed that the voice evolved out of his attempts to playfully mock the Valley Girl accent while swearing: "I have to get into [Lumpy Space Princess's accent] by cursing. That's how it started.... I'd drop the last letter of the curse word, so it's like 'Oh shi . . .' or 'Oh fu . . .'"[24] For whatever reason, Ward decided to use this goofy impression as the basis for Lumpy Space Princess's voice, and the rest, as they say, is history.

In addition to bragging about her intelligence and charm, Lumpy Space Princess often boasts about her luscious "lumps." For most of the series, it is heavily implied that these "lumps" are a euphemism for aspects of the feminine physique. However, in the ninth-season miniseries *Elements*, the audience learns that lumps are more than just physical attributes: they are "the subspace molecular lattice that binds together the scientific and magical forces of Ooo. More powerful than any one element, [lumps are] the force that orders reality into its true shape."[25] The reveal means that Lumpy Space Princess's lumps are actually a powerful anti-elemental energy, capable of combating the combined power of candy, ice, fire, and slime. At the climax of *Elements*, Lumpy Space Princess and Finn use the power of lumps to reset Ooo, unleashing a "world-healing wave"[26] that restores the elements-ravaged the land.

When she is not saving the world with her anti-elemental body (which is to say, most of the time), Lumpy Space Princess is usually shown mouthing off sassy one-liners or delivering catty insults, making her an excellent source of comedic relief. Sometimes, however, the character's selfish nature grows to such levels that it collapses in on itself, resulting in a Stygian sort of gallows humor. Consider, for instance, the fifth-season episode "Apple Wedding," which implies that the character dug up the grave of Princess Diana (yes, *that* Princess Diana) and stole her dress so that she could crash Tree Trunks's wedding.[27] Things get even darker a few episodes later in "Bad Timing," in which Lumpy Space Princess begins a romantic relationship with a lumpy person named Johnnie, before inadvertently trapping him forever in a bizarre, parallel universe.

Lumpy Space Princess is one of the show's more popular characters and is often cited as its funniest by fans and critics. Much of this love has to do with Ward's hilarious voice acting, as well as the character's self-absorbed and vivacious dialog. Gaayathri Nair of Bitch Flicks has further applauded the producers for making the character—despite her many foibles—a main heroine, writing, "To have an unlikeable female character who is not immediately cast as a villain is so rare."[28] But Lumpy Space Princess's comical unlikableness is also a double-edged sword, as her permanent immaturity means that she rarely learns from her mistakes or grows as a character. In fact, by series' end, Lumpy Space Princess is just as obnoxious as she was in her debut episode. At least she is consistent.

FLAME PRINCESS

Flame Princess[29] (birth name: Phoebe[30]) is the teenaged heir to the Fire Kingdom's throne and the flame elemental (that is, the personification of fire, which is one of the four elements comprising the Oooniverse). Despite being one of the more powerful characters in the show, Flame Princess makes her debut in Season 3's "Incendium" not as some fire-wielding valkyrie, but rather as a prisoner of her father, the Flame King, who has had her locked up in a glass lamp out of fear that she will one day possess "greater powers than [he will] ever dream of."[31] Freed by Jake inadvertently during the events of "Incendium," Flame Princess soon falls for Finn, and after a somewhat turbulent courting period, Finn and Flame Princess begin dating each other. Sadly, this relationship is cut short during the middle of the fifth season, and Flame Princess subsequently returns to the Fire Kingdom, overthrows her tyrannical father, and establishes a realm based on honesty.

Flame Princess was a late addition to the show's main cast, created during the production of Season 3 after the show's writers began to express their belief that they had exhausted all the potential storylines about Finn hopelessly pining after Bubblegum. On top of this, the writers were also increasingly uncomfortable with the age gap between the two.[32] The writers consequently decided that the best solution to these problems was to drop into Ooo a new "age-appropriate" character with whom Finn could be smitten; not only would this freshen the show by shaking up existing character dynamics, but it would also allow the writers to explore Finn's developing understanding of romance without retreading overly familiar ground. And thus Flame Princess was born.[33] Adam Muto and character designer Natasha Allegri each drafted up preliminary sketches for the character,[34] but the character's final look was designed by Rebecca Sugar, who based her design mostly on Allegri's rough drawings.[35]

Flame Princess was voiced by Jessica DiCicco, a prolific voice actress. Photo courtesy of Steve Cranston via CC Attribution-ShareAlike 2.0 Generic (CC BY-SA 2.0) license, https://flic.kr/p/jTEpV2.

With regard to characterization, the writers wanted to make Flame Princess more on Finn's level, both in terms of her age and her emotional intelligence.[36] When roughing out the character's personality, the writers were inspired by the alluring but dangerous nature of fire itself, with voice actress Jessica DiCicco revealing in a 2015 interview: "I spoke to Pen, because I wanted to get his insight into the character, and he said that [the writers and producers] wanted [her to be] like fire personified—what would fire be like if fire was a person?"[37] During the commentary for the fourth-season premiere "Hot to the Touch," Rebecca Sugar built on this line of thinking, arguing that Flame Princess's fiery nature is best understood as a metaphor for the unpredictable nature of love itself: "She's sort of the embodiment of . . . love as a . . . uncontrollable destructive force that you naturally have but you can't control—you don't really know what it is and you're kinda [sic] feeling it out . . . [Y]ou realize it's going to hurt people, but you didn't know that at first."[38]

As mentioned earlier, Flame Princess is voiced by Jessica DiCicco, an Emmy-nominated actress who has long voiced characters for animated television series and video games. Prior to her landing the role, DiCicco was only peripherally aware of *Adventure Time* and as such was not familiar with its complex characters and plot. This changed once she got an email asking if she was interested in auditioning for a new character. According to DiCicco:

> Usually they give [you] a character design, you see the character, you get the blurb about her [or] the show and you get a bunch of lines. This [audition request] just came . . . in the body of the email. I didn't have much to go off of, but I YouTubed [the series] like crazy, and I watched as much *Adventure Time* as I could, and so I started to understand the [show's] tone.[39]

DiCicco was struck by what she saw, telling media analyst Mike Gencarelli in 2013: "Immediately . . . I knew this was a show I wanted to be on."[40] When it came to the audition itself, DiCicco told me: "My audition scene was with Finn, so I was so happy I got to hear his voice and know who I was talking to. So often we get auditions for projects that are brand new and there is so much guessing involved!"[41] Much to her delight, DiCicco scored the role. "I was very happy," she told Gencarelli. "I knew that I was in for something great."[42]

Adding Fuel to the Fire: Flame Princess's Growth

Much like Marceline (with whom she has much in common), Flame Princess can readily be categorized as a manifestation of the "wild-woman" archetype, and her characterization deconstructs what it means exactly to be "evil." In her first few episodes, such as "Incendium" and "Hot to the Touch," it is suggested by characters like Flame King that Flame Princess is a depraved, wicked woman who craves wanton destruction. But by mid-Season 4, it is readily apparent that Flame Princess is not malicious—she is simply following her nature as a fire elemental, and as she puts it, "Fire's purpose is to burn."[43] As she and Finn spend more time together, she begins to realize how her flames impact nonfire persons, and—despite her father's (humorous) warning that "if she acted out of alignment . . . there'd be penalties to her experience"[44]—she works on becoming a person who helps rather than hurts others.

While Flame Princess functions more or less as a generic love interest during Seasons 3 and 4, her character begins to evolve rapidly during the show's fifth. After Finn betrays her trust by lying to her in the explosive episode "Frost & Fire," she terminates their relationship and begins an intense period of soul searching. Sometime after, she overthrows her evil father in a bloodless coup and installs herself as the queen of the Fire Kingdom. Although it takes a few seasons, Finn comes to realize how much he wronged his ex-girlfriend, and after a heartfelt apology in the eighth-season episode "Bun Bun," the two repair their friendship. Around this time, Flame Princess also begins to dabble in music, and by series' end, the character is not only a successful monarch, but also a talented rapper.

To say that Flame Princess has an impressive resume is a bit of an understatement, and from her introduction to the show's finale, the character proved to be one of the show's most dynamic. When asked about this development, DiCicco was clear:

> I think it's badass how [Flame Princess] evolved. At first I was wrapped up in the love story myself, I loved what Finn and [Flame Princess] shared. But once it was clear that Finn had a lot of growing up to do before he could be in a relationship, I was so pleased to see the direction the writers took [Flame Princess]. She's a strong, independent woman who is living up to her full potential. Although, sometimes I feel like she grew up kind of fast, and didn't get to fully live out her childhood (the little amount of childhood she had not trapped in a lantern). But I guess that's just how the cookie crumbles in the Fire Kingdom. [Flame Princess] certainly rose to the occasion and led with grace and strength.[45]

Despite being a late addition to the ensemble cast, Flame Princess was warmly received by the fandom and soon gained a respectable following. In May 2021, I reached out to DiCicco and asked for her thoughts about the character's reception and fan following, to which DiCicco kindly responded:

> When [Flame Princess] was new to the [*Adventure Time*] world, the fan reception was unlike anything I had personally experienced before. I started going to cons and meeting fans in person, and felt the excitement first hand, it was palpable. It really helped me connect more with the character knowing how many people supported her. It was incredible to be able to play [Flame Princess], and she's left a hot hand print on my heart and is now part of my identity![46]

ICE KING

Ice King (original name: Simon Petrikov) is the magical sovereign of the Ice Kingdom, who has a penchant for kidnapping princesses and trying to force them into marriage. While on the surface homicidal and insane, Ice King is really lonelier than anything else, and in many episodes, he openly wishes for someone to love him. Unfortunately, the only creatures that can stand to be around him for extended periods of time are wild penguins and other (usually dim-witted) snow creatures like ice centipedes or snow golems. Despite being an antagonist who fights the heroes, the Ice King nevertheless refers to Finn and Jake as his "best friends" and Princess Bubblegum as his "on-again-off-again girlfriend."[47] (Finn, Jake, and Bubblegum, however, would likely beg to differ.)

Series creator Pendleton Ward dreamed up the Ice King while developing a short film at CalArts that featured early versions of "Finn and Jake sav[ing] Princess Bubblegum from [an] Ice King using rocket boots."[48] When Ward revisited this short and turned it into what would later be considered the *Adventure Time* pilot, he once again featured the Ice King as the villain. This incarnation of the character was voiced by John Kassir, a comedian and actor known for playing, among other roles, the corpse-like Crypt-Keeper from HBO's horror anthology series *Tales from the Crypt* (1989–96).[49] Kassir gave the character a shrill, maniacal voice, which fits well with Ice King's behavior in the pilot, but when *Adventure Time* was picked up for series by Cartoon Network, the producers decided to recast the role. Ward initially encouraged first-season storyline writer Tim McKeon to audition for the part ("Before any roles were cast, I would do an Ice King voice while pitching stories," McKeon revealed to me in an interview), but McKeon declined the offer, citing his lack of acting experience.[50]

One of those who did audition was Tom Kenny, a prolific voice actor perhaps best known as the voice of SpongeBob SquarePants, the main character in the eponymous Nickelodeon series.[51] Kenny had been aware of *Adventure Time* largely from the beginning: "My kid was super into [the *Adventure Time* short] and his friends were some of those people that caused the pilot to get a bazillion hits on YouTube."[52] Kenny found the short's "Monty Python craziness" and its "surrealness" quite striking, and when he heard that Cartoon Network was turning it into a series, he eagerly signed up to audition for Ice King. "I really wanted to be that guy," Kenny told Britt Hayes in 2012. "I felt like I really understand this guy, you know? . . . Some stuff [that you audition for] has a . . . special feel to it. For me from the beginning, from the audition, *Adventure Time* totally had that."[53]

To develop Ice King's unique vocal pitch, timbre, and rhythm, Kenny thought about the character's warped psyche, telling MTV:

Tom Kenny, who is perhaps best known for playing SpongeBob SquarePants, also voiced the Ice King. Photo courtesy of Gage Skidmore via CC Attribution-ShareAlike 2.0 Generic (CC BY-SA 2.0) license, https://flic.kr/p/FXZKga.

My approach to the Ice King is that he's a very real psychopath. He's the kind of guy that they would do a 48 Hours Investigates about, where none of his neighbors know that much about him but they realize there's that weird smell coming from his house and they dig up a bunch of weird stuff in the basement. That's definitely the Ice King. And then when they capture the psychotic killer, he can't realize why everybody's mad at him. . . . He's one of those guys who's so pathological that he doesn't realize why anyone would be angry at him.[54]

Kenny also mentioned in this interview that he "tried not to . . . go back and look at the original short" so that his performance would not "be infected by any kind of subconscious earwigs."[55]

Ice King's design—which looks like the Winter Warlock from *Santa Claus Is Coming to Town* (1970) by way of the king from *The Point* (1971)—was largely finalized during the production of the pilot. (In fact, when *Adventure Time* went to series, the most noticeable change to Ice King's model was that character designer Robertryan Cory made the jewels on his crown more closely resemble Rupees from *The Legend of Zelda* video game series.)[56] But with regard to characterization, Ice King is perhaps the character that changes the most from pilot to finale. At the series' onset, Ice King is the primary antagonist, and the plots to many an episode are set in motion by Ice King doing something villainous. However, as the show progresses, and Finn and Jake learn more about Ice King, his character is steadily rehabilitated until he is seen by most in Ooo as a lonely but not particularly dangerous schmuck. Perhaps writer Eric Thurm said it best when he described Ice King as evolving into a "grotesque sitcom neighbor, always showing up when he isn't wanted while coming through exactly when he's needed."[57] And indeed, by the time "Come Along with Me" rolls around, Ice King is shown fighting alongside Finn, Jake, and their many "good" allies.

The Tragedy of Simon Petrikov

How is it that the series' first main antagonist—who at the start of the show was frequently written off as a hateful psychopath—became a "good guy"? The answer has to do with the character's in-universe backstory, which is first touched upon in the third-season Christmas special, "Holly Jolly Secrets": In this episode, Finn and Jake stumble upon some of the Ice King's old video diaries. These tapes reveal that one thousand years prior to the show's present, their nemesis was actually a respected antiquarian named Simon Petrikov. One day, Petrikov purchased a jewel-encrusted crown from an individual in Scandinavia. Unbeknownst to Petrikov, the ice crown was a magically-infused artifact created sixty-six million years ago by a powerful ice elemental named Urgence Evergreen. This mage had created the crown out of wish magic in the hopes of preventing a catalyst comet from plowing into Earth and causing a mass extinction event. Unfortunately, when the time came to use the crown, Evergreen was disabled in a fight. The task of wishing away the comet consequently fell to his young apprentice Gunter, a dinosaur who thought highly of Evergreen, even though his master treated him poorly. When Gunter placed the crown upon his head, however, he wished not for the comet's destruction but rather to become like his master. From that moment on, the crown was marred, and anyone who dared wear it was turned into a twisted parody of Urgence Evergreen.

Because Gunter failed to wish away the comet, it smashed into Earth, causing the extinction of the dinosaurs, as well as the temporary disappearance of magic. The ice crown, however, survived the impact and slept for millions of years, until it was rediscovered sometime during the Anthropocene. The crown eventually made its way into the hands of Simon. Knowing nothing of the crown's curse, Simon placed the artifact on his head. Unfortunately, this activated the vexatious crown, which infused Simon with maddening ice power. Simon tried to fight the crown's magic, but it was no use. To top it all off, the chaos created by the crown was so great that Simon's beloved fiancée, Betty, fled from him, leaving Petrikov distraught.

Around this time, the mutagenic Mushroom War broke out. Thanks to the magic of the ice crown, Simon was able to survive this nuclear holocaust, and in the aftermath of the war, he adopted a small, half-human, half-demon girl named Marceline, whom he found crying in the wreckage of the world. As the two struggled for survival, Petrikov continued to fight the effects of the ice crown, but he allowed himself to give into its power every once in a while, all in the name of protecting Marceline from the dangers lurking in the post-apocalyptic landscape. These occasional dabblings eventually led to the crown swallowing Petrikov whole. Thereafter he was nothing but the sociopathic "Ice King," who neither recognized Marceline nor remembered any aspect of his previous life as a mild-mannered researcher.

When *Adventure Time* began, this backstory was never part of the plan, and Ice King was meant to be nothing more than a cartoon villain. But during the production of Season 2, Patrick McHale realized that both Marceline and Ice King were one thousand years old but had yet to interact with one another in an episode. This inspired him to mock up an elaborate backstory about how the two characters had attempted to save humanity from menacing vampires centuries before the time of Finn and Jake. "My initial idea," McHale told me in an interview, "was that [Simon Petrikov] was essentially humanity's last hope—like an unlikely superhero using the power of the crown in an attempt to save humankind [from vampires], but [he was] falling further and further into insanity."[58] When McHale pitched this grand backstory, none of the writers were interested in it. But then, during the production of the third-season holiday special "Holly Jolly Secrets," McHale managed to work in portions of the aforementioned backstory by proposing that the VHS tapes Finn and Jake find contain the video diaries of Simon Petrikov, documenting his crown-induced descent into madness.[59]

"Holly Jolly Secrets" also features a short, humorous scene in which the Ice King sings Marceline's "Fry Song." This gag once again brought attention to the fact that Ice King and Marceline had yet to costar in an episode. According to McHale:

> [At this point, storyboard artist] Rebecca Sugar realized completely independently of me that Marceline and Ice King [had] never actually . . . interact[ed] with each other . . . And she came up with a more personal, beautiful backstory [for them] and came into the writers' room super excited, pitching her thoughts about it. It re-ignited the conversation and we [all agreed that her idea] was the truth of their backstory.[60]

Sugar's ideas eventually came to form the backbone for the fourth-season installment "I Remember You" (in which the audience first learns of Marceline and Ice King's shared history) and the fifth-season episode "Simon & Marcy" (which functions as a flashback, allowing the audience to actually see what their relationship was like those hundreds of years ago).[61]

The final piece of the Simon–Ice King puzzle came during the production of the show's sixth season, when storyboard artist Tom Herpich developed an intriguing backstory for Ice King's cursed crown, which later evolved into the episode "Evergreen."[62]

Many have drawn comparisons between Ice King's insanity and those suffering from debilitating neurodegenerative diseases like Alzheimer's, which impair cognitive function and destroy memory. Diseases like these are completely out of our control, so when a loved one begins to succumb to their effects and act in a manner inconsistent with their previous self, it makes no sense to fault them for anything bad they might do. The same is true for Ice King, and after learning about his condition, Finn, Jake, and the show's many characters realize that Ice King is not malicious, but rather a sick, sad old man who needs the love of friends.[63]

Of the many who have noted the parallels between Ice King and those suffering from Alzheimer's, perhaps it was Lev Grossman (the lauded author of *The Magicians*, among other works), who, in a 2013 interview with National Public Radio (NPR), said it best when he lamented:

> [Ice King] doesn't remember who he used to be, but other people [like Marceline] do . . . It's very affecting. My dad has been going through having Alzheimer's, and he's forgotten so much about who he used to be. And I look at him and think this cartoon is about my father dying.[64]

Sugar was touched to hear comments like this, and in a short 2014 interview included on the fourth-season DVD set, she confessed that "it meant the most to [her]" when people who have lost loved ones to neurodegenerative diseases appreciate what she was trying to say with episodes like "I Remember You."[65]

All things considered, Ice King is arguably one of the show's most complex characters, able to vacillate between being a heartless antagonist and an awkward weirdo—sometimes within the span of a single episode. It truly is a testament to the show's writers that such a bizarre, sympathetic character can exist.

THE EARL OF LEMONGRAB

The Earl of Lemongrab—usually referred to by the simple metonym "Lemongrab"—is one of Princess Bubblegum's many candy creations, and according to the princess, the first of her experiments to go "wrong." Ruling a fiefdom comprising Castle Lemongrab, the character nominally answers to the sovereign of the Candy Kingdom but in effect governs himself. Awkward and cantankerous, Lemongrab has problems getting along with other people and often overreacts when the slightest of things go awry. Lemongrab is one of the more popular characters in the *Adventure Time* fandom and is perhaps best known for his catchphrase: a shrill scream that things are "Unacceptable!"

Lemongrab is introduced as the antagonist of the third-season episode "Too Young," in which he usurps the Candy Kingdom throne after learning that Princess Bubblegum has regressed to a thirteen-year-old. His tenure as the kingdom's leader, however, is mercifully short, for at the end of the episode, Bubblegum reages and reclaims the throne.

According to storyboard artist and head writer Kent Osborne, the seeds of what would evolve into Lemongrab can be traced back to his watching an episode of the HBO series *Game of Thrones* that featured regency as a plot point. This inspired Osborne to pitch the idea that sometime during the first half of Season 3, Bubblegum's uncle would show up and rule in her stead until she once again reached the age of eighteen.[66]

Osborne's proposal about a Candy Kingdom proxy ruler was well-received and soon found its way into an outline for what would eventually become "Too Young." However, the episode's storyboard artists, Jesse Moynihan and Tom Herpich, were put off by the regent's aggressive and rather belligerent demeanor (on his personal website, Moynihan wrote that the character in the original outline "was just a huge asshole," and in a 2014 presentation, he likened the original version of Lemongrab to Duke Sigmund Igthorn, the cartoonishly evil villain from the 1980s cartoon *Disney's Adventures of the Gummi Bears*),[67] so they retooled his characterization. Dubbing him "Lemongrab,"[68] Moynihan and Herpich ditched the idea that he was Bubblegum's uncle and instead proposed that he was her first candy creation, who struggled with empathy. "[I] tried to play him as weirdly sympathetic," Moynihan explained online. "He does a lot of things wrong, but you can see that he's trying to do what makes sense to him. . . . I wanted the viewer to feel sympathy for him, or at least conflicted about his motivations."[69]

After "Too Young" aired, the character became popular with the fanbase, leading the show's writers to pen additional episodes in which he stars. The first of these sequels, "You Made Me," aired during the show's fourth season, and once again Herpich and Moynihan were tasked with storyboarding the adventure. While working on this episode, both artists were anxious about trying to capture lightning in a bottle, with Moynihan admitting:

> I felt a lot of pressure as a writer to re-capture what clicked with Lemongrab in "Too Young," while introducing fresh ideas about him. Sometimes

I wonder if audiences want to re-live the moments that made a character popular. If you bring someone like [Lemongrab] back, do they just want to hear the same lines he spouted off in his first appearance? Is that why the *Hangover 2* made so much money?[70]

In the DVD commentary for "You Made Me," Herpich also discussed this anxiety, claiming that he overcame the issue by consciously avoiding predictable dialogue or "catch phrases," thereby keeping the character fresh and interesting.[71]

Lemongrab is voiced by Justin Roiland, perhaps better known as the cocreator of the Adult Swim series *Rick and Morty* (2013–present). When the writers and producers of *Adventure Time* were looking for an actor to bring the character to life, Roiland was the host of *The Grandma's Virginity Podcast*—a program of which Pendleton Ward was a fan.[72] After trying and failing to contact a different voice actor for the role, Ward reached out to Roiland and asked if he was interested in voicing Lemongrab; Roiland eagerly accepted, as he happened to be a fan of *Adventure Time*.[73] Because Roiland was personally solicited by Ward, he never formally auditioned for the part, meaning that he did not know what the character was supposed to sound like. Roiland was thus forced to develop the character's unique voice at the studio while recording. "I literally just showed up and took a crack at [the voice]," Roiland explained in an interview with Benjamin Van Den Broeck. "Pen was pleased and we got to work."[74]

When Life Gives You Lemons: The Strange Story Arc of Lemongrab

Lemongrab has one of *Adventure Time*'s odder story arcs (which is really saying something). In his debut episode, "Too Young," he serves mostly as an overbearing foil for Finn and Princess Bubblegum. However, in his second episode, "You Made Me," he is played less as a villain and more as a victim who is lonely and uncomfortable with existence. This leads to Princess Bubblegum creating for him a brother. For a time, the original character is known as Lemongrab I (or "Black Lemongrab"), and his brother is called Lemongrab II (or "White Lemongrab"). After learning how to create candy life, the two Lemongrabs build up a citizenry and rule their earldom in peace. Unfortunately, in the fifth-season episode "Another Five More Short Graybles," Lemongrab I soon grows tired of and eats Lemongrab II. The sole surviving Lemongrab then becomes a veritable despot, who is ultimately deposed and blown apart by the hero Lemonhope in that character's eponymous episode. Princess Bubblegum soon thereafter creates a new composite being from the remnants of Lemongrabs I and II, who is dubbed Lemongrab III (or "Grey Lemongrab").

Lemongrab's first three episodes (all costoryboarded by Jesse Moynihan) focused on his awkwardness and his anxiety. But then, during Season 5, the

Lemongrab storyline was helmed almost exclusively by Tom Herpich and his storyboard partner Steve Wolfhard, both of whom steered the character in a much more horrific direction. While not opposing this change, Moynihan personally felt that this approach diverged from his own interpretation of the character, telling the rapper Open Mike Eagle in a podcast interview:

> So after I worked on . . . "You Made Me" . . . Tom and Steve . . . basically took over Lemongrab for several episodes, and they took him on this [dictator] arc with his brother . . . It turned into, like, a horror movie. That aspect of his personality was definitely there in the beginning, but they ramped it up—this one aspect of him—to a really high level . . . I really enjoyed watching those episodes, and I was always shocked by what they came up with, but I think if I had been working on [those episodes], I [would have approached them differently] . . . I think my tone for Lemongrab is slightly different from Steve's especially, because Steve really enjoys the horror! . . . [So] I wouldn't say [I] "disagree with" [Herpich and Wolfhard's interpretation of Lemongrab] but it wasn't a direction that I would have taken the character.[75]

After Season 5, Jesse Moynihan once again took the reins of Lemongrab's story, cowriting the heady sixth-season episode "The Mountain" with Sam Alden. "The Mountain" was something of a return to form, focusing more on Lemongrab's personal anxiety and less on his dictatorial tendencies—or his taste for lemon flesh.

Due to the character's various idiosyncrasies and his trouble relating to others, some fans and critics have interpreted Lemongrab as being on the autism spectrum. Moynihan, however, eschews this strict interpretation, arguing on his website that "Lemongrab doesn't have Asperger's. I don't know what exactly is going on with him."[76] It seems that Moynihan's comment was not made to deny possible neurodiversity in Western animation—something, mind you, that is desperately needed—but rather to avoid pathologizing Lemongrab in an attempt to figure out what is "wrong" with him. To quote Princess Bubblegum, "People get built different. We don't need to figure it out, we just need to respect it."[77]

THE LICH

The Lich is arguably the principal villain in *Adventure Time*. A powerful necromancer, the Lich has but one goal throughout the series: extinguish all sentient life from the multiverse by whatever means necessary.

During the late nineteenth and early twentieth centuries, the term "Lich"—derived from the Old English term *lic*, meaning "corpse"—had been used in works of science fiction and fantasy as a fancy (if pretentious) word for a dead body.[78] The term entered into slightly more mainstream usage with the popularization of the role-playing game *Dungeons & Dragons* (1974), specifically its expansion rulebook *Greyhawk* (1975), which defines a lich as being a "skeletal [monster] . . . of magical origin [with] each Lich formerly being a powerful Magic-User or . . . Cleric in life."[79] Given Pendleton Ward's love for this role-playing game, it is no surprise that a *D&D* enemy would come to serve as one of *Adventure Time*'s Big Bads.[80]

Ward and his creative team laid the initial groundwork for the Lich in the series' pitch bible, in which he is described as "not funny" and "absolute[ly] evil."[81] The bible also featured a somewhat macabre depiction of the Lich, drawn by Patrick McHale, which depicted the Lich as a partially decomposed corpse, with torn skin around his mouth, and massive black eyes with yellow pinpricks for pupils.[82] When I asked him what had inspired this ghoulish take on the character, McHale told me:

> I remember always thinking it was cool when Hordak entered *Masters of the Universe* as a *real* villain, [considering] how goofy Skeletor was. Pen wanted a similarly serious villain to show up in *Adventure Time* as a foil for Ice King. He had the name "The Lich," and [he] asked me to draw it because I tended to draw more scary stuff. I don't think we developed him too much until we were actually working on the series, but the intention was always that he would be a deathly serious no-nonsense villain. No personal business, just an unquenchable thirst to destroy all life.[83]

Although the character has a brief cameo in the first-season episode "His Hero," he is properly introduced in the second-season episode "Mortal Folly." Originally, lead character designer Phil Rynda drafted up a model for the Lich that resembled a stereotypical "skeleton magician," complete with a black, tattered cloak and a sinister, blackened crown on the top of his head.[84] Rynda, however, felt that the design was not "quite unique or scary enough" for the show's main villain. "He's an important character," Rynda emphasized in 2010 on his Formspring account, "and even though we only catch a glimpse of him [in 'His Hero'], it was important to me that we establish something that we [could] work with down the line."[85] Rynda consequently redrew the Lich to more closely resemble McHale's take on the character.[86] With this aesthetic tweak, the character went from menacing to down-right horrifying.

The Lich was voiced by Ron Perlman, a stalwart of Hollywood perhaps best known for playing the titular character in Guillermo del Toro's *Hellboy*

Ron Perlman voiced the Lich. As an actor, Perlman is known for his sonorous voice, which he used to masterful effect when playing *Adventure Time's* Big Bad. Photo courtesy of Gage Skidmore via CC Attribution-ShareAlike 2.0 Generic (CC BY-SA 2.0) license, https://flic.kr/p/a7QYGj.

adaptations. Prior to recording his first episode, Perlman did not know much about *Adventure Time* or the role he would be playing (his managers secured him the part, and the actor himself had not looked at any of his lines). But when he finally got a chance to read his dialogue, he was struck by the quality of the script and eeriness of his character. "Those [*Adventure Time* writers] are really smart people," Perlman declared during a question-and-answer session at the 2013 Chicago Comic and Entertainment Expo. "I was pleasantly surprised how much fun I had . . . playing [the Lich]. There was a huge amount of enthusiasm in the [studio] for the making of that show, which is always helpful."[87]

The Ceaseless Wheel: The Mythological and Thematic Role of the Lich

The Lich's origins are never directly explained, but based on clues scattered across numerous episodes, we can make a solid guess as to his backstory: According to the Lich's monologue in the sixth-season episode "Gold Stars," his essence originated from a period before time itself, when existence was nothing but a writhing mass of hideous, primordial demons. In time, the multiverse came into being, and after billions of years of celestial expansion, the essence of the Lich became infused in a catalyst comet, which careened towards Earth sixty-six million years prior to the start of the series. Despite the attempts of the ice elemental Urgence Evergreen to avert its course, the comet nevertheless impacted the planet, embedding the Lich's essence deep underground. This impact also led to the Cretaceous–Paleogene extinction event, which caused magic to all but disappear from Earth.

Eons later (c. 2000 AD), when the Mushroom War was at a cataclysmic fever pitch, human scientists dug up the essence of the Lich in the crust of the earth and used it to build a doomsday device: the mutagenic Mushroom Bomb.[88] The bomb was eventually dropped on top of a civilian subway station, possibly somewhere on the East or West Coast of the United States.[89] When the bomb detonated, it released the Lich's essence, which took over the body of a hapless victim, giving birth to the Lich proper.[90] Presumably, the Lich unleashed a reign of terror that was only stopped when the majestic hero Billy sealed the undead being away in a great block of amber, which was then stored away in the highest branches of the Candy Kingdom's great tree for safe keeping.

In the second-season episode "Mortal Folly," the Lich is freed from his prison and resumes his mission to end all life in the multiverse. After possessing a number of beings (including Princess Bubblegum and the waving snail who appears in each episode) and leaving a trail of dead bodies in his wake (including Billy the Hero and the wish master Prismo), the Lich finds himself trapped in an interdimensional prison called the "Crystal Citadel," guarded by colossal beings known as the Citadel Guardians. Despite being one of the most heavily guarded locations in the multiverse, the Citadel is no match for the Lich, and as soon as he is incarcerated, the Lich uses his nefarious powers to kill the Guardians and free the other inmates.

Although Finn tries to confront the primordial demon, he finds the Lich's power is far too strong. The only thing that Finn can do is brush some of the life-restoring blood from a recently felled Citadel Guardian onto the Lich's hand. Amazingly, this is all that is needed, and in a scene recalling the "Valley of Dry Bones" vision from the biblical Book of Ezekiel,[91] the Lich's skeletal form begins to grow organs and flesh. This revivification turns the Lich into an innocuous baby named Sweet P, who is adopted by Tree Trunks and Mr. Pig.

During the latter part of the show's run, the Lich is (for the most part) safely contained within the body of Sweet P, and while the former occasionally overpowers the latter, Sweet P is usually able to fight back and reclaim his body. But while the Lich within Sweet P is for the most part kept at bay, an alternate-universe Lich (taking the form of a hand) eventually drops into Ooo near the end of the series' run. This ghoul tries talking Sweet P into joining with him, but the child proves resilient to the alt-Lich's false promises, slaying the hand before it can cause any harm. The ghost of the alt-Lich later shows up in the *Distant Lands* special "Together Again" possessing New Death. Thankfully, the beastie is defeated (hopefully once and for all) by Finn, Jake, and—humorously enough—Mr. Fox (voiced by Tom Herpich).

A solid villain always has a purpose for their actions, so what is it that drives the Lich? Near the midpoint of the sixth-season episode "Escape from the Citadel," right after breaking out of the titular prison, the Lich delivers one of the most chilling soliloquies in children's animation, which manages to shed considerable light on his purpose: "There is only darkness for you [Finn], and only death for your people.... I will command a great and terrible army, and we will sail to a billion worlds. We will sail until every light has been extinguished.... I am the end."[92] The Lich drives his point home a few seasons later in the ninth-season episode "Whispers," when he declares: "I am the ceaseless wheel. The last scholar of GOLB [i.e., pure chaos]. I am your doom."[93]

The Lich, as he describes himself, is an entity predicated solely on turmoil, deterioration, and decay. He is nothing less than a manifestation of entropy—or general disorder in a system. According to the Second Law of Thermodynamics, entropy in an isolated system will always increase over time, eventually leading to a dead universe of unchanging randomness (this result is the so-called "Heat Death of the universe," often referred to colloquially as the "Big Chill"). This is why the Lich is so scary. The character does not just cause death; he very literally *is* death—"the destroyer of worlds"[94]—and his monstrous soliloquies can thus be seen as creative articulations of the existential dread that thoughts of death engender.

All of this means that Finn's attempt to battle the Lich are futile, as death comes for everyone in the end. But while this might seem decidedly nihilistic, I would argue that Finn and his friends' willingness to fight the unstoppable is actually an illustration of the show's "optimistically existential"[95] outlook: It does not matter if darkness one day will win—all that matters is that you fight it when you can. This resolve to do what is right in the face of looming hopelessness is something that the Lich himself will never be able to truly comprehend. And as long as that resolve exists, maybe Ooo has a chance...

4.

THE "C-LISTERS"

Other Characters of Note

Much like the expansive world of *The Simpsons*, the *Adventure Time* universe is teeming with literally hundreds of secondary and background characters—far too many to name let alone outline. As such, this present chapter briefly surveys those characters who might not be considered among the show's "major" players, but who nevertheless impact the overall plot in significant ways.

BETTY GROF

Betty Grof[1] is the magic-warped, time-hopping fiancée of Simon Petrikov. The character is introduced in the third-season episode "Holly Jolly Secrets," which reveals that she was engaged to Simon Petrikov before he wore the ice crown and became Ice King. Later episodes disclose that she was a graduate student who studied ancient petroglyphs and coauthored a book with Simon on mystical rituals.

Upon the first mention of Betty, it is suggested that she was killed during the Mushroom War, but this implication is supplanted by the revelation in "Betty" that she actually traveled through time to save Simon from the curse of the ice crown. In the sixth-season episode "You Forgot Your Floaties," Betty, while studying magic under the tutelage of Magic Man, accidentally absorbs his magical abilities—along with his insanity. For the remainder of the series, Betty exists in a half-crazed state, attempting numerous times to rewrite history or reverse-engineer the magic of the crown to save Simon, all to no avail. It is only in the series finale, after she and Ice King are consumed by the chaos deity GOLB, that the two revert to their original forms. Betty then uses the power of the ice crown to merge with GOLB, thereby keeping Simon sane and safe. GOLBetty then leaves Ooo behind, and it is implied that Simon and Betty are never again reunited.

Betty was the source of much fan speculation when her name was first mentioned in "Holly Jolly Secrets." This speculation was further fueled by a comment made by Rebecca Sugar at an *Adventure* Comic-Con panel in 2012 that an episode centering on Betty was in the works.[2] For two years, fans developed headcanon after headcanon in anticipation of the foretold episode, which finally aired in the spring of 2014. Titled "Betty" and storyboarded by Jesse Moynihan and Ako Castuera, the episode not only introduced the titular heroine, but also brought her into the thick of things by having her embark on a mission to save Simon from the clutches of Death. "Betty" was somewhat controversial upon its debut, with many in the fandom critiquing it for its brisk pacing and underdeveloped character interactions (perhaps this criticism was only to be expected, given the hype that surrounded the episode). Luckily, subsequent episodes would expand on Betty's backstory, ameliorating much of this fannish frustration.

In her first couple of appearances, Betty was voiced by the writer and director Lena Dunham, perhaps best known as the creator of the HBO series *Girls*. Dunham—who had been friends with lead writer Kent Osborne prior to her big break—agreed to be on *Adventure Time* because one of her younger relatives was a fan of the show.[3] During the ninth-season miniseries *Elements*, nerd superstar Felicia Day stepped in as the character's new voice actress, remaining on until the series' conclusion. It is not clear why Day replaced Dunham: Some fans have speculated that it was because Dunham was simply too busy to reprise her role; others, however, have hypothesized that the show was wanting to quietly distance itself from the increasingly controversial antics of Dunham. Either way, it is fair to say that Day—an actress with bona fide nerd cred who has been in everything from *Buffy the Vampire Slayer* to the CW series *Supernatural* (2005–20)—was a stellar casting choice.

BILLY THE HERO

Billy[4] is a famed hero whom Finn and Jake look up to. Before Finn and Jake became Ooo's greatest champions, it was Billy who protected the land from all manner of evildoers, including the dreaded Lich. In his heyday, Billy was often accompanied by his then-girlfriend, Canyon (voiced by storyboard artist Ako Castuera), and together the two were a heroic "power couple."[5]

In his old age, Billy became a pacifist, arguing that violence only engenders more violence. However, after the events of the first-season episode "His Hero"—in which Finn and Jake use (albeit rudimentary) consequentialist philosophy to show Billy that adherence to a strict code of nonviolence only enables evil to go unchecked—Billy returns to his heroic ways. Alas, in the fourth-season finale "The Lich," the titular villain kills Billy and possesses his corpse. It is in this way that the Lich tricks Finn and Jake into helping him open a portal to the center of the multiverse. Billy's spirit is finally allowed to rest after his bucket list is completed by Finn in the fifth-season finale, aptly titled "Billy's Bucket List."

Billy is a complex amalgamation of heroes from disparate pieces of literature, but the character's most obvious inspirations are the many heroes from twentieth-century sword and sorcery literature. Like Billy, the protagonists of these works were usually swashbuckling heroes who battled all sorts of fantastical foes.

Billy was voiced by Lou Ferrigno, an actor and former bodybuilder. While the actor is perhaps best known for playing the eponymous character in *The Incredible Hulk* (1977–82) television series, it was actually his vocal performance in the 1996–97 UPN animated *Hulk* series that made Ward want to cast him as Billy.[6]

FERN

Fern (voiced by Hayden Ezzy) is a grass doppelganger of Finn who plays a prominent role in the show's later seasons. The character has a confusing genesis, and for one to understand it, it is necessary to go back to the earliest seasons of the show. Throughout many of these episodes, there are copious visuals that suggest Finn will lose his right arm.[7] These references later prove to be prophetic, for in the fifth-season episode "Blade of Grass," Finn contracts an eternal grass curse which manifests itself as a grass sword permanently attached to his right wrist. Eventually, this curse takes over the entirety of his right arm, and while it is seemingly ripped from Finn's body at the end of the sixth-season premiere "Wake Up"/"Escape from the Citadel," it grows back as a plant-based limb indistinguishable from Finn's own flesh and bone.

A few episodes later, in "Is That You?" Finn converts an alternate-reality version of himself into a new blade that the characters refer to as the "Finn-sword." Finn uses this weapon for much of the show's sixth, seventh, and eighth seasons, until it is stolen by Bandit Princess in "I Am a Sword." Near the end of this episode, Finn tracks down the thief, and the two engage in a duel. The fight causes Finn's grass arm to partially reform into the grass sword, with which Finn accidentally impales the Finn-sword. This results in Finn's grass curse infecting the alternate-universe version of Finn within the Finn-sword, producing a new, composite being: Fern.

Fern is properly introduced in the following episode, "Two Swords," as a brutish but well-intentioned lookalike of Finn. Throughout the eighth and ninth seasons, Finn attempts to teach Fern how to be an effective hero, but Fern often finds himself outperformed by his human counterpart. Fern soon grows tired of being seen as a "lesser Finn," and this resentment causes him to go rogue. After trying to usurp the role of Ooo's resident hero, Fern is accidentally blown apart by Finn and then resurrected by Uncle Gumbald as the "Green Knight" (who is voiced by Brad Neely).[8] For much of the show's final season, Fern serves as Gumbald's evil paladin—darkly mirroring Finn's chivalric relationship with Princess Bubblegum.

According to storyline writer Jack Pendarvis, the idea for Fern cropped up organically[9] as the writers worked out the show's increasingly elaborate mythology:

> [The Fern plot] just grew naturally[10] . . . out of the story. Something was going to happen with the grass arm, and we had this [alternate-universe] version of Finn that needed to be acknowledged in some way. I can't remember exactly why or how we ended up merging the two[, but] certainly it was an interesting way of getting the curse off of "our" Finn without cheating in a storytelling sense.[11]

Indeed, Fern ultimately serves as a tidy way for the show to conclude the grass-curse saga: In the series finale, Fern makes up with Finn, and together, the two kill the grass-sword demon that has caused them both so much trouble. Unfortunately, this eleventh-hour redemption comes at a steep cost, and by destroying the demonic power that gives his body form, Fern disintegrates into nothing more than a seed. After Finn plants this remnant on the ruins of the tree fort, it grows into a mighty tree that lives for thousands of years. This means that while Fern has a sad ending, an aspect of the character manages to live on well after Finn's natural demise.

GUNTER THE PENGUIN

While Ice King is often shown surrounded by hordes of penguins whom he all calls "Gunter"[12] (the name being an unconscious reference to Urgence Evergreen's dinosaur apprentice of the same name), there is one particular penguin at whom this address is usually directed. This Gunter is an intelligent creature who communicates through duck-like vocalization (often rendered phonetically as "wenk!").

During the show's first five and a half seasons, Gunter is portrayed as a mischievous but nonetheless normal penguin. However, near the end of the show's sixth season, it is revealed that Gunter is actually a primordial space demon from before the dawn of time named Orgalorg, who long ago was banished to Earth by the power of the celestial being Grob Gob Glob Grod on behest of the King of Mars. The fall to Earth gave Orgalorg amnesia, and the gravity of the planet crushed her into the shape of a penguin. After her great fall, Orgalorg wandered Earth for some time until she was taken in by the crazed Ice King, who mistook her for an average, ordinary penguin. It is only in the episode "Orgalorg" that, after a traumatic brain injury, Orgalorg's latent personality reawakens.

While one could arguably trace the origin of Orgalorg back to the second-season premiere "It Came from the Nightosphere" (in which Hunson Abadeer refers to Gunter as the "most evil" creature in all of existence), the explicit formulation of Gunter as a space demon occurred during production of the show's fifth season. Around this time, the writers were hammering out the storyline for a television movie, and it was decided that the Big Bad should be none other than Gunter, who would turn into Orgalorg at the movie's climax. While the television movie was, for a variety of reasons, scrapped during its production, the ideas about Orgalorg were salvaged for use during the writing of Season 6.[13]

A scaly being with a trunk-like body, two contorting arms, spiny growths on the shoulders, and a head with five or so eyes, Orgalorg seems to be a broad pastiche of numerous space demons from across the popular culture spectrum, with some fans arguing that the character functions first and foremost as a parody of the horror and science fiction writer H. P. Lovecraft's famed "Eldritch abominations" like the demoniac alien-deity Cthulhu (a dreaded cosmic entity of immense power and size) or the monstrous "Elder Things" (primordial extraterrestrials who colonized Earth millions of years prior to the evolution of humankind). When asked about this connection, Andy Ristaino (the artist responsible for working out Orgalorg's final look), told me: "As far as the designs went for [the episode "Orgalorg,"] it was unintentional. They just asked me to come up with some crazy looking alien designs.... [That said] I would say it's hard for there not to be a Lovecraft influence when talking about otherworldly beings beyond our comprehension."[14]

HUNTRESS WIZARD

Huntress Wizard is a powerful mage who, like the Greek goddess Artemis, is in tune with the natural world. Designed by storyboard artist Jesse Moynihan and debuting in the third-season episode "Wizard Battle," Huntress Wizard was originally intended to be nothing more than a background character. However, after "Wizard Battle" aired, she quickly gained a cult following online, and many fans were eager for her to play a more prominent role in future episodes. Moynihan attempted to showcase her in several of his episodes, although almost all of these scenes were excised for being extraneous or unnecessary to the main plot.

For a time, it seemed as if Huntress Wizard was doomed to stay in the background. But then, during the production of Season 7, Moynihan had a deeply personal encounter with an individual that caused him to meditate on relationships, falling in love, and sacrificing desire. He then outlined a story starring Huntress Wizard, in which she and Finn begin to fall for one another but eschew a traditional relationship "in service of [their] higher calling."[15] While the ending to "Flute Spell" implies that Huntress Wizard and Finn can never be together, Huntress Wizard eventually returns in the tenth-season premiere, "The Wild Hunt," and in this episode, she and Finn reaffirm their feelings for one another. Throughout the rest of Season 10, it is suggested that the two have entered into a sort of nontraditional romantic relationship.

Initially, Huntress Wizard was voiced by Maria Bamford before Jenny Slate was cast in her stead for the seventh-season episode "Flute Spell." Slate likely landed the role due to her talent as an actress, but it certainly did not hurt that several years prior to her casting, she had praised *Adventure Time* on her personal Twitter account as "one of the best, most beautiful and special" television programs ever made.[16]

THE KING OF OOO

The "One True" King of Ooo is a con artist who travels the land with his associate, Toronto the Dog, looking for rubes to scam. Despite the commanding sound of his honorific, it is a hollow vanity title, which has earned him many political enemies (such as Princess Bubblegum), who see him as a crook. Despite his illegitimacy, he is nevertheless incredibly crafty, and he even arranges a Candy Kingdom election, which leads to the ousting of Princess Bubblegum. After this electoral coup, he assumes the full regnal name "Princess King of Ooo"—only to be almost effortlessly deposed by Bubblegum during the *Stakes* miniseries.

The King of Ooo is both a broad parody of slimy con artists (think "Professor" Harold Hill if he were a total psychopath) as well as a caricature of those silver-tongued politicians who initially campaign for things like "change" or a "return to greatness," before reneging on their promises. Designed by storyboard artist Steve Wolfhard, the King of Ooo was voiced by comedian, actor, and podcaster Andy Daly, perhaps best known for his role as Forrest MacNeil on the Comedy Central mockumentary series *Review* (2014–17). On Twitter, series storyline writer Jack Pendarvis wrote that the show was "lucky . . . to get him,"[17] and indeed, Daly's casting was inspired. Daly brings to the character a sort of jovial smarm, making the King of Ooo the sort of villain who you both hate and find funny.

LADY RAINICORN

Lady Rainicorn is Jake the Dog's long-term girlfriend and Princess Bubblegum's royal steed. A defining feature of Lady's character is that she speaks exclusively in nonsubtitled[18] Korean. According to Bert Youn (a Korean American storyboard artist who wrote for the show during its first few seasons): "[Ward] told me that he wanted [the character to speak] something he could not understand. So I suggested we use Korean. Originally, my wife was going to voice the character."[19] However, the producers eventually decided to cast Niki Yang, an artist who storyboarded during Season 1 and who also voiced the sentient robot BMO. Yang explained in an interview, "[Ward] was looking for a voice actress for Lady Rainicorn and he wanted somebody who could speak Korean. That was me. I got that role."[20] Whereas BMO's voice is processed to give the character a robotic feel, Lady Rainicorn's voice is not, with Yang clarifying, "Rainicorn is pretty much my voice and how I speak—no filter."[21]

Often, the character's inability to speak English is played up for laughs, simply because of its incongruous nature with the rest of the show. For instance, an extended scene in the fourth-season episode "Lady & Peebles" features Princess Bubblegum listening intently to a lengthy, highly emotional Korean monologue courtesy of Lady Rainicorn, only for Bubblegum to respond, "Hmm. I suppose that's true" and then immediately change the subject. (The joke being that unless the person watching the show knows Korean, Bubblegum's vague response makes the entire exchange impossible to decipher.) At other times, the show used Rainicorn's Korean dialogue as a way to add slightly risqué jokes into the show. Some commentators and fans argued that this was an example of sneaking content "past the censors,"[22] but Yang revealed in an interview: "We have a lot of freedom [with what I can say in Korean]. However, [the network executives] always triple make sure that I don't say anything bad in Korean when I read Rainicorn's lines (that I translated)."[23]

MAGIC MAN

Magic Man (voiced by Tom Kenny) is a crazed Martian wizard who spends much of the series harassing the citizens of Ooo. In his debut episode, "Freak City," Magic Man functions as little more than a one-dimensional villain who causes Finn plenty of headaches by turning him into a giant foot. It is only in the fourth-season episode "Sons of Mars" and the sixth-season episode "You Forgot Your Floaties" that his backstory is fully revealed.

Two hundred or so years before the start of the series, Magic Man was a respected Martian scientist-wizard, the brother of Grob Gob Glob Grod and a direct underling of the King of Mars himself. After the malevolent entity known only as GOLB erased from existence his wife, Margles (voiced by Gillian Jacobs), Magic Man created an AI defense system to defend Mars, M.A.R.G.L.E.S. (short for the "Magical Automated Resistance-Generating Laser Energy Supplier), which both looked like and acted like Magic Man's fallen wife. However, because his actual wife had been erased from existence, Magic Man was forced to construct M.A.R.G.L.E.S. from the wisps of memories contained only in his darkest nightmares. This meant that when M.A.R.G.L.E.S. was installed, she went haywire, accidentally attacking Magic Man and turning him into a lunatic. Following a crime spree on Mars, he was banished to Ooo by the planet's king and told to only return once he learned to care for people again. After a series of magical adventures cataloged in the episodes "You Forgot Your Floaties" and "Normal Man," Magic Man is reverted back to his "normie" self, allowing him to ascend the Martian throne, whereupon he dons the regnal name "King Man."

Much of Magic Man's story arc was developed by storyboard artist Jesse Moynihan, who often cited the character as his favorite for whom to write.[24] Moynihan first began tinkering with Magic Man's backstory during the production of Season 3. The original idea he developed connected the character with the mythology of the show's Dead Worlds and would have seen Magic Man as a "really good spirit" whose "trolling" was actually him "testing the citizens of Ooo to see if they are worthy of entering 50th Dead World."[25] When Moynihan presented his concept to the writers, it was substantially revised and divided into two outlines that became the third-season episode "Ghost Princess" and the fourth-season episode "Sons of Mars."[26] (In the comments section of his personal website, Moynihan later explained that the original outline "painted Magic Man in a light that isn't congruent with the world of Ooo after 'Sons of Mars,'"[27] and as such had little bearing on the future direction of the character.)

When it came time to tackle the outline for "Sons of Mars," Moynihan took the mantra about "writing what you know" to heart by crafting for Magic Man a new backstory that was directly inspired by a fairly "traumatic" breakup Moynihan had had with a former girlfriend.[28] Moynihan was hoping that by writing Magic Man in this way, he would be able to anchor the character's story in real emotions while also confronting his own personal issues.[29]

Magic Man's story was further fleshed out in the sixth-season episode "You Forgot Your Floaties" (storyboarded solely by Moynihan), in which the audience learns the full truth about Margles, GOLB, and how Magic Man went insane. Soon after the episode's airing in the spring of 2015, Moynihan explained on his personal website how this storyline came to be:

> I remember saying somewhere that I would never explain what happened to Magic Man [and Margles], and that maybe Ako [Castuera]

and I had already explained too much in "Sons of Mars." Tom Herpich and I talked about it on several occasions. That was definitely his feeling at the time, and after watching "Sons of Mars," I agreed with him. Unfortunately, one of my personality traits seems to be that the more I say I'll never do something, the more I think about how I could do it.... So me saying, "I'll never go into Magic Man's backstory," was really me saying, "I will definitely figure out a way to tell Magic Man's backstory!" The process of coming up with it had a lot to do with waiting and seeing how all the other episodes and character arcs were playing out, and how Magic Man's story could fit in there.[30]

Thanks largely to Moynihan's effort, Magic Man morphed over the course of the show's run from an anarchic cipher into a sympathetic (albeit dangerous) screwball. In this way, the character followed the trajectory of other *Adventure Time* foes—like Ice King and Lemongrab—who evolved from one-note villains into complex personalities.

N.E.P.T.R.

N.E.P.T.R. (short for "Never ending pie-throwing robot" and pronounced phonetically as [nep-ter]) is a neglected robot that lives with Finn, Jake, and BMO in their tree fort. Created by both Finn and Ice King in the first-season episode "What Is Life?" N.E.P.T.R. resembles a bumbling parody of Frankenstein's monster, who is not so much actively rejected by his creators as he is simply forgotten. Despite this (accidental) emotional abuse, N.E.P.T.R. still shows up from time to time and attempts to help in any way he can.

N.E.P.T.R. was voiced by comedian, actor, and rapper Andy Milonakis, who was personally asked by Pendleton Ward via Twitter to appear on the show. In a 2013 Reddit AMA, Milonakis wrote, "It was such a G [sic] way to ask someone to be on a real show. I saw his pilot and said yes immediately."[31]

PEPPERMINT BUTLER

Peppermint Butler (voiced by a pitch-shifted Steve Little) is a candy butler who serves as Princess Bubblegum's devoted *aide-de-camp*. One of the show's longest recurring jokes is that this otherwise innocuous character is a powerful occultist (in the mold of Aleister Crowley or Anton LaVey), who over the course of the series is shown performing magical rituals, summoning demons, and even demanding Finn and Jake's flesh as payment for services rendered! Despite this,

Peppermint Butler almost always aids the show's "good" characters—most of whom either overlook or are oblivious to his dark ways.

SHERMY AND BETH

Shermy and Beth (voiced by actor Sean Giambrone and singer Willow Smith, respectively) are gregarious outlaws living in the Land of Ooo one thousand years after the time of Finn and Jake. Appearing only in the series finale "Come Along with Me," Shermy and Beth might not seem notable enough for inclusion in this section. However, their one appearance is of great importance to the show's overall mythology, as the two emphasize *Adventure Time*'s driving theme that all things are circular and that even though Finn and Jake will one day die, their heroic legacy will still be carried on by others well into the future.

Much of what we know about Shermy and Beth comes to us from the (possibly extracanonical) drawings of storyboard artist Steve Wolfhard, which he shared on his personal Tumblr account after the airing of the finale.[32] According to these doodles, Beth— "Her Highness Betony [sic] Burrito Jakson [sic] IV"—is the exiled princess of the Pup Kingdom (a realm ruled by Jake's grandson Gibbon), who possesses the power to teleport objects through her belly button. Given that the pups are the descendants of Jake and Lady Rainicorn, Beth can trace her heritage all the way back to Jake himself. Shermy, on the other hand, is an adventurous cat who bears a striking resemblance to Finn.[33] This—along with the closing shot of the series finale, which features Shermy holding up the Finn sword atop the Fern-Tree à la the show's title card—implies that Shermy is likely one of the many reincarnations of Finn's soul.

SUSAN STRONG

Susan Strong is a mysterious, muscular woman who lives underground with a primitive tribe of mutated humans called "hyoomans." She is introduced in the eponymous second-season episode, in which Finn and Jake discover her existence and befriend her. At first, it is unclear whether Susan is a mutated human like her subterranean compatriots, but later episodes reveal that she is a cybernetic human named XJ-77 (better known by her friends as "Kara"), who hails from the human colony, Founders Island. Years prior to the start of the series, Kara worked on Founders Island as a "seeker" (that is, a technologically enhanced spec-op tasked with retrieving runaway humans), and after Martin and baby Finn disappeared, it was Kara who was dispatched to find them. Somehow this mission went awry, and Kara crash-landed in Ooo. Lost and amnesiac in this new world, she soon joined up with a group of hyoomans, of whom she quickly became the *de facto* leader. (Years later, she donned the name "Susan" after meeting Finn.)

Susan's story has its origins in a massively multiplayer online (MMO) game named *Blade Mistress* that Pendleton Ward and Patrick McHale played during their time at CalArts. The game featured "really buff women in torn clothing with enormous swords,"[34] and when Ward created a character, he named her "Susan Strong." Flash forward to the year 2010: Storyboard partners Adam Muto and Rebecca Sugar were starting to work on an *Adventure Time* episode that would eventually evolve into "Susan Strong" when they hit a creative snag. The episode's original outline called for Finn to discover a group of mutated humans living underground, whom Finn would then take on a grand tour of Ooo. Sugar and Muto worried that it would be hard for viewers to keep track of all these new characters, so they decided to merge them into one individual. But who would this one character be? It was then that Ward regaled his colleagues with the aforementioned story about "Susan Strong," which inspired Muto and Sugar to write her into the episode as the eponymous character.[35] (Around the time that "Susan Strong" was being storyboarded, then-creative director Patrick McHale began to block out an elaborate backstory for Susan, envisioning her as Finn's lost sister, who had been separated from him at sea. However, when Susan and Finn's backstories began to diverge in later seasons, these plans were scrapped.[36])

All of Susan's initial lines were written out in coherent English before they were deliberately corrupted into a crude pidgin by the storyboard artists. Other aspects of Susan's speech were inspired by a "made-up patois"[37] that storyboard artist Somvilay Xayaphone occasionally spoke around the production offices; the other storyboard artists found this bizarre constructed language so amusing that they decided to work elements of it into "Susan Strong" and its sequels.[38] Susan Strong was voiced by Jackie Buscarino, who—like many other individuals affiliated with *Adventure Time*—had previously worked on *The Marvelous Misadventures of Flapjack*. (Buscarino would later go on to produce *Adventure Time* alumna Rebecca Sugar's hit series *Steven Universe*.)[39]

TREE TRUNKS

Tree Trunks is a small pygmy elephant who lives in the forest and is known for her delicious apple pies. She is also married to Mr. Pig (voiced by comedian Ron Lynch) and is the adoptive mother of Sweet P. Tree Trunks was voiced by Polly Lou Livingston, an eccentric Texan who had just turned eighty in 2009 when Ward asked her to play the part. As to how she of all people landed the role, Livingston explained in a 2013 interview with podcaster Dennis Tardan:

> When [Pendleton Ward] was about 12 years old, I knew his mother, Bettie Ward . . . She had a house [near where I lived,] and I used to go see her. And there was Pen drawing, all the time. . . . I was fascinated because I've always liked cartoons and I love to draw. So we became friends—he was a very quiet, sweet person . . . After years and years and years . . . He called me from Los Angeles and asked if I [would play Tree Trunks]. I was so flattered! I cannot tell you.[40]

Tree Trunks speaks with a distinctive southern drawl, which the *San Antonio Current* colorfully described as a cross between "a hinge in quest of lubricant and Blanche Dubois as channeled by Olive Oyl."[41] What many people do not realize is that when Livingston played Tree Trunks, the actress was not inflecting her voice; in fact, it was Livingston's natural voice that made Ward want to cast her in the first place. Livingston was delighted to hear this because in the past she had been criticized for her accent, telling Tardan in his podcast: "Almost every teacher I've ever had almost kicked me out of their class because they thought my voice was so terrible."[42]

Unlike the other *Adventure Time* actors, who recorded their lines as a group in Los Angeles, Livingston recorded her lines in Texas, and in a 2013 Reddit AMA, she explained the process as follows:

> I [record my lines] from San Antonio, Texas and they're in Hollywood, but we work together through technology. I talk to a machine and it goes to Hollywood and they direct me from Hollywood . . . through earphones. . . . I can't hear what everyone else is saying, I only say my part from the script and they put it together with pictures.[43]

Much of Tree Trunks's dialog is riddled with double entendres, innuendos, or subtle sex jokes that go over the heads of children. Because of these more mature gags, many fans find Tree Trunks to be hilarious; others find the character decidedly off-putting. As for Livingston, she emphatically noted during her AMA that the dialog was "fabulous."[44]

UNCLE GUMBALD

Uncle Gumbald (voiced by Fred Melamed) is the primary villain during the show's final season, and the series finale is focused at least partially on the

"Great Gum War" between his forces and those loyal to Princess Bubblegum. While nominally Bubblegum's uncle, Gumbald is actually one of her many candy creations; this has led to a sort of reverse-Oedipus complex, in which Gumbald desperately wants to overpower his mother-niece and usurp her throne.

Much of Gumbald's backstory is disclosed in the tenth-season episode "Bonnibel Bubblegum," which reveals that Gumbald was created by Bubblegum—along with an Aunt Lolly and a Cousin Chicle—so that the lonely monarch might have a family. Throughout the episode, Gumbald is painted as a savvy businessman eager to make a profit: for instance, he fells a number of trees that Bubblegum had planted to found a new city predicated on property management. He also creates kitschy merchandise to sell to the citizens living in his new town and becomes irate when Bubblegum builds a butterscotch lake on the site of his planned gift shop. His greed for and fixation on material goods leads to him conspiring with his family to oust Bubblegum as princess. Unfortunately for Gumbald, his plan backfires, and he, Lolly, and Chicle are accidentally turned into simple-minded candy folk in the process. It is only after the events of the ninth-season miniseries *Elements* that the three are restored to their original state, whereupon they once again concoct a plan to take over the Candy Kingdom.

Gumbald's devolution from kind uncle to industrialist goon is arguably best read as a critique of capitalism, illustrating what the Candy Kingdom could have become had rampant materialism taken the wheel. Contrasting the money-hungry Gumbald with the well-meaning but micromanaging Bubblegum is important because it continues the trend of rehabilitating Bubblegum's image—a trend that began around the middle of Season 6 when Bubblegum vowed to turn off her extensive surveillance system in the episode "The Cooler." The introduction of Gumbald thus serves as a way to underline that for all the inadvertent harm her actions caused, Bubblegum's intentions were always good; Gumbald, on the other hand, only cared about capital, regardless of the pain it might cause others.

THE MANY DEITIES OF THE OOONIVERSE

In the *Adventure Time* universe, it is not a question as to whether gods and goddesses exist, as Finn and Jake have time and time again partied with deities, fought demons in space, and been snatched away by angels. Perhaps one of the most powerful of these beings is the two-dimensional "wish master," Prismo, who lives at the heart of the multiverse in the extratemporal "Time Room." Prismo is in charge of wish magic, but while he is almost omnipotent, his wishes all come with what he calls a "'monkey's paw' kind of" catch.[45] Initially aloof and impartial, Prismo quickly forms a close friendship with Jake. Prismo was voiced by Kumail Nanjiani, an actor whose laid-back vocal performance contrasts with his character's tremendous power.

Another deity that becomes more fleshed out as the show progresses is the Cosmic Owl, voiced by M. Emmet Walsh. Tasked with maintaining the dreamscapes of all those who inhabit the multiverse, the Cosmic Owl is also compelled to appear in dreams destined to become true. In religious and folkloric traditions all over the world, owls are often seen as ominous creatures, sometimes serving as harbingers of death. Other cultures believe that the bird has some sort of spooky connection to the underworld, afterlife, or the spirit realm.[46] These related traditions could explain why the writers decided to make the Cosmic Owl a prophetic dream messenger from the "great beyond." (On a less folkloric note, the character's unique beak design was based on a distinctive refraction of light produced by one of the urinals at Cartoon Network Studios.)[47]

For much of the series' run, the god of the "50 Deadworlds" (i.e., the collective name for the afterlife in *Adventure Time*) is Death (voiced by Miguel Ferrer), who lives in a "castle made of light" and enjoys playing death metal music. In terms of appearance, the character—with his cow-skull head and ten-gallon hat—is reminiscent of the Aztec god Mictlāntēcutli by way of an Alexandro Jodorowsky film. This unique look was drafted up by storyboard artist Jesse Moynihan, who initially struggled when it came time to design "such an iconic character."[48] Moynihan eventually settled on a design that he felt evoked death as a concept while nevertheless remaining unique.[49] Death's romantic partner is, ironically, Life (voiced initially by Hynden Walch and later by Corinne Kempa), whose design evokes the Aztec goddess Cōātlīcue. Life lives in a realm known as the "Underwater Gardens," and she is responsible for the transmigration of souls.

In the *Distant Lands* special "Together Again," it is revealed that Death and Life had a son, a skeleton-snake fusion (voiced by comedian Chris Fleming), who at some point killed and succeeded his father as the leader of the Deadworlds. This "New Death" becomes a tyrant hell bent on destroying the entirety of the afterlife, and thus he serves as the chief antagonist in "Together Again." By the special's end, the audience learns that, in addition to misplaced teen angst, much of New Death's aggression is due to his being possessed by the spirit of the Lich. New Death is obliterated (accidentally) by the spirit of Mr. Fox (voiced by storyboard artist Tom Herpich), who then takes up the scythe, becoming *New* New Death.

Another oft-mentioned celestial being is a four-headed Martian by the name of Grob Gob Glob Grod, whose third name is commonly invoked by Ooo's citizens as a mild swear (e.g., "Oh my Glob!"). While Grob Gob Glob Grod is viewed by some as a deity, this tetramorphic being resembles an angel more so than a god, with its four distinct faces recalling the four-fold visage of the cherubim, who according to the Hebrew prophet Ezekiel "had the likeness of a man [but with] four faces."[50] Grob Gob Glob Grod also wields a flaming sword, like the cherub whom God tasked with guarding the biblical Garden of Eden.[51] And like the Guardian of Eden, Grob Gob Glob Grod's chief duty was guarding select territory (i.e., Mars) from outside threats.

Although Grob Gob Glob Grod is a wielder of awesome power, the four-faced being is nothing compared to an entity of even greater ability: the wise King of Mars, who in the *Adventure Time* universe is none other than Abraham Lincoln himself. In the series proper, the King of Mars is introduced in the fourth-season episode "Sons of Mars" as an "all-powerful being" capable of "travel[ing] through time and different dimensions."[52] While Lincoln's appearance in this episode is an obvious call-back to the show's pilot, "Sons of Mars" also manages to work the character into the show's complex mythology: After Jake is mistaken for Magic Man and accidentally executed, the King of Mars negotiates with Death, trading Jake's soul for his own immortality. King of Mars is thus a Christ-like figure, who gives up his life so that an innocent may live, making him the closest thing Ooo has to Jesus.

But how exactly is Lincoln a godlike being, and why is he ruling over the Red Planet? An answer to this question might be found in a 2018 video interview with Doug TenNapel (a cartoonist best known for the *Earthworm Jim* video game series). In this interview, TenNaple recounts how, during the production of *Adventure Time*'s first season, he had helped storyboard an eventually scrapped episode titled "The Glorriors."[53] According to TenNaple:

> I [wrote] this giant epic story [for "The Glorriors"] where Finn and Jake . . . one of them dies, [but] they are the ones that the Earth needs to survive . . . in the future. And Abe Lincoln is an interdimensional traveler [who] shows up and says that he will insert himself back into Earth's history as [a US] president in order to die in place of one of those two guys who died and [thereby] save the universe. . . . The network canned the episode and said "We can't do any of this." . . . In [the] fourth season, they brought back some of my work and did 'Sons of Mars' and gave me writing credit.[54]

Obviously, this storyline changed dramatically when it was converted into "Sons of Mars," but TenNapel's insight suggests that in the Oooniverse, Abraham Lincoln was first and foremost the King of Mars since time immemorial, and it was only the activities of "Sons of Mars" that retroactively made him the sixteenth president of the United States. (This also explains why Pendleton Ward, during the writing of "Sons of Mars," was adamant that the character be referred to exclusively in the storyboard as the "King of Mars," rather than Abraham Lincoln.)[55]

Although many of the deities and beings of power in the Oooniverse are friendly or at the very least ambivalent towards mortal beings, this cannot be said for all of them. Chief among the more dangerous deities is the entity GOLB, a Lovecraftian abomination who embodies chaos itself. While GOLB is teased throughout the series, starting with the fifth-season episode "Puhoy," he is only introduced as a major baddie in the series finale, "Come Along with Me," when he is unleashed unto Ooo thanks to the magical antics of King Man and Betty. In this episode, the audience learns that GOLB is capable of corrupting life into almost unstoppable eldritch horrors that wreak havoc wherever they go. GOLB's deadliest power, however, is his capability to wipe people (and possibly whole universes)[56] from existence. While it is likely that GOLB cannot be killed in the traditional sense, harmony (such as that found in music) seems to weaken him. GOLB is ultimately defeated by Betty with the ice crown, although her victory is Pyrrhic, as in the end she is forced to merge with the being and leave Ooo—and Simon—behind.

A handful of times throughout the series, the Oooniverse's pantheon members make cryptic references to their "Boss." This boss is never shown, although in "Hoots," it is revealed that this entity put many of the gods in power, recalling the way Zeus is said to have divided up the universe among his siblings. Given this hint, it can be inferred that the Oooniverse's boss is a deity concerned with the division of metaphysical labor and is thus by extension interested in maintaining order in the universe.

THE FIONNA AND CAKE UNIVERSE

Fionna (a feisty girl warrior voiced by Madeleine Martin) and Cake (a magical cat voiced by Roz Ryan) are the gender-swapped versions of Finn and Jake. The two are introduced in Season 3's "Fionna and Cake," which reveals that they are actually characters in a series of fanfics penned by Ice King. Other major characters in the "Fionna and Cake" universe include:

Prince Gumball: The gender-swapped version of Princess Bubblegum, voiced initially by Neil Patrick Harris (in "Fionna and Cake" and "Bad Little Boy"), and later by Keith Ferguson (in "Five Short Tables"). In his first appearance, he serves as Fionna's main love interest.

Ice Queen: The gender-swapped version of Ice King, voiced by Grey DeLisle. The character serves as the main antagonist in "Fionna and

Cake." Much like her male counterpart, Ice Queen dabbles freely in fanfiction, writing stories about "Flynn the Human," "Jacques the Raccoon," and the "Ice President."[57]

Marshall Lee: The gender-swapped version of Marceline, voiced by Donald Glover. The character, who stars in the episode "Bad Little Boy," shares with his female counterpart a love of pranks and playing music; regarding the latter, he is both a skilled bassist and a rapper.

Lumpy Space Prince: The gender-swapped version of Lumpy Space Princess, voiced initially by Pendleton Ward (in "Bad Little Boy," part of "The Prince Who Wanted Everything," and "Five Short Tables"), and then by Peter Serafinowicz (in "The Prince Who Wanted Everything"). When played by Serafinowicz, Lumpy Space Prince speaks with a highly affected "posh" accent.

Lord Monochromicorn: The gender-swapped version of Lady Rainicorn. While Lady Rainicorn is best described as a rainbow crossed with a horse, Lord Monochromicorn more closely resembles a stallion crossed with a black licorice wheel. The character communicates with others through Morse code.

Fionna and Cake have an interesting origin story. In fanfic and fanart circles, there has always been an interest in swapping the genders and/or sexes of main characters.[58] This practice is known by various names, including "genderbending" or "genderswapping"; other fans use the catch-all designator "Rule 63" (an allusion to the infamous "Rules of the Internet").[59] Regardless of the nomenclature used to describe the practice, gender-swapped characters are usually made by fans for fans, and rarely do they make their way back into the original media object off of which they were based. It is in this last regard that Fionna and Cake are special.

The characters started life as fun doodles that storyboard revisionist and character designer Natasha Allegri had mocked up in her free time. In 2011, Allegri explained to *Bitch* magazine:

> The [genderbent] stuff I did at first wasn't for work . . . I just wanted to draw the [characters that] I wanted, and how I wanted. And I wanted to draw a cute, chubby girl in a bunny hat, and a super sexy ice queen, because why not? I wasn't getting paid to do it, so I did whatever I felt like doing at the time.[60]

Allegri eventually posted her drawings of "Fionna the Human" and "Cake the Cat" to Tumblr, where they were blogged and reblogged by many of the show's ardent fans. When Ward saw these drawings, he felt that they had creative potential, so he greenlit an official Fionna and Cake episode,[61] with Adam Muto and Rebecca Sugar tapped as storyboard artists. Sugar, in particular, was excited to work on the episode because in the past she had dabbled both in fanfiction as well as gender-swapped fanart.[62] After several extensive rewrites, Muto and Sugar turned in a finalized storyboard featuring Fionna and Cake fighting off the evil Ice Queen while trying to woo Prince Gumball.[63]

Ward thought that fans would enjoy the Fionna and Cake concept, but in many regards, he misjudged just how popular the episode would become. Upon its airing, "Fionna and Cake" became the show's most-watched installment at the time, with over 3.3 million viewers tuning in to see what a gender-swapped version of *Adventure Time* would look like.[64] In a subsequent interview with the *San Antonio Express-News*, Ward noted: "Fionna and Cake, in my mind, was a cool one-off experiment that was fun for us to dabble around in, so I didn't consider making another Fionna and Cake until [the first one] aired nine months from when we started . . . The vocal fan feedback was bangin'."[65] The success of "Fionna and Cake" led to countless pieces of fanart and numerous cosplays, and it set the stage for four other gender-swapped episodes of *Adventure Time*, as well as the *Fionna and Cake* miniseries.

Part II

COME ALONG WITH ME: A PRODUCTION HISTORY OF *ADVENTURE TIME*

5.

BEHIND THE EASEL

How an Episode Was Made

In popular discourse, *Adventure Time* is often seen as the product of a single auteur—Pendleton Ward—but in reality, the show was a team effort that required dozens of skilled artists carefully coordinating for months at a time to produce the final eleven-minute product. This present chapter takes a deep dive into the complex and enigmatic process by which an episode of *Adventure Time* was produced (a process which Ward himself once likened to a sort of magic), covering everything from initial conception to final broadcast.

A selection of the *Adventure Time* production crew at the 2015 Peabody Awards ceremony. Photo courtesy of the Peabody Awards via CC Attribution 2.0 Generic (CC BY 2.0) license, https://flic.kr/p/ukSfpZ.

DEVELOPING AN OUTLINE

Before a new season would enter production, the show's writers and producers would convene and make note of any characters who needed fleshed-out or lingering storylines that needed to be addressed. After drafting up a rough plan of the season, the writers then began to work out the details of individual episodes.[1]

All *Adventure Time* episodes originated as general outlines developed in the series' writers' room. These were relatively short story sketches—usually a page or two at most—that focused on the main "acts" of an episode (viz., beginning and rising action, climax, and resolution). Outlines were normally written by a dedicated storyline crew—directed in the show's later years by Kent Osborne—and it was common for stories to be based on the everyday experiences of the writers.[2] Other storylines were developed by the show's storyboard artists; Jesse Moynihan and Tom Herpich[3] in particular were known for helping prepare outlines, producing some of the show's strongest episodes in the process, like Moynihan's "Sons of Mars" (Season 4, Episode 15), or Herpich's "Evergreen" (Season 6, Episode 24).

Still other outlines evolved from ideas that the show's artists developed while playing writing games, of which "exquisite corpse" was arguably the most popular. This game would start with a writer drawing a goofy picture (e.g., Marceline laughing at a transmogrified Princess Bubblegum, who has been turned into a horse) at the top of an otherwise blank sheet of paper. The sheet would then be passed to a new writer, who would look at the image and then develop the first part of a story to explain what was going on in the picture. The sheet would be passed down the line, with each writer adding more and more until a coherent story coalesced.[4] While Ward once admitted in an interview that these outlines were often "terrible"[5] because they "usually devolv[ed] into boner jokes,"[6] he noted that the game would produce the occasional storyline gem. Notable episodes that emerged from games of exquisite corpse include "Puhoy" (Season 5, Episode 16), "One Last Job" (Season 5, Episode 23) "Red Starved" (Season 5, Episode 38), "Rattleballs" (Season 5, Episode 46) and "Jake the Brick" (Season 6, Episode 20).[7]

It is common to hear people describe *Adventure Time*'s stories as either "really for adults," or (more accurately) as stories that both children *and* adults can enjoy. When it came to breaking stories with such a wide appeal, Ward explained that he and the writers simply wrote plot ideas that made themselves laugh.[8] Sometimes an episode would revolve around an idea or visual that Ward felt "kids [were] really going to dig on,"[9] and at other times, episodes focused on more complicated topics like love or death. And while the show is often associated with scatological humor, Ward has emphasized in numerous interviews that he is not a fan of over-the-top gross-out comedy: "I try to stay away from gross-out humor. I like the show to be really cute. I think fart jokes"—perhaps the show's gag of choice—"are a really precise art form."[10]

THE STORYBOARDING PROCESS

Once episode outlines were finalized, they were passed off to the show's storyboard artists (often referred to colloquially as "board artists" or "boarders"). Initially, Ward wanted his show to be script-driven, so that he would have total creative control over dialogue. But as he explained in a 2012 interview with the Nerdist:

> I sat down to write my first script . . . and I wrote "Finn and Jake make funny faces at each other." I thought, "This sucks. This is not funny. I need to draw what those faces are and I need to time it out so that it feels funny." . . . I scrapped the whole idea [of having the show based around scripts] and just went [the] storyboard driven [route].[11]

As a result of this decision, it was the storyboard artists, and not the storyline writers, who had most of the creative control over pacing, action, and—most importantly—dialogue. While discussing the show in a 2013 interview with the *Daily Beast*, Osborne equated the storyboard artists to directors, saying, "They're writing all the jokes, editing the outline, picking all the camera shots . . . [and figuring out] what the episode is going to look like."[12] Structuring the show in this way allowed the artistic personalities of the various storyboard artists to shine through in finished episodes, as storyboard artist Polly Guo explained in an interview: "Each artist had their own specific voice that contributed to the show and made it the hodgepodge of art and writing that the show ended up being."[13]

Both Ward (the showrunner[14] for Seasons 1–5) and Adam Muto (the showrunner for Seasons 5–10) were interested in storyboard artists who were willing to push the boundaries of the art world, with Guo emphasizing that the storyboard artists were actively encouraged "to get weird."[15] As a result of this interest in "weird" art, Ward and Muto often recruited storyboard artists from the experimental world of independent comic books.[16] Notable *Adventure Time* storyboard artists who got their start in the indie comic scene include Derek Ballard, Michael DeForge, Brandon Graham, Tom Herpich, Sloane Leong, Jesse Moynihan, Luke Pearson, and Jillian Tamaki.

Storyboard artists almost always worked in teams of two, and how these artists approached the storyboarding process depended entirely on their sensibilities: Sometimes, the pairs would actively work with one another, coordinating their efforts so that their portions of an episode would fit together seamlessly. Other partners preferred to work in isolation, consulting each other only when necessary. For most of the show's run, it was common for there to be four pairs of "regular" storyboard artists working concurrently on their own episodes. In addition to being efficient, this division of labor also seemed to have engendered a sort of friendly competition that in turn stimulated creative growth, with Herpich telling me that when he was storyboarding, he aimed "to be as funny as Jesse [Moynihan] and as dramatic as Rebecca [Sugar]."[17]

The storyboarding process usually took about five weeks.[18] On the first week, storyboard pairs would be assigned an outline, which they would divide among themselves. Again, the method for division depended on the preferences of the artists. According to Tom Herpich:

> Different boarders do it different ways. For me it's very granular. It's always: how many pages I need to draw divided by how many days I have in which to do it, then hit those quotas as best I can. I've had partners who do one big quick take on the whole thing, and then do pass after pass refining things, but I need my schedule more concrete—it feels like less variables to worry about.[19]

Once a division was finally settled upon, the artists began to mock up a rough storyboard. According to Andy Ristaino (a storyboard artist during Seasons 5 and 6), during the first week of storyboarding, most of the emphasis was placed on dialogue, and the storyboard artists did not worry too much about perfecting their drawings; freelancer Laura Knetzger echoed this in an interview when she told me that by the end of the first week, "drawings could be really sketchy and didn't need to have every single pose drawn."[20] These rough storyboards were often doodled on Post-it Notes or on plain pieces of paper.

Following the conclusion of the first week, the storyboard artists would pitch their thumbnails to the showrunner, the various directors, and studio executives, all of whom would make comments, provide constructive criticism, and take detailed notes. During the second and third weeks, the storyboard artists integrated the suggestions they received, which inevitably resulted in dialogue being tinkered with, new jokes being added, and substandard gags being excised or tweaked until deemed satisfactory. The partners then began working on a "more polished pass" of their storyboard. According to Knetzger, during this phase of production, "drawings could still be sketchy, but [they] needed to be legible and poses needed to be completed."[21]

At the end of week three, the artists would then pitch their storyboard once again, after which they would receive a final round of notes. The fourth and fifth week were devoted to clean-up, which Ristaino described as the phase "when you're posing everything out and you're supposed to draw everything nice and put backgrounds in where needed . . . so [the production crew] can figure out all the camera angles."[22] The storyboard then spent roughly a week with the showrunner, who made final tweaks, before being passed off to the network for approval.[23] After Cartoon Network OK'ed the storyboard, it was then handed off to a revisionist, who redrew or reposed select frames so that they were on-model. As Ako Castuera (a storyboard artist who worked as a revisionist during Season 1) explained to me, "revisionists handle technical problems" and as a result, they "have minimal narrative responsibility, if any."[24]

During the storyboarding process, the production of individual episodes was overseen by a "creative director" (during Seasons 1–5) or a "supervising director" (during Seasons 5–10).[25] According to Elizabeth Ito (one of the show's supervising directors during Seasons 5–9), these directorial positions were "mostly about helping shepherd [an] episode from the outline stage, all the way through until it was sent off to be animated."[26] Also assisting at this stage was the storyboard supervisor. Ian Jones-Quartey (the show's storyboard supervisor during Seasons 4–5) clarified in an interview that in this role, his principal goals were to "break down each [story]board so every design was accounted for" and "add a lot of details [without] do[ing] anything that would detract from the original storyboard or step on any jokes."[27]

Storyboarding and revising was often an emotionally and mentally exhausting operation. Ristaino, for instance, disclosed in a podcast interview: "I was working 12–14 hours a day every day of the week. . . . And I'd be working weekends. . . . I really wanted to do a good job on my boards. . . . [Some artists' storyboards] are super rough and quick and it's all, like, short hand, and that's a skill."[28] Castuera told me something similar: "For me it was psychologically brutal, physically exhausting (so much sitting and drawing, so many all-nighters) and emotionally impactful on my personal life."[29] But the biggest hurdle was arguably the non-stop drawing required: "I struggled with the workload each time," Knetzger told me. "Drawing 200+ panels 2 or 3 times in 5 weeks is a lot, even when it's your full time job."[30] Kris Mukai, a storyboard artist who freelanced for the show during Seasons 7 and 8, likewise noted: "It's hard to figure out a good workflow for something that's so large. You have to produce just a ton of drawings for storyboards and it can be really daunting at first."[31] Luckily, the *Adventure Time* crew had a trick up their sleeves that helped make the job a bit easier: using sticky notes. As Mukai explained:

> Sticky notes are kind of translucent, so if you're drawing multiple poses you can stick a post-it over one frame to trace, and then transfer it over to the next panel. Also because sticky notes are so disposable, it makes you feel a lot less precious with the drawings.[32]

THE RECORDING AND DESIGN PHASES

After revisionists had polished up a storyboard, episode production moved into the recording phase.[33] Assistants compiled the dialogue from a completed storyboard down into a script, which was given to the voice actors. The actors would then convene in one room and record their lines together. (This method, which differed substantially from the piecemeal recording practices employed by many other animated productions, resulted in dialogue that sounded more conversational and genuine.) Recording sessions usually took about three hours, and were held every week.[34] During much of the show's run, Kent Osborne served as voice director, which required him to coach the actors, provide context for scenes, and call for re-takes. When takes were completed, an editor used video editing software to assemble an animatic by timing out the lines of dialogue and placing them over polished storyboard panels; this was then tweaked and cut down until the episode was of the correct length.[35]

A finalized (or "conformed") animatic was then passed off to a team of sheet timers, who determined the timing, down to the individual frame, for everything that needed to be animated (e.g., walk cycles, mouth movements). This timing was recorded on complex X sheets (short for "exposure sheets"), which the animators in South Korea would use to guide their work.[36] As Tom Sito notes: "Timing on X sheets is an extremely skilled operation [and] the director needs a great deal of experience to time out a film mentally before any drawing is done"[37]; it is for this reason that for much of its run, the *Adventure Time* production crew employed the skilled sheet timer Larry Leichliter, an industry veteran who had worked on a number of hit cartoons, including multiple *Peanuts* specials, *SpongeBob SquarePants*, *Hey Arnold!*, and *The Fairly OddParents*. Leichliter served as the show's director for the first four-and-a-half seasons, and after the director role was discontinued during Season 5, he freelanced as a sheet timer.

Once the animatic had been timed out, production moved into the design phase,[38] which required extensive coordination. According to Derek Kirk Kim, the show's lead character and prop designer for Seasons 6–8: "Once a week, I would meet with the other department heads to break down a completed storyboard and see what needed to be designed for that particular episode. Then the rest of the week was the actual task of designing and drawing."[39] *Adventure Time* has a very specific "look," with the characters' noodly limbs and minimalistic faces recalling the "rubber hose" animation popularized by Max Fleischer in the early twentieth century. While the groundwork for this throwback style was laid by Ward early on, it was formalized largely by character designers Phil Rynda, Tom Herpich, and Natasha Allegri during the production of Season 1. For the many seasons that followed, it was thus the job of character and prop designers to make sure that this distinct aesthetic was infused throughout all the show's many designs. (With that said, Ward and later Muto often encouraged the artists to go "off-model" if it made a scene funnier or helped sell a certain emotion.)[40]

Once character and prop designs were finalized, they were sent to a clean-up artist, such as Alex Campos, whose job was to take roughly thirty model sheets a week and polish them up in Adobe Illustrator using specialized brushes.[41] These drawings would serve as key visual aids, providing the animation studios with a clear understanding of how the characters or props were to look in a finished episode. For certain unique shots (usually those that employed off-model or unique designs), the production team would also draw out and clean-up key frames so that the animation studios would know exactly what the producers were envisioning. Once completed, the key frame, character, and prop designs were then colored in Burbank by a color stylist.[42]

Concurrent with the finalization of character and prop designs, the series' background artists met with the show's art and supervising directors to determine what set pieces needed to be designed for an episode.[43] According to Derek Hunter, who worked as a background designer during Seasons 4–8:

> At the beginning [of my time on the show], my art director [Nick Jennings] picked all the [backgrounds] I did, but he left before Season 7, and [during that season] I was put into a supervisor role, where I would go to a 2–3 hour meeting with all the department heads and episode directors to go through the storyboard page by page and identify which designs needed to be done. Then I would decide which of my background designers would do which scenes, [I would also give] them direction, reference, and inspiration photos/art to get them going [in] the right direction.[44]

Usually, the designers collectively produced between thirty to forty background pieces a week.[45] Like the character designs and key frames, these background pieces were then colored by a specialized team of painters.[46]

The entirety of the design phase was overseen by the series' art director. Nick Jennings served in this role from Seasons 1 to 6, and his successor, Sandra Lee, served from Season 6 onward. The art director worked with the lead designers, helping them navigate the complexities of the design process. The art director also worked closely with the show's color stylists and the showrunner to determine appropriate color palettes for each episode.

ANIMATION TIME

Once an animatic, a timing sheet, and all the requisite designs had been finalized, everything was sent to the South Korea animation studios SAEROM and

Rough Draft Studios; the two often studios animated episodes simultaneously to speed up production. Each studio employed roughly a dozen lead animators,[47] who focused most of their attention on key poses. These artists were in turn aided by numerous assistant animators and in-betweeners, who drew the frames that transitioned into the key poses.[48] To the untrained eye, episodes produced by the two studios look stylistically identical, but according to Tom Herpich, Rough Draft was "usually slicker and smoother . . . but, on the other hand, they also smooth[ed] away some [of the] interesting idiosyncrasies" of the individual storyboard artists. Conversely, SAEROM "studiously preserv[ed] all those idiosyncrasies,"[49] which sometimes resulted in a slightly rougher looking episode.

Unlike many modern cartoons, the animators of *Adventure Time* eschewed the heavy use of programs like Adobe Flash and instead animated episodes by hand. First, the animators penciled each frame onto paper. These pages were then scanned and loaded onto a computer, whereupon a dedicated teams of artists used Toon Boom Harmony[50] to digitally ink, color, and composite the frames.[51] The animation process was overseen by SAEROM director Dongkun Won (an industry veteran who had served as animation director for programs like *Camp Lazlo*, *Lilo & Stitch: The Series*, and *Kim Possible*) and Rough Draft director Bonghui Han (another animation veteran who in the past had worked on episodes of *The Ren & Stimpy Show* and *The Simpsons*).[52] The entire animation process for a single episode could take anywhere from three to four months, on average.[53]

When animation was finished, it was sent back to the United States, where the series' showrunner inspected it to make sure that it was of the appropriate quality. If the showrunner noticed any errors, necessary corrections were made by SAEROM or Rough Draft. According to Sandra Lee, there were two common types of mistakes caught at this stage: "technicals" and "creatives." The former included simple animation blunders or errors made by the animation studio; the latter included instances in which the producers decided to make an aesthetic change to the final cut. While major retakes were handled by the animation studios, the show's art director or showrunner would sometimes work on minor fixes from their offices in California as a cost-saving mechanism.[54]

Once the producers approved an episode's animation, it was time to create the episode's soundtrack. First, necessary sound effects were added into the episode. Following this, the series composers Tim Kiefer or Casey James Basichis dreamt up the show's chirpy score. After the soundtrack, effects, and dialogue tracks were mixed, the episode was ready to air.

From start to finish, the writing, recording, and animating of a single episode usually took about nine months to complete—an astonishing amount of time for eleven minutes of animation.

6.

THE FUN BEGINS

The Pilot and Season 1

While the last chapter emphasized that *Adventure Time* was the creative offspring of many artists, it cannot be denied that the show has its origin in one man: Pendleton Ward. Born in 1982 and raised in sunny San Antonio, Texas, Ward was an introverted child who at a young age discovered the joys of art. Ward's mother, Bettie, being an artist herself, was delighted by her son's interests and encouraged him to explore his creative impulses at every possible opportunity.[1] Ward soon developed an intense fixation with the animation medium—in interviews, he often mentions how much joy he derived from making ad hoc flip books—and in time, he began dreaming of the day that he could develop his own cartoon.[2]

Having grown up in the halcyon days of the 1990s, Ward spent hours of his free time glued to the television, watching cartoon trailblazers like Nickelodeon's *Ren and Stimpy* and MTV's *Beavis and Butt-Head*. But of all the shows in his diet of animated television, arguably the one that meant the most to Ward was Matt Groening's *The Simpsons*; in fact, so obsessed was Ward with the world of Springfield that his mother somehow tracked down Groening's home address and showed up unannounced on his doorstep with Ward in tow. Bettie explained how much Groening's show meant to her son, and she asked if he could provide any tips for the nascent artist. "I have no idea what I said," Groening later recounted to an enrapt crowd at a 2011 Comic-Con panel. "But I guess it worked out."[3]

During his teenage years, Ward's life was permanently changed when he began to dabble in the role-playing game *Dungeons & Dragons* (*D&D*). Initially released in 1974 and modeled on the miniature war games of the twentieth century, *D&D* allows players to create their own fantasy characters and go on elaborate adventures (known in the parlance of *D&D* as "campaigns"). All games are organized by a "Dungeon Master" (often simply called a "DM"), who enforces rules and keeps detailed track of game play. Known for its complex

Adventure Time was the brainchild of Pendleton Ward, who studied character animation at the CalArts during the early 2000s. Photo courtesy of Edward Liu.

logic, its Tolkien-esque monsters, and its use of polyhedral dice, *D&D* became increasingly popular in the 1980s, and by the time Ward started dabbling with the d20s, the game had become a fixture of the nerdosphere. As a game predicated on creativity and imagination, *D&D* would greatly impact Ward's artistic development, and years later, when asked about his unique writing style, he would simply liken it to "playing D&D with the characters."[4]

When a teenage Ward was not fighting fantasy creatures with his friends, he was beginning to hone his drawing abilities at San Antonio's respected North East School of the Arts (NESA)—a magnet school that boasted an arts-heavy curriculum. Ward made quite an impression on several of his teachers at NESA, including visual art director Jennifer Janak, who in 2010 told the *San Antonio Express-News* that she "remember[ed] Ward as an excellent artist and creative freethinker."[5] Ward's creative growth continued when in both 1999 and 2000[6] he attended the California State Summer School for the Arts, a summer program aimed at artistically promising high school students; then, in the spring of 2001, he was accepted to CalArts, a private university located in the Valencia neighborhood of Santa Clarita, California. CalArts is often seen as the Harvard of art schools, and for good reason. Counted among its many alumni are animation luminaries like Tim Burton, John Lasseter, and Craig McCracken.

Ward attended CalArts from 2001 to 2005, working towards a bachelor's degree in character animation. It was during these years that Ward became friends with two other artists who would later play a major role in helping him develop *Adventure Time*: Patrick McHale and Adam Muto. According to the former:

> Pen and Adam were both a grade above me [at CalArts]. I learned about Pen because some people told me that my drawings looked like Pen's drawings, except his stuff was funnier than mine. . . . I forget how we actually became friends, but we used to doodle and draw comics. We just got along really well and had a lot of similar tastes/interests. . . . [We] had a similar sense of humor and stuff. [For instance] one thing we bonded over was that we tried to create a real-world role-playing game called LifeQuest in which players walk around parking lots to fight monsters by flipping pennies.[7]

McHale also recalls:

> Adam was infamous at CalArts for being this incredible animator who would animate all day and night, but would never complete a film. Once I got to know him I realized he was just less interested in finishing a film than he was [in] exploring the possibilities of animation. It's hard to describe, but looking at Adam's animation made me realize that your animation didn't have to just be entertainment or art, but it could also be . . . literature, or poetry, or philosophy, or science or something. . . . He was almost like an animation scientist, just pushing the boundaries and testing hypotheses. Not for any purpose other than the pursuit of truth in animation. Adam animated some of Pen's wall doodles one time, which was incredible to see; at the time I hadn't really seen simple cute drawings being animated in that way. In Adam's final year I think he felt a little hopeless about handing in an actual film, so I joined in helping him sort through his stacks of animation and edit it into a watchable film. . . . We became friends during that process and we've been friends since.[8]

The importance of McHale and Muto with regard to *Adventure Time* cannot be overstated. When production for the series began in 2008, it was these two artists whom Pen called upon for help: McHale served as the series' creative director for its first two seasons and remained on as a freelance storyline writer well into its fifth, and Muto began as a writer and storyboard artist before eventually succeeding Ward as the program's showrunner during its fifth season. While Ward is rightfully considered the creator of *Adventure Time*, it is inarguable that the final tone of the show was heavily influenced by both McHale and Muto's creative sensibilities.

Ward's student work at CalArts was, as he himself admits, rough around the edges, but what he lacked in technical mastery, he made up for with creative verve and a one-of-a-kind sense of humor; in a 2014 interview with *Rolling Stone*, Muto noted, "Even back then, [Ward's] films were the funniest ones being made."[9] One of these films (created c. 2005) was a minute-long short that featured two heroes—a boy and his dog—rescuing "Princess Bubblegum" from the clutches of a wicked "Ice King." Ward later told the *Los Angeles Times* in 2018 that it "was just a sketch I kicked out into a minute-long short . . . Nickelodeon was taking pitches from CalArts students. And they didn't like it."[10]

But while Nickelodeon was indifferent to his work, others were starting to take notice, including Eric Homan, the development executive at Frederator Studios, a company that had helped produce several successful Nickelodeon cartoons, including *The Fairly OddParents* (2001–17), *ChalkZone* (2002–8), and *My Life as a Teenage Robot* (2003–9). When I inquired as to how he stumbled across Ward's work, Homan explained to me:

> Every spring CalArts holds its Producers' Show, a screening showing off the best of the year's student animated work. Pen's senior film in 2005 was a big hit with both the audience and his classmates (and with me, of course; like everyone else, I found Pen's work to be funny, good-hearted, and wildly distinctive—like Pen himself). At Frederator Studios we had just begun taking pitches for a shorts show we were producing for Nickelodeon, *Random! Cartoons*. At the Producers' Show [I] encouraged Pen to pitch.[11]

Ward—now a freshly minted CalArts grad—was delighted by the offer and dutifully showed up at the production company's offices with the idea that Nickelodeon had previously rejected.

Ward made quite the impression at the pitch by lugging in an acoustic guitar and singing a catchy theme song for his proposed short, which he called *Adventure Time*.[12] The folks at Frederator enjoyed the pitch, but many—including the company's founder and eventual *Adventure Time* evangelist, Fred Seibert—were apprehensive about Ward's work, fearing that it was too unpolished; in a 2013 interview with Dom's Sketch Cast, Seibert explained:

> I saw the pitch, loved it, and then said we weren't going to do the cartoon . . . At the time . . . I'd been making cartoons for, like, 15 years, and

Frederator executive Fred Seibert was initially reluctant to take a chance on Ward, fearing that the final "Adventure Time" short would look too much like a student film. Photo courtesy of Gage Skidmore via CC Attribution-ShareAlike 2.0 Generic (CC BY-SA 2.0) license, https://flic.kr/p/nQnyw5.

like every other idiot executive, I thought I knew what made a good cartoon. And this did not fit it on the surface."[13]

But Homan and Frederator's vice-president Kevin Kolde would not take "no" for an answer, and they continuously pressed Seibert to take a chance on Ward. Finally, after "a one-on-one meeting with Pen," Seibert came round and "became a champion" for the young artist.[14]

Given that his previous experience in animation had mostly been confined to working on student films at CalArts, Ward's opportunity to work with

Frederator—a *real* animation studio!—was something completely new,[15] and when he reflected on the opportunity in 2009, Ward noted, "It was exciting jumping into it not knowing whether I would sink or swim."[16] But enthusiasm notwithstanding, the task was still daunting, and to make it easier, Ward enlisted the help of several CalArts friends, including Adam Muto, who became the short's prop designer. Ward himself focused on designing the characters and writing the basic story beats. He also plotted out a storyboard for the short, which took roughly two weeks to complete.[17]

After months of work, *Adventure Time* was finalized in the spring of 2006.[18] In this silly short, a young boy named Pen (voiced by Zack Shada) and his talking English bulldog, Jake, (voiced by John DiMaggio) learn that the dreaded Ice King (voiced by John Kassir)—an evil wizard with frosty powers—has captured Princess Bubblegum (voiced by Paige Moss) and is holding her prisoner in his dreaded mountain fortress. Pen and Jake arrive on the scene to free the monarch, but Pen is frozen by the Ice King's nefarious magic. After being "transported back in time and to Mars," Pen receives a pep talk from a deified Abraham Lincoln (voiced by Ward), who tells him to "believe in [him] self." This provides Pen with the power needed to break out of the ice, rescue the princess, and save the day.

Adventure Time first aired on the Nicktoons Network on January 11, 2007,[19] and, despite clocking in at only seven minutes, it made quite the splash. This attention was largely thanks to Frederator, who uploaded the short onto a burgeoning video platform known as YouTube in the hopes of drumming up interest. Although Fred Seibert had received permission from Nicktoons to share the short online, the suits at Viacom—the media conglomerate that owns Nicktoons Network—were apoplectic by this "violation of copyright," and they tried to have the video removed. Their efforts, however, were ultimately in vain, for each time an "illicit" upload of the short was taken down, two more took its place. All of this drama almost certainly helped raise the short's profile, and soon *Adventure Time* had become a viral hit[20]; so popular was the short that it was even nominated in 2007 for a prestigious Annie Award![21]

Frederator, like any good production company, took notice of all this attention and inquired as to whether Nickelodeon was interested in developing the short into a full program. According to Fred Seibert:

> Nickelodeon had a two-year option [to develop a series based on the short,] so we asked Pen to create a document to pitch the series. I knew it would be a hard sell, and I tried to head off objections by citing what I felt would be the four reasons focus groups would not respond well. [Nickelodeon] came back from the groups with *five* objections and said

no to the series. We went back four more times, all to different executives. "It's not a Nickelodeon show." They all said no.[22]

It seemed that viral success mattered not to Nickelodeon, and with that final rejection, all hope seemed lost. The *Adventure Time* short reaired on December 7, 2008, as part of the Nicktoons show *Random! Cartoons*, which many believed would be the short's final moment in the limelight.

CARTOON NETWORK SAVES THE DAY
(AND THEN VERY NEARLY RUINS IT)

When the chance to develop an *Adventure Time* series seemed to evaporate, Ward was forced to get a "real job" working as a storyboard artist on Thurop van Orman's Cartoon Network series *The Marvelous Misadventures of Flapjack*. This opportunity, which Ward later called "a crash course on how to [professionally] storyboard,"[23] helped him hone his skills and provided him with experience working in a professional environment.

Concurrent with Ward growing his skillbase, Seibert set out on a quest to find a home for an *Adventure Time* series. "I had an exclusive contract with Nickelodeon in those years," Seibert explained, "[and] I asked them to cancel that deal, which was extremely detrimental to our bank account, in order to take [*Adventure Time*] elsewhere."[24] It was around this time that the higher-ups at Cartoon Network reached out to Frederator. The Cartoon Network execs said that they had seen the "Adventure Time" short and were interested in developing it into a full-fledged series under one key condition: that "Pen could prove the seven-minute short made for Nick wasn't a one-hit wonder."[25] Of course, capturing lightning in a bottle is easier said than done, but Ward was up for the challenge. After enlisting the help of his CalArts pals Adam Muto and Patrick McHale, Ward and Co. began brainstorming potential story ideas. Soon, they had roughed out a new storyboard that focused on Princess Bubblegum and the newly renamed "Finn" going on a date ("I think maybe Jake made [a spaghetti] dinner for Finn and PB?" Eric Homan recalled when I asked him about this long-lost pitch).[26]

But as Homan would later remark, "Cartoon Network wasn't having any of [that initial storyboard]. Besides their thinking the romantic aspect would alienate young boys, the network was asking—not specifically, but generally—for those things they felt made the short so special."[27] Ward, McHale, and Muto dutifully retreated back to the drawing board and began dissecting the initial short in an attempt to pinpoint the elements that made it so unique. Once they had isolated these elements—for example, the "crazy opening dance, the 'Abe

Lincoln moment," funny catchwords, and the awkward princess/kiss moment at the end"[28]—Ward and his friends did their best to transplant the short's *je ne sais quoi* into a new, somewhat unwrought storyboard that would one day become the first-season classic "The Enchiridion!"

An idiosyncratic take on the archetypical "grail quest" that sees Finn and Jake set out to find the titular "handbook of heroes," "The Enchiridion!" is a wacky romp that does a solid job of emulating the style and tone of the original short without wholesale duplicating it (standout scenes in the final episode include Finn and Jake having to deal with granny-zapping gnomes, and the *D&D*-inspired reverie in which Finn is tempted to slay an "unaligned" ant). Needless to say, the storyboard's wackier, action-heavy set pieces were exactly the things that Cartoon Network was looking for, so they ordered twenty-six episodes to go into immediate production. This was a highly unusual move, as most television shows go through a fairly detailed preproduction period, in which the writers and producers get a chance to figure out the show's world, its characters, and its aesthetics. Cartoon Network, however, was in no mood to waste time soul searching; the network needed a hit, and they needed it as soon as possible.

To make the sudden shift into production more manageable, Ward once again brought McHale and Muto into the fold, and while the trio was abounding with energy, they "had almost no experience in a commercial environment."[29] This issue was compounded both by Cartoon Network's desire to get *Adventure Time* out the door as soon as possible and the network's reluctance to fully trust Ward and his associates. It was a perfect storm that caused more than a few behind-the-scenes snafus. According to Eric Homan:

> [Ward, McHale, and Muto] pretty much launched into series production at Cartoon Network with no development time given, so the writers and artists were figuring out what the show would be while they were making episodes. And since the series was so different from anything else at the time, there was a lot of anxiety on what was seen as a pretty big risk. There were disagreements about the writing process, and having a revolving door of [Cartoon Network producers supervising the project] early on didn't help.[30]

Patrick McHale also discussed Cartoon Network's "production anxiety" during our interview, telling me:

> At the time, Cartoon Network had canceled [almost] all of their animated shows . . . [They] were [also] on the path of rebranding the network "CN" instead of "Cartoon Network" and filling it with live-action

shows instead of cartoons. *Adventure Time* was kind of the only new animated show they were making. So there was a lot of pressure for it to be *the* animated show [and] the network second guessed every decision Pen would make.... There was too much riding on it, so it's understandable why [the network was] so stressed out about it, and why they couldn't give us the benefit of the doubt... It was just unfortunate for all that it had to be so difficult in those early days.[31]

Executive producer Fred Seibert was a bit blunter when he discussed Cartoon Network's interference:

We [i.e., the executives at Frederator] fought with the network like crazy for the first year or 18 months as they demanded a variety of things that would not be in the show's interest. From creative choices to production methods.... Cartoon Network was used to bullying their creators on both the creative front and production ... [and the network] wanted to change an amazing amount of what made the series what it was. To them "adventure" was the opposite of a comedy, so "can't we change the title?" "Our target demographic is boys, we can't have girls in the show, and if we do there can't be any kissing." Stupid stuff like that.

The creative head of the network insisted that "artists can't write" (a common refrain I've heard from executives for [thirty] years, no matter how large their bonus checks were from artist-driven shows like *Dexter's Laboratory*, *The Powerpuff Girls*, *Courage the Cowardly Dog*, etc., etc.) and he and I had shouting matches about it. Eventually we [settled with] having a "story editor" they picked in the room.... There was [also] objection to having a fresh score for each episode, which was indeed different than any other show we'd produced and against common practice, until Kevin Kolde found a solution that shut that down.

The production department was used to controlling all of the players with arbitrary choices whether or not they were right for the project. No wonder Cartoon Network had had a very spotty record of success the previous decade.... Eventually [our perceived interference] resulted in some of our team [being] banned from the CN studios.[32]

This network meddling was, as one might imagine, exhausting, and during the first few months that *Adventure Time* was in production, the show was, to quote McHale, "constantly on the verge of falling apart."[33] Nevertheless, Ward and his team kept their heads down and "continued to quietly, politely fight the fight."[34]

Another creative hurdle plaguing the show's production was that, aside from McHale and Adam Muto, many of the people who were initially hired to work on the series did not understand Ward's approach to animation or his deceptively simple aesthetic. "There weren't that many people who could draw or write in [Ward's] style," McHale told me. "It *seems* very simple, and nowadays there are tons of shows that have a similar feel, but back then it was just hard to find the right crew."[35]

No one seemed to *get* it.

Noticing that the *Adventure Time* crew was struggling, Cartoon Network halted production,[36] but instead of pulling the plug, they decided to counterbalance the crew's relative inexperience by also hiring people with seasoned animation acumen. Chief among these individuals were Merriwether Williams, Nick Jennings, Larry Leichliter, and Derek Drymon, all of whom had previously worked on the hit Nickelodeon series *SpongeBob SquarePants*. Williams was stationed in the *Adventure Time* writers' room as story editor, helping Ward and his crew break episode scripts.[37] Meanwhile, Jennings and Leichliter were placed in directorial roles; the former used his creative eye for design to go over models, background pieces, and color palettes,[38] whereas the latter oversaw sheet timing.[39] Finally, Drymon was hired on as an executive producer and functioned as a creative intermediary, "tell[ing] the network what they needed to hear," while also communicating to the production crew "what [Cartoon Network] was trying to say."[40] Thanks in large part to Drymon's mediation, Ward and the writers realized that what Cartoon Network was really wanting was an animated sitcom, when all this time Ward and his crew had been "trying to write a weird action/comedy."[41] Now that the goal was much clearer, production for *Adventure Time* started to stabilize.[42]

This stabilization continued once artists were hired who intuitively understood what exactly it was that Ward, Muto, and McHale were looking for. One of these artists was Dan "Ghostshrimp" Bandit, an alumnus of Brooklyn's Pratt Institute who became the show's lead background designer. Hailing from New England, Ghostshrimp had previously freelanced long distance as a storyboard artist on *Flapjack* before moving to the greater Los Angeles area in 2008 to work in-studio for Cartoon Network. However, six months later, he was let go from *Flapjack* when a creative conflict arose between him and his then-storyboarding partner Mike Roth. The day after his termination, Ward and McHale met with Ghostshrimp and asked him if he was interested in becoming the lead background designer for their fledgling show. Ghostshrimp was touched, later declaring in a 2018 podcast: "I'll never forget that moment where Pen told me, 'I want *Adventure Time* to take place in a Ghostshrimp world.'"[43] After Ghostshrimp accepted the offer, Ward gave him relative free rein to design the *Adventure Time* universe as he saw fit.[44]

Evocative of both the offbeat architecture of Dr. Seuss and the patterned complexity of M. C. Escher, Ghostshrimp's backgrounds are off-kilter in a delightfully kooky way. Always looking to hide a joke or a piece of lore in even the simplest of backgrounds, Ghostshrimp often added strange bits of detritus—such as busted cars, oddly placed skeletons, wrecked spaceships, and deteriorating fantasy ruins—into his pieces; these hidden artifacts quickly became a defining feature of the show, and they played a key role in turning Ooo into less of a generic fantasy land and more of a postapocalyptic ruinscape. While Ghostshrimp eventually left the show as a full-time member of the production team during its fourth season, he inarguably left his mark on *Adventure Time*, and all subsequent background designers worked hard to evoke his unique style—a turn of events that Ghostshrimp later called "just crazy."[45]

Another artist who was crucial in getting *Adventure Time* off the ground was Phil Rynda. A graduate of the School of Visual Arts (SVA) in Manhattan, Rynda is a gifted character designer who can jump from art style to art style without missing a beat. When I asked him how he landed a job on *Adventure Time*, Rynda explained:

> I loved the [original *Adventure Time*] short and watched it numerous times on YouTube. I was working on [the Cartoon Network series] *Chowder*, and Pen was on *Flapjack* when Cartoon Network put [*Adventure Time*] into development. On a few occasions I ran in to Pen, asked him how development was going, and let him know that I would love an opportunity to work on the show if one ever arose. [*Adventure Time*] began testing, and I took a story test. It was probably the most fun storyboard I ever did, but it didn't land me the job.[46]

Rynda then applied for a job as a character designer, but due to a misunderstanding about what the producers were looking for, he failed that test, too.

This might have been the end of Rynda's quest to join the *Adventure Time* production crew had it not been for the actions of Larry Leichliter, the show's director. Leichliter knew of Rynda's artistic prowess and was determined to find him a design position.[47] He subsequently approached Rynda with two drawings: one that Adam Muto had designed which was very "precise," and one that Ward had made that "looked like he drew it with a crayon."[48] Leichliter then asked Rynda to draft up turn-around models[49] for both. Rynda initially thought about synthesizing the disparate art styles into one that combined the key aesthetics of both drawings, but instead he decided to do the turn-arounds in their original styles. Leichliter then took these turn-arounds and showed them to Ward, who was flabbergasted at Rynda's ability to match drawing styles while also giving the designs a sense of depth.[50] "I was able to show Pen that [not only] was I flexible enough to [incorporate] the idiosyncrasies that show up in his work," Rynda told me, "but [I could] also make [designs that are] solid, repeatable, and animatable."[51] Needless to say, Ward changed course and hired Rynda as the show's lead character designer.[52]

In this role, Rynda worked closely with Ward and McHale, both of whom stressed that the designs should "[communicate] feelings and not [be] purely aesthetic." Rynda took this message to heart, mixing emotionality in with a "modern take on what the [Max] Fleischer studios were doing in the 30s,"[53] which resulted in many of the show's iconic designs. Needless to say, Rynda's impact on the finalized look of the show was immense.

...

When it came time to build up a storyboarding crew, Ward sought out young illustrators, experimental comic book writers, or underground illustrators whose art he found entertaining.[54] As colorist and art director Sandra Lee put it, "[Pen] was looking for *artists* [who were] not bound by the rules of animation."[55] This resulted in the first-season crew being a motley group of people with a range of experience. Some, including Luther McLaurin (who had worked as a storyboard artist on the Nickelodeon programs *Rugrats* and *Rocket Power*), Armen Mirzaian (who had been a storyboard revisionist on the Cartoon Network series *My Gym Partner's a Monkey*), and Sean Jimenez (who worked in the 1990s as an in-betweener for Disney and Warner Bros.) had been working in the animation world for years. But others, like Bert Youn, Niki Yang, Elizabeth Ito, and Cole Sanchez, were newer to the world of professional animation, having just graduated (like Ward, McHale, and Muto) from CalArts.

Bert Youn was a native of South Korea who had moved to the United States to learn the art of animation. From 2003 to 2007, Youn attended CalArts, where he met and befriended Ward. Upon graduation, Youn briefly took a job as a story apprentice for Disney before securing a position as a storyboard artist on *Adventure Time*. Youn worked in Burbank for a full year on the show before life threw him the ultimate curveball: While visiting his family in South Korea, he was conscripted into the South Korean military. Youn was a dual US–South Korean citizen, so the conscription notice, while legal, caught him off guard. Nevertheless, Youn dutifully relocated to Seoul, and spent the next two years serving in the Republic of Korea Army.[56] Unfortunately, this situation precluded him from working on *Adventure Time*'s second season, but by Season 3, he managed to contribute storyboards remotely. Youn would remain a storyboard artist until the end of Season 4, after which he contributed to the show sporadically as a guest artist.

Niki Yang was also a native of South Korea who had attended CalArts around the same time as Ward, but unlike Youn, she really only got to know Ward when they were both working on shorts for Frederator. ("He was right next to my office, and we got to hang out and stuff," she noted in one interview.) When Ward began to work on the *Adventure Time* series, he asked his former Frederator compatriot if she was interested in a role as a storyboard artist—an offer which she readily accepted.⁵⁷ *Adventure Time* was Yang's first job as a professional writer for a network production, and while she enjoyed the experience, she also found it "challenging."⁵⁸ "I grew up in Korea . . . so I didn't grow up with [American] culture," Yang told Mike Gencarelli in a 2013 interview. "So it was harder for me writing jokes due to the cultural differences."⁵⁹ It did not make matters easier that the production of Season 1 was infamously tumultuous—a factor that Yang emphasized when I asked her about her tenure as a storyboard artist:

> I believe all first seasons have hectic beginnings in different ways[, but] we had an extremely rough start. I think because . . . most of us were fresh from college, [we] just needed time to learn how to communicate our ideas technically and professionally . . . The studio wanted to see what kind of the show *Adventure Time* would be right from the gate, but [*Adventure Time*] was a different beast that they had never seen before. So everyone got confused and tried to "fix" it in a panic. Thankfully, the show didn't get killed and we gained trust from "the adults" along the way.⁶⁰

Yang left her role as storyboard artist at the end of Season 1, but she remained a major part of the show by voicing BMO and Lady Rainicorn for the remainder of its run.

Like Youn and Yang, Elizabeth Ito had attended CalArts contemporaneously with Ward. The two had developed a friendship, and when Ward began seeking storyboard artists, Ito was one of the people whom he approached. Ito was partnered up with Adam Muto during the production of Season 1 and found her job to be fairly stress-free—an attitude which she readily admits was not shared by many of her coworkers:

> [Season 1] was relatively easy for me, and really fun, but I think for people higher up it was incredibly stressful. I understand that a lot better now that I've run my own show. Probably the biggest worry I had was that I wasn't going to deliver the kind of boards that Pen, Pat, and Adam had hoped for from me. Really quickly I felt like I could pitch them my silliest ideas, and they would appreciate it. It was a really fun experience being storyboard partners with Adam. We were both really awkward at first, I think because we're pretty introverted, and at least from my side of things, I was nervous that Adam was going to hate my jokes and drawings. I think I got past that pretty quick.⁶¹

Together, Ito and Muto storyboarded some of the first season's more memorable outings, including "Slumber Party Panic," "Trouble in Lumpy Space," and "Dungeon." Following the production of Season 1, Ito moved onto a job at Sony, where she worked for several years until she found herself "burnt out" and underappreciated. In 2012, she returned to *Adventure Time* as a supervising director—a career remix that she called "a no-brainer."[62] Ito stayed with the show until the conclusion of its ninth season, after which she would go on to create her own vividly experimental series, *City of Ghosts*, for Netflix.

Out of all the storyboard artists that Ward brought on during Season 1, Cole Sanchez was one of the newest to the world of professional animation, having graduated from CalArts in 2009. Sanchez—like Ward—cut his teeth working on *The Marvelous Misadventures of Flapjack* before he managed to land a gig as a storyboard artist for *Adventure Time*.[63] At a Comic-Con Paris 2016 presentation, Sanchez recounted the rather nonchalant way he found his way into the *Adventure Time* crew: "*Adventure Time* was just on the floor below *Flapjack* [at Cartoon Network studios, and once the latter show ended production] I walked downstairs, and I knocked on Pen's door, and I was like, 'Pen, can I come work on your show?' and he said, 'Yeah, come on over!'"[64] Sanchez was hired on as a storyboard artist, a position he held until Season 6, and during Seasons 2 and 3, he also served as one of the show's creative directors. Sanchez left the *Adventure Time* production staff before Season 7 to work on his friend Sean Szeles's miniseries *Long Live the Royals* (2015), but after Andres Salaff's departure, Sanchez returned to *Adventure Time*, serving as a supervising director until its final season.

Another alumnus of *Flapjack* who ended up in the *Adventure Time* storyboarding crew was Kent Osborne. Roughly a decade before working at Cartoon Network, Osborne had made a name for himself by serving as a writer and storyboard director on *SpongeBob SquarePants* during the latter part of its golden age (c. 2002–5)—a job that garnered him two Emmy Award nominations.[65] When *Adventure Time* entered into production in 2008, Osborne was working as a story editor on *Flapjack*. Osborne enjoyed his job, but after seeing the sort of stories that Ward and others were producing, he began yearning to join the *Adventure Time* crew. Unfortunately, this desire was in direct conflict with his not wanting to slight *Flapjack* creator Thurop van Orman; while discussing this quandary in a podcast interview recorded for this book, Osborne recalled: "I remember, I went down to Pen's office [and said], 'I really want to work on *Adventure Time*, but I'm on *Flapjack*! I feel like I'm dating a girl, but I want to date another girl!'"[66] Osborne ultimately decided that his best course of action was to be upfront and "respectful," and so, during the production of *Flapjack*'s second season, he told van Orman that, were the show to be renewed for a third season, he would not be returning as story editor. Soon thereafter,

Derek Drymon asked Osborne if he was interested in a job as a storyboard artist for *Adventure Time*—an offer that Osborne readily accepted.[67] Osborne remained a key member of the show's production team until its final season, and over the course of the intervening years, he would come to serve as both the show's head of story as well as its vocal director.

With all these talented artists on board, everything started to come together: a unified creative direction—inspired heavily by dungeon-crawling video games and *Dungeons & Dragons*—was decided upon, a consistent art style had been nailed down, storyboards were being approved, and a voice cast had been assembled. By the spring of 2010, the first episodes had been animated and were ready for airing.

ADVENTURE TIME HITS THE SMALL SCREEN

Adventure Time was unique in that during the production of the first season, prior to the airing of a single episode, a fan base began to form. How, you might wonder, did the show manage to develop a following *before* it had aired a single episode? As with all things in this world, there were many reasons, but one of the most critical was Frederator's ingenious choice to upload production art (like character designs and backgrounds) onto its website so readers could get a "sneak peek" of what was to come. According to Seibert:

> I have always been insistent that we share as much pre-production material as possible, even more than my own team was sometimes comfortable with. I thought the amount of people following closely were ultimately a drop in the bucket but that they were the most loyal, loudest people in the marketplace. Given the traditional bungling of marketing by most networks, and the unique nature of virtually everything about *Adventure Time*, it could only help us start up the fandom. . . . We . . . blogged regularly [about] *Adventure Time* in the years before we even had a series deal (this time on Tumblr). [In time] we had thousands of fans, just [from] the original 6-minute short, and hundreds of pieces of fan art.[68]

The lawyers and PR personnel at Cartoon Network—constantly on the lookout for any perceived "misuses" of the network's IP—often butted heads with Seibert over his decision to share production materials online, but in the end, Seibert's methods played a key role in drumming up interest. With every new post that Frederator made on its blog about the upcoming series, it seems that the fanbase only grew larger.

After a "preview" broadcast of the episodes "Business Time" and "Evicted!" on March 11 and 18[69] to drum up excitement, *Adventure Time* officially debuted on April 5, 2010, with the one-two punch of "Slumber Party Panic" and "Trouble in Lumpy Space." In the former, Finn and Princess Bubblegum accidentally unleash a group of candy zombies onto Ooo. Emblematic of the sort of humor upon which *Adventure Time* was built (the episode, after all, opens with a joke about "add[ing] three more drops of explosive diarrhea" to a scientific mixture), "Slumber Party Panic" radiates with the madcap energy of a show in bloom. "Trouble in Lumpy Space," on the other hand, sees Finn and Jake travel to a different dimension known as "Lumpy Space" after Jake accidentally catches a disease called "the Lumps." In addition to demonstrating the scope of the show's kaleidoscopic world, "Trouble in Lumpy Space" is notable for introducing audiences to a character destined to become a fan favorite: Lumpy Space Princess, a purple Valley Girl alien voiced by series creator Pendleton Ward himself.

Most of the television critics who tuned into the premiere wrote positively of the launch, with the eminent *Los Angeles Times* writer and eventual series champion Robert Lloyd applauding the show's "fantastical" setting, its "strange, somewhat disturbing characters," and its screwball dialogue—the latter of which he described as "at once so childish, so pulpy, so polite."[70] But positive reviews are only a small part of the recipe for a hit television program; the bigger question was whether the series debut had been a ratings success. By the morning of April 6, the nervous executives at Cartoon Network had their answer: *Adventure Time* was a winner. Seen by 2.5 million viewers,[71] the series' debut episodes propelled the network into the number one place for the night and led to a drastic increase in viewers for the channel across the board when compared to the same day the previous year. Delighted by the success, the network's executives did not think twice about officially renewing the series for a second season.

A Critical Look at Season 1

After its April debut, the remainder of *Adventure Time*'s first season ran until September 27, 2010. Initially, new episodes were aired in pairs (as was traditionally the case at the time for eleven-minute cartoons), but about a third of the way through the season, Cartoon Network decided to air only a single new episode each week. This not only reduced the gap between seasons, but it also put less pressure on the production crew to crank out new episodes.[72]

As a mish-mash of character introductions, wacky one-offs, and episodes that would later support the show's complex mythology, the first season of *Adventure Time* is an interesting year of television to consider in retrospect.

Perhaps more than anything, this is the season with the strongest personal tone, and much of this is due to its distinct sense of humor.

From the arithmetical exclamations ("Algebraic!") to the many cockamamie set pieces, Season 1 is thoroughly infused with an adolescent energy that combines, in equal measure, the immature, the clever, and the unexpected. One of Season 1's stylistic specialties is a narrative device that one might call *ex mediis rebus*—that is, ending episodes in the middle of some dramatic (or, more commonly, ridiculous) moment, precluding a conventional sense of narrative closure. It is a postmodern flourish that provides each episode with a final laugh while also highlighting the series' commitment to upending audience expectations. (For perhaps the best example of what I mean, look no further than the fourth episode of the season, "Tree Trunks," which ends with the titular character exploding after she eats a crystal apple!)[73]

The season's energy has led to many critics describing it as "random," but I believe it is better to view it as "playfully weird." Yes, Season 1 is wacky, but it is not the directionless morass of nonsense that a descriptor like "random" implies. Episodes all follow a coherent three-act plot structure, and characters (while eccentric) mostly function in standard narratological roles (you have your heroes, your villains, your allies, etc.). That said, to call the season "silly" is a bit of an understatement, and it is obvious that the writers spent considerable time cramming as much playful puerility into each storyboard as possible. While never fully abandoning this energy, *Adventure Time* would eventually move away from the carefully crafted weirdness of Season 1 in favor of increasingly more grounded stories. Viewers who are most fond of outsider comedy are thus likely to view this season as the show's funniest.

Arguably, no group of episodes better encapsulates the feel of the first season than the trifecta of "The Enchiridion!," "Dungeon," and "Rainy Day Daydream." In the first, Finn and Jake seek out the titular "handbook of heroes"; in the second episode, Finn bets that he can make it through a booby-trapped dungeon without Jake's help; and in the third, Finn and Jake discover that Jake's imagination is impacting reality. Replete with outrageous monsters and wacky action, these episodes share a clear interest in mixing the thrill of dungeon-crawling video games with the sprawling world of table-top gaming. But on a deeper level, they showcase and underscore the importance of Finn and Jake's familial bond—a bond that many would agree is the core of the show and the locus from which *Adventure Time*'s future greatness would grow.

But despite its flashes of brilliance and bevy of belly laughs, Season 1 of *Adventure Time* is, it must be admitted, far from the show's best. For one thing, many of the episode plots are fairly standard (e.g., Finn is jealous, Finn loses his sense of self-confidence, Finn wants to do the right thing), while others—especially those in the season's first half—are bogged down by their need to introduce us to the Land of Ooo before anything else. These shortcomings are further compounded by the thin characterization of the show's supporting characters, like Princess Bubblegum, Ice King, or Marceline, all of whom function here as little more than one-dimensional plot generators. Finally, it is worth noting that the cartoonish energy that I earlier praised can at times be off-putting, especially for viewers who are expecting the emotional and existential depth for which the series would become famous.

Having said all that, *Adventure Time* had to start somewhere, and while Season 1 might not be fully indicative of what the show would mature into, it is nevertheless a fun romp.

7.

FROM CULT FAVORITE TO MAINSTREAM HIT

Seasons 2–5

AN INFLUX OF TALENT: SEASON 2

As Ward and his crew began production of Season 2 in late 2009, it was a time of change. A fresh slate of storyline writers (including Steve Little, Mark Banker, and Thurop van Orman) had been brought on board to collaborate with Ward on episode scripts. In the art department, new recruits like Andy Ristaino were helping to further refine the look of Ooo. Even the production hierarchies were being shaken up: At the start of the season, Patrick McHale began sharing his workload as creative director with storyboard artist Cole Sanchez (a move that arguably presaged his eventual departure as a full-time member of the show's crew),[1] and Derek Drymon—the producer whose guiding hand had saved the show during the production of Season 1—stepped down from his advisory role to again focus his energy on *SpongeBob*.

Given all this reorganization, it is perhaps not surprising to learn that only a few of the regular storyboard artists from the first season were retained—namely Adam Muto, Kent Osborne, and Cole Sanchez—and the vast majority either left the show or were let go.[2] Such an exodus of talent could have been the death knell for the show, but the openings it created led to the hiring of five new artists whose creative voices would in many ways come to shape the very nature of *Adventure Time* itself: Rebecca Sugar, Tom Herpich, Ako Castuera, Jesse Moynihan, and Somvilay Xayaphone.

In the animation world, Rebecca Sugar, has become something of a household name, and for good reason.[3] The lauded creator of the smash hit Cartoon Network series *Steven Universe*, Sugar got her start working as a storyboard artist on *Adventure Time*. But long before she had fully dreamed up the Crystal Gems, she was making independent comics and directing her own independent films at SVA.[4] According to *Animation* magazine:

[Sugar's] first big break came when SVA alum and *Adventure Time* designer Phil Rynda came to the school for a panel on finding work in the industry. [According to Sugar,] "I came up to give him some of my comics after his panel, and he was like, 'Oh, we have to get a picture!' I was like, what? And I keep standing next to him for this picture . . . Then I realized he meant a picture of the panel, and I was standing in front of them! I kind of just dropped all my stuff and ran out, it was mortifying."[5]

While the experience may have embarrassed Sugar, it did not seem to faze Rynda, and soon thereafter, he recommended that the *Adventure Time* producers hire her. Sugar "aced"[6] a subsequent art test and was quickly brought on as a revisionist during the first season of *Adventure Time*, tasked with cleaning up storyboard panels.[7] Sugar was only in this position for a scant month before Pen Ward promoted her to a full storyboard artist. This was a positively nerve-wracking experience for Sugar, and in an email, she told me:

When I was given a shot at writing and storyboarding, it was with a heavy "well . . . good luck," as if it was only a matter of time until I didn't work out. So I was extremely nervous. I remember sitting in my office, just after being promoted to writer/storyboarder, and hearing someone wailing and sobbing in the writers' room next door. I kept my head down and kept working. That's how it was early on.[8]

Fortuitously, Sugar was partnered up with Ward's good friend and artistic deputy, Adam Muto.[9] The Sugar-Muto storyboard pairing was perhaps one of the show's most productive partnerships, and during the two seasons that they worked together, the duo produced a number of enjoyable episodes, ranging from the plain silly ("Power Animal," "The Chamber of Frozen Blades") to the emotionally and thematically complex ("Mortal Folly," "Fionna and Cake," "What Was Missing"). Indicative of their natural fit as storyboarding partners is the fact that the first episode that they costoryboarded, "It Came from the Nightosphere," was later nominated for an Emmy for "Outstanding Short-Format Animated Program."[10]

While Sugar is a gifted storyboard artist—capable of striking a deft balance between emotional honesty and the silliest of humor—she is also a talented songwriter. When she was a young adult, Sugar had only felt comfortable sharing creations with her closest friends,[11] but after she landed her job on *Adventure Time*, Sugar began to open up about her music, thanks largely to encouragement by Ward. This eventually led to her composing Marceline's now-famous "Fry Song," first heard in "It Came from the Nightosphere." After the episode aired, fans and critics alike praised the song for its emotional honesty, and this success was just the encouragement Sugar needed. During her remaining tenure as a storyboard artist, Sugar became something of the show's master songwriter, composing memorable tracks like "I'm Just Your Problem" (a song from the episode "What Was Missing" that first hinted at Marceline and Bubblegum's romantic feelings for one another), "Remember You" (a duet sung by Marceline and Ice King from the episode "I Remember You," in which the audience first learns of their tragic history), and "Bacon Pancakes" (a goofy, twelve-second ditty from "Burning Low" that has been hailed by many fans as something of a *chef-d'œuvre*). Given her music-writing abilities and her storyboarding prowess, it is no wonder that in 2012, *Forbes* magazine named her one of their "30 under 30" and credited her with writing "many of the best episodes" of *Adventure Time*.[12]

Much like Sugar, Tom Herpich was an SVA graduate and indie comic maker before coming to work on the show during its first season[13] on the behest of Phil Rynda.[14] When asked about his start on the show, Herpich recounted:

> I was living in Brooklyn in 2008, trying to make it as an illustrator, but not having much luck with it. It wasn't a good fit, but I didn't have the experience or imagination necessary to envision any other sort of career in which I'd be able to draw all day. Right when things were at their worst (the economy had just crashed, and I'd just quit/gotten fired from my part-time job), I got an offer to move out to LA to work ... on *Adventure Time*. I barely knew what I was getting into (and a lot of what I thought I knew I was wrong about), and didn't expect it to last for more than the 6 months of work they were guaranteeing, but it all clicked.[15]

Herpich was initially hired as a character and prop designer who whipped up models for the show's countless characters. Looking back at this time, Herpich noted, "I had so many ideas and so much energy, the design position couldn't contain it all. (I'm sure I was really annoying at the time—I had opinions about every aspect of the show and stuck my nose into everyone's business—I didn't have much experience with working on a team.)"[16] Pendleton Ward, however, recognized Herpich's boundless vigor, and when the show began production on its second season, he asked Herpich if he would be interested in a job as a storyboard artist. "Pen suggested storyboarding might be a good fit for me," Herpich told me. "And Pen was right: storyboarding turned out to be a really great, really fulfilling fit."[17]

If Rebecca Sugar's strength lay in her expert use of music and emotion, then Tom Herpich's strength lay in his masterful use of dialogue. Indeed, many of Herpich's episodes come across as *A Clockwork Orange*-like in their imaginative use of fictional, idiomatic language. For instance, it was Herpich who developed the memorably nonsensical line "This stink-ups mega bam-bam to the J-stop" (translation: "This stinks!"),[18] as well as the slang adjective "bloobalooby" (equivalent to "awesome"),[19] among many others. Herpich relished any chance he got to create new slang terms (in fact, he once noted in an interview, "I have the most fun when I get to play around with language, and write weird abstract poetry stuff"[20]), and his unique use of language eventually led to many of his crewmates calling him the undisputed master of *Adventure Time*'s wacky vernacular.[21] Herpich also gained a reputation for storyboards that dabbled in what one might call "pensive philosophy." These often took the form of "allegorical escape stor[ies],"[22] with the epitome being Season 7's masterpiece "The Hall of Egress," which sees Finn having to escape from the titular dungeon by trusting in his mind rather than his physical senses. Herpich would go on to be one of the show's most-lauded storyboard artists, and by the time the series finale aired in late 2018, his work on *Adventure Time* had earned him two Emmy awards (among a total of seven nominations).

During Season 2 and parts of Season 3, Herpich was paired up with Ako Castuera, an artist who had grown up in Los Angeles and had studied at the California College of the Arts (CCA). The story that Castuera recounted to me about landing a job on the *Adventure Time* crew was proof positive that talent and a hint of networking can take you to incredible places:

> [After college] I moved back to LA, [and] a neighbor I had become friends with hired me to do character designs at Titmouse Studios. [At the time,] I was still working on my own stuff, including a comic about a radioactive cactus girl, which made its way to Pen via my friend Jackie [Buscarino] (voice of Susan Strong and many other characters). Pen liked the comic and invited me to take a storyboarding test. I was hired as a revisionist and learned the technical craft of storyboarding. By the end of [Season 1], I was promoted to storyboarder.[23]

Castuera's episodes often emphasized the "physical and tactile," to quote her long-serving storyboard partner Jesse Moynihan: "She likes to do a lot more visual jokes—especially with Jake—and she likes to manipulate/mutate environments."[24] This fascination with physical action or states of materiality was likely due to her interest in sculpting; indeed, aside from her work on *Adventure Time*, Castuera is perhaps best known for her quasiabstract clay sculptures depicting fantastical animals and primeval humanoid figures.

During her time working with Tom Herpich, Castuera costoryboarded several memorable episodes, such as "The Other Tarts," "Guardians of the Sunshine," "Go with Me," and "Memory of a Memory." Ironically, while the two artists were and remain close friends, and the episodes that they made were often strong, Castuera admitted to me that their "dynamic as partners wasn't ideal."[25] In an interview with the background designer Ghostshrimp, she elaborated further by saying: "Tom and I . . . we just are on opposite ends of everything"; Castuera specifically cited their divergent approaches to the creative process and their differing work ethic as being the main reasons why they struggled to gel as a pair.[26] Consequently, in the middle of Season 3, Herpich began to storyboard with Bert Youn, and Castuera began working with Jesse Moynihan—a partnership that would go on to be quite fruitful.

Moynihan joined the production crew at the beginning of Season 2, and unlike the artists discussed so far in this section, he did not have an art degree, having studied at the Pratt Institute for a year before transferring to and earning a film degree from Philadelphia's Temple University.[27] Moynihan, however, was well-known in indie comic circles for his unique sensibilities, and he had first landed on Ward's radar after the two met at a Small Press Expo comics convention. Ward was drawn to Moynihan's aesthetic and hired him on as a storyboard revisionist.[28] On the strength of his work, Moynihan was soon promoted to full storyboard artist midway through Season 2. He worked alongside Season 1 veteran Cole Sanchez (whom Moynihan credits with "show[ing] [him] the ropes" during this time).[29] While Moynihan's first episode, "Crystals Have Power," received a mixed reaction among fans and critics due to its heavy use of off-model design, Moynihan would soon work on several Season 2 classics, such as the Orphean "Death in Bloom" and the down-right terrifying "Mortal Recoil."

Prior to his joining the *Adventure Time* crew, Moynihan had long been interested in religion and spiritualism (as perhaps best evidenced by his webcomic *Forming*, which attempts to present a syncretic account of many of the world's disparate religious traditions). He consequently brought these interests along with him when he was promoted to storyboard artist, liberally sprinkling esoterica and "symbols . . . that have deep ancient meaning" throughout many of his greatest episodes.[30] This fixation with the mystical led Moynihan to help develop elements of Ooo's afterlife[31] and the mythology of the catalyst comets, among other topics. While a group of detractors online sometimes maligned his work for being "2deep4u,"[32] a vast majority of the fandom praised Moynihan as one of the show's strongest artistic voices. Television critics, too, often found his episodes to have a certain depth and philosophical richness that made unpacking them a treat.

The final storyboard artist hired at this time is something of an enigma: Somvilay "Somvi" Xayaphone. A CalArts classmate of Pen Ward and Patrick McHale (both of whom cite him as a direct influence),[33] Xayaphone had initially served as a storyboard revisionist during the show's first season before he was partnered with Kent Osborne for Seasons 2 and 3. More so than perhaps anyone else on the show, his style is eccentric and hard to define; avant-garde may be the best descriptor. Xayaphone finds humor in what one might call "awkwardness": his storyboards often feature purposely stilted poses, strange pacing, and bizarre facial expressions. Xayaphone also has a deep fascination with sound,[34] and many of his episodes dabble in this interest to some degree, whether it be noise music ("Dream of Love"), sound effects ("James Baxter the Horse"), or beatnik poetry ("The Empress Eyes"). Due to these peculiarities, he often polarized audience members, some of whom loved his decidedly offbeat style, whereas others lambasted him for being weird for weirdness's sake.

It is important to note that of the five storyboard artists just discussed, only Xayaphone and Herpich remained storyboard artists until the show's end,[35] meaning that in many ways their personal styles and distinct artistic voices became thoroughly infused into the very DNA of the show—more so than perhaps any other artists aside from Ward, McHale, and Muto.

A Critical Look at Season 2

Season 2 of *Adventure Time* debuted on October 11, 2010, with "It Came from the Nightosphere." A little over half a year later on May 9, 2011, the season aired its *de facto* finale, "Heat Signature."[36]

On the surface, Season 2 is in many ways similar to its predecessor, with regard to both aesthetic design and humor (fart jokes, for instance, remain a staple). But with this batch of episodes, there is an immediate shift towards the characters and their emotional connections to one another. This change is readily noticeable in the second-season premiere, "It Came from the Nightosphere," which sees Finn try to help Marceline reconcile with her demon dad, Hunson Abadeer (voiced delightfully by Olivia Olson's actual father, Martin). Underneath a veneer of juvenile humor and Lovecraft-meets-Cronenberg-style body horror, the episode is firmly founded on the complicated relationship between Marceline and her absentee father. The tension is made clear when Marceline performs her now-iconic "Fry Song." On the surface, the incident about which Marceline plaintively sings might seem trivial, but that root frustration the song expresses—that feeling that your parent does not really love or understand you—is likely something to which many viewers can relate. "It Came from the Nightosphere" thus serves as a creative juncture—one in which the *Adventure Time* writers started to view wackiness as a means to an end, rather than an end in and of itself.

From this point forward, the season mixes Finn and Jake's one-off adventures—like their screwball trip to the underworld in "Death in Bloom," or their desperate attempts to stop a creepy horse from staring at them in "The

Eyes"—with key episodes that can only be described as increasingly personal. Finn's crush on Bubblegum is scrutinized in episodes like "To Cut a Woman's Hair," "Go with Me," and "The Real You." On one hand, these episodes make it plain to see that "Fubblegum" is a doomed "ship," but on another, they begin to hint at the deeper, more familial affection that unites Finn and Bubblegum. Likewise, Finn's friendship with Marceline is explored in episodes like "It Came from the Nightosphere," "Heat Signature" and "Go with Me"—the latter of which diffuses any romantic tension between the two and shows that boys and girls can indeed just be friends. Even Jake begins to show a vulnerable side, such as when he begins fretting about meeting his girlfriend's mom and dad in "Her Parents."

Make no mistake: The episodes that I just listed are all quite comedic, as the show has only just started to move past the nutty energy of the first season. But when Seasons 1 and 2 are compared side by side, the latter feels a bit less flippant and more heartfelt. It is readily apparent that at this stage of production, the writers were pushing past *Adventure Time*'s surface premise and beginning to explore its full potential.

Adventure Time's stylistic evolution would continue with the season finale *de jure*, "Mortal Folly"/"Mortal Recoil," which introduced one of the show's main villains, the Lich, and by extension the concept of continuity. Prior to this two-parter, many *Adventure Time* episodes felt as if they existed in their own self-contained universes; this tendency to "reset" at the start of each episode fit with the "wacky" style of the early show. But during Season 2, the writers began to flesh out and explore the in-universe histories of the show's main characters—a move that coincided with their increasing desire to tell stories that could not be fit into a pithy eleven minutes. "Mortal Folly"/"Mortal Recoil" seems to have been the one-two punch that broke the proverbial floodgates, as the addition of the Lich suggested that Ooo had a definite mythology and that this mythology was far bigger than could be explored in one episode.

"Mortal Folly"/"Mortal Recoil"—in addition to being an adrenaline-pumping two-parter full of both sight gags and bursts of horror—was thus the direct catalyst for the backstory episodes and multiepisode story arcs in Season 3 and beyond, which by their very nature necessitated a consistent linkage between episodes. After a few seasons, *Adventure Time* would grow from a string of wacky one-offs into a complex web, with episodes referencing previous installments, minor characters showing up in various episodes, and characters learning from their past adventures. This newfound interest in continuity was a key development, and one of many developments that would help transmute *Adventure Time* from a fun kid's show into one of the great television programs of the twenty-first century.

CONTINUED EVOLUTION: SEASON 3

In late 2010 (roughly around the time that Season 2 debuted on televisions across the country), Cartoon Network renewed *Adventure Time* for a third season. In a press release sent out a few months later, the network boasted that the show consistently "ranked #1 in its timeslots on all of television—broadcast and cable—among kids and boys [aged] 2–11, 6–11, and 9–14."[37] While the network was waxing poetic about their pet program, the writers and producers of *Adventure Time* were hard at work ensuring that the show's third season would be better than what had come before it.

Fans and critics alike often see *Adventure Time*'s third season as a watershed period in which the show began to actively eschew the over-the-top wackiness of its first two seasons in favor of a "deeper" approach to its storytelling. What exactly was the reason for this shift? According to Rebecca Sugar:

> [When Season 1 was in production] there was a lot of pressure to turn [*Adventure Time*] into something more conventional, with catch phrases and a clear appeal to 6–11 year old boys (our target demographic,) and there was a lot of staff turnover, especially writers and storyboaders. Things started settling down in season two, crew wise, and the pressure to turn the show into something more accessible let up more and more once the show came out and did well, so by [Season 3] we were really finding our stride. And it also felt like everyone was inspiring each other. The outlines were starting to reflect ideas that storyboarders had come up with, the storyboarders were bouncing off each other, I was trying to compliment/contrast/build off ideas that other boarders had established, and we had some foundation to stand on, by season three.[38]

In a podcast interview recorded for this book, storyboard artist Kent Osborne noted something similar, telling me:

> [During] Season 3, I remember we had a meeting—it was [Kelly Crews, Pendleton Ward, Patrick McHale] and me—and we were talking about the writer's room. And they were like . . . "The execs . . . are just now starting to leave us alone." . . . There was a sense that we were on the air, [*Adventure Time*] was doing well, [and the network executives] were kind of like, "OK you guys are off and running." We had one executive who was keeping an eye on us, but there wasn't the sort of close-up chaperoning that was going on in Seasons 1 and 2 . . . That's when . . . we were hitting our stride.[39]

As both Osborne and Sugar note, Cartoon Network's willingness to trust the show's writers led to the storyboard artists collectively "finding their grooves," so to speak.

Season 3 is thus in many ways when the unique voices of the individual storyboard artists started to really bubble up to the surface. Sugar began to take episodes into increasingly more emotional places, producing fan favorites like "Incendium" (which sees Finn break down and sob about his crush on Bubblegum) and "What Was Missing" (which smashed the metaphorical champaign bottle and set afloat one of the show's most famous ships: "Bubbline"). Meanwhile, Moynihan began to lean into his spiritual interests and helped focus the episode "Ghost Princess" on aspects of the Ooo afterlife. Finally, Herpich contributed his first solo storyboard for the episode "Thank You," demonstrating his bourgeoning talent at helming quiet, contemplative stories.

According to Osborne, alongside this flowering virtuosity, "suddenly, all of this world-building started happening."[40] Indeed, if Season 2 of *Adventure Time* was the first to really hint at a larger, more consistent world in which the characters lived, then Season 3 was the first that began to actively construct the history of that world. The show's writers and storyboard artists accomplished this by focusing on the often-mysterious backstories of the show's various characters. The first to receive this treatment was Marceline; in Season 3's "Memory of a Memory," the audience learns that sometime when she was a little child, Marceline had lived through the Mushroom War—a mysterious nuclear cataclysm that had ravaged modern society, unleashed magic back upon the world, and drove humanity to the brink of extinction. Additional Season 3 episodes like "What Was Missing" and "Marceline's Closet" would continue to provide bits and pieces about Marceline's past, specifically regarding her relationships with other characters, like Princess Bubblegum.

The next major character whose backstory the show began to tease out was Ice King, with much of this development occurring over the course of the two-part Christmas special "Holly Jolly Secrets." At the start of the episode, Finn and Jake discover old VHS tapes long ago disposed of by the Ice King, which they soon learn contain the personal home movies of their oddball foe. As Finn and Jake watch tape after tape, they come to slowly piece together the Ice King's backstory: their nemesis was once an ordinary human antiquarian named Simon Petrikov who was cursed one thousand years prior to the start of the series after placing the ice crown upon his head. The decision to give the Ice King a tragic backstory was a masterstroke, as it not only provided depth to a formerly one-note villain, but it quickly expanded upon the show's budding mythology in a way that felt organic, instead of forced.

A Critical Look at Season 3

The third season of *Adventure Time* premiered on July 11, 2011, with "Conquest of Cuteness," and concluded later the following year on February 13, 2012, with "Incendium" (the latter of which introduced a new main character: Flame Princess, the irascible heir apparent to the Fire Kingdom, voiced by Jessica DiCicco).

Season 3 was important for *Adventure Time* as it not only marked a change in the show's tone, but also its popularity. While Seasons 1 and 2 had each averaged just around 1.9 million viewers per episode, Season 3's episodes were surpassing this mark with ease. The season's ninth episode, "Fionna and Cake," even managed to reel in 3.32 million viewers—at the time, a record for the show![41] Thanks to this increased viewership, the show's fandom quickly began to outgrow its "cult" label. Soon, *Adventure Time* fanart and fanfics were growing in number, Tumblr accounts dedicated to the show were sprouting up left and right; and an increasing number of people were logging onto sites like Reddit to chat about the series.

Season 3 was also around the time that established media outlets began to take notice, too: "*Adventure Time* has rightfully solidified itself as a Cartoon Network primetime staple and a genuine cult sensation," Mike LeChevallier of *Slant* declared in a largely positive review of the season.[42] Concurrently, media critic Will Pfeifer of the *Rockford Register Star* praised the series for being "well-written and nicely animated, with plots that are surprising and characters you care about.... It's funny, smart and—best of all—completely unpredictable."[43] Arguably, when "Incendium" aired in early 2012, *Adventure Time* had ceased being an underground success and had officially become a mainstream hit.

Was this popularity boom due simply to luck, or is there something about the season itself that can explain the boom? Many of the fans to whom I spoke while writing this book favored the latter, arguing that the popularity was due to the season's increased interest in world and mythology development. The Ooo of Seasons 1 and 2 had been a fun backdrop, but after the reveals of Season 3, the world had a solid sense of depth; it had a *history*. And this history was mysterious—full of gaps and lacunae that drew in the viewer. *Where did the ice crown come from? How did Marceline become a vampire? Was Susan Strong related to Finn? What's up with Bubblegum and Marceline?* Whenever the season revealed a piece of lore, more questions were often raised than answered, so viewers began to wildly speculate about the riddles of this world. This speculation engendered hype, which encouraged more and more new viewers to give this weird little show a try.

Another quality that may have attracted and held new viewers is this season's comedic, dramatic, and creative equipoise. This balance is readily apparent upon rewatch. While Seasons 1 and 2 can feel a bit too silly at times, and later seasons like 6 can be a bit too maudlin, Season 3 does a solid job harmonizing all the goofiness with a more nuanced approach to storytelling. But what caused this balance? In the DVD commentary to the third-season episode "Conquest of Cuteness," Tom Herpich argued that the season's evenness was the result of the production crew's growing skills overlapping with their enthusiasm: "[Season 3] is actually . . . the most balanced season, where . . . there was a novelty and an ambition still, but we were sort of figuring out . . . how to say what we want[ed] to say and make it work." Season 3 is strong, simply because it is a "nice mix" of "youthful energy and professional chops."[44]

FIGHTING THE "FOURTH SEASON BLUES": SEASON 4

In April 2011, *Adventure Time* began production of its fourth season, which, being set to comprise twenty-six episodes, would include the one hundredth installment of Finn and Jake's adventures in the Land of Ooo.

One hundred episodes is quite the achievement for any show, and the show's producers were rightfully proud of their creation. But when work began on this new batch of episodes, the writers hit a problem. "We were starting season four, and we were sort of exhausted with trying to come up with 11 minute stories," head writer Kent Osborne admitted in a 2012 WonderCon panel. In an oft-quoted interview with io9, Ward explained that this necessitated that he and his writers "dig a little deeper" when they began writing stories for Season 4. "Not to say that anything's unoriginal," Ward clarified. "Everything's still coming out super weird and interesting—but it just gets a little harder."[45] Ward and his writers referred to this trial as surmounting the "season four blues."[46] Years later on, storyboard artist Jesse Moynihan would reference this problem on his personal website, using language reminiscent in many ways of Ward's: "All the ideas I had in the beginning [of my time on *Adventure Time*] were right there on the surface of the well water. It was pretty easy to scoop up. Once that material was gone though, I felt obliged to dip further down, essentially holding my breath for longer and longer stretches of time."[47]

One method the writers embraced to "dip further down" was to flesh out newer characters, chief among them being Flame Princess.[48] Upon her debut in the third-season finale "Incendium," the character was a relative cipher, devoid of any real personality other than a vaguely-defined "evilness." The writers consequently used Season 4 as an opportunity to more fully develop her character and integrate her into the Land of Ooo. Over the course of several episodes—including the Season-4 premiere "Hot to the Touch," as well as "Burning Low," and "Incendium"—Flame Princess grows from a generic love interest to a vibrant character with her own skills, challenges, and worries.

In addition to working with new characters, the show's writers also took a note from the writers of *The Simpsons* by developing stories that starred not just Finn or Jake, but also the show's supporting characters. In a 2012 interview with Fast Company, Ward explained:

> We are just trying to expand the characters. I look to the *Simpsons* and see what they did. I feel like at a certain point the *Simpsons* expanded on their secondary characters, you'd know more about Krusty or you'd know more about Professor Frink. So that's what we are trying to do, dig into some more of the secondary characters . . . and show off their secret lives, what they do in their spare time, their pasts.[49]

In the black-and-white, hardboiled parody "BMO Noire," for instance, the titular robot—who prior to this episode had usually played second banana to Finn and Jake—takes center stage and shines; likewise, in "You Made Me!" the Earl of Lemongrab (last seen in Season 3's "Too Young") returns, this time played less like a shrill villain and more like a misunderstood weirdo. Even one-off characters as inconsequential as NEPTR (the robotic sad-sack last seen in Season 1's "What Is Life?"), and Ricardio (Ice King's sentient heart, who served as the main antagonist in the eponymous first-season episode) are brought back and given something productive to do in the episodes "Hot to the Touch" and "Lady & Peebles," respectively.

The decision to "spotlight"[50] these already-introduced characters was arguably an outgrowth of the show's interest in continuity and worldbuilding, and in retrospect it was a smart move. Bringing back characters as minor as Gunter's Kitten or the King Worm helped underscore the idea that Ooo was not some random cartoon world that ceased to exist in the liminal space between episodes. Instead, the show went to great lengths to emphasize that Ooo should be seen as a real, "lived in" place whose inhabitants did things and had lives outside the boundaries of each episode.

The final method that Ward and his crew used to fight seasonal rot was to play around "with [a] more experimental approach to storytelling."[51] Once again, the writers looked to *The Simpsons* for guidance. After drawing inspiration from the *Treehouse of Horror* Halloween specials and the episode "22 Short Films About Springfield,"[52] the *Adventure Time* writers started to develop an episode made up of shorter stories. The result was "Five Short Graybles," a goofy little installment that is hosted by a mysterious being named Cuber (voiced by the king of oddball comedy, Emo Philips) and composed of five seemingly disparate vignettes that are all united by a common theme. While certainly an odd way to structure an episode, the "grayble" format was quite freeing as it provided the writers with the opportunity to focus on a smattering of smaller stories that might not otherwise support full episodes. Because of this, additional grayble episodes were produced during Seasons 5, 6, and 8, and by the time the series ended, the format had arguably become something of an *Adventure Time* tradition.

Other storytelling innovations were more subtle. For instance, in a 2015 post on his person website, Jesse Moynihan argued that Season 4 was, in his experience, the year that the writers began to increasingly reject "the idea that we had to explain everything a character was going through."[53] The emphasis, Moynihan argued, began to shift from telling to showing—a move that freed the show from the "narrative handholding that embodies not only kid's television, but almost all television."[54] This shift is most noticeable during the season's latter half, with episodes like "BMO Noire," "King Worm," and "I Remember You" eschewing expository dialogue in favor of more abstract methods of storytelling.

Behind the scenes, Season 4 also bore witness to a substantial production crew shuffle. Adam Muto left his position as a regular storyboard artist and became one of the show's creative directors, serving alongside former storyboard supervisor Nate Cash; this shift allowed Pendleton Ward to scale back his involvement in the day-to-day operations of the show and instead focus mostly on "put[ting] notes on things [and] chop[ping] down episodes."[55] Meanwhile, Muto's old storyboard partner Rebecca Sugar was teamed up with comedy master Cole Sanchez, who returned to storyboarding after spending the last two seasons as a creative director. Likewise, Bert Youn was partnered up with Somvilay Xayaphone, and Tom Herpich was paired with Skyler Page, the latter of whom had just earned his degree from CalArts and would eventually go on to create the Cartoon Network series *Clarence*. It is possible that this reconfiguration of the production crew shook things up, helping to give this season a distinct "feel."

A Critical Look at Season 4

Adventure Time's fourth season debuted on April 2, 2012, with "Hot to the Touch," and concluded a little over six months later on October 22 of that year with "The Lich."

Upon its initial run, Season 4 was warmly received by the fandom, and today, in discussions of the show's best season, many fans still consider the fourth one of the strongest. Surely one reason for this steadfast love is the season's continued interest in world building, demonstrating that there is much more to Ooo than meets the eye. Consider, for instance, "Sons of Mars," in which Finn and Jake get roped up into one of Magic Man's nefarious schemes, which results in their being teleported to Mars of all places. This may sound like your standard cartoon goofiness, but "Sons of Mars" is actually one of the show's most ambitious examples of world building: Not only does it give Magic Man a backstory that fits nicely into the overarching mythos of the show itself, but it also introduces several characters of cosmological importance, such as the oft-mention-but-never-before-seen Glob, as well as the all-powerful King of Mars—who is none other than a nigh-omnipotent Abraham Lincoln.

Another fine example of this sort of world-building comes to us in the season finale, "The Lich," which prominently reintroduces the titular villain. This character had last been the focus of Season 2's "Mortal Folly"/"Mortal Recoil" two-parter, whereupon it was plain to see that he was a being of unimaginable malevolence. But other than his unwavering allegiance to evil, the Lich was a tabula rasa, whose motives were unclear; sure, we knew he wanted to destroy life itself, but why? And through what means? The Season-4 finale begins to unravel these mysteries by giving the Lich an explicit mission: to steal the *Enchiridion* and travel to the center of the multi-dimensional Oooniverse. In the closing minutes of the episode, when the Lich finally reveals his plan, the stakes truly feel like they have never been higher. To top it all off, this whizbang episode culminates in a cliff hanger that sees Finn, Jake, and the Lich zapped to a different reality, literally fulfilling the show's promise to take us to "very distant lands."

Another strength of Season 4 is the masterful use of emotion, which adds additional layers of complexity to already well-written characters. Of course, this is most obvious in overtly dramatic episodes, like "Hot to the Touch" and "Burning Low" (which detail Finn's experiences with the strange and sometimes painful feelings of teenage romance), or "Princess Cookie" (an allegory about accepting transgender people which sees Jake moved to action by the plight of a male criminal, whose only desire is to become a princess). But emotional development can be found in even the silliest of episodes. Consider, for instance, "You Made Me," which features the return of fan favorite Earl of Lemongrab. This episode may feature its fair share of wacky humor, quotable dialogue, and bizarro set pieces, but the overall story is written in a way that forces you to feel for Lemongrab. (Sure—the episode seems to say—he is a screaming mass of citrus, but he is a screaming mass of citrus *with existential anxiety*.)

But out of the season's twenty-six episodes, arguably none is more touching than the penultimate installment, "I Remember You." This episode, storyboarded by Cole Sanchez and Rebecca Sugar, is an absolute heart tugger that showcases the until-then-unexplored relationship between Ice King and Marceline. The setup for the episode is simple: Ice King asks Marceline to help him write a song. But while things start off innocuous enough, "I Remember You" soon grows darker, and through expert use of diegetic music and flashback, we are privy to a shocking development: One thousand years prior to the events of the series, in the direct aftermath of the cataclysmic Mushroom War, Simon Petrikov—the Ice King's former self—had adopted a young Marceline and used his magical crown to protect her from the dangers of the postapocalyptic world. Unfortunately, the crown eventually corrupted Simon's mind, and he forgot all about poor Marceline. When the episode ends, the irony of its title is palpable.

When "I Remember You" debuted, most *Adventure Time* fans—accustomed to the show focusing almost exclusively on the escapades of Finn and Jake—were blindsided by the episode's quiet, devastating sadness. (Sure, we all knew that Ice King had a sad backstory, but we did not know it was *that* sad!) Thanks to the raw emotion of its climactic reveal, "I Remember You" has regularly been hailed by many fans and critics as not only one of the show's best episodes, but also an exemplar of modern animation in general.

PEAK POPULARITY: SEASON 5

In late winter and early spring of 2012, the producers, writers, and storyboard artists for *Adventure Time* began working on the show's fifth season. At first, members of the show's production staff were under the impression that Cartoon Network wanted twenty-six new episodes—the same number of episodes that had comprised each of the show's four previous seasons. However, according to head writer Kent Osborne, Cartoon Network eventually "let [the team] know that [they] were extending the fifth season to make it twice as long."[56] The result was a behemoth of a season comprising fifty-two episodes.

Once again charged with the arduous task of writing new episodes, the writers first attempted to build off that which had been successful in the past in a way that still felt innovative and original. This resulted in the writing and storyboarding of a second Fionna and Cake episode entitled "Bad Little Boy" (which focuses on Marceline's male counterpart, Marshall Lee), two new Graybles episodes, and a follow-up to the Season 4 classic "I Remember You" entitled "Simon & Marcy" (which builds upon the familial link between Marceline and Ice King while also expounding upon the show's intriguing postapocalyptic mythology). But to keep things fresh, the show also began foregrounding character development: Jake and Lady Rainicorn, for instance, were given children near the start of the season, and Finn's understanding of teen romance was fleshed out in episodes like "All the Little People" and "Vault of Bones." And on the production side of things, guest artists such as James Baxter, Graham Falk, and David OReilly were brought in to put their own unique spin on select episodes, inaugurating a tradition that would last until the show's end.

It was during the early part of Season 5 that the show also began to feature the regular storyboarding of artist Steve Wolfhard. Born and raised in Canada,

Wolfhard had learned the art of visual storytelling while attending Sheridan College's prestigious animation program. After college, he landed a position with Studio B Productions, working as a character designer on its animated series *Being Ian* (2005–8), *Pucca* (2006–8), and *Kid vs. Kat* (2008–11). Like many of the other storyboard artists who worked on *Adventure Time*, Wolfhard was also active in independent comic circles, and according to Wolfhard himself, it was in this way that he found himself on Ward's radar:

> I knew Pen from the indie comics scene, and he had asked me to come onto the show when it was starting, but I was taking a break from animation at the time, so I said no. Then a few years later I got married and decided I needed more regular work, so I asked him if the offer was still available.[57]

Luckily, the deal was still good, and Wolfhard was brought on as a storyboard revisionist during *Adventure Time*'s third and fourth seasons, working remotely from his native Canada. Wolfhard's next big break came near the tail end of Season 4's production cycle, as he explained to me via email:

> After doing revisions on "King Worm," Adam [Muto] asked if I had ideas for how the climax could play out. I sketched out some ideas and was surprised later to find out that I was given storyboard credit and that my drawings went straight to production. It had been kind of an invisible trial. I was shocked to see those drawings on TV.[58]

Wolfhard's scenes were of such quality that in November of 2011, Ward offered him a job as a storyboard artist. There was just one catch. The promotion would require him and his wife, Leslie, to relocate to Los Angeles. Wolfhard initially rejected the offer before reconsidering at the eleventh hour, and once in Burbank, he was partnered with Tom Herpich. While Wolfhard and his wife eventually moved back to Ontario during the production of Season 6, he remained on as a storyboard artist, working remotely with Herpich until the show's end.

A talented Cintiq artist, Steve Wolfhard is known for his distinctive digital illustrations that tend to combine uniform cel shading with thick, sometimes patchy line work. Wolfhard is also fond of designing cute, chubby characters that in many ways evoke the key features of Pendleton Ward's original design aesthetic. But Wolfhard's fondness for endearing characters belies a fascination with darker topics (indeed, many of Wolfhard's storyboards include some of the show's bleaker jokes, tucked in among all the candy and fluff). During his tenure as an *Adventure Time* storyboard artist, Wolfhard worked almost exclusively with Tom Herpich, and together the two produced several highly lauded installments, including the Emmy-nominated episodes "Be More" and "Ring of Fire."

In 2012, as Wolfhard was settling nicely into his role as storyboard artist, the production crew was simultaneously preparing to say goodbye to one of their own: Rebecca Sugar. About a year earlier, in 2011, Cartoon Network had solicited potential pilot ideas from several of their employees. Sugar was one of the artists approached, and she quickly began working on a cartoon proposal—inspired equally by her beloved brother Steven and her fondness for video games, musicals, and anime—about a young boy with special abilities who lives with a group of superpowered alien women. Sugar called her pet project *Steven Universe*. The executives at Cartoon Network were intrigued by Sugar's creativity and eventually ordered a *Steven Universe* pilot before greenlighting it for full-series production. Within no time, Sugar had become the first nonmale[59] to create a show on Cartoon Network.[60]

But because she cared so much for Finn, Jake, and the many residents of Ooo, Sugar attempted to work as a storyboard artist for *Adventure Time* while also developing *Steven Universe*. Unfortunately, this arrangement was not viable in the long term, and by the time Sugar was working on the second Fionna and Cake episode, "Bad Little Boy," she realized that if she wanted to see *Steven Universe* achieve its full potential, she was going to have to step down from *Adventure Time*.[61] The final *Adventure Time* episode that Sugar worked on was the aforementioned "Simon and Marcy," which received near-universal acclaim from television critics upon its airing. While many in the fandom lamented Sugar's departure, most agree that she could not have chosen a better episode with which to end her tenure as an *Adventure Time* storyboard artist.

The Abandoned Television Movie

Near the middle of the production for Season 5, the writers and producers of *Adventure Time* decided to try something new: creating a forty-five-minute television movie—a decision that arguably presaged the show's dabbling with the miniseries format several seasons later. In a 2011 interview with journalist Tim Surette, Ward explained:

> The network is interested in longform stories now, because they can call them "specials," so they can feel more special than a regular episode and can be advertised easier. So they're interested in us doing longer stories . . . maybe a 45-minute episode or something. It's tricky, though, because so many of our episodes have epic storylines, where it's life and death situations or Finn is saving someone. To find something more epic for a feature would be kind of difficult.[62]

"Difficult" is something of an understatement! At the time of its production, the movie was the largest project that the *Adventure Time* staff had yet undertaken, and it necessitated intense coordination and contributions from all of the show's regular storyboard artists.

Described by former writer and creative director Patrick McHale as "an *Adventure Time* version" of both Herman Hesse's *Siddhartha* and Richard Bach's *Johnathan Livingston Seagull*, the movie was slated to begin with "Finn's finger getting blown off in a battle, leading to him having a spiritual crisis and setting out alone to find the meaning of life."[63] During this journey, Finn "abandon[s] his bear hat [and] ends up beheading a Snake King . . . [He then uses the snake's head] as a hat for a while."[64] At some point, Finn encounters a swarm of Sea Lards and sings a song that ripped off *The Little Mermaid*'s "Under the Sea" entitled "Under the Sea Lards."[65] He then "ascends into outer space and meets the Space Lards, as well."[66] While all of this is going on, Jake notices that Finn is missing, so he "turns into a bus, and he and Tree Trunks and a bunch of candy people" track down Finn.[67] The movie would have ended with Finn "question[ing] everything about what it means to be a hero while climbing a mountain into space and having a confrontation with Orgalorg inside a weird cube portal to the many Dead Worlds."[68]

Unfortunately for all involved, the movie was never finished. Problems first started when the storyboard artists found themselves unable to settle on a consistent tone for the special; in a 2014 online post, the storyboard artist Jesse Moynihan confessed that the movie, when considered as a whole, "was a mess and needed so much work to get in shape. All the individual parts were really cool, but they weren't hanging together right, and the end seemed impossible to figure out."[69] Much of this was due to the movie's aforementioned scale, which threw the crew for a loop. When the cracks in the movie's foundation began to grow, the decision was made to push it back, with the hopes that Ward would be able to "put his magic on it . . . and make it make sense."[70] Alas, this last-minute Hail Mary was not enough, and the movie was officially canned.

When production of Season 5 wrapped, and it became clear that the movie was not going to be made, elements of the four-parter were subsequently repurposed for use during the show's sixth season. Finn losing a body part featured heavily in the climax to "Escape from the Citadel," Finn experiencing an existential crisis became the season's main story arc, and Orgalorg emerging and becoming a major antagonist was repurposed for "The Comet."[71] Additionally, a sizable chunk of the movie's first ten or so minutes was cannibalized to serve as the backbone for the episode "Something Big,"[72] the road-trip portions of the special served as loose inspiration for "Thanks for the Crabapples, Giuseppe!,"[73] and the visual of Finn encountering "Space Lards" would wind up in "Astral Plane." Herpich also revealed in the aforementioned email exchange that he had planned to recycle parts of his section—in which "Finn bec[ame] a servant to a crew of crash-landed aliens pretending to be Greek gods"—but unfortunately, he "never found the time."[74]

By the time production for Season 6 was over, almost all the good ideas had been strip-mined from the dead movie's carcass. The roughed storyboards for the movie were then boxed up and, like the proverbial Ark of the Covenant, mothballed into the bowels of some Cartoon Network archive.[75] Where these storyboards reside today is something of a mystery, and in a 2020 Reddit AMA, Adam Muto confessed that "there was so much reboarding and revising that I'm not sure a complete version of the special was ever scanned in. I haven't been able to find it, at least. Maybe Pen's got a stack of thumbnails lying around somewhere."[76] Perhaps one day the storyboards will turn up, but for now, they remain lost.

The Dawning of the Adam Muto Era

In 2012, roughly around the time that the production crew was struggling to make its television movie come together, Pendleton Ward stepped down as series showrunner. A year later, in an interview with the music and pop culture magazine *Rolling Stone*, the auteur explained:

> Dealing with people every day wears on you . . . To spend that extra energy and time you don't have, to make something that's worth making, to make it awesome, wears you out . . . It's a beast of a show. And the more popular it gets, the more the ancillary things—like the merchandise and games and everything—keep getting bigger. . . . For me, having quality of life outweighed the need to control this project and make it great all the time.[77]

While Ward never truly left the series (he remained on as a regular storyline writer until Season 7, continued to storyboard the occasional episode into its eighth, and retained informal "veto powers"[78] until production wrapped in 2018), he completely relinquished his role as lead decision maker. Ward has never discussed the exact catalyst for his decision, but many of those involved with production have suggested that Ward simply did not enjoy all the stress and bureaucratic minutia that came with showrunning a hit cartoon.

Such a high-profile departure might have kicked off a messy succession struggle in a lesser production, but thankfully the *Adventure Time* crew was spared a civil war when Ward's position was quickly filled by the only man for the job: Adam Muto. Muto had been working on the show since the pilot episode, and at the time of Ward's resignation, he was a supervising director who

Adam Muto succeeded Pendleton Ward as showrunner of *Adventure Time* during the production of the show's fifth season. Photo courtesy of Joel Feria.

oversaw much of the production already. Pensive, talented, and dedicated to his craft, Muto was Ward's natural successor, and because of this, Kent Osborne noted that "Pen . . . felt fine leaving because he knew Adam was taking [the show] over."[79]

Despite being friends and long-time creative associates, Muto and Ward favor divergent approaches to the showrunning process. In a podcast interview recorded for this book, Ghostshrimp expounded on these differences, explaining:

> Pen was really good at putting the right people in place and then just letting them go wild. . . . With Adam, he has much more of a very specific thing he is looking for, and he is going to ask you to make changes

to that and he is going to try to get that out of you.... In my opinion, [both Pendleton Ward and Adam Muto are] absolute creative heavyweights: [Ward] appreciate[s] what other people are bringing to the table, and [Muto] has a laser focus of what the end vision of something is. [Ward] allow[s] people to do their thing, and [Muto] demand[s] excellence from a group of people. Both things are equally captivating and motivating and I think both guys are equal in creative genius stature.[80]

Osborne echoed these ideas later in the same interview when he told me that Ward usually made key decisions "in the moment," whereas "there was a technical side to Adam."[81]

Given Ward's inclusive, bottom-up approach to showrunning and Muto's more top-down style, a reader would be forgiven for assuming that the *Adventure Time* production crew had a hard time adjusting to their new boss, but actually the opposite was true: Muto's transition into his new role was, as Osborne put it, relatively "smooth,"[82] with the day-to-day operation of the show continuing much as it had under Ward. Muto's ascension did, however, affect the show's tone. In fact, the latter part of Season 5 is a noticeable shade darker than previous years, with episodes focusing on heavy topics like loss (e.g., "James," "Bad Timing"), the pains of teen romance (e.g., "Frost & Fire," "Earth & Water," "The Red Throne"), and the meaning of sacrifice (e.g., "Sky Witch," "Betty"); other installments dabble freely in horror ("Red Starved," "James") or heady philosophy ("Lemonhope").

It was roughly around the time of this slight tonal shift that two new storyboard artists were brought on board: Andy Ristaino and Seo Kim. Ristaino—an alumnus of Rhode Island School of Design who had made a name for himself in the indie comic scene—had gotten his start on the show during Season 2, when he was hired on as a character designer. Ristaino excelled in this position—it was his character designs, after all, that garnered the series its first Emmy award win in 2013—but he had long wanted to try his hand at storyboarding episodes.[83] Needless to say, when a storyboarding slot opened up midway through Season 5, he jumped at the chance.

Ristaino brought his talent to the storyboarding table, and during production of Seasons 5 and 6, he alongside Cole Sanchez worked on some of the show's most mythologically-important episodes, like "Wake Up," "Joshua & Margaret Investigations," and "The Cooler." Ristaino would ultimately step down from being a storyboard artist at the end of Season 6, citing the grueling hours and the emotional exhaustion that came with the position. Nevertheless, he remained a part of the show's production crew, working as both a background designer and a storyboard revisionist. By the time the final season of *Adventure Time* aired, Ristaino had become the show's jack-of-all-trades.

Kim, on the other hand, was brand new to the show when she worked on her first episode. A native of Toronto, Canada, and an alumna of Sheridan College's animation program, Kim was somewhat nonchalant when asked about how she landed a job on *Adventure Time*:

> I went to animation school [and] learned how to storyboard there, and about a year after graduating I somehow acquired a storyboard test for [*Adventure Time*], though I was not immediately offered work after submitting the test. I spent the next few months making comics for my Tumblr, and I think they saw and liked my comics, and then I was offered work.[84]

Indeed, Kim's online work—noted for its loose, somewhat sketchy look that recalls the aesthetic of colored pencils—impressed Adam Muto enough for him to ask her to work on the fifth-season episode "Earth & Water."[85] Kim was subsequently brought on as a permanent storyboard artist, working almost exclusively with Somvilay Xayaphone until the show's end. While some of Kim and Xayaphone's early episodes are hit or miss, by the time the show entered into the production of its last three or so seasons, they were one of the more consistently funny storyboarding partners.

Just prior to Ristaino and Kim joining the storyboard ranks, Patrick McHale departed as a storyline contributor, leaving the writers' room one member short. To fill this void, Kent Osborne reached out to Jack Pendarvis, an instructor at the University of Mississippi who happened to be one of Osborne's favorite authors.[86] In an interview, Pendarvis explained:

> Kent asked me if I could help out in the writers' room for a couple of weeks . . . I didn't realize that it was sort of an audition for a permanent position, so that was a nice surprise. They told me I was hired in such a laid-back manner that I didn't realize I had a job at first. The following Monday I got a lot of phone calls from Kent: "Where are you? You're not in the meeting!" And it finally dawned on me that I had been hired.[87]

Unlike many who landed a role in the *Adventure Time* production crew, Pendarvis was not an illustrator. He was, however, an accomplished writer, a well-read individual, and a die-hard fan of twentieth-century cinema—especially the work of comedian Jerry Lewis. Pendarvis would go on to contribute to the scripts for almost half of the show's episodes, diffusing his distinct sensibilities far and wide.

A Critical Look at Season 5

Season 5 debuted on November 12, 2012, with the two-parter "Finn the Human"/"Jake the Dog," which was seen by a whopping 3.4 million viewers.[88] The season concluded on March 17, 2014, with "Billy's Bucket List," which drops the bombshell that Finn's biological father is still alive, trapped somewhere in the infinite cosmos.

Looking back, Season 5 is something of a chimera, given that it is essentially two seasons fused into one. The first part of the season (comprising those episodes helmed by Pendleton Ward[89] and often called "Season 5.1" by fans) is a mostly lighthearted frolic that spends considerable time building off the gimmicks introduced in previous seasons: for instance, we are privy to a second Graybles episode, and a follow-up to Season 3's "Fionna and Cake" called "Bad Little Boy," starring Marceline's counterpart, Marshal Lee. These "sequels" are all serviceable, with their own moments of brilliance, but when considered in retrospect, they do give the impression that the season was playing it safe by retreading familiar ground.

Another weakness of Season 5.1 is the disinterest in overturning the show's status, with several episodes promising big changes only for everything to go back to normal in the end. Consider, for instance, the season opener, "Finn the Human." At the start of this episode, Finn is zapped to a parallel universe, wherein he accidentally starts the apocalypse and unleashes an alternate version of the Lich. It is heavy stuff, but none of it is permanent because everything is neatly reset—by a wish of all things!—at the close of the following episode, "Jake the Dog." Another offender is "Jake the Dad," in which Jake and Lady Rainicorn have a litter of puppies. This could have been a transformative moment for Jake's characterization, forcing him to mature in his quest to be a good father. Unfortunately, the writers decided to have the puppies grow up (literally) overnight, torpedoing a rare opportunity to develop Jake into something more than just "Finn's magic dog-friend."

But while Season 5.1 occasionally struggles to reach its full potential, when it was good, it was *very* good. Case in point: Rebecca Sugar and Cole Sanchez's "Simon & Marcy," which builds off the drama of Season 4's "I Remember You" by further exploring the relationship between a pre-Ice King Simon Petrikov and a young Marceline. Considering just how much "I Remember You" had endeared itself to the show's fans, to say that the expectations for its Season 5 sequel were sky-high is a bit of an understatement. But somehow "Simon & Marcy" met fan expectations, combining zombies and the *Cheers* theme song in a way that not only works, but is downright heartbreaking. Another emotional winner is Tom Herpich and Steve Wolfhard's "Puhoy." Functioning like a cross between the *Star Trek: The Next Generation* episode "The Inner Light" and L. Frank Baum's Oz series, the episode sees Finn find himself trapped in an alternative pillow universe. Unable to find an exit, Finn starts a family, grows old, and dies in this world—only to wake up back in Ooo, whereupon he quickly forgets about his alternate life. By equating lived experience with the transience of dreams, "Puhoy" is a melancholic episode that reminds us that, in the end, all things are impermanent.

The back half of Season 5 (produced under the leadership of Adam Muto[90] and referred to as "Season 5.2" by fans), while still quite silly, shows an increased interest in systematizing the lore of Ooo and taking it more seriously. The episode that best epitomizes this shift is arguably Ako Castuera and Jesse Moynihan's "The Vault," which reveals that Finn's spirit has been reincarnated throughout the ages and that in a past life, he was a thief named Shoko who had befriended and then betrayed Princess Bubblegum. Not only did this episode allow viewers to "reflect on how we carry our wounds through time and space and generations,"[91] but it also laid the groundwork for key mythological developments (e.g., the confirmation that Bubblegum is well over eight hundred years old) that would play a crucial role in subsequent seasons.

This interest in long-term narratives is arguably one of Season 5.2's strongest attributes. Sure, previous seasons had featured the occasional two-parter, but Season 5.2 was really the first to begin plotting out narrative arcs that lasted more than just a few episodes. Key storylines established in this part of the season include the fall and rebirth of Lemongrab (featured in "Two Old," and "Lemonhope" parts I and II); Finn and Flame Princess's dramatic break up (as detailed in "Frost & Fire," "Earth & Water," and "The Red Throne"); and the loss of the demon blood sword and the rise of its grass-based replacement (as seen in "Play Date," "The Pit," "Blade of Grass," and "Rattleballs"). By the time the season finale, "Billy's Bucket List," aired, these story arcs had all become somewhat intertwined with one another, forming a knotty whole that gives Season 5.2 narrative heft and a solid sense of structure.

Season 5.2's continued storytelling maturation was also accompanied by a subtle drift into darker waters; indeed, if Season 5.1 has bursts of gloom here and there, Season 5.2 feels like the metaphorical storm clouds are gathering in the distance. This change was largely the result of the writers' idea to begin focusing on Finn's tumultuous passage into puberty, starting with Somvilay Xayaphone and Luke Pearson's "Frost & Fire." In this episode, Finn manipulates Flame Princess in the pursuit of pleasure, leading to their break up. Subsequent episodes such as "The Red Throne" and "Too Old" would continue to emphasize Finn's more base hormonal desires and how they clashed with his otherwise heroic resolve.

While many fans and critics applauded the fifth season's increased interest in mythology building and narrative serialization, there were also those who disliked the show's tonal shift. (These fan grumblings were, in many ways, portents of the civil war that Season 6 would bring.) But criticisms notwithstanding, Season 5 was quite popular with viewers overall, and in the span of the season's sixteen-month run, the show blossomed into a legitimate cultural phenomenon.

By early 2014, when the season was nearing its end, *Adventure Time* was decidedly in vogue. Episodes were regularly being watched by two to three million viewers; publications such as the *A. V. Club*,[92] IndieWire,[93] and the *New Yorker*[94] were writing thoughtful odes to the show; *Adventure Time* merchandise was quickly becoming more accessible; attendees of comic conventions could be commonly spotted cosplaying as the show's characters; and a balloon of Finn and Jake had even been added to the Macy's Day Parade in the fall of 2013![95] Today, there are quite a few *Adventure Time* fans (myself included) who look back at this time with a sense of wistful nostalgia. Season 5 may not be a perfect season of television, but it did mark the apex of *Adventure Time*'s popularity.

8.

COMING OF AGE IN OOO

Seasons 6 and Beyond

THE AGE OF ENLIGHTENMENT: SEASON 6

In July 2013, production for the show's sixth season began,[1] and immediately, the writers got to work crafting a satisfying continuation of the fifth-season reveal that Finn's father was still alive. It was while the writers meditated on how to build off this plot twist that they had an idea. Instead of featuring him in an episode or two, why not explore the nature and role of Finn's dad over the course of a season long, multiepisode story arc?

The writers decided to establish this plot thread in the double-length sixth-season opener "Wake Up"/"Escape from the Citadel," but how exactly would they break this story arc? While mulling over options, the writers thought back to the production of the fourth-season finale, "The Lich." In the original storyboard, there had been a short scene that introduced Finn's father as a majestic hero who had been unjustly trapped in a celestial prison.[2] The scene had been excised from the storyboard at the last minute, but it soon found new life when the writers decided to use it as the springboard for the sixth-season premiere. This time, however, the premise was turned on its head. Finn's father would not be some great hero who had been unfairly locked away for a crime he did not commit, but rather an indifferent space criminal who likely deserved celestial punishment for whatever he might have done.

Although Finn learns that Martin is not the father that he had hoped for, in "Escape from the Citadel," he tries to bond with his dad nonetheless. Alas, Martin wants nothing to do with his son, and he runs away. The emotional trauma of this turn of events is compounded when Finn dramatically loses his grass-cursed right arm in the closing minutes of the episode. While a lesser show might have played all this off in a funny way or quickly brushed it all aside, the *Adventure Time* writers were interested in "trying to approach this situation realistically"[3]; a child of Finn's age, after all, would not be in a position to process and overcome all of this trauma in just a few episodes' time.

The events of "Escape from the Citadel"[4] would thus prove to be a major turning point for the show, with Finn's loss drastically affecting the show's tone, and while many of the season's episodes still focused on the hijinks of Finn and Jake, others eschew overt humor in favor of quiet contemplation and sometimes outright seriousness. Epitomizing this shift are episodes such as "The Tower" and "Breezy," which explore heavy topics like the agony of loss and the inability to feel pleasure in the wake of depression.

But it was not all doom and gloom. In an interview at Comic-Con in 2014, Adam Muto argued that the season was also a celebration of "creativity,"[5] and when considered in retrospect, this is readily apparent. After all, Season 6 also saw the producers freely toy around with different art styles (e.g., "Food Chain," "Ocarina," "Nemesis," "Water Park Prank"), make use of unique plot devices (e.g., "Sad Face," "Graybles 1000+"), and focus more attention on minor or background characters (e.g., "Little Brother," "Thanks for the Crabapples, Giuseppe!," "The Diary"). This experimentation was amplified by the producers' choice to bring on several guest storyboard artists such as Derek Ballard, Masaaki Yuasa, Madéleine Flores, Jillian Tamaki, Sam Alden,[6] Sloane Leong, Brandon Graham, and David Ferguson. Most of these artists were mavericks from the world of independent comics, and each brought different sensibilities to the show, all of which contrasted nicely with the more "established" style of the show's regular storyboard artists. Given that guest storyboard artists worked on a staggering one-fourth of the season's episodes, it is not hyperbole to say that their aesthetic impact was immense.

Season 6 also saw a handful of regular storyboard artists such as Tom Herpich, Kent Osborne, Steve Wolfhard, and Jesse Moynihan work on episodes by themselves. Previously, solo storyboards had been something of a rarity, with usually only a handful appearing in a season, but Season 6 bucked tradition by featuring a whopping eleven. These episodes are all noteworthy in their own right—both Kent Osborne's "Jake the Brick" and Tom Herpich's "Walnuts & Rain"[7] netted the show Emmy awards,[8] and Steve Wolfhard's "Graybles 1000+" is a remarkable episode that deepened the show's mythology by taking us far into Ooo's future[9]—but it is arguably Moynihan's solo episodes that are the most distinctive. Captivated by the darker tone of the season and the cosmic scale of its overarching plot, Moynihan worked hard to make each of his solo episode (viz., "Something Big," "Is That You?," and "You Forgot Your Floaties") weirder and more abstract than the last. In fact, so distinctive are Moynihan's episodes that many within the fandom view him as the unofficial voice of the show's sixth season.

A Critical Look at Season 6

Adventure Time's sixth season debuted on April 21, 2014, with the two-parter "Wake Up"/"Escape from the Citadel" and came to a close on June 5, 2015, with the two-parter "Hot Diggity Doom"/"The Comet."

By all traditional metrics, the season was a success. Numerous media outlets continued to heap praise onto the series—Eric Thurm of the *A.V. Club* lauded the season as "the series' best yet" and dubbed its crew "a perpetual motion machine generating an awe-inspiring number of great episodes"[10]—and the season also scored a number of coveted awards, including an Emmy, an Annie Award, and even a prestigious Peabody Award for Best Children's Programming—the latter of which was awarded to the show for its "animated alchemy, an impossible mash-up of comedy, horror, fairy tale and coming-of-age fable."[11]

Given all the accolades, it would be reasonable to assume that fans loved the season, too. The strange truth, however, is that Season 6 actually fractured the fandom and instigated something of a civil war, which largely raged on in online spaces. In one camp, you had the fans who reveled in the season's "existential funk."[12] These fans applauded the season's gloomy, more experimental outings, and they argued that the show's willingness to explore more mature stories was a testament to its creative depth. Conversely, there were also fans who bemoaned the show's darker, more intellectual turn. *Adventure Time*, they argued, was supposed to be about *adventure*. It was supposed to be a show about fighting monsters, cracking jokes, and acting silly—not about daddy problems, teen angst, and depression. These fan-critics also tended to see the season's headier episodes as pretentious at best and masturbatory at worst.

As Season 6 wore on, the more intense the online battle between the fans and the critics became. And while several sixth-season episodes fomented robust debates about quality ("Chips and Ice Cream," for instance, was decried as boring, despite a promising guest spot by musical comedy duo Garfunkel and Oates, and "Water Park Prank" was lambasted for its simplistic writing and its somewhat-disquieting animation style), perhaps no other sixth-season episode divided the fandom more than "Breezy." While some viewers appreciated the episode's meditation on using sex (allegorized as kissing) as a "self-medicine" for depression, others found the premise off-putting. There were also fans who were disturbed by the scene featuring Lumpy Space Princess and Finn "taking [things] to the deep end," which some interpreted as the former sexually assaulting the latter. But for some fans, the show's unforgivable sin was giving Finn his arm back after only four episodes, which was seen as a lazy regression to the status quo. The divide in opinion was most evident online, where both those who enjoyed and hated the episode clashed on sites like 4chan and

Reddit. When the digital dust began to settle near the end of the season's airing, a number of disgruntled viewers left the fandom, never to return.

The polarizing nature of the season was compounded by Cartoon Network's poor handling of the episodes' airing schedule. This all started early in the season, when the network moved *Adventure Time* from its long-held Monday timeslot to Thursday nights, catching some viewers off guard. Then Cartoon Network aired only a single new episode between August 14 and November 24, 2014, throwing off the momentum of the season; the airing of the season was further disrupted in November 2014 and June 2015, when the network decided to burn off handfuls of episodes by releasing them in "bombs" (that is, short clusters of episodes that are aired back-to-back, sometimes during a single week, and sometimes on a single day), rather than airing new episodes once per week.

Further exacerbating this disordered airing schedule was Cartoon Network's tonally flawed promotional strategy. *Adventure Time*'s sixth season was, after all, darker and more serious than any of its previous seasons, but the network refused to showcase this tone shift in their advertisements. Many years later, on his personal blog, Jesse Moynihan would lament this turn of events:

> In the later seasons [*Adventure Time* was] winning Emmys, getting Peabody awards, being called one of the best shows on TV by the *New Yorker*, etc . . . and the [public relations (PR)] department of CN did not adjust their marketing strategy to take advantage of the critical praise. [*Adventure Time*] was a cult hit with a rabid fanbase that could have completely exploded but CN PR didn't [use anything outside] their previous success models. Online articles were comparing us to shows like *Louie*, but our advertisements were promoting us like we were *Phineas and Ferb*. . . . PR could have tried to make adjustments as the show evolved but maybe that was asking too much. I think it meant way more to us, since we were ripping our guts out trying to make the best thing we could.[13]

Moynihan's comments about Cartoon Network's promotional (non)strategy echo the thoughts of an anonymous *Adventure Time* staffer who in early 2017 told Eric Kohn of IndieWire: "[*Adventure Time*] never really fit into a category, so Cartoon Network didn't really have a model in which to manage its ever-growing popularity."[14]

Cartoon Network's lack of a promotional strategy combined with its messy handling of timeslots and airdates impacted the show's popularity and cut into its once-impressive Nielsen ratings. While the season debut was watched by almost 3.32 million viewers, the finale scraped only 1.55 million[15]—a staggering

50 percent decrease in raw viewership numbers. Meanwhile, those fans who remained with the show during this turbulent time could do nothing but gawk at the network's imprudent decisions. For many, it felt like Cartoon Network was *trying* to scuttle its flagship series. When all this drama was happening in 2014–15, it was easy for fans to jump to hasty conclusions about the show's direction and the network's decision making. Now, over half a decade later, it is far easier to judge the season with a modicum of objectivity.

For one thing, many of the problems that some viewers had with the season now seem thoroughly overblown, chief among them being the near-hysterical condemnations of "Breezy." While there is a solid case to be made that the show should have at least waited a few more episodes before giving Finn a new limb, criticisms about the episode's conclusion ended up being premature, given that the saga of Finn's grass curse was far, *far* from over. (Arguments often heard on 4chan or Reddit that "Breezy" single-handedly destroyed the show are so lacking in nuance that they do not even deserve a retort.)

Other critiques, however, are more valid. Consider, for instance, that while many of Season 6's more experimental episodes succeed in showcasing the show's background characters, this was often at the expense of fan favorites like Ice King, Marceline, Flame Princess, and BMO—all of whom received hardly any screen time.[16] And while the season's experimentation led to some philosophical and artistic masterpieces (e.g., "The Mountain," "Astral Plane"), it also diffused a sort of existential despondency throughout the entire season, resulting in some episodes that play as straight dramas. For fans who just want to watch the humorous adventures of a boy and his dog, the seriousness of the season can sometimes make rewatching it an emotional chore.

But perhaps the most deserved critique had to do with how the show handled its seasonal arc; indeed, *Adventure Time*'s sixth season often struggled at points to tell a cohesive story. Part of this was the clunky way the show integrated Martin into the fold. Martin functioned little more than a chaotic cipher and whose arbitrary characterization left something to be desired. The season also struggled in its pacing, choosing to follow up game-changing episodes with nonconsequential installments (e.g., the excruciatingly mediocre "James II" directly following on the heels of the game-changing "Escape from the Citadel") or purposeful anticlimaxes (e.g., the season finale, "The Comet"). This issue with pacing may have also been exacerbated by the near-constant revolving door of guest storyboard artists, whose presence resulted in a unique but sometimes disorienting mélange of aesthetic voices.

Be that as it may, one ought not to forget that at this point in its run, *Adventure Time* was not known for having a single, guiding story arc; even Season 5's increased interest in multi-episode plot lines paled in comparison to Season 6's ambitions. What is more, the show's mythology had previously evolved at a snail's pace. (For perspective, it took the show almost two full seasons before it returned to the paradigm-shifting Lich plot introduced at the end of Season 2!) Season 6 thus marked *Adventure Time*'s first foray into the art of season-long plot development. It therefore seems only fair to view the season as a trial run, and for a first attempt at this sort of storytelling, it is certainly an admirable one.

But regardless of its strengths and weaknesses as a whole, Season 6 inarguably contains several of the show's strongest episodes. Perhaps the greatest is Tom Herpich and Steve Wolfhard's melancholic "Escape from the Citadel." This episode, wherein Finn meets and is rejected by his human father, functions like *Adventure Time*'s very own *The Empire Strikes Back*; by delivering the usually-unstoppable Finn an emotional and physical blow, the show stresses his humanity, reminding us that Finn has his limit too.

Jesse Moynihan also deserves praise for his aforementioned string of solo storyboarded mindscrews, chief among them being "You Forgot Your Floaties." Combining the visual aesthetic of Alejandro Jodorowsky's *The Holy Mountain* (1973) with the magic of Aleister Crowley, this episode explores Magic Man's damaged psyche in an abstract way. There is a fundamental weirdness to this episode that is hard to express—Is it somber? Is it unnerving? Is it profound?—and in many ways "You Forgot Your Floaties" feels like the apogee of Season 6's dalliance with creative unorthodoxy.

In a run-down of *Adventure Time*'s best seasons, its sixth sharply divides the fandom, and you will either find fans out there who love it or downright hate it. At the end of the day, I believe it is best to see the season as something of a flawed masterpiece—a complicated coming-of-age story, at times messy and melancholic, which reflects the difficulties of growing up. Season 6 is far from perfect, but when taken as a whole, it nevertheless illustrates *Adventure Time*'s raw creativity and its willingness to explore adolescence in bold, unexpected ways.

THE RENAISSANCE: SEASONS 7-8

During the summer of 2014, it was officially announced by Cartoon Network that *Adventure Time* would return for a seventh season. Whether it was the split reaction of the fandom to early sixth-season episodes like "Breezy," or simply a desire to try something different, the writers decided that with the show's seventh season, they would move away from the dark and sometimes serious tone that many associate with the show's sixth. When directly asked as to whether this was a conscious shift on his part, Jesse Moynihan noted on his website, "I can say that on my end, while going into [Season 7] I decided to steer my boat away from philosophical notions and focus a bit more on jokes and adventurous scenarios. This is because I feel like the end of Season 6 gives Finn a reason to embrace the temporary, material life."[17] Moynihan's comments were later echoed by Tom Herpich, who explained in an interview that his writing for the season was "more grounded" than that of the show's sixth.[18] Adam Muto too expressed a similar sentiment when at a panel in 2015, he noted that with Season 7, the writers consciously decided to eschew "really heady and philosophical" storylines.[19]

Raising the Stakes

In November 2014, around the time that the season's first batch of episodes were being storyboarded, former *Adventure Time* production crew member Patrick McHale's event series *Over the Garden Wall* aired to both critical acclaim and solid viewership numbers. Executives at Cartoon Network immediately thereafter began contacting the showrunners of their biggest shows, inquiring if they were interested in working on stories that could be delivered in a "longer, more serialized format": the miniseries.[20] One of the shows that the network approached was *Adventure Time*. According to Adam Muto, the writers were equally as interested in the idea as the network, as it would allow them to "dig into one idea and really explore it."[21] As they began mulling over story ideas that the program could focus on, they eventually remembered a long-hibernating story about Marceline the Vampire Queen's origin.

At the onset of the series' production, Marceline's honorific "the Vampire Queen" was seen by the writers simply as a title that rhymed with her name and provided her with spooky superpowers. In a show full of weird beasties and even weirder characters, it needed no elaborate explanation. After all, what was so special about a plain old vampire? But as production wore on, Marceline and her vampirism became a larger and larger question mark. Finally, during the production of Season 2 in 2010, then-creative director McHale decided it was time to hash out how exactly Marceline had gained her bite marks. In a 2019 interview, he explained:

> I realized . . . that we'd never actually had Marceline and Ice King interact with each other in the same episode, and we'd also established that they were both 1000 years old. I thought that was meaningful, and so I started coming up with this whole elaborate backstory [explaining that] Marceline was the daughter of a demon and a human . . . [and that roughly one thousand years prior to the start of the show] Marceline and Ice King were working together to save humanity [from vampires]. But Ice King was losing himself [to the ice crown], and it all landed on Marceline to fight off the vampires as the humans were escaping on an ark, set for some unknown shore. . . .

So in the final struggle, as a mutated horde of monsters and vampires come to kill the last remaining humans . . . [Marceline] goes and fights the vampires with her demon powers so that the boat can leave. The humans make it, but Marceline is turned into a vampire. So she's stuck looking [like a teenager] forever, and Ice King is stuck being crazy . . . and it's too heartbreaking for [Marceline] to ever even go near him, so she avoids him and lives in a cave . . . Anyway, I pitched this whole huge elaborate thing to the writers room and they were like, "That's cool, Pat." But it was too much plot. Nobody was very excited about it.[22]

McHale's ideas quickly fell by the wayside and were archived away in some file cabinet, where they languished for years in a state of undead limbo.[23]

Fast forward to 2014: while trying to think up a storyline for a possible miniseries, the writers suddenly remembered McHale's earlier attempt to delineate Marceline's origin story. Adam Muto and the show's writers decided that the time was right to "[roll] with that [original idea] and [expand] that into eight episodes."[24] The result was the first *Adventure Time* miniseries, *Stakes* (originally titled *Return of the Vampire King*),[25] which began production at the tail-end of 2014. For fans of Marceline, this could have come at no better time, for during the show's fifth and sixth seasons, the character—despite being a fan favorite—had started to slowly be sidelined by the writers, appearing in only a handful of scattered episodes.[26] While some might argue that this was because the show was wanting to focus most of the action on Finn, there is evidence that Marceline's absence might have been because the show's writers did not exactly know what to do with her character anymore.[27] *Stakes* thus gave Marceline a *raison d'être*.

The cast and crew of *Adventure Time*—when told of their new project—were immediately energized by the creative challenge (Tom Herpich perhaps best summed up the collective elation when he told me: "I was really excited about the Marceline miniseries and couldn't shut up about it around the office for the longest time. I really drew my heart out on that one").[28] The miniseries also functioned as something of a homecoming for a few artists: former storyboard artist Rebecca Sugar contributed a new song for the miniseries, Ghostshrimp (whose backgrounds in Season 1 had arguably set the stage for the series' post-apocalyptic nature) designed a few background pieces, and former storyboard artist Ako Castuera returned to work once again with Jesse Moynihan, producing three of her all-time best episodes. The miniseries also saw storyboarding contributions from long-serving revisionist Lyle Partridge, frequent guest storyboard artist Luke Pearson, and newcomer Hanna K. Nyström.

The miniseries was initially slated to air during the Halloween season of 2015, but for whatever reason, it was pushed back a month. *Stakes* finally aired during the week of November 16 (with new episodes debuting every day in pairs) and follows the adventure of Marceline, Princess Bubblegum, Finn, and Jake as they attempt to eliminate five recently resurrected vampires whom Marceline had killed long ago. Along the way, Marceline loses, regains, and then comes to terms with her vampirism, growing over the course of the eight episodes from a "messed up kid" to an adult.

For the most part, the miniseries received positive reviews from television critics, many of whom lauded its storyline and its focus on one of the show's most beloved characters. Other outlets—including some that normally did not review television, like *Pitchfork*[29]—penned gushing prose about Rebecca Sugar's new song. That said, more than a few critics and fans were disappointed that the miniseries did not fully elucidate "the ghosts of Marceline's past" (as was promised in the miniseries' official press release).[30] Much of this disappointment can arguably be chalked up to the way Cartoon Network (mis)advertised the miniseries as a movie-length flashback, rather than an interconnected but nevertheless episodic monster hunt.[31] In hindsight, *Stakes* is a delightful long-form adventure story that combines the humorous dialogue and exciting action sequences of the show's earlier seasons with the character development and philosophical musings seen in the show's fifth and sixth. It is by no means perfect (compared to later miniseries, for instance, *Stakes* does at times feel a bit disjointed, and at other times too flippant in its storytelling), but it illustrates the continuing evolution of the series even in its later years.

Artists Come, Artists Go

When production started on Season 7, the *Adventure Time* crew was several storyboarders short; Cole Sanchez, a stalwart artist who had worked on the show since Season 1, had left the series at the end of Season 6 to become a supervising director on the miniseries *Long Live the Royals* (2015); his partner, Andy Ristaino, had decided to move from storyboards to background designs; Jesse Moynihan was still without a permanent partner after Ako Castuera's departure at the end of Season 5; and following the writing of *Stakes*, Pendleton Ward decided to scale his involvement with the series back even further, which led to an open spot in the writers room. The subsequent search to fill these vacancies would end with the hiring of four talented artists whose aesthetic sensibilities noticeably impacted the tone of *Adventure Time*'s final few seasons: Hanna K. Nyström, Sam Alden, Aleks Sennwald, and Ashly Burch.

The first of these artists, Hanna K. Nyström, was a freelance illustrator and member of the Peow Studio art collective who hailed from Sweden.[32] "Adam got in touch with me after reading [my] small comic . . . *New Frontier: Third Wheel*," Nyström explained to me through email. "He asked if I had ever done any storyboard work before (I had not) and if I'd be interested in doing a test for the show."[33] Nyström indeed was interested—she had long been a fan of the show—and after passing the test, she was hired in 2014 as a guest storyboard artist during the production of *Stakes*; after a few more guest storyboards, she was eventually promoted to full-time status. Nyström remained in Sweden during her time on the show, and the five-thousand-mile distance between her and Burbank necessitated that she use synchronous and asynchronous technology to communicate with her peers. While Nyström admitted to me that the remote storyboarding experience could be "a bit lonely" and that "the time difference could be kinda [*sic*] rough too,"[34] she nevertheless surmounted these hurdles and in time became one of *Adventure Time*'s strongest latter-day storyboard artists.

Also joining the show around this time as a permanent storyboard artist was Sam Alden. An alumnus of Washington state's Whitman College, Alden had cut his teeth producing independent comics and Risograph-like illustrations for publications such as the *Seattle Times* and *Slate*. Alden first got involved with the production of *Adventure Time* in early 2014, when he emailed Adam Muto and inquired if he could take a storyboard test for the show. There was only one problem: Alden had never really watched the series. "I spent about as much time just binge-watching *Adventure Time* . . . as I did drawing [the storyboard test]," Alden revealed at a DePaul Visiting Artists Series in 2014. "It was a really weird week. . . . I was walking around in my apartment in my underwear drinking coffee and living and breathing *Adventure Time*."[35] All this cramming evidently paid off, for Alden was subsequently hired on as a freelance storyboard artist, working with Jesse Moynihan on one of the sixth season's trippiest episodes, "The Mountain." Alden was again asked by the *Adventure Time* producers to freelance a few months later, this time working with Kent Osborne on the seventh-season episode "President Porpoise Is Missing!" On the strength of his freelance work, Alden was soon offered a permanent storyboarding position.[36]

The third new storyboard artist to join the show was Aleks Sennwald, whose first contributions for the series were the Fionna and Cake episode "Five Short Tables" and the mythologically significant "Preboot." Like Alden before her, Sennwald had gained critical exposure by landing illustrations in prestigious publications like the *New York Times*, the *Washington Post*, and *GQ Germany*. Sennwald also had experience in the video game industry, having been one of the prop designers for the highly lauded video game *Gone Home* (of which Pendleton Ward was a major fan),[37] and this interest in video games can clearly be seen when one looks at the promotional art pieces that she designed for her episodes of *Adventure Time*, most of which featured simple CGI animation made with modeling programs like Blender. Sennwald was partnered with Hanna K. Nyström during the show's final few seasons, and together the two worked on several stand-out episodes including "Hide and Seek," "Bonnibel Bubblegum," and "The First Investigation."

Season 7 also saw the debut of Ashly Burch as one of the show's storyline writers. Prior to her hiring, Burch was a voice actress well known in the video game world for having provided the voice of Tiny Tina in the first-person shooter *Borderlands 2* and Chloe Price in the time-travel adventure game *Life Is Strange*.[38] Burch's journey in becoming an *Adventure Time* writer was relatively serendipitous. During the show's sixth season, she provided a number of voices, including Breezy the bee from the eponymous episode. During the recording session for that episode, Burch and lead writer Kent Osborne got to know each other and became friends. Then, during the middle of Season 7's production, when Pendleton Ward scaled back his commitment to the show even more by no longer regularly working in the writers' room, Osborne reached out to Burch and asked if she was interested in working as a storyline writer—a job that she eagerly accepted.[39] Burch would ultimately serve as a writer for most of Season 8, as well as a few episodes in Seasons 9 and 10, including the series' four-part finale.

While prior to her tenure in the writers' room, *Adventure Time* had been a fairly progressive show, Burch's hiring in many ways injected into it a new streak of feminism; in an interview with John Moe, she explained, "I just love the female characters on the show. It is important to me that female characters [like Princess Bubblegum and Marceline] are highlighted on any show."[40] This emphasis is perhaps most notable in episodes like "The Thin Yellow Line," "Broke His Crown," "Bun Bun," and "Ketchup," which portray the show's lead female characters as competent, strong, and understanding, while still managing to showcase their complex emotional dimensions.

But as in seasons past, the addition of talented voices like Alden, Nyström, Sennwald, or Burch often preceded the departure of more experienced crew members. This time, the individual leaving would be Jesse Moynihan, who had been storyboarding for the series since Season 2 and who had developed a reputation online as a veritable auteur for his unique brand of spiritual episodes. Unfortunately, the extreme experimentation that Moynihan embraced during the production of Season 6 (discussed earlier in this chapter) led to a severe mental and emotional breakdown. "[I] reached some level of emotional exhaustion that was so intense," Moynihan wrote on his personal website. "It felt like I'd lost all mental defenses or sense of personal space. . . . I felt like a raw nerve that was tied symbiotically to . . . how I was judging my own work."[41] The distress of this nearly caused Moynihan to resign from *Adventure Time* after its sixth season, but eventually, he decided to remain on as a storyboard artist for a final season, treating that year like his victory lap by "scaling back a lot of experimental aspects and just pushing for jokes and excitement."[42] He explained, "I felt like if I could pull that off, it would be a nice end cap to my time on [*Adventure Time*], and then I could feel good about leaving."[43]

Moynihan's seventh- and eighth-season contributions are notably lighter than his sixth-season episodes, with a heavier emphasis placed on silly dialog and comedic set pieces. Some might argue that during this time, Moynihan artistically regressed and "phoned it in," but I would argue the opposite—that his final few episodes show evidence of substantial creative growth and flexibility. After all, episodes like "Crossover," "Flute Spell," "I Am a Sword," and his final storyboarding contribution "Normal Man" all manage to tell stories that are neither pretentious (as some of Moynihan's sixth-season contributions were wont to be) nor frivolous. They thus serve as a creative synthesis of his past work, merging the hilarity of Moynihan's earliest episodes with the profundity of his fifth- and sixth-season creations.

A Critical Look at the "Original" Season 7

Adventure Time's seventh season debuted on November 2, 2015, with the episode "Bonnie & Neddy." Initially, thirty-nine episodes had been ordered by Cartoon Network, and the season was slated to conclude with the two-parter "Preboot"/"Reboot" (which would eventually air on November 19, 2016). However, in the summer of 2017, the network completely reorganized how the official seasons were divided, retroactively making the twenty-sixth episode of the season, "The Thin Yellow Line" (which had aired on March 19, 2016), the "official" Season 7 finale. The network then grouped the following thirteen episodes of the original Season 7 order with the start of Season 8. The "Preboot"/"Reboot" two-parter thus became the midseason finale for the show's eighth season. A strange decision made for no clear reason, this divisional snafu caused many a headache and gave *Adventure Time* fans plenty to argue about online. While I have respected Cartoon Network's post facto renumbering scheme throughout this book, in the present section, I will consider the thirty-nine episodes from "Bonnie & Neddy" to "Reboot" as one unit, given that they were produced as such.

...

Season 7 was in the unenviable position of airing right after the show's sixth had fractured the *Adventure Time* fandom. Fans who had enjoyed the previous season hoped that the show's seventh would continue to take risks by exploring the emotional side of its characters. Conversely, fans who had been disappointed by Season 6 openly yearned for episodes that would eschew drama in favor of humor and excitement. Needless to say, the stakes were as high as the expectations. Making the situation all the more volatile was Cartoon Network's decision to separate Seasons 6 and 7 with a five-month hiatus. At the time, this was the longest the show had gone without the airing of new episodes, and it is almost certain that this content drought depressed interest in the show, continuing the fandom's shrinkage. And for the fans who had stuck around, lack of content was causing expectations to mount. *Adventure Time*'s seventh season was at a critical risk of being overlooked by some and overhyped by others.

Season 7 finally debuted with a "bomb" of episodes during the first week of November 2015, and with each new premiere, the fandom—which had been collectively holding its breath up until this point—sighed in relief: Gone was the overwhelming sense of existential gloom that pervaded Season 6. In its place was a balanced approach to storytelling that synthesized much of the show's past strengths. Some episodes, like the season premiere "Bonny and Neddy" or the Marceline-Bubblegum classic "Varmints," buzzed with an emotional energy that matched the best of Season 6's weighty excursions, whereas other episodes, like "Football" and "Mama Said," were mirthful in a way that recalled the clownishness of the show's earliest seasons. Put another way, the first few episodes of Season 7 had something for everyone, with neither the silly nor the serious being neglected.

This tonal equilibrium runs throughout the entire season, but it is perhaps best displayed in the season's cynosure: the *Stakes* miniseries. Across these eight episodes, the show focuses on Marceline's journey to shed her vampirism and "grow up," while pondering the nature (or the existence) of fate and free will along the way. These might not sound like the happiest of concepts, yet *Stakes* is never a depressive slog. Instead, the miniseries contrasts its weighty themes with a bevy of humorous set pieces (e.g., the vampire king parleying with Marceline in his underwear) and the show's trademark dialogue ("These guys will crack up ya sacrum!"). This allows *Stakes* to make solid philosophical points—such as Marceline's observation that history repeats ad nauseum because no one ever lives long enough to see the patterns replay—without ever lapsing into the pretention or morosity that, at times, affected Season 6.

Some might take all this talk about the return of levity to mean that Season 7 is thematically impoverished. This is far from the truth. If Seasons 5 and 6 were interested in the tumultuous passage of adolescence, and thus by extension, the process of growth, Season 7 focuses much of its time on triumphantly recognizing that growth. This is most evident in the characterization of Finn, who eschews the narcissistic self-pity that had enveloped him in Season 6 and instead prioritizes the feelings of others. The clearest demonstration of this maturation occurs in the episode "Bun Bun," in which Finn heartfully apologizes to Flame Princess for the way that he treated her in the past. This apology is motivated neither by a hormonal desire to "get back together" with Flame Princess, nor by an egotistical want to save face. Instead, Finn is driven by the simple recognition that his misbehavior had hurt his friend.

Finn is not the only character who recognizes their growth this season. At the end of *Stakes*, for instance, Marceline muses that the events of the miniseries provided her with a way to process the trauma of her vampiric turning and finally "grow up." Princess Bubblegum, too, uses her time in exile to become a kinder, more emphatic ruler—growth which she later demonstrates in episodes like "The Thin Yellow Line" and "Scamps." Even Jake (a character who often functions as the personification of Peter Pan Syndrome) takes the time in "Daddy-Daughter Card Wars" to accept that he is no longer a wild mad lad in his twenties. Season 7 truly is, for most of Ooo's residents, a year of self-recognition.

With its balanced tone and competent character development, Season 7 is often held in high regard by the show's fandom, and many (including myself) view it as a renaissance of sorts. Considering that even the greatest of series usually begin to stagnate after a half a decade on the air, it is a major accomplishment that the seventh season of *Adventure Time* saw the show not only survive but creatively and emotionally thrive.

THE DÉNOUEMENT: SEASONS 8–9

The production of what was originally supposed to be the show's seventh season ended with the storyboarding of the "Preboot"/"Reboot" two-parter. In terms of plot, these episodes blow the mythology of the series wide open: Finn, we learn, is not the only human! Instead, there is a whole human colony somewhere out there, beyond the farthest reaches of Ooo. Likewise, we learn that Susan Strong is a cyborg who had at one time worked with the mysterious Dr. Gross, a villainous scientist obsessed with "upgrading" living organisms. But perhaps the most important development comes near the very end of "Reboot," when the grass curse merges with the broken Finnsword, producing a new, mysterious being. While previous season premieres and finales had introduced novel plot points, there was something about the "Preboot"/"Reboot" story reveals that felt different. Instead of raising more questions, it was as if the show was interested in finally answering them.

In the fall of 2015,[44] the *Adventure Time* writers and producers reconvened to work on the two-parter "Two Swords"/"Do No Harm." These episodes (originally intended to serve as the eighth-season premiere) reveal that the mysterious being teased at the end of "Reboot" is Fern, a grass doppelganger of Finn voiced by Hayden Ezzy. This plot turn shed considerable light on the nature of the grass curse that had long plagued Finn, and in doing so, it seemed to further suggest that, indeed, the show was shifting into answer mode. For this reason, the "Two Swords"/"Do No Harm" two-parter can be seen as the transition point from the show's Renaissance to the beginning of its grand dénouement. On his personal Tumblr, Herpich wrote something similar, noting that after the production of these episodes "everything start[ed] rolling into one big snowball that roll[ed] and roll[ed] all the way to the end" of the show.[45] *Adventure Time*'s overarching story—which had been built up over the course of well over two hundred episodes—was finally coming together.

Visiting the *Islands*, Braving the *Elements*

While working on the batch of episodes that followed "Two Swords"/"Do No Harm," the producers decided that the time was right to explore one of the show's biggest mysteries: Finn the Human's origin story. While bits and pieces of Finn's backstory had been teased out over the years, the show had yet to offer a definitive answer that tied these loose strands together. In an interview with IndieWire, Muto explained: "For a long time, Finn's origin story didn't seem like one of those threads [that needed to be resolved] . . . [But] the more seasons we got, the more glaring that mystery became."[46] It just so happens that the writers and producers began thinking about this plot thread after *Stakes* aired in late 2015. The miniseries was a ratings success, which made Cartoon Network eager to greenlight more long-form projects.

So, during the winter of 2015–16, the *Adventure Time* writers' room convened to start working on a second miniseries. It was during these brainstorming sessions that the writers once again reached into their file cabinet of ideas and dusted off a rough backstory for Finn that had been tentatively outlined during the production of the show's second season. Although plot developments in subsequent seasons had rendered unusable almost all of this initial backstory, there remained one key idea that had yet to be contradicted: that a colony of humans had managed to survive the cataclysmic fallout of the Mushroom War by hiding on a mysterious island.[47] Muto, in particular, seized upon this kernel of an idea and combined it with a meditation on transhumanism (a topic that had caught his eye after he read about it in a magazine article). The result was a new eight-part epic focusing on Finn's genesis, which was eventually dubbed *Islands*.[48]

Unlike with *Stakes* (which Cartoon Network had announced months prior to its airing and had eagerly promoted throughout 2015), the network barely did anything to promote *Islands*. In fact, the first official reference to the miniseries came via an obscure Comixology post from November 2016 that was passed around fansites. This was followed up by an official press release a month later.

(This lethargy on the part of the network is likely due to the announcement in late 2016 that *Adventure Time* had been canceled; it seems that the network did not want to expend too much energy on a show it had just axed.) *Islands* eventually aired the week of January 30, 2017, with new episodes debuting every day in pairs.

Islands follows the sea voyage of Finn, Jake, Susan Strong, and BMO, as they travel to the quasimythical "Founders Island" to learn more about Finn's human family—and also meet his long-lost mother. Similar in structure to Vergil's *Aeneid*, the miniseries is a sprawling epic whose first half sees our heroes meandering across the sea in search of their "destiny," and whose second half focuses on the heroes coming face to face with that which they seek. Replete with meditations on the impact of technology and what it means to keep someone you love safe from harm, *Islands* is a touching batch of episodes that not only explores the mythology of the series but also provides Finn with some emotional closure regarding his family. In a 2017 interview with IndieWire, showrunner Adam Muto mused:

> I'm glad we were able to tell this story . . . In a way, it sort of frees [Finn] to have a completely unexpected ending. He's not a chosen one with a grand destiny or the last anything. He's the son of a doctor and a con man trying to figure stuff out in a colorful magical land.[49]

A few weeks after *Islands* debuted, the *Adventure Time* fandom was caught off guard by wonderful news: another miniseries, entitled *Elements*, would be airing mid-2017, and it would continue almost right where *Islands* ended, with the two miniseries separated by what became the postfacto Season 9 premiere, "Orb."

As to how this third miniseries came about, head writer Kent Osborne explained in a podcast interview: "*Elements* [was largely] my idea. I was like, 'Well, what's going on in Ooo while [Finn and Jake are off] doing *Islands*?'" Likewise, in a 2019 interview, storyline writer Jack Pendarvis, told me:

> *Elements* . . . came up organically, and if I recall correctly, we surprised ourselves with the realization that we were basically writing another miniseries on the heels of *Islands*. . . . [*Elements*] came from talking about what was going on in Ooo while Finn and Jake were gone. I believe it was Ashly Burch's idea that [Patience St. Pim's] scheme should come to some sort of fruition . . . and that's how that sort of foreshadowing episode ("Jelly Beans Have Power") came about. Ashly worked on "Orb," too, in which we have the big reveal (at the very end) which leads into *Elements*.[50]

Osborne also noted in the aforementioned interview that he initially wanted the miniseries to be an "epic" showdown in which all the characters "are all battling . . . everyone is fighting each other, and you get to see the extent of everyone's powers."[51] The final version of *Elements* is likely more subdued than what Osborne had originally intended, but nevertheless the miniseries still features its fair share of action—especially in bombastic episodes like "Happy Warrior" and "Hero Heart."

Cartoon Network once again took a cagey approach when it came time to advertise the miniseries, publicizing the string of episodes via a press release that preceded the miniseries' airdate by only a month. *Elements* eventually ran during the week of April 24, 2017, with two episodes debuting each day. In this event series, Finn and Jake return to the Land of Ooo to discover that it has been transformed into a nightmare realm, with each quarter of the land being overtaken by a different universal element (viz., candy, ice, slime, and fire). Finn and Jake subsequently team up with Ice King, Magic Betty, and a begrudging Lumpy Space Princess to restore the land that they call home. Compared to the mythological tidal waves that were *Islands* and *Stakes*, *Elements* is a little less significant to the series' overarching story, and more or less plays as a fun "simple fetch quest."[52] While this means there is a certain superfluousness to *Elements*, it nevertheless has a solid ending, and the entire thing recalls the light-heartedness of the show's earlier seasons, making it enjoyable in a nostalgic sort of way.

Just before the writers started to outline *Elements*, Burch left the series and a new artist (who would soon go on to become a Cartoon Network series creator herself) was hired to take her place: Julia Pott. A half-American, half-British animator, Pott hailed from London and had studied animation at both Kingston University and the Royal College of Art.[53] After making several short films, Pott was hired by Cartoon Network to create a pilot short, which would serve as the springboard for her soon-to-be picked up series *Summer Camp Island*. It was during this time that she was also tapped to be a writer for *Adventure Time*.[54] Because the show was at that point over half a decade old, Pott told the *Los Angeles Times* that upon her arrival, she "felt very new, like [she] was walking into a high school in the last year."[55] Pott was nevertheless ecstatic about the opportunity, as she was a self-professed "huge fan of *Adventure Time*,"[56] having first seen the pilot while an undergraduate student in London years prior.[57] Fellow storyline writer Jack Pendarvis wrote on his personal blog that Pott "showed incredible spirit and ingeniousness" after joining the writing crew, providing them with a jolt of energy that helped them fully block out the *Elements* miniseries (as well as the remaining twenty-two episodes of the series).[58]

A Critical Look at the "Original" Season 8

Originally, the twenty-eight episodes from "Two Swords" (which aired on January 23, 2017) to "Three Buckets" (which aired on July 21, 2017) had been ordered together as part of a projected eighth season. However, in the summer of 2017, when the network rearranged the season divisions, the first fourteen episodes of the original order (i.e., "Two Swords" through the *Islands* miniseries) were lumped together with the final thirteen episodes of what had initially been the seventh season; this new string of twenty-seven episodes (i.e., "Broke His Crown" through *Islands*) became the "official" eighth season. The remaining fourteen episodes (i.e., "Orb" through "Three Buckets") were then christened the "official" ninth season. As with the "original" Season 7, I believe it only makes sense to critically appraise "Two Swords" through "Three Buckets" together, given that they were produced together.

In doing so, the first thing to note is the thematic cohesion. Indeed, this episode string collectively represents the show's most successful attempt at long-form storytelling, with arcs flowing into one another in a way that is both satisfying and affective. The excitement all begins in the "Two Swords"/"Do No Harm" two-parter, which introduces viewers to Finn's grass doppelgänger, Fern. This drama quickly segues into the epic *Islands* miniseries, which culminates in Finn reconnecting with his mother, Minerva. But Finn is not given much time to process this parental reconnection before he is thrust into the events of *Elements*, a miniseries predicated on the elemental takeover of Ooo. Containing well over half the season's episodes, the *Islands* and *Elements* miniseries are the keel of the season, guiding everything in one narrative direction.

The season culminates with the bombastic "Whispers"/"Three Buckets" two-part finale. In the former, the Lich returns and attempts to lure Sweet P to the dark side so that the two can rule as "twin kings of ruin." The Lich, wedded as he is to a nihilistic sort of fatalism, is certain that his return is inevitable, but Sweet P surprises the demon by rejecting his offer and ultimately killing him. "Whispers" thus ends by emphasizing volition and our capacity to be a hero, even when the circumstances seem dire. From here, "Three Buckets" begins, and the focus shifts to Fern—a character who has always been subordinate to Finn. Try as he might, Fern cannot find a way to substantially differentiate himself from his fleshy counterpart. Soon, Fern's frustrations grow into jealousy, which further mutate into hate. By the end of the episode, Fern has become Finn's literal opposite, his shadow. The season ends with a Good Finn–vs.–Bad Finn dynamic clearly established, suggesting that the following season will dabble heavily in themes of conflict, opposition, and possibly even reconciliation.

In the past, *Adventure Time* was critiqued for having its story arcs move at a glacial pace, but the twenty-eight episodes of the original Season 8 order prove that the show was more than capable of telling a complex story at a clip. Unfortunately, all this long-form storytelling came at the price of "stand-alone" installments, and of the season's twenty-eight episodes, only four episodes (i.e., "Wheels," "High Strangeness," "Horse and Ball," and "Fionna and Cake and Fionna") can rightfully be considered one-offs, uninformed by the season's overarching narrative developments. For fans who watch the show chiefly for Finn and Jake's random adventures, this season might be something of a disappointment, but for those who enjoy the show's lore, Season 8 will almost certainly become a quick favorite.

THE LAST ADVENTURES(?): SEASON 10

On July 21, 2016, Kent Osborne tweeted a quick doodle of Tree Trunks (dressed like then-presidential candidate Donald Trump, saying, "This apple pie is gonnna be yuuuge!"), along with a hashtag indicating that *Adventure Time* had been renewed for a tenth season.[59] Compared to previous renewal announcements, this one was met with a relatively muted reaction (probably due to the low-key way in which the news was delivered), but for the show's most devoted fans, it was cause for celebration. The writers soon thereafter began crafting up new episodes, many of which focused on Princess Bubblegum's recently restored Uncle Gumbald and his plan to conquer the Candy Kingdom.

The show's writers, producers, and cast members were under no delusion that *Adventure Time* would go on forever. With the epic reveals in *Stakes*, *Islands*, and *Elements*, many of the show's biggest mysteries were being answered, resulting in an increased discussion about wrapping the show up. As Olivia Olson (paraphrasing Adam Muto) put it: "The ending of the show was getting stretched and stretched and stretched out because of how softly they let us know. There were definitely talks for a long time of 'Okay, this might be the last season.'"[60] In fact, as work on Season 10 started, the writers and producers truly believed that the end was near: Cartoon Network had only ordered sixteen episodes, a drastic departure from previous years, in which as many as fifty-two episodes had been ordered.[61]

Nevertheless, the series cancellation in September of 2016 caught the show's crew members off guard.[62] According to Kent Osborne, the writers and producers were under the assumption that following the production of a truncated tenth season, Cartoon Network would order one final season (comprising twenty-six episodes) to wrap everything up. The writers had a number of story ideas they were interested in pursuing—some of which involved Sweet P, Susan

Strong, Finn's mother, and presumably, Fionna and Cake—and so as to segue into what they believed would be the show's swansong season, the writers tasked Tom Herpich with plotting out a four-part story that wove elements of the Uncle Gumbald storyline with new plot points that he had for a long while wanted to work into an *Adventure Time* story.[63] Alas, the "timing was no good," to quote Herpich,[64] and these plans were disrupted by Cartoon Network's decision to axe the program with only four episodes left to be written.[65]

The *Adventure Time* writers were suddenly left with the almost Herculean task of wrapping up the show's myriad plot threads in less than a half dozen episodes. As Adam Muto told the *Los Angeles Times*, "I freaked out a little because endings are so hard on TV shows. So it was like 'What is the perfect ending?'"[66] The first thing that they did was completely retool Herpich's epic season finale premise, keeping some of his ideas, but sadly jettisoning most of the more novel ones.[67] Thankfully, the impossible task of crafting the "perfect finale" was made easier by Cartoon Network, who gave the show's writers several additional months to hammer out the finale's plot points by pushing back the air date of the *Islands* miniseries.[68]

The series' writers eventually worked out a four-part finale entitled "Come Along with Me" (after the show's ending theme) that focused on Princess Bubblegum and her Uncle Gumbald preparing for battle, only to be interrupted by the arrival of the malevolent entity GOLB. When it came time to actually storyboard this behemoth of an episode, all hands were called on deck: Tom Herpich and Steve Wolfhard were tasked with setting up the Great Gum War plot as well as introducing viewers to the far future of Ooo; Seo Kim and Somvilay Xayaphone focused most of their attention on an extended nightmare sequence; Hanna K. Nyström and Aleks Sennwald storyboarded the arrival of GOLB and the reactions of the various characters (including a long-waited "Bubbline" smooch); and Sam Alden and Graham Falk brought it all home by not only writing a satisfying ending to the episode, but also working on an elaborate montage showing what becomes of the show's many characters.

A Critical Look at the Final Season

Adventure Time's tenth and final season debuted with four new episodes on September 17, 2017, the first of which was "The Wild Hunt." For the remainder of the season, Cartoon Network continued to make use of this one-day "bomb" method, releasing additional quartets of episodes on both December 17, 2017, and March 18, 2018, respectively. It is not exactly clear why the network eschewed the tried-and-true method of debuting new episodes once every week. Regardless, this peculiar treatment of the series led many fans to speculate that the network was trying to burn off the few episodes that remained of its former flagship series.

Season 10 is, for certain fans, something of a disappointment after the creative heights of Seasons 7–9. This is largely due to its abbreviated nature, which precluded the sort of closure a final season of twenty-six or so episodes may have offered. This issue is perhaps most noticeable when one looks at the development of the season's antagonists—Uncle Gumbald and the Green Knight—neither of whom receive the screen time needed to feel like genuine "big bads."

The cramped feel of the season was further exacerbated by the decision to produce several OK-to-middling "bad dad" episodes (viz., "Son of Rap Bear," "Marcy & Hunson," "Jake the Starchild"). These episodes make up a disproportionate chunk of the season, and while they have their moments, they mostly retread ideas that had been better explored in previous episodes.

But as "disappointing" as the season may be, it still has its moments. Aleks Sennwald and Hanna K. Nyström's "Bonnibel Bubblegum," for instance, is a triumph of an episode, covering huge swatches of Bubblegum's backstory while also explaining Uncle Gumbald's origin; what is more, the episodes does this in only eleven minutes. In lesser hands, "Bonnibel Bubblegum" could have felt like a hack job, but Sennwald and Nyström make it work.

Another of the season's stronger installments, Sennwald and Nyström's "The First Investigation," sees Finn and Jake investigate the "haunted" offices of their deceased parents, Joshua and Margaret. Radiating with a Henry James-esque spookiness that culminates in a fun sci-fi twist, the episode provides Finn and Jake with the chance to show their late parents how much they love them.

And we cannot forget about the charming entry that is "Blenanas," the show's final one-off storyboarded by Sam Alden and former creative director Patrick McHale. In this episode, Finn and Ice King join forces to revive the comedy magazine *Ble*, despite their both being terrible at comedy. While the setup might seem a bit banal for a "best of" list, the fact that it sees Finn amicably team up with a character who had once been the series' primary villain shows how much *Adventure Time* had evolved over its ten seasons.

When all the episodes are taken together, it is inarguable that Season 10 works, but it is nevertheless a somewhat frustrating experience—a string of decent-to-great episodes retroactively blemished by the thoughts of what could have been.

THE FUN WILL NEVER END: "COME ALONG WITH ME" AND BEYOND

In late August 2018—just days before the premiere of the series finale—dozens of laudatory pieces celebrating the series as a whole were run in high-profile publications like the *Los Angeles Times*, *Entertainment Weekly*, and the *New York Times*. Online, fans were understandably bittersweet in their postings to social media: many were delighted that their beloved show was getting a proper conclusion, while at the same time bemoaning that *Adventure Time* would soon pass into the annals of television history. For others, the finale represented a sort of homecoming. As was discussed earlier, during the height of the show's experimentation (c. Season 6), many fans had jumped off the *Adventure Time* bandwagon as their tastes and the show's tone began to diverge. Some of these former fans, curious as to what would become of Finn and Jake, resolved to return one final time to watch the epic conclusion to the series. All of this interest meant that *Adventure Time* message boards—many of which had seen a decrease in traffic ever since the show began to wane in popularity around 2015—lit up with activity as fans began to excitedly speculate. For the briefest of moments, it was like the glory days of 2013, when *Adventure Time* was the talk of the Internet.

On September 3, 2018, *Adventure Time*'s four-part finale, "Come Along with Me" was broadcast to almost a million domestic fans, many of whom were watching with bated breath. Detailing the resolution of the great "Gum War" between Princess Bubblegum and her Uncle Gumbald before morphing into a battle against the cosmic chaos deity GOLB, "Come Along with Me" is a tour de force of storytelling, replete with touching character moments, wacky dialog, and inspired design choices. Television critics for the most part gushed about the finale, and the majority of fans were happy with how things turned out for our heroes.

Now it must be admitted that "Come Along with Me" is not a perfect episode of television—the anticlimactic resolution to the Gum War is disappointing, and the episode's lengthy nightmare sequences mess with its pacing—but *Adventure Time* never pretended to be a perfect show. Instead, as Eric Kohn argues, it often "embraced [a] messy aesthetic" so as to convey "the complicated nature of the human experience,"[69] and this attitude is clearly on display in "Come Along with Me." The finale is a heartfelt mix of (sometimes contradictory!) emotions, which are presented in a way that, while not flawless, is definitely sincere. All things considered, "Come Along with Me" is a fitting end to *Adventure Time*'s run.

After the airing of the finale, members of the *Adventure Time* fandom mourned their loss for several months before eventually carrying on with their lives. Such is the natural order of a beloved TV series. But in our age of reboots, revivals, and reinterpretations, many suspected that *Adventure Time* was unlikely to remain forever in its television grave; perhaps this sentiment was expressed most famously by Tom Kenny, who sometime after the final episode was recorded, told Kent Osborne: "Just this week, I'm doing voice work on *Teenage Mutant Ninja Turtles*, *Powerpuff Girls* and *Samurai Jack*"—all of which were shows that had been canceled and then brought back sometime later—"This isn't the end of anything."[70]

Kenny's words proved prescient. In late 2018, fans learned that Adam Muto was beginning work on a mysterious new project for Cartoon Network. Then, on July 24, 2019, the animation industry insider Steve Hulett let slip on his personal website that Cartoon Network Studios was working on a special— codenamed "Rumble Jaw"—that was supposedly "based on the characters from *Adventure Time*."[71] It was not exactly clear what this meant (Was this special a spin-off of the original series? Or was it more of a reinterpretation, à la the 2014 CGI *Powerpuff Girls* sequel?), which led to fan speculation. Who would it star? What would it be about? Was Pendleton Ward involved? Was this Adam Muto's new project? What is up with that name? The questions continued to build.

In the weeks that followed Hulett's leak, the online *Adventure Time* fandom began tracking down the tiniest of digital clues. The fans eventually concluded that this mysterious "Rumble Jaw" was likely a one-hour *Adventure Time* special. The promise of a new Finn and Jake adventure was enticing and soon the fandom began to bubble with excitement. But then, on October 23, 2019, Cartoon Network made an announcement that proved the fans wrong: "Rumble Jaw" was not the codename for a new *Adventure Time* episode—it was the codename for *four Adventure Time* episodes, collectively dubbed the *Distant Lands* specials. Each of these episodes was an hour long, and they were slated to debut exclusively on the HBO Max streaming service sometime starting in 2020. Needless to say, fans were floored by the news.

How did such a bounty of new content come to pass? As Adam Muto explained during a 2020 Comic-Con@Home virtual panel, the *Distant Lands* specials had their origin in a series of story ideas that the writers developed near the tail end of *Adventure Time*'s run:

> [The core of *Distant Lands* is] actually kind of an older idea.... Towards the end of the show, we had gotten our [final] season order, and we had had some success doing miniseries with the characters. So we pitched a few more miniseries ideas to kind of fill out the back-half of a longer season. One of those was [focused on] BMO and one of those was [focused on] Marceline and Bubblegum.[72]

In a Reddit AMA interview, Muto further explained: "At the time, the network was enthusiastic [about the miniseries ideas] but there wasn't really an appropriate venue or immediate desire to make more."[73]

The ideas were thus shelved until 2018,[74] when, for reasons unclear,[75] executives at some level of the WarnerMedia hierarchy decided to revive *Adventure*

Time as a series of specials, each of which would be released via the conglomerate's new HBO Max streaming service. Adam Muto was once again tapped to showrun these specials, and Hanna K. Nyström and Jack Pendarvis were brought on to help further develop the project as a whole. Production continued in secret for months (with the crew using the aforementioned codename "Rumble Jaw" to throw people off the scent) until the whole project was officially announced in October 2019.

On May 25, 2020, over six months following this grand reveal, the first *Distant Lands* special, "BMO" was released exclusively through HBO Max. This special, which functions as a prequel to the main series, follows the titular robot's adventure on a dying space station called the Drift. Over the course of this special, BMO befriends a rabbit-humanoid named Y5 and the two decide to take on Hugo, the exploitative Elon Musk-esque techno-billionaire who serves as the *de facto* leader of the Drift.

When asked at the 2021 *Adventure Time* Comic-Con virtual panel why the writers decided to focus the first special on BMO, Adam Muto reasoned:

> Part of it is that BMO is a very recognizable and cute character and that felt like an easy access point. And [his] being in it would make the episode feel younger kind of by default, just because BMO's perspective is a bit younger and more naive . . . And it [also] felt funny to throw a very young and old kind of character [like BMO] into a situation where he would probably do very poorly.[76]

Aside from a short coda, which establishes how Finn, Jake, and BMO were introduced to one another, "BMO" does not really tell us anything new about the eponymous character, making it feel at times superfluous. Nevertheless, it still manages to deliver a fun BMO-centric story that critiques social inequality and lifeboat ethics in one robotic swoop.

In contrast, the second of the *Distant Lands* specials, "Obsidian," is one of the most impactful, delving into the history of Marceline and Princess Bubblegum's complex relationship as well as the story of Marceline's mysterious mother, Elise. This special debuted on November 19, 2020 and follows Marceline and Bubblegum's quest to save the Glass Kingdom from a lava monster named Molto Larvo—all while dealing with the turbulence of their past. By exploring Marceline's childhood trauma, her and Bubblegum's romantic past, and their domestic life after "Come Along with Me," "Obsidian" highlights the characters' vulnerabilities while also emphasizing the healing power of their love—a love that is displayed (unlike in the original series) without ambiguities or euphemisms covering up its explicit queerness. "Obsidian" is further bolstered by the musical contributions of guest artists like Zuzu, HALF SHY, and Amanda Jones.

Neither overly maudlin nor saccharine, the music of "Obsidian" radiates with the powerful message that *amor vincit omnia*.

The penultimate *Distant Lands* special, "Together Again" (released on May 20, 2021), is perhaps the most ambitious of the four, as it follows Finn and Jake's "final adventure" in the afterlife. That's right: Finn and Jake are dead! At the 2021 Distant Lands Comic-Con panel, Muto explained how this shocking plot coalesced:

> As soon as we found out that we were getting specials, we wanted to see if there was an opportunity to do something with Finn and Jake ... [We said to ourselves] OK, we don't want to step on [the finale], but maybe if we just did a special focusing on their friendship [in a way that] we couldn't in the main series, that would also feel special and worth revisiting.[77]

So Muto and the writers decided to throw Finn and Jake into the hereafter! The "twist" reveals that "everyone is dead" could have easily felt tired or tacky in the hands of lesser writers, but the *Distant Lands* production crew takes the idea and artfully mixes it with the show's longstanding fascination with the cyclicality of existence. The result is a grand finale that sees Finn and Jake reincarnated together. The "open-ended finality" of the episode is ingenious, assuring the audience that while the story of the Finn and Jake that we know might be over, the story of their souls will never end.

Initially, the bosses at WarnerMedia had only ordered three *Distant Lands* specials, but at some point during production, the powers that be decided to extend this order by one. So the writers began to hammer out an episode focusing on a young Peppermint Butler and his adventures at wizard school. Peppermint Butler was a character on whom the writers had long wanted to focus, but for whom they could never develop a strong story idea. That rapidly changed following Peppermint Butler's accidental deaging in the penultimate main series episode "Gumbaldia," as Adam Muto explained in an interview:

> A lot of that came from just the opportunities that were opened up at the end of the series because where we left Peppermint Butler ... he was kind of restarting. ... [We wondered if we] could we tell a story with this ... closer-to-a-ten-year-old character? We [also] hadn't gone to wizard city a whole lot; we just [got] a couple episodes [set there], so [this special] was a chance to explore the lore of that place and to see more of it.[78]

The result was "Wizard City," a murder mystery set on the campus of the previously unmentioned "WizArts" that debuted on September 2, 2021. Fans of the Harry Potter novels and Julia Potts's *Summer Camp Island* will likely enjoy this special's spoofing of the "magical boarding school" trope, but because it effectively stars a whole new cast of characters, "Wizard City" feels more like a backdoor pilot than anything else; further sinking the special is its climax, which sees a demon-possessed Peppermint Butler brutally murder a bevy of (to be fair, evil) wizards. It seems so strangely cynical in a way that *Adventure Time* never was. These defects do not ruin "Wizard City"—the whole thing still works out in the end—but they do prevent it from reaching the heights of "Obsidian" and "Together Again."

...

As I am finishing up this chapter, the *Adventure Time* fandom has been energized once again with the reveal that Adam Muto is developing for HBO Max an eight-episode miniseries focused on Fionna and Cake. Needless to say, the show's fans have been speculating wildly as to how this miniseries will unfold. While predicting the future is always something of a fool's errand, one thing seems certain. The adventure is far from over.

9.

GOOD JUBIES

The Guest-Animated Episodes

Across the show's ten-season run, the producers of *Adventure Time* were always looking for ways to push beyond the boundaries of animation. This was perhaps best exemplified by their willingness to hand over the reins of episode production to select guest animators once a season. Given total creative control, each of these directors put their own unique spin on the Land of Ooo, and needless to say, their episodes are, as a group, perhaps the show's most visually arresting. In this chapter, I will catalog each of these guest-directed episodes, detailing the fascinating stories about how each came to be.

"GUARDIANS OF SUNSHINE" (SEASON 2, EPISODE 16)

Adventure Time's first foray into the realm of guest animation occurred during production of the Season 2 episode "Guardians of Sunshine." In this episode, Finn and Jake are teleported inside BMO so that they can play the titular video game. Given this plot and its unique setting, the show's producers were hoping to animate portions of the episode in a way that emulated the 8-bit, low-resolution graphics of old-school Atari video games like *Adventure* (1980), *Pac-Man* (1982), and *Pitfall!* (1982). But despite their best efforts, the show's production crew and animation houses were having trouble getting the CGI aesthetic right.[1]

Jacky Ke Jiang learned of this struggle while auditing a class at CalArts taught by *Adventure Time*'s lead character designer Phil Rynda. An animator who had previously served as a lead modeler for the PlayStation 3 video game *Journey*, Jiang was interested in working on the series, so he mocked up a few short clips that illustrated his technical capabilities. Jiang subsequently showed the reel to the show's producers, and they were impressed enough with his ability to hire him on as a freelance artist. Jiang was initially slated to serve as a "style supervisor," who would merely oversee the animation process and provide input when necessary, but the producers soon decided that it would be far easier for him to animate the scenes himself.[2]

Jiang was given about a month to build digital models of the characters in the 3D modeling program Autodesk Maya and then render whole portions of the episode in the desired style. While Jiang followed Herpich and Castuera's storyboard closely in regard to the action, he was given substantial creative control over the character designs and the aesthetic look of the CGI elements. This led to him "add[ing] lots of animation . . . easter eggs in each scene."[3]

Jiang eschewed the use of a production manager or animation assistants, instead choosing to do all the work himself. He also worked from the first scene to the last scene instead of jumping around so that "each character's emotional arcs [would play out] in a nice orderly fashion, like actors performing . . . a live stage play."[4]

It took Jiang five weeks to animate his portion of the episode, with a few extra days budgeted for implementing feedback provided by the show's writers and producers. In the end, Jiang's scenes comprise five minutes and forty-five seconds of screen time—almost half the length of the full episode.[5]

"A GLITCH IS A GLITCH" (SEASON 5, EPISODE 15)

The second time *Adventure Time* dabbled in guest animation occurred during the writing of the show's fifth season, when the episode "A Glitch Is a Glitch" was storyboarded and animated by the experimental Irish filmmaker David OReilly. Prior to the production of this episode, OReilly was known for his avant garde animated films, which, in addition to their slick 3D aesthetic, are infamous for juxtaposing cute, charming characters with dark or taboo topics like sex, murder, suicide, drug use, or spousal abuse. Pendleton Ward had been a fan of OReilly's work for some time, and around 2010 (roughly during production of *Adventure Time*'s second season), he had actually reached out to OReilly to see if he was interested in contributing 3D animation to an episode. OReilly—who was a fan of Ward and several of the artists working on the show—was indeed interested, but his responsibilities at the time (namely, his work on the film *The External World*) precluded a collaboration from happening. A few years later, OReilly emigrated from Europe to Los Angeles, where he ran into Ward. Ward once again extended to OReilly an invitation to work on an episode, and this time OReilly accepted.[6]

Inspired by his past experiences with glitch art, and "want[ing] a narrative idea to justify [his episode] being in 3D,"[7] OReilly developed a story in which Finn and Jake attempt to stop a computer virus that has been programmed

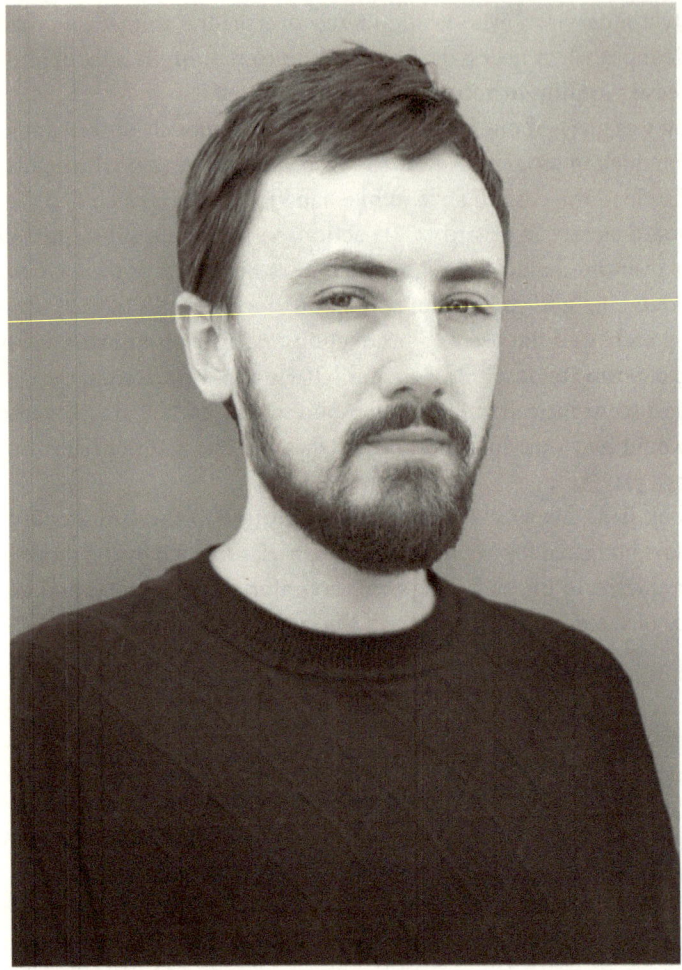

"A Glitch Is a Glitch" was the brain-child of datamoshing wizard David OReilly. Photo courtesy of David OReilly.

by Ice King to delete everyone—sans himself and Princess Bubblegum—from existence. To simulate the virus taking its toll on reality, the animation in "A Glitch Is a Glitch" starts off smooth and on-model, before devolving into bursts of random pixels, streaks of misaligned animation, compression artifacts, and heavy sound distortion. To simulate the near-complete breakdown of reality, OReilly also made liberal use of a technique known as "datamoshing," which is the "distortion of [an] image, audio, or video, generated by an application of data compression that causes a diminishing of quality."[8] In an interview with Rhizome, OReilly admitted: "In general, doing stylistic glitch is easy compared to doing good character animation. Mixing the two gets very tricky though."[9]

Some of OReilly's initial jokes were too risqué (or, as Ward put it, "too funny"), forcing him to excise or rewrite certain sequences. Preserving his unique artistic voice while also avoiding content to which the network might object was often a stressful balancing act. This was a particular challenge when it came time to craft a scene in which Finn and Jake receive a disturbing video via email that makes them feel physically ill. In an interview with game designer and academic Colleen Macklin, OReilly later said, "You got to [think like a] lawyer. What . . . can you show a kid [on television that] still make[s] them throw up?"[10] Using obscene shock sites like goatse.cx, LemonParty.com, and TubGirl as inspiration, OReilly eventually animated a short video of a young woman eating her hair (which, while gross, is nowhere near as offensive as the aforementioned sites).[11]

A different scene, featuring Princess Bubblegum kissing her hand, caused an issue with the censors at Cartoon Network for a reason OReilly did not understand. In his interview with Macklin, the artist explained:

> There was a scene . . . where Bubblegum was kissing her hand . . . [Cartoon Network] said she is not allowed to moan when she kisses; she can only make [light] kiss sounds but she's not allowed to [make passionate kiss sounds] . . . so I had to go into a waveform editor and cut out moans for that version. I was like, "What do you think? Do you think hearing a moan is going to make some kid . . . shoot up a school or something?" There was no logic there.[12]

Later in 2020, OReilly expressed his irritation at this sort of network-mandated censorship, telling me: "Some things [in the episode] were cut back, or edited out without my input. . . . It was extremely frustrating. When you reach the edges like that you realize you're actually working in a very conservative environment pretending to not be."[13] OReilly's (mis)treatment at the hands of the network left a decidedly sour taste in his mouth, and in an email, he told me that "the experience was so awful that [he] will never work with them again."[14]

When it came time to score the episode, OReilly reached out to Bram Meindersma, a sound editor and composer who had contributed the music to *The External World*. OReilly had also wanted to craft a new intro for the show and have his friend Steven Ellison, better known by his stage name Flying Lotus, provide the music, but due to budgetary and time constraints, this did not come to pass; instead, Flying Lotus contributed the song "About that Time," which plays over the episode's ending credits.[14] A hyperbolic chiptune track—replete with sporadic, glitchy chirps and a fuzzy synth bass—"About that Time" is a perfect finish to a truly madcap episode.

"A Glitch Is a Glitch" took most of 2012[15] to produce and was (appropriately) released on April 1, 2013. Upon its debut, the episode immediately garnered praise from those in both the animation and game design industries. Fans of *Adventure Time* were a bit more divided, with some being put off by the episode's writing and its distinct animation style. (This later led OReilly to joke in an interview with Macklin that his episode is "probably one of the most hated . . . by the most hardcore fans" of *Adventure Time*.[16]) Other fans celebrated the entry's inventiveness and OReilly's unique take on the universe.

"JAMES BAXTER THE HORSE" (SEASON 5, EPISODE 19) AND "HORSE AND BALL" (SEASON 8, EPISODE 18)

Around the time that OReilly was working on "A Glitch Is a Glitch," the show was busy collaborating with another guest animator: James Baxter. While his name might not be a household one to the average Joe or Josephine out there, in the world of animation, Baxter's name is legendary, and for good reason. Baxter is a gifted character animator and an industry veteran who has worked on dozens of features such as *The Little Mermaid* (1989), *Beauty and the Beast* (1991), *The Hunchback of Notre Dame* (1996), and *Spirit: Stallion of the Cimarron* (2002). And what *Adventure Time* episode was Baxter asked to work on? Why a jaunty installment entitled "James Baxter the Horse" of course! What is more, the producers also hired Baxter to voice the eponymous character, who, as his epithet suggests, is a horse that brays its own name in a comically posh accent while rolling around on a beach ball.

Often cited by fans as one of the show's funniest episodes, "James Baxter the Horse" has its origins in something relatively mundane: a university lecture. In the early-to-mid 2000s, when Ward was still a student at CalArts, one of the school's professors invited Baxter to deliver a guest talk, in which he explained his unique take on the fundamentals of character animation. Hoping to demonstrate by doing rather than simply by saying, Baxter reached out to the audience and asked for a concept that he could animate before their very eyes. As Baxter put it:

> I usually ask for suggestions from the students of what they would like me to animate for them, so they can see the thought process. At that lecture someone yelled out, "Do a horse balancing on a ball!" . . . I guess as a goof, knowing that might be a little tricky for a quick demo. I remember asking for something a little simpler, please.[17]

It just so happened that Ward was a student in that class, and the idea of a large, awkward horse trying to delicately balance on a beach ball of all things "stuck with [him]."[18]

Years later, when he was busy working on *Adventure Time*, Ward received a call from none other than James Baxter himself. According to the animator:

> I . . . told [Ward] how much I liked *Adventure Time*, and I . . . told him that if he ever needed me to do anything to give me a call. I guess he heard me because later he asked me to meet him at a tiny sandwich place that was on Flower St. and Sonora in Burbank. . . . There, he pitched me the idea for the character and he gave me a quick sketch of James Baxter the Horse. I said, "Yes, absolutely I would love to animate and voice that for you, that sounds amazing."[19]

Most of "James Baxter the Horse" was animated in South Korea, but the scenes featuring Baxter's character were penciled by the animator himself at his home studio in California:[20]

> I saw the storyboard, and they gave me a printed copy of it, as well as some exposure sheets for the shots that the horse was in. I spent a little time working out some different cycles that I could move between, James balancing in place, James turning in a circle, etc. I was trying to do cycles that could be reused over and over in different shots to save on work. It was all animated on paper and all the clean up drawings were done by my wife Kendra. . . . I guess it took us about a month or six weeks, but I was only working on it evenings and weekends. . . .
>
> I was given a lot of freedom. I just had that one sketch that Pen had drawn, but he had suggested that I give it a more flowing mane and tail. I remember sending a drawing of mine back to the team at Cartoon Network so that they could do a color model for him. As far as key poses went, I just had the boards to go from, which were clear but not super detailed, so I had a lot of freedom to make up the animation as long as I stayed true to the staging and to the length of the shots. By the time I got the exposure sheets, the dialogue tracks had already been written on them, which is common practice, so I could animate to the sound.[21]

Speaking of sound, Baxter was also hired on to voice his equine counterpart:

> The voice is me just trying to be horsey, and a little posh, and British. [James Baxter the Horse] only ever says his name (no trouble remembering the lines!), so it's a little hard to really define an accent, but I'm British so that's where I went. My natural accent hovers somewhere over the mid-Atlantic since I've lived in the US for over thirty years. The whinny is just me trying not to cough as I'm trying to make horsey

noises! Voice acting is not my talent, but it was a lot of fun, mostly because it was so surreal just saying my own name in different ways for half an hour! They were very nice and patient with me.[22]

Once Baxter's animation and vocal takes were completed, the domestic material was composited with the animation produced overseas, forming a final, cohesive whole (that said, the scenes that Baxter animated are readily apparent, due to their distinctive dynamism).

"James Baxter the Horse" debuted on May 6, 2013, and became almost an instant fan favorite, thanks largely to its eccentric comedy and its fluid animation. In fact, so popular was the episode that James Baxter (the animator) would later contribute animation to a sequel, the eighth-season episode "Horse and Ball," which aired on January 26, 2017. This follow-up not only sees the return of Baxter's equine character, but it also provides him with a surprisingly touching backstory while commenting on the importance of creative self-satisfaction. When asked about working on the sequel, Baxter told me:

> I was very pleased to get another chance to do more James Baxter, but there was more footage of him in the second episode, and I had less time to do it. That meant that I only animated a few shots of him in that episode, not all of him as I had done in the first one. I would have loved to have done it all, but there just wasn't time. But it was just as fun to animate, especially falling off the ball and the dance at the end.[23]

As with the earlier "James Baxter the Horse," "Horse and Ball" is a stand-out episode due to its distinctive animation, courtesy of an industry veteran. And what does Baxter himself think of all this? "I've got to say, it's very gratifying having this amazing alter-ego [in *Adventure Time*]," he explained in an interview, "especially since he's such a benevolent character. I'm glad Pen didn't decide to make him a jerk! All he does is ride around cheering people up, how amazing is that!"[24]

"FOOD CHAIN" (SEASON 6, EPISODE 7)

When news broke in early 2014 that *Adventure Time* would begin airing its sixth season in the spring, information also leaked that the season would include a new guest-directed episode. The fandom reacted largely with delight and immediately began to speculate as to whom the guest director was and what unique style the episode would be in.

It turned out that the episode in question was named "Food Chain," and it was directed by Japanese animation whiz Masaaki Yuasa.

"Food Chain" was written, storyboarded, and directed by lauded Japanese animator Masaaki Yuasa. Photo courtesy of Dick Thomas Johnson via CC Attribution 2.0 Generic (CC BY 2.0) license, https://flic.kr/p/NJVyLn.

According to TV Tropes, Yuasa is "one of the most prominent figures of alternative anime" because "his visual style is immediately recognizable as it significantly differs from standard anime iconography."[25] Indeed, Yuasa is set apart from other anime directors due to his fondness for vibrantly wild animation, a fluid approach to character designs, and a willingness to make use of new styles in service of a story. This approach to animation gives all of Yuasa's productions a distinctive flair. Standouts of Yuasa's oeuvre include the feature film *Mind Game* (2004) and the television series *Ping Pong* (2014).

Yuasa's collaboration with the *Adventure Time* producers happened accidentally. According to *Adventure Time* character designer Michelle Xin, sometime in 2013, Yuasa hosted a Google Hangout session to talk directly to his fans about his film *Kick-Heart*, which had recently been funded via a ground-breaking Kickstarter campaign. Xin was one of the fans taking part in this Hangout, and during the session, she mentioned that she was a character designer on *Adventure Time*. Much to her amazement, Yuasa mentioned that he was a fan of the program,[26] having long been captivated by the show's unique character designs and its overall "adventurous feeling."[27] Soon after this chance online encounter, Yuasa and his longtime associate Eunyoung Choi contacted Cartoon Network, inquiring about a possible collaboration. According to Choi, "We reach[ed out] and asked . . . 'What if Yuasa worked [on] one episode?' And [the producers of *Adventure Time*] talked and said, 'Yeah, why not!'"[28]

Cartoon Network itself was understandably a bit leery about green lighting the project, given that it was not yet attached to an established animation studio, and to ameliorate these concerns, Yuasa and Choi cofounded Science SARU[29] studio.[30] Yuasa focused his attention on "director things" like storyboarding, whereas Choi took on a "producer-like" role by handling the day-to-day operations of the studio; she also served as the episode's creative director.[31]

After brainstorming for a bit, Yuasa visited the Cartoon Network offices in 2013 to show the producers his preliminary ideas, most of which were focused on exploring the food chain.[32] Yuasa also brought with him large watercolor illustrations that he had mocked up to better showcase his budding ideas. The show's producers, delighted to be working with an artist of Yuasa's caliber, were receptive to his ideas, and while they helped him refine the story to a certain degree, Yuasa was given almost total creative control over the direction of the episode's plot and its final look.[33] (According to Choi, the only major change that Cartoon Network asked of Yuasa was to alter the color of brown candy in one scene so that it looked less like feces.[34])

Dialogue for the episode was recorded in California, and to ensure it matched his vision, Yuasa, with the help of a personal translator, coached the actors himself.[35] According to voice actress Minty Lewis (perhaps better known for her role as a storyboard artist on the Cartoon Network series *Regular Show*), who voiced Erin the worm:

> The recording session was pretty bananas, too. There were multiple steps of communication between Masaaki Yuasa, his translator, the director, and the actors, so it was kind of like playing [a game of] telephone so I had no idea if what I was delivering was what was desired.[36]

After the voice sessions were finished, Cartoon Network gave Science SARU all the recorded takes so that the studio could choose the ones that captured the right "mood."[37] When it came time to work on the episode's soundtrack,

Yuasa solicited the help of Soichi Terada, a chiptune composer known in the video game community for his scores to the *Ape Escape* series.

While most episodes of *Adventure Time* were animated on paper and then scanned into a computer, Yuasa's studio animated the entirety of "Food Chain" using the now-deprecated Adobe Flash software. In the 2000s and 2010s, it was fairly common to hear Flash disparaged in some artistic circles as a poor animation platform,[38] but when one looks at Yuasa's work, it becomes apparent that under the right direction, Flash can be used to create breathtaking pieces of media. Cartoon Brew writer Amid Amidi expressed such a sentiment in a 2015 analysis of Yuasa and Science SARU's animation setup, writing, "The studio appears to have a flexible production pipeline that allows them to come up with inventive solutions for each shot. Some of their scenes are puppeted, while others use full animation techniques. All of it looks good."[39]

"Food Chain" aired on June 12, 2014, and in no time became a darling among media critics, with Oliver Sava of the *A.V. Club* calling the work "an engaging sensory experience" and "an unforgettable installment of this series."[40] In early 2015, the episode was nominated for a coveted Annie Award, and later that summer the parade of accolades continued when the episode was screened at the prestigious Annecy International Animated Film Festival in Annecy, France.

"Food Chain" would not be the last time the *Adventure Time* producers worked with Science SARU, as the studio would also animate the unique title sequences for the *Stakes* (2015), *Islands* (2017), and *Elements* (2017) miniseries, as well as the show's series finale, "Come Along with Me" (2018). Unlike with "Food Chain," each of these intros was done in the show's established aesthetic, and the ease with which they blend into *Adventure Time*'s regular style is further testament to Yuasa and Science SARU's animation prowess.

"WATER PARK PRANK" (SEASON 6, EPISODE 37)

Near the end of Season 6, production on another guest-directed installment began. This episode, which would eventually be named "Water Park Prank," was written and directed by David Ferguson, who prior to working on the show had been one of Pendleton Ward's favorite experimental animators. Ferguson was based out of Glasgow, Scotland, and known mostly for what reporter Amid Amidi called "fun . . . naive animation [that is often paired with a] borderline incomprehensible Scottish accent."[41]

Interestingly, "Water Park Prank" was not originally slated to be a full episode. Back in 2014, Ferguson had been contacted by *Adventure Time*'s production company, Frederator, and asked if he was interested in animating their online short *Spacebear*—a job that he accepted. Soon after work on *Spacebear* wrapped, Ferguson received an email "out of the blue" from Cartoon Network, inquiring if he would be interested in working on an *Adventure Time* project. The network explained that it was wanting a five-minute "miniepisode" that would be released exclusively online; according to Ferguson, the intention was for this short to come across as a "bootleg version of *Adventure Time*," with Ferguson himself voicing all the characters.[42] Ferguson agreed to the project and worked diligently to mock up a storyboard—featuring Finn and Jake going to a water park and running into Ice King—which was approved by the show's producers and the network.

Cartoon Network eventually decided that it was no longer interested in producing web shorts, and when the news reached Ferguson, he was understandably worried that all his hard work was about to go up in a puff of smoke. Luckily, Adam Muto intervened, petitioning the network to salvage Ferguson's creation. Ferguson had to endure "two or three nervous weeks" before he learned the fate of the project: his five-minute short had been upgraded to an eleven-minute episode that would air on Cartoon Network proper.[43]

But this presented additional challenges. Because Ferguson's storyboard had been intended for a five-minute short, the upgrade forced him to "build [more scenes] around [his initial story] rather than try to redo the whole lot," as the latter option would have not only forced him to bin what he had already created, but would have also eaten up far too much time. In an interview with podcaster Terry Anderson, Ferguson explained:

> Even though I'm working in a simple style, I'm still usually on a tight deadline, and that's why [producers or networks] might pick me to do something, because you can get away with something in that style . . . this looked like it was going to be something that I could actually spend quality time [on] and maybe put a bit more animation in, but then it became twice as long, and . . . it wasn't twice as long for the deadline. So I thought, "Right, I'm going to have to work even harder than I've ever worked before for something that is a huge thing."[44]

Despite the extreme time crunch, Ferguson managed to expand his episode by drafting up a B story about "Princess B'Onangutan" and Finn being infected by parasitic "Daddy Sad Heads."

Ferguson animated the entire episode in Glasgow, never actually journeying to California while the episode was in production. He did, however, listen in on the voice recordings that took place in Burbank via phone—an opportunity that he called "a surreal experience."[45]

"Water Park Prank" aired on May 21, 2015, near the tail-end of Season 6. At the time, the fan reaction to the episode was largely negative, with Ferguson telling Anderson in late 2015, "If you go looking for it, [the reception] is not great. [Many fans called it] the worst episode of *Adventure Time* ever, but some of the actual artists . . . seem to like it, so I think that's the main thing—as long as you haven't ruined it for the people who work on it."[46]

A few years later, while working on the *Distant Lands* special "BMO," Adam Muto again reached out to Ferguson, asking if he would be interested in animating a short piece of exposition projected by the knock-off MO robot CGO. Muto was drawn back to Ferguson after seeing his glitchy, 2D "soaked leggings glitch 2017" video. "It felt like something similar would work for CGO's display since she's supposed to be a bit less high tech than BMO," Muto explained in a 2020 Reddit AMA.[47] While fans reacted negatively to "Water Park Prank," the reception to Ferguson's work in "BMO" was largely positive. Why the change of heart? It is hard to speak for the entire fandom, but I would argue it is because "BMO" used Ferguson's unique style in such a way that worked with, rather than against, the show's normal style.

"BAD JUBIES" (SEASON 7, EPISODE 20)

In early 2014—when production of *Adventure Time*'s seventh season began—the show's producers let slip that they were interested in working with a stop-motion animator for their next guest directed episode. Soon thereafter, Kirsten Lepore—an experimental artist who had developed a distinct style while studying at both the Maryland Institute College of Art (MICA) and CalArts—came onto the show's radar after releasing her breathtaking stop-motion short *Move Mountain*. The film, which details the story of a young girl who climbs a volatile mountain to locate an herbal balsam, is a work of pure creativity, whose lamination of whimsy and emotion recalls the established aesthetic of *Adventure Time*; the show's producers seemed to have thought the same thing,[48] for soon after Lepore released her short film, Adam Muto contacted the animator and asked if she would be interested in working on a special stop-motion episode of the show. Lepore responded with a resounding "Yes!" In an interview, she explained:

> [After receiving the offer] I was very giddy with excitement—both because it was an opportunity to work on a phenomenal show and also because it felt like a huge stepping stone in my career. At the time, I had actually only seen a few scattered episodes of *Adventure Time* (my husband was actually a big fan and had shown me a few over the years)

so I was also pondering all the TV I would have to watch to catch up on the entire series and educate myself on the [*Adventure Time*] world!

Initially I pretty much had free rein to explore whatever concepts I wanted for the episode. Adam Muto even encouraged me to consider an episode without any of the traditional characters, as well. I brainstormed for a bit and came up with around 8 or 10 potential loose concepts that I pitched to the writers in a meeting and they gave their input. I feel like that was the only point at which I learned which things I should probably steer away from. For example, one of my main ideas was to have the characters transition from 2D to 3D (stop-motion) and be aware that their physicality had changed and comment on it. Pen Ward had big reservations about that one since he felt that we should treat the characters like they were real, rather than cartoons, which was understandable. . . . [In terms of characters,] I knew we had to have a limited cast due to the budget . . . so I picked my favorites that I thought would play off each other well for the story. For a while I really wanted to include Marceline, because I love her, but [I] couldn't find the right spot for her in this particular story . . . In the end I wound up coming up with an entirely new idea . . . that was then approved by Kent Osborne.[49]

The story that Osborne and the producers approved—detailing Finn, Jake, BMO, and Lumpy Space Princess's attempt to build a bunker and avoid the destruction wrought by a tempestuous storm (played by veteran voice actor Kevin Michael Richardson)—took Lepore roughly "five or six months" to draft up, block out, and storyboard.[50] This task was quite difficult, with Lepore confessing, "Storyboarding is exhausting and super hard . . . you basically have to do the job of the writer, cinematographer, editor, designer, and fine draftsman all in one."[51]

After several revisions, Lepore's storyboard was accepted, but just as she began to shift from writing to directing, a crisis of sorts occurred: Cartoon Network trimmed the episode's initial budget down substantially. As can be guessed, this put a major strain on Lepore and the show's producers, forcing them to find a stop-motion production house that would agree to work with a smaller-than-usual budget. Eventually, Bix Pix Entertainment stepped up to the plate, promising to work with the show and problem-solve any budgetary issues that might arise.[52] (Lepore later called Kelly Bixler, the production house's owner, a "saint," as she was kind enough to "gift" Lepore an additional week to work on miscellaneous aspects of production.[53])

The stop-motion animating finally began in November of 2014: five weeks were dedicated to creating a set and the necessary puppets, and another five weeks were dedicated to the actual animation. To help develop the set pieces,

"Bad Jubies" was written and directed by stop-motion animator Kirsten Lepore, who secured the position after the *Adventure Time* producers saw her short film, *Move Mountain*. Photo courtesy of Joyce Kim and Kirsten Lepore.

backdrops, and props, Lepore reached out to the talented Jason Kolowski, who among other things, rigged up a stop-motion stream and designed a replica of Finn and Jake's tree fort.[54]

Stop-motion animation itself is extremely time-consuming, with sometimes only a few seconds of workable footage being produced in a single day. To make the daunting task of animating eleven minutes of footage more manageable, the animation was divided among four stages, each of which was helmed by a lead animator.[55] While this sped up filming by a factor of four, it did necessitate the creation of four puppets for each of the main characters.[56]

After the bulk of the animation was finished, Lepore spent February through April 2015 working from her house on the "finishing touches," such as special effects and postproduction cleanup. Lepore also took this time to work on a stop-motion intro for the episode, which she animated entirely by herself.

When it came time to hire a composer for the episode, Lepore sought out the talents of Richard Vreeland, an experimental electronic musician known professionally as "Disasterpeace." While Vreeland arguably gained prominence after scoring the indie horror film *It Follows* (2014), it was actually his score to the 2012 video game *Fez* that prompted Lepore to contact him. She explained:

> Towards the end of the animation process, I was obsessively listening to the Fez soundtrack, and it dawned on me one day that Rich would probably be the perfect person to score the episode. It felt like a total pipe dream, and I never expected him to say yes, but I just reached out to him by email and he agreed . . . I love the score he created so much and was incredibly happy to have him on the project.[57]

In an interview, Disasterpeace told me that the feeling was mutual, and he was "ecstatic to be involved" with the episode.[58] When I inquired as to what the scoring process was like, the artist responded:

> The score took a few months [to compose]. It was a bit of an on-and-off again process, in part due to the creation schedule for the episode. . . . I worked entirely remotely, and Kirsten was my only point of contact. It can be quite nice to hash out music for something like this with just a single person. Sometimes when there are a lot of voices involved it can make the process more difficult. . . . Kirsten gave me lots of freedom to explore different ideas and as she has a musical background herself, we got to collaborate a bit on some different sections of the episode, specifically Jake's nature rapping segment. . . . I wanted to try sourcing sample material from friends for the score, and so what you hear in the end result is a collection of sources, various people playing instruments, answering machines, Gameboys, and other eclectic sounds which helped to create the sound of the episode.[59]

"Bad Jubies" aired on January 4, 2016 (many months after it was completed), and like the guest episodes of the past, it was immediately lauded by fans and critics alike. In fact, so positive was the reaction that the episode later netted both an Emmy Award for Outstanding Individual Achievement in Animation and an Annie Award for Best Animated TV/Broadcast Production for a Children's Audience. It is not hard to see why the episode was showered with these accolades: "Bad Jubies" is a sprightly excursion that successfully transposes the show's *je ne sais quoi* into a three-dimensional environment.

"BEYOND THE GROTTO" (SEASON 8, EPISODE 3) AND "KETCHUP" (SEASON 9, EPISODE 11)

During the middle of 2015, the *Adventure Time* writers developed an episode entitled "Beyond the Grotto," in which Finn, Jake, and their pet "sea lard" get trapped in an odd parallel dimension. Storyboarded by *Adventure Time* veterans Seo Kim and Somvilay Xayaphone, the middle portion of this episode features Finn and Jake interacting with bizzaro versions of Ooo's denizens and becoming increasingly disoriented as their minds are manipulated by hallucinatory "purple stuff." Given that "Beyond the Grotto" was ripe for trippy visuals, the show's producers thought it best to bring in a guest animator to make the episode stand out. It was in this way that the show came to work with Lindsay and Alex Small-Butera.

A husband-and-wife art duo, the Small-Buteras had met one another when they were students of animation at Massachusetts College of Art and Design (MassArt) in the late 2000s.[60] After graduation, they made a name for themselves online with their whimsical web series *Baman Piderman*. Around 2014, Cartoon Network contacted the duo, inquiring if they were interested in animating parts of the *Clarence* episode "Tuckered Boys," in which the main characters stay up all night and, in a sleep-deprived state, begin to wildly hallucinate. The Small-Buteras were fans of the show and naturally agreed to take part.[61]

One thing led to another, and soon the two were approached by *Adventure Time* showrunner Adam Muto, who asked if they were also interested in contributing animation to "Beyond the Grotto." Muto had long been an admirer of the Small-Buteras' work (in the past, he had even donated money to a *Baman Piderman* Kickstarter campaign), so he was eager to work with them.[62] The Small-Buteras were likewise excited by the opportunity and eagerly signed on.

According to Lindsay, Cartoon Network and the show's producers "trusted [them] to take care of the seven minutes of full animation" and gave them "incredible" creative control over the finished look of the episode.[63] "The only thing we couldn't alter," Lindsay revealed to me in an email, "was the dialogue, since it had already been recorded.... We received sketchy [story] boards and ended up redoing most of them, while using [the originals] for inspiration."[64]

The Small-Buteras animated the episode in Flash, but strived to make the animation feel both "other worldly" and as "'un-Flash' as possible."[65] In regard to the latter point, the two decided to use a line thickness recalling the distinctive

Alex (left) and Lindsay (right) Small-Butera at the 2018 Primetime Emmy Awards ceremony. For her work on "Ketchup," Lindsay won an Emmy for Outstanding Individual Achievement in Animation. Photo courtesy of Lindsay Small-Butera.

look of graphite. When it came to coloring in the individual cels, Lindsay explained online:

> I had [an] idea to do an offset printing style of color starting after Finn and Jake consume the purple stuff and start forgetting themselves. Before that point, they're colored how they normally would be in a traditional [*Adventure Time*] episode, but as they descend into an [out of body] experience, I thought it would be neat if the colors were literally out of body and slowly became more purple as the episode progressed.[66]

Lindsay and Alex worked on "Beyond the Grotto" for about three months.[67] The resulting episode, complete with wiggly lines and strong cel shading, is reminiscent of the "Squigglevision" programs developed in the 1990s and early 2000s by animation pioneer Tom Snyder, such as *Dr. Katz, Professional Therapist* and *Home Movies*. And of course, it also echoes the off-beat quirkiness that made so many fall in love with *Baman Piderman* in the first place.

Around mid- to late 2016, the producers of *Adventure Time* once again reached out to the Small-Buteras and asked if they could contribute animation for the episode "Ketchup," in which Marceline and BMO entertain one another by taking turns telling allegorical stories.[68] On their personal Tumblr, the Small-Buteras wrote that it was "extremely flattering" that the *Adventure Time* producers enjoyed their work enough to ask for their return.[69] Unlike "Beyond the Grotto"—in which Lindsay and Alex worked in only one style—"Ketchup" vacillates between four dissimilar aesthetics: the show's regular look, a "tropical" but slightly "unsettling" look for BMO's first story, a "cinematic" look for Marceline's puppet show, and a "theater" look for BMO's tale of the "Moonlady."

Lindsay worked closely with Matt Cummings (a painter who had designed backgrounds for "Beyond the Grotto") to develop these individual styles, striving to make each distinct but not jarring.[70] Per Lindsay:

> I wanted each story to have its own unique feeling [and to] emotionally resonate in very specific ways. BMO's initial story is child-like and humorous, and clearly quite off from what had really "happened" during *Islands*. I wanted to have a kind of curious broken line style and bright color palette that sort of described a tutti fruiti child's brain . . . For this we also did everything on 1's, which means there's a full 24 frames drawn per second rather than a more traditional 12. It gives it a strange, dream-like effect, although [it] adds a lot of time and difficulty.
>
> Marceline's story is still a fairy tale, but I wanted to go a [cleaner], traditional route because she's a bit more mature than BMO, even though she's trying to explain a complicated situation to him through the lens of "puppets." Here we relied more heavily on slowly changing color[s] to describe a turn of events.
>
> For Moonlady, [we] wanted it to feel like a stage play, and contain a lot of theatrical flourish and decoration. It feels more like it's happening on a set, rather than in a real space, since BMO's story feels sort of like a legend or a fable. I had a lot of fun with the design of this one, particularly Moonlady herself.[71]

As with "Beyond the Grotto," the Small-Buteras worked tirelessly on "Ketchup," with production lasting for roughly five months.[72] The result was a poignant peek into Marceline's psyche, which later earned Lindsay an Emmy Award for Outstanding Short Form Animated Program in 2018.

"DIAMONDS AND LEMONS" (BONUS EPISODE)

While it was not strictly guest directed, the *Minecraft*-themed episode "Diamonds and Lemons"—produced after the finale of *Adventure Time* was written and storyboarded—is distinctive in terms of style. It thus seems appropriate to discuss the episode's creation in a section focused on aesthetically unique installments of *Adventure Time*.

Unlike many tie-ins that are the product of cold, capitalistic calculation, the idea for an *Adventure Time/Minecraft* crossover developed organically. It all started in early 2017, when Mojang, the Swedish video game development hub that had created the popular sandbox game *Minecraft*, began working with Cartoon Network to develop a "Mash-Up Pack" for *Minecraft* players, which painstakingly translated the Land of Ooo into a *Minecraft* context. This collaboration was fruitful, and soon there was talk of working on a special *Minecraft*-themed episode of *Adventure Time*. According to Lydia Winters, Mojang's chief storyteller:

> We heard from the Cartoon Network team that the *Adventure Time* team loved *Minecraft* and wanted to do an episode—this sounded great because we were all *Adventure Time* fans and thought a collab episode would be perfect. Also, we always want to partner with other people who love *Minecraft*, then we know the collaboration will be authentic.[73]

While many of the writers and designers on *Adventure Time* indeed were devoted fans of the game, Adam Muto admitted in an interview that his main reasons for wanting to work on the episode were "pretty selfish." "Production was wrapping on the final [*Adventure Time*] season," he explained, "and I wanted an excuse to work with the crew one more time."[74]

Regarding the aesthetic look for the episode, Mojang told the producers that while they wanted the episode to celebrate all things *Minecraft*, the final episode "shouldn't look exactly like the game."[75] Winters explained:

> Originally, [the *Adventure Time* producers] thought it would be fun to make it look like [the episode] was all done in *Minecraft*, but since we have lots of our community making *Minecraft* videos online, we thought the coolest thing would be to see *Minecraft* in the *Adventure Time* style. They took that idea and ran with it creating all of the sketches and ideas.[76]

To meld the cubic, 8-bit world of *Minecraft* with the aesthetic of Ooo, the show tried out a variety of artistic approaches before settling on a style proposed by

Joe Sparrow, a UK-based freelancer with whom Adam Muto had long wanted to collaborate.[77] On his personal Tumblr, Sparrow explained that "the idea was to get a look that felt recognisably *Minecraft*-y whilst also fitting in with the aesthetic of the show, which was a fun challenge."[78]

To generate the basic story, Muto and the other writers consulted with former art director Patrick McHale, storyboard artist/supervising director Cole Sanchez, and series creator Pendleton Ward—all of whom had passionately played *Minecraft* in the past. The episode was storyboarded and written by *Adventure Time* veteran Hanna K. Nyström in partnership with the tenth-season storyboard revisionist Anna Syvertsson (both of whom, coincidentally, hail from Sweden). The folks at Mojang, meanwhile, served in an advisory capacity, "reading the script, looking at storyboards, watching the animatics, and . . . giving approval along the way from the viewpoint of making sure that everything was correct for *Minecraft*."[79]

"Diamonds and Lemons," which aired on July 20, 2018, was very much a labor of love—the product of two groups of artists who were fans of one another. When I asked her what the folks at Mojang thought of the finished episode, Winters had nothing but positive things to say:

> We all loved the episode and did a viewing party in our office cinema. All the inside *Minecraft* jokes that the *Adventure Time* team added in made the episode great. The community reaction to the episode was amazing too, and it was a pairing that felt natural, and I see that being because the *Adventure Time* team loved *Minecraft*! It's still one of my favorite projects.[80]

For fans of the show who are otherwise unfamiliar with *Minecraft*, the plot to "Diamonds and Lemons" might not make total sense. Nevertheless, the writers did a solid job keeping the whole thing accessible, allowing those who somehow avoided *Minecraft* fever to still be in on the fun. And for the more seasoned *Minecraft* veterans, the writers also sprinkled in myriad easter eggs that allude to the game's mobs, its various mechanics, and the larger culture surrounding it. (The episode's biggest flaw is that we do not get to see Finn take on a Creeper.)

As the creative cherry on top of the whole thing, "Diamonds and Lemons" also features a special 8-bit style intro, animated by Ivan Dixon and Paul Robertson. In 2015, the two had produced a memorable pixel-version of *The Simpsons* intro which went viral and was later aired as part of the twenty-sixth-season episode "My Fare Lady."[81] The two later inquired as to whether the *Adventure Time* producers were interested in an intro of this sort, but according to Muto, the idea "didn't feel quite appropriate" until "Diamonds and

Lemons" entered into production.[82] As a celebration of all things 8-bit, Dixon and Robertson's intro nicely compliments the episode's video game theme.

POSTSCRIPT: THE GUEST EPISODES THAT COULD HAVE BEEN

At the 2018 San Diego Comic-Con, writers for the website Comics Beat asked showrunner Adam Muto if there were any other guest animators with whom he and producers had wanted to collaborate. Muto answered: "I really wanted to do a Don Hertzfeldt directed episode. We were even talking to him during the last season but it got canceled. So that was the one director I wanted to get in before the show ended."[83] Hertzfeldt is an experimental animator perhaps best known for his cult classic short film *Rejected* (2000), which satirizes television culture by taking the form of "rejected" wraparound segments and commercial shorts for the (fictitious) Family Learning Channel. Replete with eminently quotable dialogue, over-the-top cartoon violence, and clever metahumor about the medium of animation, the film has developed a fan following on video streaming sites such as YouTube.

In April 2021, I reached out to Hertzfeldt and asked him about this "lost episode." Hertzfeldt kindly responded to my inquiry, telling me:

> Things didn't get too far down the road. [Adam Muto and I] talked about possibly writing or directing an episode, or even just a sequence, and Adam and the *Adventure Time* gang sent me the box set of the show on DVD because I wasn't actually that familiar with it and wanted to binge as many episodes as I could. It was sort of just a general, wide open possibility with no parameters yet. This was back in 2016. My friend Julia Pott was working on the show at the time, too. Adam and I kept in touch but a few months later they announced the plug had been pulled, and they were winding the show down sooner than expected. It would have been fun though. It's a great show.[84]

Given the creative absurdity of Hertzfeldt's work, it is not hard to imagine how madcap his episode could have been.

...

In July 2021, a few months after I spoke with Hertzfeldt, the King of Ooo Tumblr account revealed that during the production of the show's sixth season, the producers of *Adventure Time* had also toyed with the idea of working on an episode with Basil Twist.[85] An experimental puppeteer who trained at the

École Supérieure Nationale des Arts de la Marionnette (ESNAM) in France, Twist is known for his 1998 *Symphonie Fantastique*, which is best described as an "abstract underwater puppet show" set to the music of Hector Berlioz's 1830 symphony of the same name.[86] In August 2021, I reached out to Twist and asked him about this abandoned collaboration, to which he responded:

> [Cartoon Network executive producer] Rob [Sorcher] was a friend of a friend. He became aware of my work . . . and he kept wanting to engage me in different [projects]. . . . He had this runaway success with *Adventure Time*[, and] he thought: "Hey, how cool. I just want to get Pendleton [Ward] and Basil in a room together and just see what happens!" He was just one of those kinds of producers, like, "This would be neat to get these two minds together!" . . .
>
> So, I came to the Cartoon Network headquarters and hung out with Pendleton and just kind of brainstormed for a while. . . . I didn't really know *Adventure Time*, either. I hardly knew anything about it. I had seen pictures of that guy with the backpack and his dog, [so] I had to learn a little bit about the cosmology of these characters. . . . [When I was brainstorming with Ward, we] were trying to imagine an episode that would be a combination of live action and animation like in *Space Jam* or *Who Framed Roger Rabbit*—that kind of real world with animated characters in it.
>
> The thing that I remember [we came up with] was a [scene that took place in] some sort of ritual space, with all the characters around. [There was] some sort of object in the center that was continually unpeeling like an onion, with lots of layers. And that would be an actual three-dimensional puppetry object . . . [The object] kept transforming and opening up and peeling away until at the center there was a beautiful jewel. That's what was at the heart of this psychedelic artichoke that everyone was around, worshipping.[87]

Ward and the writers would later refine this nugget of an idea, transforming it into a more structured story about Cinnamon Bun making a deal with Hunson Abadeer to sell the Oooian equivalent of girl scout cookies. Ward even thumbnailed a very rough cut of the episode, which would have framed the work as a performance in a theater full of animated spectators.[88]

Unfortunately, for reasons that are unclear, the episode never moved out of the development stage, and Twist told me that after the initial brainstorming sessions: "I got on a plane and left, and then I never heard anything else about it!"[89] Will the world ever get a glimpse of the psychedelic artichoke that Twist and Ward schemed up? Perhaps one day, but for right now, it remains only the ghost of an episode that could have been.

Part III

THE WIDER WORLD OF *ADVENTURE TIME*

Chapter 10.

THE INSTITUTE OF SO UND

The Music of *Adventure Time*

Any consideration of *Adventure Time*'s production would not be complete without a discussion of the show's music—an aesthetic element many would agree not only accents but also helps sell the show's zany energy. The first part of this present chapter discusses the importance of the composers who crafted *Adventure Time*'s chiptune score: Casey James Basichis and Tim Kiefer. The chapter comes to a close with an outline of the major musical numbers featured in the series, complete with production information and critical commentary.

THE COMPOSERS OF *ADVENTURE TIME*

Adventure Time's soundtrack was the product of two electro-wizards named Casey James Basichis and Tim Kiefer. Like Ward, both Basichis and Kiefer had attended CalArts in the early 2000s. Thanks to their shared interest in experimental music, Basichis and Kiefer became friends and often collaborated on idiosyncratic school projects.[1] Meanwhile, Basichis and Ward got to know one another thanks to a web comic and fortuitous living circumstances: "Pen and I haunted the same [CalArts] dormitory hall," Basichis explained via email. "I was stalking his web comic 'Bueno the Bear' and eventually, [I] awkwardly approached him to tell him I adored it."[2] This moment of sincere admiration led to collaborations between the two, which eventually grew to include Kiefer.

When the *Adventure Time* short was being written, Ward asked Basichis to compose the background music, and when Cartoon Network picked up the full series, Basichis was naturally hired as series composer.[3] During the early production of Season 1, Basichis worked on musical compositions by himself—a task he later described as "over the top [and] unnecessarily monastic"[4]—and so, to make the process less taxing, Basichis began reaching out to Kiefer for assistance.[5] "I . . . help[ed Basichis] out every now and then," Kiefer explained, "like recording weird vocal sounds for his 'Jiggler' score or making video game music for a BMO game in 'My Two Favorite People.'" Pretty soon I was arranging some of Casey's musical sketches ('The Witch's Garden,' 'Wizard')."[6] Roughly around the midpoint of Season 1, the producers decided to bring Kiefer on board as an additional composer, with his first episode being "When Wedding Bells Thaw." This was a wise choice because, as Kiefer noted, it ensured that "each episode got the musical TLC it deserved, despite the crazy TV deadlines."[7]

The soundtrack to *Adventure Time* can broadly be categorized as electronic dance music (EDM), but arguably this label collapses down the numerous dimensions that make Basichis and Kiefer's music so charming. According to Kiefer, during Season 1, he and Basichis worked together to figure out "*the sound*" of the show,[8] and while Pendleton Ward often had specific notes about the music he was envisioning in the final cut, he was also interested in letting the composers work their own magic; "We would be given a decent amount of direction," Kiefer clarified at a 2018 WonderCon Q&A session, "but . . . we were free to interpret . . . the simple direction from Pen [Ward]."[9] Basichis seconded this point, telling me: "Generally we were given an unreasonable amount of freedom and patience—Pen, Adam, and the rest are inscrutable angelic beings."[10] As one might imagine, this flexibility quickly led Basichis and Kiefer to experiment with other genres of music,[11] and by the time the first half of the series was finished, Kiefer noted, "every single episode [sounded] completely different."[12]

Despite both being electronic producers, Basichis and Kiefer approached composing from slightly different angles. For Basichis, the process involved both "intellectual" and "performative" phases. In a featurette included with the first-season DVD, Basichis explained the "intellectual" phase as follows: "I usually start[ed] by looking at the characters and the things that [were] specific to an episode, and [I tried] to find the real attitude of it, and how I could represent it musically."[13] When he entered into the "performative" phase of recording, Basichis was wont to employ the wonders of technology, either by creating computer programs that helped him dream up new melodies, or by assembling a "component orchestra" of mechanized instruments that "play[ed] differently than the way you expect them."[14] Basichis's experimentation later led him to describe his "more WTF soundtrack efforts" as being "littered with prototypes on the way to a new musical mathematics and cognition."[15]

Of the many songs in his *Adventure Time* oeuvre, perhaps Basichis's more famous background tracks are those that he composed for the show during its first season, such as the energetic party song that both opens "The Enchiridion!" and sets the mood of the series; the score to "The Jiggler," bursting forth with computer-modulated yelps and warbles; or the purposefully-vapid hyperpop that saturates "Trouble in Lumpy Space" (the sound of which Basichis later likened to "shoplifting from Claire's").[16] Basichis also produced the music for many of the show's diegetic character songs, including the positively infectious "House Hunting Song" from the first-season episode "Evicted!" and Marceline's famous "Fry Song," first heard in the second-season premiere "It Came from the Nightosphere."

Kiefer too was enthralled with electronic music, but he also had a special affinity for more traditional instruments. In fact, many of the characters' iconic instruments (e.g., Finn's flute, Jake's viola, Marceline's bass) were played by Kiefer.[17] In terms of distinct genres, Kiefer cites Chicago juke, footwork,[18] and skweee[19] as his main influences.[20] Some of Kiefer's best-known background tracks include "Manlorette Party" (the smooth dance track that plays over a montage in the first-season episode "When Wedding Bells Thaw"), "Chip Dip Triple Flips Are Hip" (the chiptune magnum opus that opens Season 2's "Power Animal" with an 8-bit bang), and the high-spirited rave music heard in the second-season episode "Belly of the Beast."[21] Kiefer also produced the instrumentals for the Rebecca Sugar classics "Time Adventure" and "Everything Stays" (the latter of which has, as of September 2019, almost a third of a million streams on Kiefer's personal Soundcloud).[22]

When Basichis and Kiefer first started to work on the series, the network provided them with about two weeks per episode; this gave them plenty of time to think of fun background tunes. But as the show got more and more popular, the network began to tighten their deadlines, and by the time the show reached the apex of popularity during its fifth season, the composers only had four to five days to work on an episode. The drastic reduction in turnaround time caused both musicians stress, but interestingly, Kiefer did note that it sometimes led him to experience a "weird Nirvana": "I think the crazy intensity of the network TV deadlines . . . helped . . . [I would say to myself] 'Stop thinking. . . . You can't overthink this. There isn't enough time. Just go with your instinct. Just kind of be reflexive about it.'"[23] In a 2019 retrospective about the series, Kiefer once again alluded to this state of mind, arguing that while stressful, the crunch nevertheless allowed him to tap into the "creative sublime."[24]

Throughout the show's run, Basichis and Kiefer split composing duties between themselves, each working on their own set of episodes.[25] This division of labor was not because Basichis and Kiefer disliked collaborating with one another—in fact, the latter noted that "collaborations are a sweet . . . thing"— but rather due to simple logistics. For the first five or so years of the show's production, Basichis was based out of Los Angeles, whereas Kiefer lived in San Francisco. Due to this distance, working one-on-one together was a difficult endeavor to coordinate.[26] And even after he moved to Los Angeles during the show's later seasons, Kiefer told me that collaborations were still hard to coordinate because of the show's "prohibitive production schedule."[27] When a fortuitous collaboration did come to pass, it "look[ed] something like sending recordings and parts back and forth, infusing them with [the composer's] zany styles each session."[28]

...

For years, *Adventure Time* fans clamored for a full soundtrack, containing the electronic bleeps and bloops that gave each episode so much atmosphere. While Spacelab9 released a smattering of limited-run vinyl records (including a Marceline minialbum in 2015, followed by a partial soundtrack in 2016), these releases compiled only the songs sung by the show's characters and excluded Basichis and Kiefer's distinctive score. These releases also used audio ripped directly from the episodes, meaning that the sound quality was shoddy. For a time, it seemed that fans would never get what they wanted, but in November 2018, Cartoon Network finally acquiesced to the audiophiles by releasing a double-LP soundtrack of the *Adventure Time* finale "Come Along with Me"; this was followed up by the release of *The Complete Series Soundtrack* box set in July of 2019. According to Kiefer (who also coproduced the set):

> Working on the [project] the past year and change was pretty surreal. For one, Casey and I were the last holdouts of the [*Adventure Time* production] staff, digging through nine years of memories by ourselves! A weird experience while the rest of the world was moving on from the series ending. Olivia Olson [also] joined in the fun to resurrect "Everything Stays"—we made an extended version exclusive to the Complete Series soundtrack. Breathing new life into a dozen or so old tracks—"A Blip and a Bubble," "Party with the Chief," "Thinking of Butts," [etc.]—was my fondest memory of the process.[29]

Spread across four LPs, a ten-inch vinyl record, a CD, and a cassette tape, *The Complete Series Soundtrack* is truly a mammoth set that assembles more than two hundred of the songs featured in the series, including not only the ones sung by characters but also selections from Basichis and Kiefer's eclectic body of work.

A RUNDOWN OF MAJOR SONGS

Adventure Time is not a musical in the conventional sense, but many of its episodes feature a song or two. These numbers are often used by characters to deliver exposition or express complex emotions, and thanks to their usual catchiness, many have endeared themselves to the show's viewers. In this section, I will take the reader on a musical journey by considering *Adventure Time*'s merriest and most memorable melodies. (Note that due to the number of songs featured in the series, not every ditty will be discussed—only those about which much has been said by fans, critics, or the show's crew).

The Theme Song (Also Known as "Adventure Time")

Before Pendleton Ward had even storyboarded the initial "Adventure Time" pilot, he had already written a theme song. In fact, during the initial pitch to Frederator, Ward even brought in a guitar and played the tune to Fred Seibert and the other big-wigs at the production studio.[30] Seibert was completely caught off guard by this ad hoc concert ("In ten thousand pitches that we've gotten, nobody's been in there [with a] guitar," Seibert remarked in a 2013 interview),[31] and Ward's novel song-and-pitch tactic was one of the main reasons that Frederator eventually took such a chance on him.

When it came time to record the track for the pilot, Ward asked a friend of his to play the guitar. During a 2014 interview, Ward revealed that just before recording the guitar part, his friend "farted really loud."[32] Ward caught this errant sound effect during the mixing process, but instead of excising it from the final cut, he actually *increased* the volume because he thought it was funny.[33] (In many ways, this creative decision portended the comedic direction the show would eventually take.)

A few years later, when Ward was working on the official series opening, he recorded a temporary version of the theme "on a bad microphone in the animatics bay" so that he could turn in a rough demo of the intro's animation for network approval. In a hurry, Ward sang this version in falsetto and accompanied himself on a ukulele, resulting in the track's eccentric (and now-iconic) sound. Ward had intended to go back and record a slicker version once the opening was OK'ed, but when he tried redoing the song, he found himself drawn to the almost antifolk nature of the original.[34] After Casey James Basichis added a few additional effects, the temp track then became the final version.

"Baby" (from "The Jiggler," Season 1, Episode 6)

While not the first song composed for the series (that honor belongs to "House Hunting Song," which is discussed next), "Baby" was the first that aired. A euphoric mélange of auto-tuned vocals, pitch-bent instrumentation, and blippy samples, the track is in many ways epitomic of the show's wild and wacky first season.

In an email chat, Basichis explained to me that the song's soundscape was the result of extreme musical experimentation: "'Baby' and [the score to] 'The

Jiggler' were the most counter intuitive compositions on the show. I made a giant sample library of vocal fry, breakup and other raspy artifacty effects, and [then I] autotuned them into modem speak. They were then mapped to a keyboard, controlled by dynamic—so what sample was triggered depended on hitting the key at an exact hardness. Why? Reply hazy, try again."[35]

"House Hunting Song" (from "Evicted!" Season 1, Episode 12)

"House Hunting Song" was the first song written after *Adventure Time* entered into production. In the original storyboard for the episode "Evicted!" the notes specify that the scenes of Finn and Jake looking for a new home were to be accompanied by simple "montage music."[36] At some point during the episode's development, Pendleton Ward decided to replace the generic music cue with an actual song, so he whipped up some lyrics that bemoan Finn and Jake's plight. Ward recorded an a capella version of this tune before handing it over to then-creative director Patrick McHale, who trussed it up by composing a guitar part.

McHale then recorded a simple demo of his arrangement, accompanying himself on the acoustic guitar. According to McHale, this version of the song was intended to sound "lame," like a "singer songwriter guy who's into Dave Matthews but isn't nearly as talented."[37] Ward enjoyed McHale's take and petitioned for his version to be used in the episode, but McHale vetoed this decision. Ward subsequently recorded two versions: The first was a soft, restrained interpretation of the song, which Ward described as sounding "nice [and] normal."[38] The second version (which Ward sardonically referred to as the "fake energy guy" version, and which Basichis called "stentorian") was loud and punchier,[39] having been directly inspired by the sound of the pop punk band blink-182.[40] Ward favored the former, but on behest of executive producer Derek Drymon, the latter was selected.[41]

The song then passed to Basichis, who spruced up the instrumentation by adding undulating drums, warm strings, and bursts of zigzagging synthesizers. According to the composer, the final version was produced in a hurry: "I think this was also one of the first nightmare crunches where I was still composing the song while [the producers were] mixing the episode wondering where the music was. The first of many falling skies."[42]

Luckily, all this hard work paid off, and "House Hunting Song" is arguably one of the season's strongest musical interludes. For that reason, it might come as a shock to learn that after working on the song, Ward expressed an interest in scaling back the show's use of music, arguing that *Adventure Time* should live up to its name by "go[ing] in a more straight adventure way."[43] ("I'm not really into musicals," Ward later explained at the Toronto Comic Arts Festival in 2012. "It sorta works against the sincerity when you're singing your every word, right?"[44]) But Ward's crew did not share this sentiment, and as Adam Muto related in a 2018 interview, they eventually "talk[ed] him into" embracing the potential of numbers like "House Hunting Song"—a decision that in time led music to become an integral part of the series' DNA.[45]

"Fry Song" (from "It Came from the Nightosphere" Season 2, Episode 1)

Out of all of *Adventure Time*'s many songwriters, perhaps none is more respected than Rebecca Sugar, who first gained attention for her songwriting abilities after storyboarding the second-season premiere, "It Came from the Nightosphere." In this episode, Marceline the Vampire Queen sings the "Fry Song" about the strained relationship with her father.

Sugar's initial draft of the song featured lyrics that focused overtly on Marceline's father being a neglectful parent.[46] Ward was concerned that this version would be a bit too serious for the show, so he worked closely with Sugar to make the track a bit funnier. The two latched onto a lyric in Sugar's original version—in which Marceline bemoans how her father does not "take [her] to get a burger and shake-y [sic]"—and rewrote the entire song to be about a past incident in which Marceline's father ravenously ate some of her french fries without asking.[47] While these lyrics are superficially silly, deep down they explicate the sort of relationship that Marceline and her father share: he is a deadbeat dad who is worried only about himself, and Marceline feels that while he might say he loves her, his (in)actions speak louder than words.

At the storyboard pitch for "It Came from the Nightosphere," surrounded by crew members and many of the higher-ups at Cartoon Network, Sugar nervously performed the song on ukulele; Ward assisted by beatboxing. From Sugar's perspective, it was almost certainly an excruciating experience, but when the pitch was over, everyone in attendance agreed that her song was a winner. (Eric Homan of Frederator even "apologized" on the company's official blog for not filming the pitch because he had found it so enjoyable.)[48]

"Fry Song" was then handed off to Casey James Basichis, who whipped up a bass-heavy instrumental; when discussing with me his thoughts on the track, Basichis lauded Olivia Olson's "unbelievably good" vocal performance and poetically referred to the finished track as "daddy issues in an atmosphere of delicious golden crisp."[49]

After "It Came from the Nightosphere" debuted on October 11, 2010, "Fry Song" became a massive hit with the show's fanbase—as evidenced by the dozens upon dozens of amateur covers uploaded onto video streaming sites like YouTube.[50] It seems that something about the song's absurd premise and Olivia Olson's vocal performance resonated strongly with viewers, and even today, when asked what song has stuck with them after all these years, many fans will enthusiastically reply, "Fry Song"!

"Susan Strong" (from "Susan Strong" Season 2, Episode 18)

The melody of this song derives from an earlier tune that a young Pendleton Ward had composed when he was a student at CalArts. Written when Ward and his friends were enthralled with an online game called *Blade Mistress*, the tune was an ode to Ward's character, Susan Strong. Years later, when Ward and the *Adventure Time* crew were working on "Susan Strong," Ward decided to recycle his old ditty for the episode. But because Ward's original was "not at all safe for television," storyboard artist Rebecca Sugar was tasked with rewriting the lyrics.[51] The end result is therefore a complex amalgamation of both Ward and Sugar's playful creativity.

"Friends Don't Fight" (from "Video Makers" Season 2, Episode 23)

"Video Makers" is a somewhat overlooked second-season episode that follows Finn and Jake as they attempt to film a home movie. Alas, because the brothers cannot decide on what type of movie they would like to make, they end up in a bitter feud. Poor BMO, caught in the middle of this fight, decides to whip up "Friends Don't Fight," an electro-ditty about the importance of friendship and forgiveness. Written by storyboard revisionist David C. Smith, the song was a last-minute addition to the episode, replacing a red-carpet reveal party that storyboard artist Kent Osborne felt was too unrealistic (even for Ooo).[52]

Recording "Friends Don't Fight" was a new experience for Niki Yang (the voice of BMO), who told me via email:

> Singing at karaokes is my only public singing experience.... The friendship song was my very first song ever recorded in my life. Of course, I was deadly nervous and [it] took a while to finish recording the song. But Pen wasn't happy about the result. [So he] called me later that day, and we went to the composer's house and had to re-record.[53]

Production issues aside, the end result is a pleasant juxtaposition of acoustic guitar and robotic autotune, which manages to tug at the listener's heart strings while also worming its way into their ear.

"Puncha Yo Buns" (from "Memory of a Memory" Season 3, Episode 3)

After being swept into Finn's mind in the third-season episode "Memory of a Memory," Marceline witnesses a baby version of Finn singing a ridiculous song entitled "Puncha Yo Buns" to himself in a mirror. This tune was not originally in the episode's storyboard, and in its stead, writer and artist Tom Herpich had drafted up a quick scene featuring Finn talking to himself in the mirror "like a cool guy," à la Robert De Niro in the film *Taxi Driver* (1976).[54] During the revision phase, Herpich replaced this scene with a slightly more absurd sequence in which Joshua the Dog consoles Finn after he threw up a love letter meant for his elementary school teacher.[55] When the storyboard got to Ward, he "vetoed" these ideas, replacing the scene with the "Puncha Yo Buns" song. To ramp up the scene's humor, character designer and storyboard revisionist Natasha Allegri then posed out Finn's distinctive dance.[56]

As with other quick and inane *Adventure Time* ditties, "Puncha Yo Buns" has endeared itself to members of the *Adventure Time* fanbase, and when attending conventions, voice actor Jeremy Shada is often begged by fans to perform the song. The song has also permeated the larger pop culture landscape, and in 2018 the Chicago-based rapper Tobi Lou recorded a song entitled "Buff Baby" that prominently samples the lyrics to "Puncha Yo Buns." The music video for this track also features a re-creation of the "Puncha Yo Buns" scene from "Memory of a Memory," with Tobi Lou standing in for Finn.[57]

"Oh, Fionna" (from "Fionna and Cake" Season 3, Episode 9)

"Oh Fionna"—written by storyboard artist Rebecca Sugar—was intended to serve as an "homage" to classic "cartoon musical" moments,[58] drawing specific inspiration from Alan Menken and Tim Rice's "A Whole New World" (a song written for an iconic scene in the 1992 animated Disney film *Aladdin*, in which the title character and his love interest, Princess Jasmine, ride the world over on a magic carpet). "Oh Fionna" was sung by Neil Patrick Harris (the voice of Prince Gumball) and Madeleine Martin (the voice of Fionna), the former of whom Sugar lauded on her personal Tumblr, writing that he "sang the song beautifully."[59]

Songs from "What Was Missing" (Season 3, Episode 10)

"What Was Missing" focused on Finn, Jake, Princess Bubblegum, BMO, and Marceline's collective attempt to track down a thieving "door lord" who has stolen some of their beloved possessions. Unfortunately, this being seals himself behind an imposing door that will only open to the sound of a "genuine band." Marceline, a natural musician, decides to take a stab at the challenge, so she launches into a bass-heavy song entitled "I'm Just Your Problem." In the series, Marceline rarely opens up to others, but "I'm Just Your Problem" is deeply personal, suggesting that at some unspecified point in the past, Princess Bubblegum and Marceline may have been in a romantic relationship—a relationship that evidently turned sour. Due to its explosively truthful lyrics, the song not only shocks Marceline's friends, but it also nearly opens up the doorlord's hidey-hole.

"I'm Just Your Problem" was written by storyboard artist Rebecca Sugar, who based the song on a strangely emotional experience she had had with a former roommate sometime after graduating from SVA: Sugar and this acquaintance did not get along very well, but despite the increasing acrimony between the two, Sugar desperately wanted to make up and become friends. In the DVD commentary for "What Was Missing," Sugar explained: "I found myself just trying and trying to make it up to her, while at the same time being angrier and angrier that I was stuck with this person who was just making me crazy."[60] It was while attempting to empathize with Marceline that Sugar remembered these paradoxical feelings, eventually channeling them into the final song.

The sort of honesty featured in "I'm Just Your Problem" is later reprised in Finn's song, "Best Friends in the World." At this point in the episode, Marceline, Bubblegum, and Jake have gotten mad at one another and are storming off. Finn does not want to see his three best friends leave, so he begins to air his worries via song; he admits that while he cares deeply about them, he worries that they do not reciprocate this feeling. When Finn starts singing, Marceline, Bubblegum, and Jake are all taken aback by Finn's earnestness, but then one by one they join in on the song, implicitly conveying that they consider Finn their friend, too. The door then responds to this genuineness, opening with a spectacular flash of light!

The song is quite sweet on its own, but its affective nature is amplified when one realizes that Rebecca Sugar wrote the song to channel emotions and doubts that she herself felt about the *Adventure Time* crew:

> This song is really about how I felt working on the show. This was . . . my first job and I just loved everyone I was working with so much—especially . . . [my storyboarding partner] Adam [Muto]—and it was really strange for me because everyone was a cartoonist and [it] meant so much to be friends with all these amazing cartoonists. But it was work, too. So I just couldn't tell where work ended and friendship began. I felt like Finn is in a similar position.[61]

Fans and critics are wont to consider "I'm Just Your Problem" and "Best Friends in the World" as being among the show's strongest songs, and it seems almost certain that this love is in part due to their raw, emotional honesty.

"Journal Song" (from "Marceline's Closet" Season 3, Episode 21)

"Marceline's Closet" features a scene in which Finn and Jake accidentally eavesdrop on Marceline while she records a private song about her "life and stuff."[62] Entitled "Journal Song," this nonconventional ditty was written by storyboard artist Jesse Moynihan, who drew inspiration from the eccentricity of twentieth-century classical music. On his website, Moynihan expounded:

> The demo I submitted to Tim [Kiefer] and Casey [James Basichis] was loosely inspired by the composer Louis Andreissen's piece "De Staat," except dumbed down. Basically I tried to write the kind of thing that I've never heard on TV before. I kept a consistent beat throughout, but didn't let the melody repeat in any way. It's sort of a wandering, linear phrase with all the instruments reinforcing Olivia Olson's vocals in unison.[63]

Soon after he sent his demo recording to the show's composers, Moynihan grew nervous that his song was *too* weird for television, so as an emergency back-up, he crafted a version that he defined as "straight pop." However, Moynihan's worries were for naught, for Ward quite liked the original,[64] comparing it positively to the music of David Byrne.[65] (Moynihan's band Make a Rising later used elements of the pop version in some of their subsequent songs.)[66]

When it came time to record dialog for the episode, Moynihan attended the session so that he could provide musical direction to Olivia Olson, given his song's peculiar nature.[67] During a Twitch livestream celebrating the tenth anniversary of the show in April 2020, Olson was asked her thoughts about the song; she responded that it was "really, really tough to" record because the timing was "all over the place," and she kept "want[ing] to do it so straight and melodic."[68] Nevertheless, she called it an "interesting challenge"[69] and has cited it as one of the songs that "sticks the most in [her] mind."[70]

"Dream of Love" (from "Dream of Love" Season 4, Episode 4)

"Dream of Love"—the fourth-season episode based almost entirely on Tree Trunks and Mr. Pig's obnoxious public displays of affection—is something of a divisive topic within the fandom, with many viewers being put off by the episode's excessive on-screen smooching. That said, the episode's eponymous song, in which Tree Trunks and Mr. Pig express their love for one another, is well-regarded for its catchy hook and its affecting energy.

The song was written by storyline writer Patrick McHale because "nobody else wanted to write" it.[71] McHale initially intended the song to sound like a heartbreaking duet between country music legend Dolly Parton and rock singer Meat Loaf—a sort of "I Will Always Love You" by way of "I'd Do Anything for Love (But I Won't Do That)." In a 2014 interview, however, McHale admitted: "In my head, when it [was] Dolly Parton and Meat Loaf singing, [I thought], '[My demo is] gonna sound really good!' [But then I realized] 'Ah . . . I don't sound as good as Dolly Parton and Meat Loaf.'"[72] While McHale's reservations about his singing ability might *technically* be true (I mean, how many of us can say we sound just like Dolly Parton?), the catchiness of "Dream of Love" proves that he does at the very least have solid songwriting chops.

"Political Rap" (from "Daddy's Little Monster" Season 4, Episode 6)

In the fourth-season episode "Daddy's Little Monster," Finn and Jake find themselves faced with one of their greatest challenges yet: waiting in a Kafkaesque line to talk to the leader of the Nightosphere. To disrupt hell's agonizing bureaucracy, Finn and Jake decide to free-style a rap, thereby instigating a demon uprising.

The soundscape of "Political Rap" is relatively sparse, featuring Jeremy Shada shouting random sociopolitical buzzwords (e.g., "Ride bikes!" "Science!") over John DiMaggio's beatboxing, with the joke being that despite the song's randomness, it nevertheless inspires a "woke" demon insurrection. The track was written by Jesse Moynihan, who on his website explained: "It was [inspired by] a running joke my friends and I had for a while, where we'd try to freestyle terrible political raps at each other."[73]

While a product of Moynihan, the track appears in an episode storyboarded by Rebecca Sugar and Cole Sanchez. This is because the track was intended to appear in the preceding episode "Return to the Nightosphere" but was cut for time. Sugar, however, liked the rap so much that she petitioned for it to be included in her episode.[74]

"Let Me Show You Something Special"
(from "Princess Monster Wife" Season 4, Episode 9)

"Let Me Show You Something Special" was written by former creative director and then-storyline writer Patrick McHale for use in the episode "Princess Monster Wife." Because the song is featured in an extended sequence in which Ice King and his bride survey the entirety of the Ice Kingdom, McHale—like

Rebecca Sugar when she worked on "Oh Fionna"—drew inspiration from Alan Menken and Tim Rice's song "A Whole New World" from *Aladdin*.[75] Originally, it was planned for the song to be a duet between Ice King and Princess Monster Wife (voiced in tandem by Steve Little, Hynden Walch, and Pendleton Ward), but according to McHale:

> I recorded [my demo track] with Ice King's voice and then a [placeholder] falsetto voice for the female part. I think [the producers] just thought it was funny [to] instead have the Ice King pull out a tape recorder and play his own voice in falsetto, 'cuz it feels crazier for the Ice King to be, like, "I already created this whole song. We don't have to sing it together! I can do it!"[76]

The result is an ostentatious ballad that is equal parts romantic and disquieting (which, for Ice King, is par for the course).

"Bacon Pancakes" (from "Burning Low" Season 4, Episode 16)

Written by Rebecca Sugar, "Bacon Pancakes" is a relatively short ditty, clocking in at only twelve seconds, and it was written to bring a little bit of levity to an otherwise serious episode. When pitching the song to the show's producers, Sugar was self-conscious that the fandom would be repulsed by its "hacky" nature.[77] Much to Sugar's surprise, however, the song became immensely popular with *Adventure Time* fans, and for a time, it seemed as if no comic convention at which Sugar appeared was complete without a performance of the song.

"Bacon Pancakes" even became an online meme in 2012 when a clever YouTuber remixed the track with Jay-Z and Alicia Keyes's 2009 hit single "Empire State of Mind." (It certainly did not hurt when actor Hugh Jackman uploaded a Dubsmash video of himself lip-syncing to the song in 2015.) Given that today, "Bacon Pancakes" is one of the most well-known and beloved songs from *Adventure Time*, it is somewhat ironic that Sugar was so worried it would be poorly received.

Songs from "I Remember You" (Season 4, Episode 25)

"I Remember You"—the Rebecca Sugar and Cole Sanchez–penned masterpiece that broke millions of hearts—is a veritable musical, featuring a grand total of four songs, including a Gunter-centric parody of Marceline's "Fry Song," a frivolous ode called "Oh, Bubblegum" that extols the titular princess, the song "Nuts" which details Marceline's mixed feelings about Ice King, and "Remember You," a musical climax that finally begins to unpack the heart-breaking relationship shared by Ice King and Marceline. Rebecca Sugar, when discussing the tragic lyrics to "Remember You," explained:

> It's a note that Ice King as Simon was writing to Marceline but she never got it.... We'd always wanted to do a Marceline/Ice King musical [episode], and Pen really took it to that emotional place. He was the one who came up with the idea of them having this shared history, and then we really took it from there.... Somehow music can transcend memory loss and so can your feelings about people. Like it's just there—he's really jamming on the drums and he's really proud of this thing that they're making even though he doesn't really know what it is. And that she gets to have all the catharsis of knowing that he really cares about her in the form of this song. And seeing him happy is simultaneously the best and the worst part.[78]

With the exception of the "Fry Song" parody, all the songs in the episode prominently feature Sugar's very own omnichord (that is, a synthesized autoharp that can play major, minor, or seventh chords with the push of a button). The instrument that Sugar owned while working on the episode was old and a bit unreliable, and when she used it to pitch the episode's songs to the show's producers, the device began to lose power near the ending of "Remember You." As the instrument struggled to play, warbling eerily in and out of tune, the producers pointed out that the distorted notes nicely paralleled Ice King's mental degeneration. This "accident" was eventually replicated in the studio and worked into the episode's final score,[79] making the final mix all the sadder.

Songs from "Bad Little Boy" (Season 5, Episode 11)

A sequel to Season 3's "Fionna and Cake," "Bad Little Boy" is a fun fanfic excursion that features two catchy songs, both written by storyboard artist Rebecca Sugar. The first, entitled "Good Little Girl," is a relaxed doo-wop track, complete with a slick "Heart and Soul"-esque chord progression and prominent backup vocals. On her Tumblr account, Sugar explained that she and fellow storyboard artist Cole Sanchez were wanting "to do a gritty '50s bad boy story with Marshall Lee (a little *Dirty Dancing*, a little *Cry-Baby*) as opposed to [another] fairytale prince whirlwind adventure."[80]

The second song in the episode, the titular "Bad Little Boy," is a rap, delivered courtesy of Marshall Lee, Marceline's male counterpart, who is voiced by Donald Glover. In addition to his work as a stand-up comedian, actor, and writer, Glover also records hip hop and R&B music under the moniker "Childish Gambino." In a 2013 interview with the *San Antonio Express-News*, Pendleton

Ward expressed his excitement at getting the chance to work with Glover, saying: "Donald [has] . . . got awesome funny chops and singing chops and we spotlight all his chops in the episode. I was super stoked when he came in, and he's told me he's super stoked to have worked on [the episode], which makes me extra stoked."[81]

"Good Little Girl" and "Bad Little Boy" would be the last songs Sugar contributed to the show's fifth season, for following the production of the episode "Simon and Marcy," she departed from the *Adventure Time* crew to begin working on her own series, *Steven Universe*. While legions of *Adventure Time* fans cheered on Sugar's well-earned success, many also lamented the loss of a gifted songwriter. Although it is simplistic and a bit essentializing to say that Sugar had a musical *je ne sais quoi* not possessed by any other artist, this line of thinking nevertheless became a popular one among some groups of fans—especially those who posted to online message boards like 4chan or Reddit. A cursory browsing of these sites will turn up thread after thread in which fans bemoaned the "decline" of the show's music following Sugar's departure. While the premise of this cataclysmic opinion is questionable (given that it ignores the existence of post-Sugar classics like "Get over You" and "Food Chain"), it cannot be denied that the loss of Sugar was a definite blow to the series.

"Where Everybody Knows Your Name"
(from "Simon and Marcy" Season 5, Episode 14)

Season 5's heartbreaking masterpiece "Simon and Marcy" concludes with Simon Petrikov singing "Where Everybody Knows Your Name" in a desperate, and ultimately futile, attempt to fight the ice crown and retain his sanity. The use of this song—which had been written by Judy Hart Angelo and Gary Portnoy to serve as the theme song for the NBC sitcom *Cheers* (1982–93)—is notable, as it marks one of the few instances in which *Adventure Time* directly alludes to "real world" pop culture. But unlike other shows that use pop culture references as a lazy form of joke telling, *Adventure Time*'s use of "Where Everybody Knows Your Name" is not funny—in fact, it is heartbreakingly sad.

How did an eighties theme song make its way into a cartoon like *Adventure Time*? In a 2020 podcast interview with background designer Ghostshrimp, the show's writer and vocal director Kent Osborne claimed that he had originally pitched the idea as a joke, but Ward latched onto it, insisting that it be used.[82] A competing story, shared by Rebecca Sugar's father, Rob, on his YouTube channel, is that "Where Everybody Knows Your Name" was originally a placeholder that the show's producers eventually decided to use in the finished cut.[83] Regardless of which explanation is "correct," Adam Muto clarified that the song was selected because "it fit . . . and had the right emotional punch."[84] (Curiously, despite being born in 1962, Tom Kenny was not familiar with the *Cheers* theme when he went in to record "Simon & Marcy," and Olivia Olson had to queue up a YouTube video of the song so that he would know how it went.[85])

For a time, another song that was "in the running" for use in "Simon and Marcy" was "According to Our New Arrival" (also cowritten by Angelo and Portnoy), better known as the theme song to the ABC sitcom *Mr. Belvedere* (1985–90).[86] This track was later used in the *Stakes* episode "Everything Stays," during a scene in which Marceline befriends a tribe of humans by performing the song on her bass. In early February 2020, I reached out to Gary Portnoy and asked for his opinion on the use of his songs in the series, to which he responded:

> I had never heard of *Adventure Time* when they used "Where Everybody Knows Your Name." I watched ["Simon and Marcy"] and even though I had no understanding of the plot or the back story, I definitely connected with the nostalgic and poignant aspects of it. I read at the time that it was the first time they had used a "real world" song on the show. [Later, when] they used ["According to Our New Arrival" in *Stakes*], I was . . . flabbergasted. Why did they do it? There is no shortage of TV themes in the world. Why two of mine? Coincidence? I have no idea.[87]

"Get over You" (from "Love Games" Season 5, Episode 35)

"Love Games" was the first episode on which Andy Ristaino worked as a storyboard artist, and to mark the occasion, he decided to write a song for inclusion in the episode. Entitled "Get over You," the track is sung by Finn during a crooning competition in the titular Love Games. According to Ristaino:

> Cole Sanchez was my storyboarding partner at the time. We had storyboarded our first pass [of "Love Games"] and pitched it, but I hadn't written the song yet, so in our first pitch [the storyboard] had a section that said "insert heartfelt song here." After our first pitch was over, we sat in the pitch room and figured out a simple melody on a guitar that was just lying around the studio, and what the song was going to be about. I hashed out the lyrics over the evening.
>
> The song was about Finn pouring out his feelings about still being stuck on Flame Princess. You want songs like that to feel like they're coming from the heart, so I just pulled on past experiences of mine, being hung up on a girl that dumped me and how it felt. I ended up playing it for the writers and storyboarders when we did our second pitch for the episode. I was really happy with how it turned out.[88]

A soft, acoustic track focused largely on young love and the pain of a breakup, "Get over You" is touching, feeling in many ways like a spiritual cousin to the songs that Rebecca Sugar had previously written for the series.

"Hanging Out Forever" (from "We Fixed a Truck" Season 5, Episode 39)

While blocking out Season 5's "We Fixed a Truck," storyboard artist Andy Ristaino felt that the episode could use a short song. And thus he began writing "Hanging Out Forever," a song in which Banana Man waxes poetic about having friends. When he first sat down to write the track, Ristaino was wanting the final product to sound like "an early Beach Boys song."[89] However, after noodling on his guitar for a while, Ristaino scrapped this initial idea when he came up with a jangly riff to which he "was immediately able to conjure up lyrics."[90] These initial lyrics were serious, mixing in car- and truck-related metaphors to express how friendships are built and maintained. Ristaino's storyboard partner, Cole Sanchez, later helped him fine tune the lyrics and make them a bit sillier.[91]

"Hanging Out Forever" was sung by comedy legend "Weird Al" Yankovic, who is best known for his parodies of popular songs. In an interview, Ristaino told me:

> We added the song specifically because Al was the voice of Banana Man, and we wanted to have him sing in an episode. It was very fun to write ["Hanging Out Forever," which is] much more lighthearted and idiosyncratic than "Get over You." I am also a huge Weird Al fan so it was a big deal to not only write a song for Al to sing but get to watch him sing the song in person! Al was super kind, gracious, and professional. I had made a little demo as placeholder of the song for the episode's animatic. They sent Al a copy of it so he could familiarize himself with it before he came in to record. Al . . . came into the recording studio with sheet music he made of the melody! I still have it somewhere.[92]

"Young Lemonhope" (from "Lemonhope" Season 5, Episodes 50–51)

This song, softly sung by Princess Bubblegum, plays at the end of the fifth-season two-parter "Lemonhope" over a flashforward sequence depicting Ooo one thousand years after the time of Finn and Jake. The track's instrumentation is hauntingly sparse, and its lyrics, while happy on the surface, ring out in a somber, melancholic way. When combined with the visuals of a future Ooo, the song does a solid job reminding the viewer that death, loss, and decay are waiting for us all. "Young Lemonhope" was written by storyboard artist Tom

Herpich, and when I asked him what inspired the song, he told me it was supposed to sound like a "sweet lullaby"—a decision, he joked, that "was shaped . . . by [his] lack of any kind of musical aptitude."[93]

"Baby's Building a Tower into Space"
(from "The Tower" Season 6, Episode 4)

Thanks to the power granted to him by a spectral arm, Finn spends most of the sixth-season episode "The Tower" constructing the titular edifice in a hair-brained attempt to locate his space-faring father. To keep his focus during this arduous task, Finn repeatedly sings "Baby's Building a Tower into Space." A buoyant carousel of a song, "Baby's Building a Tower into Space" has a looping structure reminiscent of car trip favorites like "She'll Be Coming 'round the Mountain" or "99 Bottles of Beer." Lyrically, however, things are a bit darker, and "Baby's Building a Tower into Space" is nothing short of oedipal, revealing that Finn wants to find his father and rip his arm off. (Luckily, the situation is resolved before any blood is spilled.)

The lyrics to "Baby's Building a Tower into Space" were written by storyboard artist Steve Wolfhard and his wife, Leslie, the latter of whom also composed the song's music.[94]

"Lost in the Darkness" and "Oh So Beautiful"
(from "Breezy" Season 6, Episode 6)

The sixth-season episode "Breezy" is one of the show's more controversial installments, as it painfully documents Finn's descent into melancholy following the loss of his father and arm in the season premiere. When storyboard artist Jesse Moynihan was writing a few songs for the episode, he turned to his brother Justin for help. Justin had long been a student of piano music and ballet accompaniment, and Jesse figured that his brother's training would prove invaluable when it came time to channel the episode's mature emotions into song form. The result of this collaboration was two tracks—"Lost in the Darkness" and "Oh So Beautiful"—which serve as bookends, framing the start and culmination of Finn's depressive spell.

The songs were written in a time crunch, with Justin and Jesse given about two days to hammer out all the details. Justin focused on developing the tracks' melodies and piano arrangements, and the brothers worked on the lyrics together: "Jesse had the [storyboards] written with temp lyrics," Justin told me via email. "I pulled from them and created something new that expressed the same feelings."[95] Justin developed several drafts for each of the songs, which

Jesse reviewed and reworked if necessary. When the compositions were finalized, Justin handed them off to Casey James Basichis and Tim Kiefer, who "definitely punched [them] up nicely."[96]

In terms of style, Jesse wanted "Lost in the Darkness" and "Oh So Beautiful" to be "'romantic' in the Old World sense,"[97] citing as direct inspirations the French composer Claude Debussy's orchestra piece *Prélude à l'après-midi d'un faune* (*Prelude to the Afternoon of a Faun*), as well as Erich Wolfgang Korngold's intertextual score to the 1935 film adaptation of *A Midsummer Night's Dream* (1935).[98] In a 2014, Reddit AMA, Justin revealed that he was mainly inspired by the music from John Boorman's 1981 fantasy film *Excalibur*, musing: "Something about middle ages, opera, and starry nights made that work."[99] In a later 2020 interview, Justin also cited the influence of the German composer Richard Wagner,[100] perhaps best known for his operatic works like "Ritt der Walküren" ("Ride of the Valkyries").

"Food Chain" (from "Food Chain" Season 6, Episode 7)

The sixth-season episode "Food Chain"—storyboarded and directed by anime legend Yuasa Masaaki—comes to a close with a show-stopping tune, also entitled "Food Chain." In this song, Finn and Princess Bubblegum wax poetic about the wonders of this natural cycle in the style of a lively show tune. While the lyrics for this track were written by the staff at Science SARU (Yuasa's production company), the music was composed by Soichi Terada.[101] A 1988 graduate of the University of Electro-Communications in Chōfu, Japan, Terada had developed a love for New York–style house music while in school, leading him to found the record label Far East Recording after he graduated. In the 1990s, Terada gained a reputation as a talented electronic musician, and by the 2000s, his scores for the *Ape Escape* video game franchise were being lauded by fans and critics alike.[102]

During the production of "Food Chain," Science SARU, reached out to Terada, asking if he was interested in working as a composer for the guest episode. Terada excitedly took the offer and soon thereafter met with Yuasa to discuss the technicalities of the situation. Over email, Terada told me that while he had almost total creative control over the episode's background music, when it came time to develop the closing tune, Yuasa had a specific vision: He wanted the song to recall the jaunty glitz of the music from the 1985 film adaptation of *A Chorus Line* (based on the Broadway musical of the same name). Terada rose to the occasion, melding this flamboyant style with elements of gospel music.[103] The result is a glamourous show tune soundalike that explicates the wonders of the food chain in under two minutes.

"A Kingdom from a Spark" (from "The Cooler" Season 6, Episode 22)

"A Kingdom from a Spark" is a song that Flame Princess sings in the sixth-season episode "The Cooler." Perhaps best described as a Fire Kingdom hymn, the song is a bit cryptic, with lyrics that detail the mythological cosmogony of Flame Princess's people. According to Andy Ristaino (the storyboard artist who wrote the song): "[The track is] about the origins of the Fire Kingdom. Their gods are the Sleeping Giants [which were] giant weapons from the Great Mushroom War. . . . The Fire Kingdom was birthed from the use of those weapons."[104]

Ristaino's first pass at "A Kingdom from a Spark" "sound[ed] like an ancient Dwarven war song."[105] Ristaino took this approach because he felt that over hundreds of years, a war song like this would have been popularized until it was more or less a Fire Kingdom folk song. This version was eventually scrapped because it did not fit the final feel of the episode,[106] and Ristaino composed a new version that was shorter and more accessible in terms of its lyrics.[107] The finishing touches were applied by series composer Tim Kiefer, who whipped up a "medieval chant-y" instrumental to emphasize the song's primeval subject matter.[108]

"A Kingdom from a Spark" was Flame Princess's first solo song in the series. When I asked her about her experience recording the track, Jessica DiCicco (the voice actress of Flame Princess) told me:

> I was very nervous to sing because I was always in such awe of how well Marceline sings. But I just tried to really focus on feeling the words to the song, and however my performance came across was how [Flame Princess] was meant to sing! I loved that song though, it was haunting when I first heard the demo, and I was actually excited to start to work on it. But yes [I was] nervous at first.[109]

"Yeah, Girl, It Stinks" (from "Astral Plane" Season 6, Episode 25)

Just before the climax in the sixth-season episode "Astral Plane," as Finn's projected spirit rises through the atmosphere of Earth, he spies Marceline floating among the clouds, singing a melancholic song entitled "Yeah, Girl, It Stinks." The lyrics to the song are pessimistic, detailing how eternity will inevitably destroy all memory and that the only chance for an immortal like Marceline to stay sane is by suppressing her emotions; it is not any fun (hence the titular line), but what can you do? These downer lyrics offer viewers a peek into Marceline's worldview, suggesting that she is indifferent to the world and has resigned herself to loss.

According to storyboard artist Jesse Moynihan, the line "Dutch-boxing up the palace" was originally supposed to be "hot-boxing up the palace"—a reference to, as Moynihan colorfully put it, "filling a [closed-off] room with your fart smell."[110] However, the phrase "hot-boxing" can also refer to the act of smoking marijuana in an enclosed room. Cartoon Network was understandably wary about having a possible drug reference slip through the cracks, so they requested that the line be modified. Moynihan obliged, as he never meant to insinuate anything illicit with his original lyrics.[111]

"Everything Stays" (from *Stakes*—"Everything Stays" Season 7, Episode 7)

During production of *Stakes*, series showrunner Adam Muto reached out to Swedish artist Hanna K. Nyström and invited her to work with him on the miniseries' second episode, "Everything Stays." Soon after Nyström accepted the offer, she was given the daunting task of composing an affective lullaby for Marceline and her mom to sing together. Nyström began to worry; this was a Marceline miniseries after all, and Marceline was going to need a show-stopping tune to bring it all home, but unfortunately, Nyström did not know that much about writing music. Luckily, her worry turned out to be a boon for the show, for when she relayed her reservations to Adam Muto, he reached out to his good friend and former storyboard partner Rebecca Sugar for assistance.[112]

Even after departing *Adventure Time* during the production of its fifth season, Sugar had remained a fan of the series and a friend of Muto, and consequently she was both "excited" and touched when he asked her to pen the lullaby. The first song idea Sugar drafted up was fairly "literal," written as if "someone [were actually] talking to their daughter."[113] However, Sugar was unhappy with this result and abandoned it, instead opting to make the final lyrics more ambiguous and poetic.[114]

While pondering how exactly to do this, Sugar remembered that when she was a child, she had lost her favorite toy—a stuffed rabbit—somewhere in her family's verdant garden. Months passed before Sugar finally found it, and when she picked her toy up, she was startled to see that the top had been bleached by the elements, but the bottom was the same dark color it had always been. At that moment she realized, "It wasn't worse and it wasn't better. It was just *different*."[115] This memory appropriately dovetailed with the meditation on change and the eternal return on display in *Stakes*, so Sugar ran with it, eventually producing a haunting song dubbed "Everything Stays." Due to the deeply personal memories into which she tapped to pen the tune, Sugar later claimed in a 2016 interview with *Comic News Insider* that "Everything Stays" was the "most personal" song that she had at the time written.[116]

The instrumental for "Everything Stays" was arranged by Tim Kiefer, who based its dark soundscape on "the musical profile [he had] developed for Marceline over the years."[117] A swirling mixture of rich bass guitar, synth pads, and reverb-heavy strings, Kiefer's melancholic instrumental is a nice compliment to Rebecca Sugar's pensive lyrics.

The version included in the *Stakes* miniseries runs about forty seconds and features only a single verse, but an extended version, released on *The Complete Series Soundtrack Box Set* (2019), contains a second, with lyrics that mention beaches, the tide, and the moon. It is not exactly clear to what these lyrics are referring, although it is possible that they are allusions to the photographs of Marceline's mother that are found on an old USB drive in the ninth-season episode "Ketchup."

"Robot Cowboy" (Season 7, Episode 17)

While wandering the deserts of Ooo in the seventh-season episode "Angel Face," BMO—in the guise of the titular character—begins to sing a melancholic ballad entitled "Robot Cowboy." The song, which outlines the rather lonesome and demanding life of a computer cowhand, was written by storyboard artist Seo Kim, with assistance from Cyrus Ghahremani (of the band Hot Karate) and Ryan Kattner (who performs under the stage name Honus Honus). The track was musically inspired by "Blue Shadows," a song written by Randy Newman for the 1986 comedy film *Three Amigos*; Kim explained to me that she based "Robot Cowboy" on Newman's song because she wanted hers "to feel wistful but also cute and goofy."[118]

"Robot Cowboy" was Niki Yang's biggest song for the series since "Friends Don't Fight" (from the second-season episode "Video Makers"). While Yang had been quite nervous when she had previously been asked to sing for the show, she explained to me that by the time "Robot Cowboy" was recorded, she "felt comfortable being a BMO." Needless to say, recording this time around went "much smoother."[119]

Songs from "The Music Hole" (Season 8, Episode 10)

In the eighth-season episode "The Music Hole" (storyboarded by Polly Guo and Andres Salaff), Princess Bubblegum and Jake organize a battle of the bands to cheer up a recently demoralized Finn. A whole slew of characters consequently take to the stage, performing a wide variety of songs in the hopes of wowing the crowd.

One of the tracks is a rap duet courtesy of Flame Princess and NEPTR (or, as they are known in certain hip hop circles, "Flame P" and "MC NEPTR").

This track was written by Salaff, who was inspired by the hip hop memories of his youth: "As a kid growing up in Ohio," he told me, "I used to attend a yearly festival called Scribble Jam. I tried to make FP and NETPR's song/performance as close to that as I could remember."[120]

Another stand-out song is Marceline's contribution: the moody ditty "Francis Forever." Savvy indie rock fans will likely recognize this as a song written by the musician Mitski. As to how this song—which had originally been released on the Mitski album *Bury Me at Makeout Creek* (2014)—found its way into *Adventure Time*, Polly Guo explained:

> I pitched the idea to use a Mitski song for a Marceline number . . . It was always Mitski and only Mitski for Marceline. I'm pretty sure Mitski fans had long been making the comparison between [the two] (both bass players). Mitski just gets so much raw emotion through her music, and Marceline is a character with immense unexpressed angst, so it was kind of a no brainer.[121]

According to Guo, she settled on "Francis Forever" because it is

> a song about longing . . . Marceline [has] got all this longing and unresolved regret in her relationships with both Princess Bubblegum and Simon, so "Francis Forever" seemed to fit the tone. I had a friend who regularly worked with punk musicians who had worked with Mitski previously, so she introduced us through email. [We] got informal permission through email, and then Adam Muto transferred her agent through to [Cartoon Network]'s people.[122]

At the end of "The Music Hole," Finn crowns the titular being the winner of the contest, and together, the two sing "I Look Up to You," a song by Ashley Eriksson's band LAKE. According to Guo, it was showrunner Adam Muto's idea to include a LAKE song in the episode:[123]

> ["The Music Hole"] was always going to be music heavy, so Adam Muto actually provided me (and [Andres] Salaff) with a couple choices for songs from Ashley Eriksson (responsible for the Adventure Time [end] song) and LAKE to use throughout the episode to help me in the process, just so I didn't have to come up with or write my own songs if I didn't want to.[124]

Other catchy songs featured in the episode include the Ice King's funky cover of "Do the Boogaloo" (which was originally performed by the early 1980s disco act Quango & Sparky), Susan Strong's power ballad entitled "Power of Myself," and Jake's silly ditty about the miraculous universality of dumplings (written by Guo).[125]

"Slow Dance" (from "Marcy and Hunson" Season 10, Episode 7)

Season 10's "Marcy and Hunson" revolves around Marceline's father crashing one of her concerts and interrupting the performance of a hauntingly beautiful ballad entitled "Slow Dance." The lyrics to this song are somewhat cryptic, but they heavily suggest that Marceline has feelings for a likely female someone—and given the events of the series finale, this someone is almost certainly Princess Bubblegum.

Penned by alt-country musician Evil,[126] "Slow Dance" was actually dreamed up long before "Marcy & Hunson" was written. According to a post on the artist's Tumblr:

> I wrote "Slow Dance" about this girl I had a big crush on, and she liked me too but she had a boyfriend. The girl in question is actually the person talking in the intro of the original demo of "Slow Dance" . . . She had a boyfriend and I wasn't a boy . . . (to her). I identify as genderfluid, and I feel very he/him most of the time. I was so heartbroken because I knew I wasn't a "boy" in her eyes but I thought I could be, if she let me. Hence, "I know all the other boys are tough and smooth." It's okay [though], she's a very lovely girl and I wrote a really good song out of it.[127]

Evil recorded a rough cut of the track over a sampled Santo and Johnny instrumental and then published it to their Soundcloud, where it became "a lot more popular than [they] expected."[128]

It was around this time that the show's writers and storyboard artists were busy working on the ninth-season miniseries *Elements*. One of the artists involved, Polly Guo, was tasked with, among other things, storyboarding the introduction of "Marshmaline the Campfire Queen" (i.e., the candified version of Marceline) in the episode "Skyhooks." The script called for the character to sing a song, and, according to Guo: "I wanted her to be singing something a bit uncharacteristic of Marceline—something both sweet and eerie. My initial pick was "Green Sleeves," but Adam [Muto] wanted something a bit more original, so I suggested we use [Evil's music]."[129]

It just so happened that Evil was a big fan of the series, having written in a 2016 Tumblr post that the show was "with [them] during one of the worst times of [their] life."[130] Integrating one of Evil's songs into the series seemed like a perfect fit, but alas, for reasons unclear, Evil's track never made it into the final cut. Flash forward to production of Season 10's "Marcy & Hunson." Once again, the script called for Marceline to sing an affective song, so Adam Muto reached out to Evil again and asked if the show could use "Slow Dance." According to Evil, "[The producers] explained the scene to me beforehand so I was definitely down for them using it.... [I] was very happy it ended up happening."[131]

Since the debut of "Marcy and Hunson," "Slow Dance" has become very popular with fans of the series; Cartoon Network's official YouTube clip of the scene featuring the track, for instance, has almost 1.5 million views as of January 2020.[132] Evil was both shocked and moved by the response, telling me:

> It was crazy, it's def gotten the most attention of all my songs for obvious reasons. The song ended up being much bigger with the show's fan base than I had expected, which was really sick ... It was really flattering to see people enjoy the song so much.[133]

Due to heavy implications that the song is a love ballad directed toward Bubblegum, "Slow Dance" has also been warmly received by many in the LGBTQ+ community, with *them.* magazine perhaps epitomizing this sentiment when it argued that the song is Marceline's "most clear and direct love song to Bonnibel ... capturing the essence of queer love and complicated relationships in a few simple lines."[134] When I asked Evil how they felt about "Slow Dance" being associated with one of the most famous queer relationships in modern animation, the artist responded:

> I think being able to have a gay song on a prime network TV show for kids is very cool. I think it's very cool kids get to see queer cartoon characters.... [I]t's the best thing ever to be and feel represented by the things that mean a lot to you.[135]

"Time Adventure" (from "Come Along with Me" Season 10, Episodes 13–16)

In the fall of 2016, the *Adventure Time* crew learned that the show would be ending and that they had only four episodes left to turn into a series finale. The writers and storyboard artists immediately got to work, drafting up a story that would serve as a satisfying cap to the series' near ten-year run. To make the episode as strong as it could be, Muto once again reached out to Rebecca Sugar, asking her if she would be willing to write a song for the finale. Because Sugar was still busy with her own series, Muto worried that by asking Sugar, he would be "creating more work for her."[136] These worries, however, were mostly misplaced, for when he asked her, she happily accepted. After mulling over ideas, Sugar eventually penned a tune titled "Time Adventure," which—in addition to spoonerizing the show's title—meditates on heavy topics like the passage of time, memory, and existence. Regarding the song's inspiration, Sugar told me:

> [When I was working on the song,] I was tapping into the time I spent storyboarding with Adam Muto, [which was] one of the happiest times of my life. Every day I'd come to work, and be in the office with Adam, [and we would be] bouncing ideas off each other, drawing all day, and being encouraged by Pen to do the most interesting, personal, experimental work possible. I think back on those times so fondly, and so I like to think about how I'm still in that office with Adam, at those particular moments in time.
>
> I was also being forced to move while I was writing the song. Ian Jones-Quartey and I had been living in a cabin for 5 years, in Elysian Park, but someone bought the place while we were living in it, and we had to leave. I couldn't stand it, I loved living in that place, so I was thinking every day about how I'd still be there, with Ian, in the past.
>
> But the truth about "Time Adventure" is that it's about animation. Every drawing in every episode exists, and keeps existing, but you can only experience animation if those drawings are flying by fast enough to give the illusion of motion. Technically you could print out every frame of Finn and Jake and hang them up like pictures on a wall, and see the whole thing all at once. But that's not how you experience animation. You need the passage of time. And I was thinking then, that life is similar, and I am still in that office with Adam, and still in the cabin with Ian, but in order to experience life, it has to go by. Animation is the time adventure. Life is, too.[137]

Once Sugar finalized the song's lyrics and the cast recorded their lines, the tune was passed off to Tim Kiefer, who produced the final track:

> "Time Adventure" was emotional from the start. Even [just] working on it I was a wreck, crying in the studio. Style-wise, it was the culmination of something I had been exploring for a couple years—making beats without conventional drums. In their place I used percussive instruments, negative space, and pitch to convey rhythm. With "Time Adventure," I took one of the trademark [*Adventure Time*] sounds—blippy, tuned 808 toms—and made them the epic centerpiece.[138]

Of the show's many affective songs, "Time Adventure" is one of its most emotionally compelling. Starting with a verse and chorus that discuss eternalistic "block time,"[139] the song ultimately builds to a tear-jerking bridge in which the characters express their desire for a way to capture and replay the past through thousands of "tiny frames"—a poetic metareference to the art of animation itself. Most fans and critics would agree that "Time Adventure" is a fitting cap to the series and one of Sugar's greatest achievements as a series songwriter.

"Island Song"

For many fans, the series' closing tune, "Island Song" (known also as "Christmas Island" and "Come Along with Me"), is just as beloved as the show's opener. The track was written by the Langley, WA-based singer-songwriter Ashley Eriksson c. 2007–8 before being re-recorded by her band LAKE for their album *Let's Build a Roof* (2009). As to how the song came to serve as *Adventure Time*'s closing theme, Eriksson relayed via email:

> I grew up across the street from [CalArts] and made friends with [the] students through a mutual interest in music. As an 18-year-old, I would go there to drink coffee and hang out with friends I had made, mostly Andrew Dorsett[140] and Patrick McHale, who were roommates their first semester. I was writing songs and recording a lot around that time and my music started circulating in the animation department. I was told that my music was sometimes background music in figure drawing class. Once that happened, I suddenly felt like everyone knew my music. Eventually, animators started asking me for music for their student films. I should also note that students needed to find copyright-free music for their films, so this also played a part, for sure. Pen Ward, Patrick McHale, Vi Dieu Nguyen,[141] and J. G. Quintel[142] all used my music in their student films! It was so fun. I loved it. . . . Fast forward four or five years, Pat and Pen got in touch with me about music for *Adventure Time*. I sent five or so songs that seemed like they could work, and they chose "Island Song" [to be the show's ending theme].[143]

However, the producers did request one change to the lyrics: "Pen thought some of the original lyrics didn't quite fit, so he suggested . . . that I change my lyrics about 'a town beside the sea' to 'the butterflies and bees.'"[144] This complimented the animation for the show's ending credits, which feature an animated butterfly, a bee, and a ladybug.

The series finale turns the meaning of the track on its head when it is revealed that the track actually exists in-universe, and is the creation of the Music Hole (introduced in the eighth-season episode of the same name and voiced by Eriksson herself). "Come Along with Me" concludes with the Music Hole singing the song, and while this happens, the audience is privy to a final montage, illustrating what became of the characters in the future. It is a tear-jerking moment, as it manages to take a song that for so many epitomized the joyfulness of the show, and infuse it with an element of melancholy.

Songs from "Obsidian" (*Distant Lands*, Episode 2)

It is not hyperbole to say that the second *Distant Lands* episode, "Obsidian," is filled to the brim with some of the show's strongest musical compositions. This was largely a result of the show's production staff inviting guest musicians to write the special's emotionally-charged tracks. One of those musicians was Zuzu, a Liverpool-based indie rocker. The artist had come onto Adam Muto's radar when in a 2019 interview with *Clash* magazine, Zuzu mentioned her fondness for *Adventure Time* and expressed a desire to one day write music for Cartoon Network. ("That's the dream . . . Literally the dream," she told the magazine).[145]

Zuzu was in luck because only a few months later, the *Distant Lands* specials entered production, and one of those specials, "Obsidian," called for several musical numbers. When Muto began to think of musicians who might be interested in helping compose these songs, he remembered Zuzu's interview with *Clash* and decided to reach out. According to Zuzu herself:

> The first message I had about writing the songs for the show was via a Twitter DM! Adam Muto had hit me up saying he was working on a new project and there were a few Marceline type songs that would play an important role in the episode. . . . Never in my wildest dreams did I imagine this would happen . . . Adam went on to send us some specific parts of the script . . . to give us context [about the episode]. From there we had creative reign to just do what came naturally.

For Zuzu, writing songs for *Adventure Time* was a task made all the easier by her impressive grasp of the show's aesthetic, its tone, and its characters:

> My writing partner [Kurran Karbal] and I have been long term fans of the show so we are so familiar with the instrumentation used on previous [*Adventure Time*] tracks and Marcy tracks in particular. . . . I have spent a long time with both characters . . . over the life span of *Adventure Time*, so I feel like I really know Marcy as if she were a friend. I can really relate to her, so it wasn't too hard when I sat down to write [the songs]. The words just came tumbling out of me pretty fast.[146]

Zuzu and Karbal whipped up two songs: "Woke Up" (the episode's emotive "break up" song), and "Eternity with You" (a more traditional love ballad). Unfortunately, there was a problem, as Zuzu revealed:

> We actually misunderstood [the request] and wrote two songs thinking we were meant to write both Marcy songs [i.e., the break up song, and the Bubbline love song] . . . We weren't, but Adam ended up wanting to use "Eternity with You" for Glass Boy! I was pretty embarrassed about that at the time, but I guess it all worked out well in the end![147]

When I asked her about the lyrical and musical inspiration for "Eternity with You," Zuzu explained:

> When I [wrote] the lyrics for "Eternity with You," I was putting myself in the mindset of being remorseful after being cruel to the person you love. The lyrics [to the song] were inspired by [Marceline and Bubblegum's] eternal love and the ups and downs [in their relationship] over thousands of years. I originally wrote it from the perspective of Marceline singing to [Bubblegum] but I adjusted the lyrics slightly to fit for Glass Boy. The instrumentation on this one was inspired by the Glass Kingdom! We used all types of different glass bottles for the percussion.[148]

Zuzu and Karbal's other major contribution, "Woke Up," is a bass-heavy diss track that nicely marries the pop-industrial sensibilities of Garbage with the emotional angst of pop punk queen Avril Lavigne. Zuzu explained that when she and Karbal began putting the song together:

> [W]e started with the bass on "Woke Up," which felt like the obvious first. Kurran got this awesome distorted tone and these really cool glitchy sounds along with these really aggressive sounding rave synths. We did go back and forth on a few little things with Adam, mostly just making "Woke Up" even more cutting lyrically.[149]

Indeed, the lyrics to "Woke Up" are perhaps some of Marceline's most pointed, making "I'm Just Your Problem" seem positively polite in comparison!

Another musical highlight from "Obsidian" is "Monster," the love song that Marceline plays for Princess Bubblegum when they are trapped in a collapsing magma cave with Molto Larvo. A tender ballad that expresses both the pain of ostracization and the happiness of finding your true love, "Monster" was written by Seattle-based musician Karen Havey, who records music under the moniker HALF SHY. Prior to working on the special, Havey (like Zuzu) had long been an *Adventure Time* devotee, and the story of how she landed a job working for the show is nothing short of a fan's fantasy becoming reality. According to Havey:

> I keep a log of "Song Starters" with neat things I've heard in the world, and I would look through it every now and then and notice just how many came from *Adventure Time*. Eventually I thought well, I have to make a song about this show that just keeps breaking my heart. It was around the time I was nearly done with the first [*Adventure Time*-inspired] song "In My Element" that I got an email from Bandcamp saying "someone bought your album (*Bedroom Visionaries*)."
>
> I get maybe one or two of these a month at most so I love to go in and say hi to the person and say thanks, be curious about who they are, [and] what they're all about. Turns out it was Adam Muto, the executive producer of the show.... So I sent him an email saying, "Hey wow thanks for checking out my tunes. Also ... holy crap you've made the best show I have ever seen in my life." [I] played it real cool like. After finishing up writing my second [*Adventure Time*-inspired] song "Betty" I couldn't help but fangirl real hard [and I sent him another message saying], "I'm sorry this is probably awkward, but I really love your show and I wrote these songs about it." He was incredibly kind and shared them with his Twitter Universe, and a while after that I got a random email from him saying basically, "Hey, I'm working on this thing I can't talk about, would you be interested?" ...
>
> [Adam and I] chatted a bit about what the project was going to be and the direction. He mentioned there [would be] two Marceline songs in the special, [and he asked if I would] be interested in giving the love song a try? Trying real hard to suppress my instant imposter syndrome I was like, "Yea, totally I'd be into giving that a shot!" So I read through the story and loved the idea of the dragon mirrored in Marceline, thinking through how they've both built up a protective shell, how she grew tough for a reason, but now she can open up and be vulnerable with PB.[150]

Havey was energized by the opportunity to work on her favorite show, but of course coming up with the right lyrics and chords for such an important track was no easy task:

> I filled about 5 little pocket notebooks just thinking through the story, ideas, and trying to get this song right. I wanted it to feel familiar and

honor the past songs of the show ([e.g.,] using the ukulele and referencing a few of the familiar chords from "I'm Just Your Problem") but also be pretty open and vulnerable and different for [Marceline]. [I wanted to] show that she's going through some tough emotions but also figuring herself out and growing.... From there I wrote the initial demo with the first two verses mostly intact and we went back and forth a few times editing it down into the final version. I recorded the final parts for the show in my little home studio in Seattle.[151]

Contrasting nicely with the viciousness of Zuzu's "Woke Up," Havey's "Monster" is a sweet, vulnerable song that sees Marceline finally express in lyrical form her deep love for Bubblegum. While the song's sparse ukulele soundscape and its confessional lyrics recall Rebecca Sugar's emotive style, "Monster" has a striking quiddity that allows it to stand on its own. The National Academy of Television Arts and Sciences was wont to agree, and in 2020, "Monster" was nominated for an "Outstanding Original Song for a Preschool, Children's or Animated Program" Emmy at the 48th Daytime Creative Arts Emmy Awards.

...

It is evident that without Marceline and Bubblegum's queer relationship, songs like "Woke Up," "Eternity with You," and "Monster" would not exist. When I asked Zuzu how she felt knowing that her music is now a key part of this groundbreaking pairing, she told me:

> I am beyond proud my song is connected to such an important point in the relationship of Bubbline. I believe it's incredibly important to normalise all types of LGBTQ+ relationships in animation and all other aspects of life. As a fan I have been waiting for this moment along with the rest of the world for the back story of their relationship. To get to be directly involved in writing the music really is a dream come true. I got a Bubbline tattoo, that's how much the most iconic gay duo in animation history mean to me.[152]

HALF SHY likewise stressed just how much the characters' relationship means to her and how important Bubbline is in terms of media representation:

> Oh, I'm a total fan girl of Bubbline. The whole story of how Rebecca Sugar and Muto slowly morphed it into this deeper relationship is just great. As a part of the LGBTQ community myself it really means so

much to see the representation of characters like yourself portrayed in an intelligent way. Growing up I was too young to fully understand what was going on but I saw *Ellen* getting cancelled, and [I] heard people around me saying they'd never watch her show again after she came out. That stuff sinks in as a kid and so to have these characters who are not only intelligent, but funny, complex, and unapologetically strong who also happen to be queer is really great. I love that the story here isn't about their orientation, but that they're people struggling with how to be open and vulnerable in a relationship.[153]

Amanda Jones's Score for "Obsidian" and "Together Again"

The *Distant Lands* specials "Obsidian" and "Together Again" are notable not only for their tear-jerking moments of raw emotion, but also for their orchestral scores, which were composed by Amanda Jones, an Emmy-nominated composer based out of Los Angeles. Prior to her working on *Adventure Time*, Jones had provided the score for several television programs, including HBO's *A Black Lady Sketch Show* and BET's *Twenties*. As it so happens, one of Jones's fans was Adam Muto, who reached out to her via her website and inquired if she would be interested in a scoring gig. Initially, Muto wanted Jones to score only one of the *Distant Lands* specials, but likely due to the quality of her work, she ended up scoring both "Obsidian" and "Together Again."[154]

Jones worked closely with Muto to "[define] the sonic framework for each episode," after which she was given "a ton of creative freedom" to experiment with what she thought was appropriate.[155] Regarding the specifics of her work, Jones told me:

> For "Obsidian" I pitched some ideas for a score that covered all sorts of genres: spaghetti western vibes à la Ennio Morricone, . . . sweeping orchestral textures, electronic music, noise rock and punk rock. . . . I definitely associated Glass Kingdom with glass mallets and sweeping orchestral textures to give it that feeling of awe and wonder. I also tapped into Marceline's punk rock energy for some of her cues. . . . Adam was down for it all!
>
> "Together Again" was its own sonic universe as well. . . . It takes place in . . . Death's Kingdom, so sonically we harkened back to some of the earlier episodes that explored that setting [like Season 2's "Death in Bloom"]. . . . The music was a mixture of death metal, southern metal, haunting orchestral cues, wooden/metal percussive cues and a little bit of new age.[156]

With mallets and guitar, Jones infused "Obsidian" with a unique energy that captures both the exoticism of the Glass Kingdom and the repressed pain of Marceline's past. Likewise, her score to "Together Again" is dynamic, emotional, and occasionally spooky—qualities that accentuate the special's poignant subject matter. All things considered, Jones's scores are solid additions to *Adventure Time*'s musical canon.

11.

THE ANCILLARY ADVENTURES OF FINN AND JAKE

Comics, Video Games, and More

Adventure Time is not just a television series; it is a media empire that has spawned a variety of ancillary media, like comics, games, toys, and the like. Unfortunately, these supplementary works are often overlooked by fans who are more interested in the source material. This is something of a shame, for while many of these creations might seem subordinate to the television program, they are still works of human labor overflowing with the same sort of artistic effervescence that made the *Adventure Time* television series so remarkable in the first place. In this chapter, I would like to make up for years of neglect by taking a closer look at three of *Adventure Time*'s most important ancillary offsprings: the mainline comic book series, the *Adventure Time* video games, and the abandoned film adaptation.

THE *ADVENTURE TIME* COMIC SERIES (2012–18)

Perhaps the most successful of the show's ancillary products was the main *Adventure Time* comic line, published by KaBOOM! a kid-centric subsidiary of BOOM! Studios. This monthly series, which launched in 2012 and concluded in 2018, earned itself a loyal following, sold hundreds of thousands of copies, and won over a slew of critics during its six-year run.

The Ryan North Era (2012–14, Issues 1–35)

The *Adventure Time* comic series has its origin largely in Shannon Watters, an inventive editor at BOOM! Studios. In 2011, the publisher secured the rights to the *Adventure Time* license, and Watters was tasked with helming the comic series. A fan of underground comics,[1] Watters reached out to one of her favorite artists, Ryan North, who at the time was best known for his web comic

The first thirty-five issues of the *Adventure Time* comic series were written by Ryan North, an illustrator also known for his online work *Dinosaur Comics*. Photo courtesy of Okras via CC Attribution-ShareAlike 4.0 International (CC BY-SA 4.0) license, https://w.wiki/5Qtr.

Dinosaur Comics.[2] North had been an *Adventure Time* fan since the pilot leaked onto YouTube, and needless to say, he hurriedly accepted the offer.[3] North soon thereafter met with Pendleton Ward, and the two decided that the comic series should stick to the tone of the television show while "do[ing] its own thing"[4]; this meant that North was free to play around with the characters and the lore of the world, without adhering perfectly to the show's canon. (That said, North challenged himself to remain true to the established logic of Ooo—a challenge he called "a fun change." "I don't think that *Adventure Time* is a show or a comic that should be choked by its own continuity," he clarified in a 2011 interview with Jimi Jaxon, "but I'd rather have something right if I can!")[5]

While North's comics may seem conventional on the surface, a closer inspection will reveal numerous flourishes that helped him standout from other writers. One of these was his penchant for "secret notes," often inconspicuously placed at the bottom of an issue's pages, by which he sneaked in subtle jokes or quips about the reader. (This was inspired by his use of alt-text in *Dinosaur Comics*, which he used to hide non sequitur jokes and metacommentary about the comic itself.) North was also fascinated in the possibilities of the comic book format, and he often played with its affordances and constraints. Perhaps his greatest experiment with the comic medium was the series' tenth issue; entitled "Choose Your Own *Adventure Time*," the work was a riff on the popular *Choose Your Own Adventure* book series, published by Bantam Books. North's take on the concept allowed comic book readers to choose how the plot of the issue unfolded. (To make sure that the story's strands would line up, North used the computer program Twine to create a digital "insanity wall" of interconnected plot points.)[6]

Other issues that North wrote follow the main cast as they fight the Lich, hack their way into a computer game, fight off a gummy science experiment gone wrong, and travel time.

During North's tenure as lead writer, almost all the comics were illustrated by Shelli Paroline and Braden Lamb (except Issue 5, which was illustrated by Mike Holmes, and Issues 26–29, which were illustrated by Jim Rugg). Paroline and Lamb, a married couple hailing from Massachusetts, got their start in the comic industry by working on BOOM! comic book adaptations of popular media franchises. According to Paroline:

> Braden and I had worked on some other all-ages comics with Boom. I illustrated some Muppet comics, and Braden colored Duck Tales. . . . I think Boom got the *Adventure Time* comics license right around the time of [San Diego Comic-Con], 2011. We were at their booth doing sketch covers, which was a good way to show that we could do good, fast, imaginative art. [BOOM! Editor] Shannon Watters asked us if we wanted to work on it, and we jumped at the chance!
>
> At first, we were a little intimidated, because it seemed like a hip show, and we don't really feel hip, ourselves. But we quickly realized that more than anything, *Adventure Time* is silly, weird, and sweet, which is very much our speed.[7]

In a 2014 Tumblr post, Lamb also expressed appreciation for the show's "all ages content," as well as its radical promotion of "creative freedom."[8]

When asked about their approach to illustration, Lamb explained online that he and Paroline "share all the art duties on the *Adventure Time* comic pretty evenly."[9] Lamb later elaborated on these methods in an interview, telling me:

> Our process depends on the project, but we tend to alternate on the stages of making comics. For *Adventure Time*, we sat down together and designed the look of new elements, like outfits for Bubblegum and Marcy, princesses and monsters, and whole new lands. We worked out the page layouts in ClipStudio together, nailing down the right flow and emphasis, and even peppering in some visual gags and interest. Then we divided up the pencils, Shelli inked, and I colored.[10]

Paroline and Lamb's style matches closely with that of the animated series—so much so that were a casual viewer to glance at a comic panel stripped of dialogue bubbles, they might mistake it for a frame from the show! This aesthetic similitude was due largely to the artists' unique strengths: Paroline had an eye for "consistent character designs," whereas Lamb sought "to incorporate more elements into a panel to reinforce the scene or the action."[11] When combined, these qualities were instrumental in translating both the distinct, frenetic feel of the original series into a static, two-dimensional space.

Paroline and Lamb enjoyed a close, productive friendship with North (in an interview with Comics Alliance, North was emphatic when he declared that near the start of his tenure, he "stopped writing *Adventure Time* comics and started writing *Adventure Time* comics for Shelli and Braden to draw").[12] North was also fairly open to Paroline and Lamb's suggestions about a story's plotting, characters, or locations, as Lamb noted:

> We chatted with Ryan a few times about things we were interested in drawing, or notions we wanted to explore. I walked him through some interesting corners of *Dungeons and Dragons*, which is a big influence on the show, but which Ryan wasn't all that familiar with. That was the starting point for the "Dungeon Crawl" storyline (volume 4), which included some nods to classic monsters and situations from the game. But Ryan took it a huge step further by making it a deep dive into Ice King's psyche that was really sad and sweet and amazing.[13]

Under North, Paroline, and Lamb, it was if the *Adventure Time* comics could do no wrong. Fans devoured the series, with many issues selling so fast that BOOM! had to quickly reprint copies to keep up with demand.[14] Critics, too, were pleased: In 2012, the series was included on many "Best of" listings[15]; in 2013, the series won a coveted Eisner Award for "Best Publication for Kids";

and in both 2013 *and* 2014, the series won Harvey Awards for "Best Original Graphic Publication for Younger Readers," and Ryan North won special awards for "Humor in Comics."[16] By 2015, however, North, Paroline, and Lamb decided it was time to move on. "We talked with Ryan about how we all wanted it to remain fun," Lamb explained, "and that we didn't want to grow to resent it, so [we all] took our leave after thirty-five issues."[17] Soon thereafter, the search was on for a new writer-illustrator team that could continue the good work that North, Paroline, and Lamb had started.

The Christopher Hastings Era (2015–17, Issues 36–61)

When North announced his departure from the *Adventure Time* comic series, Whitney Leopard, one of the editors at BOOM!, reached out to web artist Christopher Hastings and inquired if he was interested in filling North's shoes. Hastings is perhaps best known for his surreal comic *The Adventures of Dr. McNinja*, which follows the escapades of the titular hero who practices both medicine and the art of ninjutsu. The series is eccentric in a way reminiscent of *Adventure Time*, and it is for this reason that Hastings believes he landed a job on the BOOM! team: "[Leopard] thought that my experience with combining action and absurd humor with a smidge of heart might be a good fit for the book."[18]

North and Hastings were both members of the independent art world, and had long been friends before either started to work on the *Adventure Time* comic. This made the "transfer of authorship" a bit less painful than it could have otherwise been. The two worked closely to ensure that Hastings's comics would remain faithful to the series that North had established. According to Hastings:

> Ryan and I . . . had a very fun time talking about the job, and how the baton pass would go. We talked about his original character, Penelope, who is implied to be one of Finn's potential reincarnations in the future, and how I could continue her story. We talked about how Ryan liked to do one shot issues in between arcs that really focused on things comics could do that the show couldn't, and how I might continue that. And he revealed that he didn't really know what to do with Tree Trunks, so you only see her once in his first issue, and then she was gone from the rest of his run, so I was able to make a joke about that when she returned in my first issue.[19]

While North and Hastings are two different writers with two different writing styles, the transition between their issues is an otherwise smooth one—a testament to Hastings's ability to quickly match the tone of a series that was otherwise new to him.

The *Adventure Time* line was the first monthly comic series that Hastings worked on, and his approach to the job evolved as he grew more familiar with its unique requirements:

> In the beginning, I think I would work on the scripts a little bit almost every day across a month. Once I got more comfortable on the series, I was able to get it down to about a week or two of focused attention.... In the beginning, there was [also] a lot more hand holding, notes, and corrections from both Boom's editorial, and from the licensing folks at Cartoon Network. "BMO wouldn't say this," "Make sure not to do that," etc. By the time I was wrapping up, things got signed off on without any friction. I was very comfortable, and [I] wrote pretty much whatever I wanted.[20]

When writing conversations between the characters, Hastings aimed to "capture the 'voice' and feel of the TV show" in a way that was organic, rather than forced. To do this, Hastings employed a clever sort of "dialogic free-style," which he described to me as follows:

> Once I had my outline, I would just free-write dialogue between the characters, especially Jake and Finn. I didn't worry about panel or page counts, I would just let everybody talk to each other in the most naturalistic way possible, trying to imagine the voice actors in my head. Once I had something that "felt" right, I would cut the dialogue down to something more tight and manageable for a comic, and introduce the panel descriptions and actions.[21]

During Hastings's tenure as writer, the art for the comics was handled by Zachary Sterling (Issues 36–42 and 44–48), Phil Murphy (43–45, and 49), and Ian McGinty (50–61). Unlike the fairly close working relationship that North, Paroline, and Lamb shared, the relationship between Hastings and the artists who worked on his books was a bit more hands-off:

> I didn't really need to talk too much with [the artists] during the work process. They ... had such intense deadlines, they really just needed the freedom to hit the ground running and not to look back. I'd check in with them to see if there was anything they were particularly excited to draw or would dread drawing (which led to Finn and Jake riding snails in the wild west instead of horses. Snails [are] far easier to draw

than horses). That said, I always write my scripts knowing that they are essentially letters to the artist and editor as they are pretty much the only people who read them. So it's a lot of one-sided conversation in those scripts.[22]

Hastings served as the comic series' lead writer for Issues 36–61, penning a number of imaginative story arcs that see Finn and Jake fight a demon chef named Arklothac, discover that they have a new (alternate dimension) sister named Gata, and find themselves trapped inside of BMO's programming! But after twenty-six issues, Hastings decided it was time to let someone else take a crack at the comic. When I asked what made him step down as lead writer, Hastings explained:

> The answer is simply that I had run out of things to say about *Adventure Time*, or more specifically, the relationship between Finn and Jake. I found myself outlining an arc that was designed to give me an excuse to focus on other characters, realized that was wrong, and instead of following it through, I emailed Whitney [Leopard] and told her I was ready to instead execute my last arc that would wrap up every loose end I'd put down through my prior issues.[23]

The Twilight Issues (2017–18, Issues 62–75)

Following Hastings's resignation, the *Adventure Time* comics never again had a consistent lead writer for more than four issues. And thus began the series' twilight. Lead writers at this time included Mariko Tamaki, coauthor of the graphic novel *Skim* (Issues 62–65); fantasy and sci-fi writer Delilah S. Dawson (Issues 66–69); graphic novelist Kevin Cannon (Issues 70–73); and Conor McCreery, creator of the *Kill Shakespeare* comic series (Issue 74). This era of the comic also saw a similar rotation of lead illustrators, with BOOM! veteran Ian McGinty providing the illustrations for Issues 62–69, Joey McCormick working on Issues 70–73, and Jorge Monlongo illustrating Issue 74. Unfortunately, this revolving door of writers and illustrators means that Issues 62–74 feel artistically disjointed, and while these issues are not without merit (Issue 74's do-it-yourself coloring gimmick, for instance, is a clever way to play with the format), they pale in comparison to the more unified approaches of North and Hastings.

In late 2017—around a year after Cartoon Network pulled the plug on their flagship series—BOOM! decided that the *Adventure Time* comic series, too, had run its course. The "series finale" of the comic line, Issue 75, was the joint creation of Christopher Hastings, Ryan North, and Mariko Tamaki. When asked about this finale, Hastings explained:

> Whitney told me, Ryan, and Mariko that it would be the comic series' finale and wanted to see if we'd be up for writing a collection of shorts together. We all chatted about what we wanted to do, and basically wanted to focus on the idea of the world continuing with other characters, showing that there is always potential for more stories in Ooo. I was excited to get to collaborate with Ryan and Mariko, and it was nice for us all to get to put a cap on this thing we'd all spent so long working on individually at different times.[24]

Issue 75 was also something of an illustrator's homecoming that saw Ian McGinty team up with Zachary Sterling and the comic's original designers, Braden Lamb and Shelli Paroline. According to Lamb, he and Paroline were "happy" to return for the finale and "had fun dropping in little farewell cameos from characters that were introduced in the comic."[25]

THE VIDEO GAMES

Adventure Time's aesthetic, with its penchant for pastel colors and its chirpy score, has long been compared to that of video games (in particular, those from the 1980s and '90s). As such, it should come as no surprise that during the show's run, it inspired five major video game releases. In this section, I will take a look a closer look at these games, exploring how each came to be and how each was received by the public.

Hey Ice King! Why'd You Steal Our Garbage?!! (2012)

Almost as soon as *Adventure Time* debuted, fans of the series began to eagerly call for a video game adaptation. It was an understandable want, given how much the show felt like a fantastical level of some open-world video game, and when asked if such a project was in the works, Pendleton Ward would often stress that he was more than interested in seeing the Land of Ooo brought to life in a burst of 8-bit pixels. "I'd be stoked to work on an *Adventure Time* video game," he stressed in a 2011 interview with Critical Hit. "I think games are amazing for telling stories. I don't think that people do that very often."[26] Luckily, Ward's desire would quickly come to pass, for later that year, Cartoon Network signed an agreement with WayForward (a developer perhaps best known for their game *Shantae*) to develop an *Adventure Time* game for the Nintendo DS and 3DS.[27] James Montagna, a designer who had worked on a bevy of WayForward games, was tapped as director. As to why the company chose him to helm the project, Montagna reasoned:

> Despite being the youngest director, I had some experience working on games like the *Shantae* series, as well as other cartoon licenses. In fact, the first project I helmed myself was a *SpongeBob SquarePants* title with Nickelodeon and the publisher THQ. So with side-scrolling action games, and working with a publisher to make sure a cartoon brand's guidelines were met both being under my belt, WayForward's management felt I'd be a good fit to take on a project with those criteria involved.[28]

Production of the game started with Ward, who developed a "rough pass" of the game's plot.[29] Montagna then took Ward's ideas and from them began to extrapolate a more fleshed-out game. In an interview, Montagna explained:

> I started by writing the GDD (Game Design Document), which, in the case of *Hey Ice King!* was a 100+ page document detailing everything to know about the game we planned to make . . . The GDD defined stuff like which characters would cameo, where the heroes would go location-wise, and in what order. . . . During the month or so spent writing it, I would spend hours in solitary watching every episode of *Adventure Time* . . . I was fueled by an enormous amount of passion to make the first *Adventure Time* game, so, I singlehandedly made a playable prototype of the gameplay alongside the GDD to allow everyone on the team to get a feel for the speed and rhythm of gameplay and combat.[30]

Once the GDD was finished, Montagna wrote up a draft of the game's script. This was sent to Ward, who rewrote portions of it as necessary to better fit the style of *Adventure Time*—a process Montagna called "putting the . . . script through the 'Pen filter.'"[31] Montagna and Ward further refined the game's dialogue by bouncing ideas off one another, leading Montagna to stress that this phase of development was an "iterative" one.[32]

When the GDD was finalized and the script's details were hammered out, the WayForward team began to code the game. Montagna's role as director meant that he

> [spent] hours every day playing the game and offering the programmers incredibly nuanced notes on their progress. . . . If this was really going to be an *Adventure Time* game, I wanted Finn to feel as dynamic as he can be in the show itself, so at first it was a lot of just running Finn around

an empty room to get a feel for movement speed and jump height while telling the programmers how to fine tune it all. . . . I also put together plans for the music, gather[ed] references and specif[ied] the details of where everything would be used, and even got my hands dirty with some level design work as well.[33]

Ward once again played an active role during this phase of development; occasionally, he would even drop by the WayForward offices to draft up ideas in-person, as Montagna related to me:

> The real magic of *Hey Ice King!* had everything to do with how hands-on Pen was in its development. . . . He would swing by the studio impromptu to hang out sometimes, and we'd set him up with a desk to work at. He would then silently slip out when done at the end of the day, and we would end up with an email full of countless concepts he drew for us. His excitement about this project motivated the entire team, and gave us a lot to consider while coding the game mechanics. . . . All in all, [his] creativity [and his] easy-going attitude made Pen just really delightful to work alongside.[34]

As production of *Hey Ice King!* wore on, Ward began to find himself with less and less time to guide the game's direction. Nevertheless, he still managed to provide input by emailing Montagna sketches of funny ideas that he wanted to include in the final product.[35]

The finalized version of *Hey Ice King!* is a quest game that follows Finn and Jake as they try to get their garbage back from Ice King (who has been using our heroes' rubbish to create his own "Garbage Princess"). Many fans and critics have noted that the aesthetic of the game borrows heavily from Nintendo's 1987 game *Zelda II: The Adventure of Link*, most notably in how the player sees the game world: When Finn and Jake are exploring the overworld of Ooo, the player is privy to a top-down view of the map; however, when the characters enter select locations, the perspective shifts, and the game becomes a side-scroller. In an interview with GeekDad, Montagna readily admitted that *Zelda II* was one of WayForward's main inspirations, but he also stressed that he and the production crew did not "set out to mold the entire experience after [that] one particular game."[36] Instead, the WayForward team drew inspiration from myriad games released in the 1980s and '90s. For instance, Montagna himself noted that the "quirky humor" of Nintendo's *Mother* series informed the comedic tone of *Hey Ice King!*[37] and the bouncy way that character sprites idle seems to be a clear reference to the ground-breaking aesthetic of Capcom's hit arcade game *Street Fighter II* (1991).[38]

Hey Ice King! Why'd You Steal Our Garbage?!! was released on November 20, 2012, by D3 Publisher for the Nintendo 3DS and DS. The game received a decent if somewhat muted reception. Of the critics who did take notice, most appreciated how the game managed to translate the *Adventure Time* aesthetic into a 3DS world; any criticism had largely to do with the game's relatively short length, its lack of difficulty, and its overreliance on nostalgia for games like *Zelda*.[39] In retrospect, the game does feel a bit too derivative, but it is important to remember that *Hey Ice King! Why'd You Steal Our Garbage?!!* never claimed to be some sort of radically original, intricate creation; instead, it is a game that happily wears its inspiration on its sleeve. And while it might be a bit short, it is a fun romp while it lasts. *Adventure Time* fans looking for a snappy, nostalgic video game adaptation of their favorite show will likely be satisfied.

Explore the Dungeon Because I Don't Know! (2013)

Following the release of *Hey Ice King! Why'd You Steal Our Garbage?!!*, Way-Forward was signed on to produce a follow-up for D3 Publisher. And this time, Tomm Hulett—a former employee of Konami who had worked on games like *Silent Hill: Origins* (2007) and *Contra 4* (2007)—would serve as the game's director. Hulett believes he was brought on board because:

> WayForward had . . . taken on a lot of projects so they needed to hire a new team to make the game. [WayForward and I] had worked together before on *Contra 4*, so they reached out to see if I was interested. I was! So they let me know [the new *Adventure Time* game] would be my first game as director. They hired me just before Christmas break, and I didn't start until mid-January, so I spent my entire break catching up on the series (which was in Season 3 at the time I believe).[40]

To start off on the right foot, WayForward paid close attention to the feedback that *Hey Ice King!* had received. Because many players had wanted the game to be longer and "more challenging,"[41] Pendleton Ward suggested that the new game be an "endless dungeon game" in the spirit of *Gauntlet* (1985) and *Diablo* (1997). Cartoon Network—at that time interested in developing games with multiplayer potential—felt that a dungeon crawler was in line with their vision, and so they threw their support behind Ward's idea.

With a format decided upon, Hulett and his team got to work hashing out "the core idea and concepts of the game."[42] During this phase of production, Hulett worked closely with Ward to develop *Explore the Dungeon*, as the former related:

Pen was pretty hands-on for *Dungeon*. . . . I met with Pen several times at the beginning and tried to understand his vision for [*Adventure Time*] and what an [*Adventure Time*] game should accomplish. . . . Pen [even] came and worked in our office for a few days! . . . He approved all of my boss designs, and we presented to Cartoon Network management several times throughout development.[43]

Ward also collaborated with Hulett and *Hey Ice King!* director James Montagna when it came time to work on the game's script, as Hulett explained:

Pen set the premise and storyboarded the intro scene. From there I wrote the bulk of [the game's script], but Pen reviewed and added some flavor throughout. Later on, when we had to write all the battle call-outs and things for our huge roster of playable characters, I asked James Montagna if he would help since he knew all the characters (being a fan, and having worked on [the previous game]). It was really fun writing for these characters with the blessing of their original creator!

Since *Hey Ice King!* Had largely been based on the first two seasons of *Adventure Time*, Ward also requested that *Explore the Dungeon* "hit the later seasons" by referencing them throughout.[44] Hulett rose to the task and "tried to fit as many characters and fan-service surprises as [he] could into the game."[45]

As the game director, Hulett had great say over the tone and overall look of the game, but he stressed in our interview that "because [the game] was a random dungeon crawler, we had more of an emphasis on programmers to get all the content in, and animators. It was a huge team, honestly."[46] This had much to do with the how many unique characters the game featured: After all, each character required custom animation, and this animation also needed to be multidirectional so as to provide the character sprites with a sense of depth. "It was my first project as director," Hulett explained, "So it hadn't really hit me how many frames of animation would be needed in a top down game . . . Near the end of production we needed to pull in a lot of extra programmers as well, to complete the bosses."[47]

One key aspect of *Explore the Dungeon* that breaks from the precedent established by *Hey Ice King!* is the increased use of voice acting. Hulett, in an interview with Shack News, explained that when WayForward had interviewed players of *Hey Ice King!* to better guide the production of the game's follow-up, the developers discovered that "people wanted voice acting! They wanted lots and lots of voice acting!"[48] Hulett took this to heart, and when codeveloping the game's script, he made sure to write plenty of dialogue for the show's regular cast.[49] Hulett also told Shack News that when the cast convened to record their lines, "they did a ton of ad lib in the studio," thereby upping the dialogic variety even more.

Released domestically on November 19, 2013, by D3 Publisher, *Explore the Dungeon Because I Don't Know!* features a straightforward premise: Princess Bubblegum orders Finn and Jake to journey into the Candy Kingdom's deepest, darkest dungeons to discover how the criminals that the princess has locked up keep breaking free. Our heroes eventually learn that it is Princess Bubblegum's progenitor—the Mothergum—that is behind all the hubbub. Located at the dungeon's lowest level, this one-thousand-year-old blob of "sentient pink soup" had recently begun expanding. This weakened the structural integrity of the dungeon around it and provided criminals with escape routes. The game ends with the Mothergum sublimating into bubbles and floating into the heavens.

Prior to its release, the hype for *Explore the Dungeon Because I Don't Know!* was palpable, and the game looked destined to be a hit. Unfortunately, when *Explore the Dungeon* dropped, reception was largely negative: Keza MacDonald of IGN, for instance called the game "deeply boring and devoid of imagination"[50]; Carolyn Petit of *GameSpot* seemingly agreed when she blasted the game for its "unadulterated drudgery."[51] What was it about *Explore the Dungeon* that earned it such scorn? For many, the game's critical flaw is that the player never really has a sense of progress or development. The opponents one encounters are of a limited variety, and the game's one hundred levels are an almost identical loop of monster fighting; eventually, the levels start to blur, and the whole ordeal feels Sisyphean! Of course, the game does have its bright spots—namely, its lively cutscenes (which were storyboarded by Pendleton Ward), as well as the end reveal that Bubblegum is 827 years old (a development of truly mythological proportions)—but for many, these positives were not enough to make up for the game's monotony.

The Secret of the Nameless Kingdom (2014)

Explore the Dungeon Because I Don't Know! may have been something of a critical lemon, but this did not deter Cartoon Network from greenlighting a third video game adaptation. WayForward and Tomm Hulett were again tapped as the developer and director, respectively. Having carefully considered past criticism, Hulett went into this project hoping to synthesize *Hey Ice King*'s "quest-based structure" with *Explore the Dungeon*'s "challenge-based" progression.[52]

In terms of gameplay design, *Nameless Kingdom* owes much to *The Legend of Zelda: A Link to the Past* (1992). This was based largely on Pendleton Ward's fondness for the *Zelda* series, per Hulett:

Pen suggested that [Cartoon Network] leave the genre and style of game up to WayForward. I had heard from various people that Pen's vision for an [*Adventure Time*] game was something like *Zelda*, but modern *Zelda* games obviously take enormous teams and a much longer development schedule than we would have. So I wanted to do a more modest version of Pen's vision and recreate a 2D *Zelda*-type game.[53]

The *Zelda* influence is readily apparent with regard to *Nameless Kingdom*'s story, which was written almost entirely by the WayForward team; this more "hands off" approach was due in part to Ward's decision to step down as series showrunner. Having said that, WayForward was never on its own, and Hulett emphasized that Cartoon Network and the show's writers were involved, in some capacity, throughout:

> [While] there was a bit less involvement at that point, [the show's writers and producers still] read over our story and game design to give some feedback. They actually changed the names of the Princesses to what we used in the final game (Nightmare, Lullaby, and Slumber Princess were originally Fear, Song, and Dream Princess).[54]

Cartoon Network also provided Hulett and his team with access to then-unreleased episode scripts and concept art from future episodes. This ensured that the WayForward team would have a solid understanding of where the game was to fit in the show's chronology.

As Hulett explained to me, he and his team put great care into designing the game's new characters and ensuring that their aesthetic fit in with Ooo's established look:

> I took a ton of inspiration from the show and any time a new character or creature showed up, I would try to come up with an enemy or boss design. It made me double-excited to watch each new episode, both as a fan and then as someone designing an [*Adventure Time*] game. . . . Since we had created so many pixel characters for *Dungeon*, I thought we could modify and reuse them to stretch our budget a bit further, to get in as much content as possible.[55]

While some fans with whom I spoke were a bit frustrated that WayForward decided to reuse characters from *Explore the Dungeon*, Hulett's reasoning is sound, and it was a smart way to include characters who would have otherwise been omitted.

The Secret of the Nameless Kingdom was released by Little Orbit on November 18, 2014, to a much warmer reception than its immediate predecessor. Critics largely enjoyed the game's *Zelda* homages and felt that, while derivative, its gameplay mechanics made sense. Conversely, criticism was aimed at the game's (lack of a) clue-giving system and the glitches that could disrupt playthrough.

Finn & Jake Investigations (2015)

When it came time to produce the fourth major *Adventure Time* video game, Cartoon Network decided to contract the work to Vicious Cycle Software, and Dave Ellis, a media writer who had worked on several lauded games like *Dead Head Fred* (2007) and *Eat Lead: The Return of Matt Hazard* (2008), was brought on board as developer. Prior to working on this game, Ellis was familiar with several Cartoon Network properties, but *Adventure Time* was not one of them, he admitted to me via Twitter DM:

> *Finn & Jake Investigations* was one of the last games I worked on at Vicious Cycle Software. We got the contract like we did with most of our games: our publisher got the game rights to the license, and assigned the game to us.... I had to take a crash course in *Adventure Time* before [working on the game]—my job for weeks was just watching the show and taking notes for ideas to base the game upon. I had never seen it prior to Vicious Cycle getting the contract to make the game![56]

After boning up on the series, Ellis began to develop the basics of the game, its script, and its mechanics:

> I was the game designer as well as the writer. I came up with the idea for the type of game, I designed the overall game flow (with our level designers in charge of the individual levels and puzzles), and came up with the basics for the interfaces and so on. I also came up with the idea for the story—in collaboration with the *Adventure Time* creative team—and wrote the story and [voiceover] script.... We went through several iterations of story with the team. Originally, the story involved Maja as the primary villain. There were a couple of other ideas as well. The [sixth-season] episode "Joshua and Margaret Investigations" had just aired while we were going back and forth on the story, and we all agreed that—given the fact that the game was an old-school point-and-click kind of adventure game—the idea of Finn and Jake following in

their parents' footsteps and investigating mysteries was a great way to go. It rooted the story in the world of the series really nicely.[57]

Finn & Jake Investigations is set roughly during the show's sixth season and is divided into five stories (or "cases"), each of which takes around three or so hours to complete. Over the course of these cases, the player guides Finn and Jake around different locales, looking for clues to resolve the story in question. This focus on clue-finding is refreshing and sets *Finn & Jake Investigations* apart from its predecessors, which were largely based around combat.

Finn & Jake Investigations further breaks from its predecessors by featuring 3D graphics. While the geometry of *Adventure Time* is fairly simple, all things considered (most characters are just a combination of tubes and orbs, after all), taking a 2D world and giving it a real sense of depth is often easier said than done. Eric Peterson, the game's art director, emphasized as much in an interview with Gaming Bolt when he noted that it took the development "a lot of time to properly translate [Ooo] into the third dimension."[58] Vicious Cycle's efforts were ultimately worth it, though, as the graphics for *Finn & Jake Investigations* are both visually appealing and faithful to the source material.

Finn & Jake Investigations is, as mentioned earlier, a point-and-click game that revolves around finding clues. Players do this by hovering over and clicking on key items, which will cause Finn, Jake, or one of the game's many characters to say something aloud. This feature of the game required the voice actors to record over six thousand lines of observational dialog—an arduous task, to say the least. (While he did not direct the voice recording sessions, Ellis was nevertheless on hand to help out if necessary: "My main task was to explain to the actors the situations in the game so that the actors would have context for the lines. . . . I had to explain what was going on so the dialog would make sense."[59]) The hundreds of dialog snippets featured in *Finn & Jake Investigations* help make for a varied experience, further setting this game apart from its predecessors.

Finn & Jake Investigations was published by Little Orbit on October 20, 2015, for PC, PlayStation 3 and 4, Wii U, Xbox 360 and One, and Nintendo 3DS. The game was mostly well received by critics, many of whom enjoyed its format, tone, and understanding of the source material. When compared to the previous *Adventure Time* games, *Finn & Jake Investigations* is a definite step up in both quality and creativity. Ellis's script is spot on, with each case feeling like its own bona fide episode, and the investigative nature of the game also helps it stand out among the pack. While the game does lack robust replayability (once you have cracked a case, subsequent run-throughs are unlikely to veer wildly from your first go), it scores points for creativity, and of the five games discussed in this section, I believe it to be the best of the lot.

Pirates of the Enchiridion (2018)

The last of the major *Adventure Time* games to be released was 2018's *Pirates of the Enchiridion*. Billed as an open world game that would allow players to more thoroughly explore Ooo, *Pirates of the Enchiridion* was developed by Climax Studios, a company perhaps best known for its contributions to the *Silent Hill* franchise. Ian Hudson, a veteran of the company, served as lead designer, and Dave Ellis (the writer and designer of *Finn & Jake Investigations*) was brought on to hammer out the game's storyline and script. When discussing his contributions to the game, Ellis explained:

> [I worked on] *Pirates of the Enchiridion* . . . after I was out of the game industry (at least in a full-time capacity). We had worked on a lot of Cartoon Network games at Vicious Cycle—3 *Ben 10* titles plus *Adventure Time*—and I had remained friends with Angel Sisson, our producer at Cartoon Network. [Climax Studios] designed and built *Pirates of the Enchiridion*, but [it] didn't have a writer on staff. Angel recommended me to [the studio] since I knew the license so well at that point.[60] . . . I helped flesh out the story and helped to match the story sections to the levels and flow of the game, as well as writing the [voiceover] script.[61]

While Ellis told me that he "had nothing to do with the game design," Rhys Cadle (the game's design director) seemed to counter this in a 2018 interview with Fandom when he said that Ellis's "encyclopedic knowledge of *Adventure Time*" was a boon for production: "[Ellis] was in effect . . . our benchmark for testing out things [to make sure they were] on tone."[62]

The developers sought inspiration for *Pirates of the Enchiridion* from a variety of sources, including: *Finn & Jake Investigations*, Atlus's *Persona 5* (2016), Double Fine's *Costume Quest* (2010), and Nintendo's classic *Paper Mario* (2000). But of all the games that the designers considered, arguably the biggest inspiration was Nintendo's *The Legend of Zelda: The Wind Waker* (2002), which prominently features the game's main character, Link, sailing between islands. While discussing the mechanics of *Pirates of the Enchiridion* with Well-Played, associate producer Orcun Adsoy confirmed that the Nintendo game "was . . . a solid frame of reference when [Climax Studios was] looking at how the boat would function and feel on the open sea."[63] Interestingly, lead designer Ian Hudson also revealed in the aforementioned Fandom interview that the Ubisoft series *Assassin's Creed* influenced how the Climax developers approached their own open world. "You're never short of something to do," Hudson explained, likening *Pirates of the Enchiridion* to the Ubisoft series. "[In both] you've got mainline quests, but you can spend just as long on the side quests [and] 'sub-activities'"[64]

In terms of story, *Pirates of the Enchiridion* is set during the show's final season and follows Finn and Jake (and later, BMO and Marceline) as they sail to different kingdoms in an attempt to understand why Ooo has mysteriously flooded. Because of this inundation, players are required to use a boat to sail around looking for clues. (This unique plot was engendered by the developers' desire to give Finn and Jake "some kind of vehicle" to make travel easier, as well as their interest in focusing the game around "some kind of huge impact to the land of Ooo like a giant flood.")[65] It is important to note that players are free to travel wherever they wish, making *Pirates of the Enchiridion* the first of the major *Adventure Time* video games to feature an open world. And even though much of the game map is flooded, the navigable area is still quite large, as Hudson emphasized to Jason Stettner of Gamer Headquarters in a 2018 interview:

> If you look at a map of Ooo you can get a sense of scale for our game. Players will be able to sail from the Ice Kingdom in the north all the way down to the Fire Kingdom in the south. Then from the Candy Kingdom in the west to the Evil Forest to the east. In between these main land masses, players will be able to stop off at smaller locations designed exclusively for the game, as well as seeing well known landmarks popping up through the water such as Lady Rainicorn's house.[66]

In addition to open-world exploration, *Pirates of the Enchiridion* allows players to fight off foes with a turn-based combat system. Players can also use the game's unique "interrogation" function to secure useful information. Huson was particularly proud of this feature, arguing that it was "fast and fun" and allowed the developers to "[show] off the character's personality and humour as they try to charm their way to victory."[67]

Pirates of the Enchiridion was published by Outright Games on July 17, 2018, for PC, PlayStation 4, Xbox One, and the Nintendo Switch. Like the other games discussed in this chapter, it was met with largely mixed reviews. As with previous *Adventure Time* games, critics appreciated *Pirates*'s occasional flourishes that recalled the cleverness of its source material, but they were more critical of its simplistic mechanics and its limited explorability. In truth, the restricted nature of the game's "open-world" are rather disappointing (throughout *Pirates*, Ooo is underwater, severely limiting where a player can go), but thankfully the game does balance some of this out with solid animation and another solid script. While far from perfect, *Pirates of* the *Enchiridion* is a serviceable game that especially younger fans are likely to enjoy.

THE THEATRICAL MOVIE

On February 27, 2015, the online news site Deadline published an article that made the *Adventure Time* fandom collectively gasp: According to Hollywood insiders, Cartoon Network was developing *Adventure Time* into a feature film! Additionally, Pendleton Ward himself was working on a script, and Chris McKay (who served as an animation codirector for 2014's *The Lego Movie*) and Roy Lee (one of the producers of *The Lego Movie*) were lined up to produce the film. This was for many fans the dream team—the creator of one of TV's smartest animated programs teaming up with two of the people who helped bring *The Lego Movie* into the world? What more could be asked for?

Alas, it seems Deadline had jumped the gun with their big scoop. Cartoon Network representatives almost immediately began to stress that the network had never actually greenlit a movie—they were merely exploring the *possibility* of such a production. Adam Muto reiterated the same point at the 2015 New York City Comic-Con later that year, telling attendees that while Ward was "working on the premise," there was "nothing official to announce yet."[68] In the months that followed, fans held onto the possibility that all this talk would finally coalesce into a definitive production. Unfortunately, it seems that it was never meant to be, and a little over a year after all this gossip circulated, Cartoon Network canceled *Adventure Time*—a testament to the fickleness of the entertainment industry.

12.

UTTER FINNDEMONIUM!

The Ins and Outs of the *Adventure Time* Fandom

On May 8, 2019, while browsing my Twitter, I stumbled across a tweet made by the absurdist musician Neil Cicierega, in which he encouraged every major fandom to create "a long tapestry, depicting its whole history—major events, flamewars, times of peace, prominent mods and admins."[1] This tweet reminded me of the performance fan studies theorist Francesca Coppa's book chapter "A Brief History of Media Fandom," in which the author noted that while much has been written about the history of media fandom as a whole, "very few histories of *individual* fandoms and the works of art they produce" exist.[2] Cicierega and Coppa's points quickly collided in my mind, and in no time, I had an idea: "Why don't I write a history of the *Adventure Time* fandom?"

I grabbed my computer and furiously began researching. Soon I had mocked up a textual outline of what was basically the *Adventure Time* fandom's very own Bayeux Tapestry. Unfortunately—and I say this in a loving way—there are only so many pages of fancrufty minutia, myopic shipping wars, and ofterroneous fan speculation you can document before you put even the most dedicated of fans to sleep. I thus reformulated my approach, and instead of detailing the entirety of the fandom, I decided to focus specifically on the common behaviors of the fans within that fandom, as well as the websites that helped the show balloon in popularity. To enliven things even more, I interviewed dozens of passionate fans, who shared their insight into the show's fervent following. The result was this chapter, which serves as a useful snapshot of the show's sprawling and diverse fandom.

MAJOR FANDOM BEHAVIORS

Fanfiction

Even to those unacquainted with the jargon of fandom studies, the term "fanfiction" will likely sound familiar. Defined by the fandom scholar Francesca Coppa as "creative material featuring characters that have previously appeared in works whose copyright is held by others,"[3] fanfiction (sometimes called "fanfic" or simply "fic") is a broad term referring to a vast sea of creative texts, all of which are united by the fact that they are penned by fans and based on some pre-established media object. Works of fanfiction usually revolve around a media object's main characters, although many others focus on background characters or even new characters that the fan writer has created. (For anyone who is still in the dark as to the practice, simply watch *Adventure Time*'s third-season episode "Fionna and Cake." This episode—which stars the titular characters—is both a lampooning and celebration of fanfic culture, and watching it should clear up many of the misunderstandings a reader might have of the behavior discussed in this section.)

When it comes to the question of motivation, most of the *Adventure Time* fans to whom I spoke reasoned that fanfic serves as a way for fans to, as media scholar Henry Jenkins once put it, "fill in the gaps in the broadcast material," either by "provid[ing] additional explanations for the character's conduct" or by "expanding the series timeline."[4] Consider, for instance, what the fan Biggerboot told me in a Discord chat: "Since *Adventure Time* constantly left loose threads as it tied up new ones and had this whole vast lore that was only in the background, I think it got a lot of people wanting to complete that puzzle in their head."[5] Building off this idea, others argued that fanfic functions as a sort of productive wish fulfillment. Perhaps this understanding was best articulated by fan Instagrammer Sophie,[6] who told me: "I believe [fanfic writers] like to create situations that they wish would've occurred in the show."[7] Despite their differences, the assertions expressed by both Biggerboot and Sophie lend credence to Jenkins's argument that "fan writers do not so much reproduce the primary text as they rework and rewrite [that text], repairing or dismissing unsatisfying aspects, [or] developing interests not sufficiently explored."[8]

In the popular consciousness, fanfiction is often associated with the practice of "shipping." Short for "relationshipping," this fannish term originated with *The X-Files* fandom in the 1990s and refers to "the desire to see two particular characters in a work of fiction engage in a romantic and/or sexual relationship."[9] In the *Adventure Time* fandom, popular romantic pairings (or "ships") include the following: "Bubbline" (a portmanteau of Princess Bubblegum and Marceline), "Fubblegum" (Finn and Princess Bubblegum), "Finnceline" (Finn and Marceline), "Flinn" (Finn and Flame Princess), and "Finntress" (Finn and Huntress Wizard). Many fans take their ships personally, and some will go to extreme measures to defend them.[10] Given shipping's popularity in the larger fandom, it is perhaps unsurprising to learn that many of the most popular *Adventure Time* fanfics are what can be called "ship fics," including Ruby Sword's *The Last Human* (which at least partially centers around Finn and Marceline falling in love),[11] Annalynn Roe's *Change Everlasting* (a romantic drama about Marshall Lee and Fionna),[12] and we4retheincrowd's *A Love Like War* (a fic that focuses on Marceline and Bubblegum's relationship).[13]

A substantial number of *Adventure Time* fanfics—including the aforementioned *A Love Like War*—take place not in Ooo but in "alternate universes" (often abbreviated as "AUs"), with the most common settings being "real-world" locations such as high schools or universities. This sort of "character dislocation"[14] can sometimes be hard to understand, especially for those fans who are attached to the Land of Ooo as a setting. In a Discord discussion about why AUs are popular, the fan Gale argued that "the main appeal here is basically to speculate 'how would these people behave if they lived in a different life?'"[15] Gale's emphasis on behavior is strikingly similar to what the fanfic writer myqueenmarceline had told me a few months earlier when we were discussing the popularity of fanfic in general:

> I think [AUs are a product] of what fanfiction primarily is: character-driven fiction. The fanfictions I've read are usually based on characters from the piece of media in question, rather than the specific world they're in. Fans like to mix things up because they want to imagine how their favorite characters would interact in other places. The setting always impacts the story, but when the focus is on the characters and their relationships with each other, the specific setting isn't as important. Honestly, fanfiction is one of the best spaces I've found where you can really practice character exploration. I think people being creative enough to "mix it up" and examine how these characters would act in another universe is just a part of that character exploration.[16]

On the topic of character exploration, myqueenmarceline also told me that, for her, "the most important thing for good fanfiction is a strong grasp of the characters" and that "authors have to make sure they're actually treating the characters like the complicated and multifaceted people they are, and not just as blank slates to project on whatever they want."[17] This lines up with what fan theorist Ann McClellan argues in her book *Sherlock's World* (2018): "Even though [fanfic] writers may change virtually every aspect of the setting, time periods, details, whatever, the one thing that most critics and fans agree must stay consistent is characterization."[18] For many readers, fics that struggle with characterization indicate that the author has a poor grasp on the characters, is not familiar with the story world, or is simply a weak writer. A major exception is usually made for fanfics about "background characters" (that is, characters upon whom the spotlight does not normally focus); with these works, readers are often more forgiving of radical experimentations with characterization. This is because these background characters are tabulae rasae, whose characterizations are often not firmly established in canonical texts.

Prior to the Internet, fanfic was often published in fanzines or by "apas" (short for "amateur press associations").[19] With the emergence of the online world, fans were no longer bound by material restraints and were free to distribute their creations via digital channels.[20] This has certainly been the case for *Adventure Time* fanfic, and today most works are uploaded to websites like FanFiction.net or Archive of Our Own (AO3). In fact, as of September 2019, the former site hosts over 7,400 *Adventure Time* fics[21] and the latter hosts 1,708.[22] Other works of *Adventure Time* fanfiction can be found on sites like Tumblr and Twitter.[23]

Fanart

Fanart is the catch-all name for derivative artwork based on a media object's characters, locations, or events. Delineating what is and is not fanart can be somewhat tricky—given that the term "art" denotes a variety of unique media—but in this section, I will be using Fanlore's "colloquial" definition: "Fanart... refers to the art for a [media object] that is drawn or painted either traditionally or digitally" by fans of said media object.[24]

Adventure Time fanart is almost always character-focused, with Finn, Jake, Ice King, and the show's female characters being particularly popular models. When I asked Sophie (a fan who occasionally posts fanart on her *Adventure Time*-themed Instagram account) what she found so appealing about the show's characters and why she liked to draw them, she told me:

> The colors and designs of the characters are just simply so much fun. Each character is individual and there is a plethora of characters to choose from when drawing! You cannot get bored drawing them: Wanna draw an animal-like character? Gunter or Jake. Wanna draw a vampire Queen or demon? Have a go at Marceline or one of her demon forms. Wanna draw something really crazy? Think of an item of candy (or sweet as we say in England), add some arms, legs, eyes, a mouth and you have a candy person! There's so much scope for experimentation, because the characters are already so fabulously unusual and brilliant.[25]

As an amateur fanartist myself,[26] I concur with Sophie. I delight in doodling the show's characters because they are all so unique, which provides me with ample amounts of room for creative exploration.

In terms of style, some fanart remains faithful to the show's noodly aesthetic, whereas other pieces deviate wildly from the show's style, embracing aspects of everything from anime to photorealism. In a discussion about this stylistic variance, Jagm (who also makes pixel art when he is not hard at work updating the AT Chronology page) opined:

> Since the very beginning, simplicity has been at the core of *Adventure Time*'s designs. I remember old style guides made by Pendleton Ward and the crew that described Finn as being made of a set of bendy tubes. Anyone can draw a tube, and therefore anyone can draw Finn the Human. This simplicity also affords a lot of variation. Finn can be depicted in any way, from anime to pixel art to cosplay, and will always be instantly recognisable. . . . So fan artists can easily impose their own personality and art style onto all the characters in the show without losing the charm of the original designs.[27]

Another reason for this deviation may be that it provides fans with the chance to experiment with new artistic techniques, develop their own style, or even explore aspects of their own identity, all while using familiar characters from a media object that they enjoy.[28]

Fanart is often seen as the "visual counterpart" to fanfiction, and while the practice should not be written off simply as "fanfic with pictures," the graphic novel expert Robin Brenner does point out that fanart "often fulfills the same desires as fanfiction . . . by allowing the artist to create moods, relationships, and character shifts according to what they desire from a story."[29] Brenner also writes that those who pen fanfiction and those who draw fanart are united because they "take the leap from speculation to creation [by] . . . us[ing] their talents to fill in the gaps, to create alternative timelines, and mix universes."[30] Brenner's point about fanart "fill[ing] in the gaps" was echoed by many of the fans to whom I spoke. For instance, the artist "loycos," who gained prominence in the fandom for her inventive comics, told me: "A lot of fanart is actually exploration of things that aren't canon or aren't addressed in the [source] material. Basically, it's both a story on its own and a translation/extension of the original media."[31] Likewise when discussing how they first got into fanart, the artist "Otto" explained: "[I] wanted certain characters to interact (such as Flame Princess and Fionna), but they never did—so I made my own drawings."[32] These quotes suggest that indeed, fanart can function like a tool that allows fans to expand or remix the *Adventure Time* canon to suit their needs or wants.[33]

For much of the 2000s and 2010s, the hub of all things fanart was DeviantArt, a website founded in 2000 that self-describes itself as the "largest online art gallery and community."[34] As of May 2021, DeviantArt hosts roughly 85,200 pieces of art that are labeled with the "adventuretime" tag.[35] Gigabytes of other *Adventure Time* fanart can also be found across the Internet on sites like Tumblr, Twitter, Pinterest, Imgur, Pixiv, and Reddit.[36] All of the aforementioned sites are free to access and use, and as a result, most *Adventure Time* fanart is released for free online. With that said, some artists do upload their creations onto online marketplaces like Etsy and sell them "under the table" as t-shirt designs, stickers, prints, and more. Other fans have eagerly embraced the possibilities of programs like Redbubble's Partner Program or Amazon's Merch Collab, both of which allow fans to create and sell officially-licensed designs after an approval process.

Cosplay

Another behavior endemic to the *Adventure Time* fandom—and one that, in general, fan scholar Paul Booth calls "the most visible in the mainstream press"[37]—is cosplay, or the practice of dressing up as fictional characters from popular media franchises. The costumes used for this activity tend to be sewn or assembled by fans themselves, and often, fans will compete in elaborate cosplay competitions at fan conventions ("cons").[38]

Cosplay (a portmanteau of "costume" and "play") has an elaborate history that the costume theorist Theresa Winge traces back to the United States at the turn of the twentieth century. At this time, masquerade balls were popular, at which guests would wear fantastic masks or dress up as historical characters. In the 1930s, when science fiction conventions began to gain popularity in the United States, con-goers began following the lead of masqueraders by dressing up, but instead of wearing masks or donning the look of real people, these fans dressed up as their favorite fictional characters. For decades this practice flourished in the fandom scene, but it went without an official name. This changed in 1984, when the Japanese writer Nobuyuki "Nov" Takahashi dubbed the practice "cosplay."[39] In the years that followed, cosplay flourished in Japan and was eventually repopularized in the United States. Today, the practice is so ubiquitous that it is usually considered an integral part of any fandom's culture.

Scholars have for decades now debated the meaning of cosplay, although many are in agreement that the behavior has something to do with identity and identity formation. Booth, in his book *Playing Fans* (2015), writes that "cosplay is inherently about performance . . . Cosplay enacts identity play for both the fan and for the character [whereby] we learn about both through the unique interaction of the two."[40] Nicolle Lamerichs builds off this thinking

Adventure Time has spawned legions of cosplaying fans, many of whom go to considerable lengths to ensure that their costumes are show-accurate and of the highest quality. Photo courtesy of James H. Greyloch via CC Attribution-ShareAlike 2.0 Generic (CC BY-SA 2.0) license, https://flic.kr/p/edvM3w.

in her monograph *Productive Fandom* (2018) but goes further than Booth by arguing that cosplay is really a performative performance (à la Judith Butler) that allows the cosplayer to construct their identity through costuming, make-up application, and prop construction. Echoing the idea of Booth, Lamerichs writes, "By stating [through cosplay] that a narrative or character is related to me . . . I make a statement about myself," but she emphasizes that this connection has a real impact in affecting how the cosplayer is viewed in what we often call the "real world."[41] Lamerichs thus concludes that cosplay is a special behavior that provides us with the "transformative potential . . . to express who we are through fiction."[42]

Lamerichs also argues: "Similar to fan fiction, fan movies, and [fanart], cosplay motivates fans to closely interpret existing texts, perform them, and extend them with their own narratives and ideas."[43] However, unlike fanfic or fanart, cosplay is a behavior almost always predicated on a physical creation (i.e., a costume).[44] This is important to note, and many of the fans to whom I spoke connected their enjoyment of cosplay to the physical construction of their costume. Sophie, for instance, mentioned that when she cosplayed as Fionna for FanExpo Canada in 2015, she did it "because it was fun to make a costume from scratch."⁴⁵ This is similar to what Celina, a German cosplayer who runs the Novalee Cosplay social media accounts and who cosplayed as Princess Bubblegum in 2016, told me: "Joy . . . [comes from] creating something from nothing. I'm always surprised that in the end, there is a costume I can wear."⁴⁶

Cosplay has long been an undeniable part of the *Adventure Time* fandom, and at the zenith of the show's popularity, hundreds of cosplayers donned green backpacks, spray-painted ice crowns, or papier-mâchéd their own ax basses so that they could dress as *Adventure Time* characters at conventions. In fact, so fashionable was the show amongst the cosplay crowd that in 2013, Olivia Olson told the Mary Sue:

> At Comic-Con [in 2011, when the show was not yet a phenomenon] . . . a lot of people still dressed up like Finn around the convention center. . . . I think I saw two people dressed up as Marceline and I just thought, "This is so awesome!" Fast-forward to this year at Comic-Con . . . Literally, anywhere you look, anywhere in your range, you're going to see at least two people dressed up like Finn. It's crazy.⁴⁷

Indeed, a quick Google Image search, or a perusing of Flickr will show you that in the 2010s, *Adventure Time* characters were well-represented at fan conventions, with Marceline, Bubblegum, Finn, and Fionna being among the more popular cosplay choices.

Fancams

While video manipulation has long been a part of the fandom experience,⁴⁸ the "fancam" is a relatively new concept. Fancams emerged from the world of K-pop and originally referred to compilations of fan-captured footage that focused on one musician (usually the compiler's "bias"—that is, their favorite K-pop musician); a musical track featuring the musician in question often accompanied the footage. Fancams initially thrived on video-based sites like YouTube, but much of the attention shifted to Twitter when savvy K-pop fans realized they could include their fancams when replying to other tweets, thereby boosting views. As the K-pop fandom grew more and more ubiquitous online, the art of the fancam grew in popularity. Soon, individuals from other fandoms were creating their own fancams that focused not on K-pop musicians, but rather on individuals important to their respective fandoms.⁴⁹ When this behavior migrated to "Animation Twitter" (that is, the loosely defined network of Twitter users who enjoy animation, of which "*Adventure Time* Twitter" is a subsection), fans began compiling videos of their favorite animated characters. Because of this evolution, the word "fancam" has become something of an umbrella term that has (to the chagrin of some) subsumed many older practices, like fanvids, fan edits, and anime music videos (AMVs).[50]

In the *Adventure Time* fandom, fancams are not a monolith. "There are a wide range of fancams," Twitter user Foeyia told me. "Some are simple scenes from a show (or fanart!) with music playing [in the background], however, there are also edits with complex transitions and coloring [that] can take hours [to make]."[51] Foeyia noted that these videos might even try to tell a story: "For example, I might edit Marceline and PB, and show how their relationship has changed over time—or maybe Finn's journey as a hero."[52] One feature that seems somewhat constant across all fancams, however, is the use of musical backing tracks—a likely holdover from when fancams exclusively celebrated musicians. While some fancams use tunes from the show, others pair clips from *Adventure Time* with popular music. When discussing how she picks the backing tracks for her fancams, Twitter user Bee explained:

> A lot of times I'll hear a song and be like, "Oh that fits this character perfectly," or I'll see clips and think, "Oh, that would be so cool set to music." I try to make the song somewhat fit the character or at least have it be upbeat or more calm depending on the vibe I'm going for.[53]

Like the K-pop fans that preceded them, *Adventure Time* fancammers often post their edits onto popular Tweet threads to boost circulation. Others use their video edits like digital advertisements, posting them onto popular threads to cleverly entice people to watch the show.

Fan Documentation

In addition to the sprawling "What if?" category that is fanfic, there is also what fan theorist Jason Mittell calls the "What is" category of fantexts that seek "to extend the fiction canonically, explaining the universe with coordinated precision and hopefully expanding viewers' understanding and appreciation of the storyworld."[54] Often, fans who put together these sort of encyclopedic works do so to "arrive at the singular, correct account of complex narrative material,"[55] or to make sense of a media object's sometimes confusing continuity. An excellent example of a "what is" paratext in the *Adventure Time* fandom is the *Adventure Time* Wiki (discussed in detail in the latter part of this chapter), which solicits contributions from readers to construct a holistic understanding of the show's canonical universe.

There are many *Adventure Time* fans out there who spend their free time cataloging the show's complex lore, but perhaps no one else is as dedicated as a fan who posts online using the pseudonym Jagm. Once described on Reddit as the "all knowing lord of [*Adventure Time*] knowledge,"[56] Jagm is the creator of another important "what is" paratext: the meticulously curated "AT Chronology" website,[57] which catalogs every canonical happening in the Land of Ooo, from the time of primordial monsters to the death of the solar system.

Jagm began working on the site in September 2017, after being frustrated by the lack of an exhaustive text detailing *Adventure Time*'s in-universe history. In an interview, he told me:

> I'm a bit of a perfectionist, and it began to nag at me that there was no central place documenting all the show's history. The fan wiki is an amazing resource, but it's severely lacking in a lot of areas, especially when it comes to the later seasons and the comics. Another awesome member of the fandom named RedLionKing had made a large and very well written timeline, but it hadn't been updated since the Stakes miniseries, and again included nothing from the comics and also nothing from the show's "present day" era, and skipped a lot of events that the author didn't consider "important."
>
> So over the course of 2017–18, AT Chronology evolved from a simple bulleted list of historical events I was just going to post on Reddit, into a 70,000 word monstrosity of a website that rivals a lot of novels in size. I'm very pleased with the result.[58]

Finally published at the start of 2018, the AT Chronology website is a remarkable achievement that can only be described as a labor of love. (And so accurate is the site that it was even cited in the official Frederator YouTube video "The Complete *Adventure Time* Timeline"!)[59]

Other works of fan documentation—including much of this book that you are now reading—detail not the canon of the series, but rather facts about how it was created. Once again, the *Adventure Time* Wiki is an excellent example: a cursory browsing of the site will reveal page upon page replete with storyboard PDFs, character designs, story notes, and episode backgrounds. Why do fans (like myself) derive pleasure from collecting tidbits about production? The question of motivation, like all other behaviors discussed in this chapter, is a complicated matter, but I believe that it has to do with a want to vicariously participate in the production of the show. Perhaps I am speaking for myself, but when I track down a bit of production information, I often feel as if I have gained some sort of esoteric, insider knowledge of *Adventure Time* about which only those closest to the show's production know. And by collecting those production facts in one place (such as this book), I am hoping to share that sense of insider knowledge with other fans, too.

Criticism and Commentary

Henry Jenkins wrote in his seminal 1992 monograph *Textual Poachers* that when it comes down to it, "organized fandom is, perhaps first and foremost, an institution of theory and criticism."[60] The *Adventure Time* fandom serves as an excellent illustration of Jenkins's point, for in addition to the myriad fans penning fanfics or drawing elaborate comics, there are also legions who express their love for *Adventure Time* by critically analyzing the source text and posting these thoughts for others to read. These sorts of critiques come in many styles and flavors; some, for instance, are think-pieces about characters, whereas others are critical dissections of key story arcs. Most of these critiques are text based, but there are others that take the form of video essays or hypermedia assemblages that blend otherwise "conventional" elements of criticism with aspects of new technologies. Often the fan writers who pen these works don the label "reviewer," which indexes their primary mission: critically evaluating a show that is dear to them in a complex and interesting way.[61]

On the surface, being a reviewer might sound easy, but in practice, it can be a tough act. Too often do inexperienced fan critics[62] "evaluat[e] . . . individual episodes against an idealized conception of the series, according to their conformity with the hopes and expectations the [fan] has for the series' potential development."[63] While a common practice, this sort of criticism (i.e., deriding an episode because it does not live up to overhyped expectations or does not conform to one's "headcanon"[64]) is not exactly lauded in the *Adventure Time* fandom. Instead, to be well-regarded, a reviewer needs to be eloquent and interesting, and—perhaps most important of all—they must possess the ability to see how something that one person might not like can nevertheless have artistic merit (and vice versa).

What is it that drives these Oooian Siskel and Eberts to critique that which they like? According to the popular reviewer UncivilizedElk (who gained prominence in the fandom by posting episode reviews and storyline analyses to his YouTube channel), critiquing and commenting on *Adventure Time* served a metacognitive exercise, providing him an opportunity to contemplate why he likes or dislikes certain media:

> For myself, it's a more involved method of merely thinking thoroughly about what I watch. I tend to have thoughts form as to why I liked/didn't

like something automatically when reading [or] watching entertainment media, but a lot of times they are rather haphazard and jumbled, and sometimes poorly formed.

Taking that swirling mass of thoughts and trying to structure them into a [critical review] can be a fun process to better understand how you engage with media, as well as (to an extent) how your own mind works. So personally, critiquing [and] reviewing allows me to engage with media in a more robust and detailed manner than if I was to just keep my thoughts to myself.[65]

UncivilizedElk also emphasized that *Adventure Time* criticism was "one of the many ways to initiate/engage in discussion" with other fans.[66] This point was also brought up in a separate interview by Eric Stone (the critic behind the popular *Adventure Time* Reviewed site) when he told me that with his reviews, he was hoping to start "a dialogue that encourages unique takes and doesn't limit found meaning to one specific source."[67]

And when it came time to explain why fans enjoy reading critiques, Stone speculated:

Fans like reading . . . analyses because *Adventure Time* is such a vague show where so much can be left to your interpretations. Part of the reason I like to read into other reviews [or] analyses is because they often offer up a point-of-view that is completely different from mine, but still really unique and interesting. . . . [For instance] I've seen about a million different takes on season five's "Puhoy," and I think that's why that episode has such a strong following. There are so many unique spins you can take with its story, and I think every last theory has its own strong points.[68]

All things considered, fan criticism is appealing because it offers viewers a way to express the reasons they like (or dislike) an episode (or character, story arc, design choice, etc.). In turn, those who consume critiques or analyses are provided with an opportunity to consider different perspectives. Fan criticism and commentary is thus fundamentally predicated on the sharing and circulation of different points of view.

KEY FANDOM WEBSITES

Previous research on *Adventure Time* has often commented on the show's strong Internet following, but hardly any of that research has considered in detail the specific sites that the fandom uses. This is disappointing to say the least, given the enormous impact the online fandom has had on the show. With this section, I hope to take readers on a fantastic journey of the online fandom, exploring everything from fan-run wikis to anonymous 4chan threads.

The *Adventure Time* Wiki

In an outline of key websites, it is perhaps best to start with one of the largest and most heavily trafficked: the *Adventure Time* Wiki.[69] Supported by a hosting service known as Fandom,[70] this site uses the MediaWiki software, allowing anyone with an internet connection to modify content on the site,[71] much like the famous encyclopedia Wikipedia. Founded in 2009, the *Adventure Time* Wiki was the brainchild of a web developer named Tavis Lam. In an online interview, Lam explained how the site got its start:

> [I was] a contributor and adopter of multiple wikis on Fandom (formerly known as Wikia), [and] most of the work on those wikis was completed by 2009, as their respective TV series had finished airing. In my ambition to further expand the community with new and qualitative wikis, I set out in search of a new TV series. As a Cartoon Network fan, it wasn't long before my research brought me to a new, upcoming series on their network known as *Adventure Time with Finn and Jake*, based on the 2007 viral Nicktoons short *Adventure Time*. I went straight ahead in creating the new wiki. After designing and writing pages based on what I already knew from the short, it was only a matter of waiting for the time to come when more information was released or when the new series would finally air a year later in 2010.[72]

Indeed, soon after the first episodes aired, the wiki started to fill up with plot synopses, production artwork, and screenshots.

Most fan wikis are based on the ethos of documentation and thus oppose the posting of what is called "original content."[73] In other words, editors are encouraged to document a media object's "canon," the production that went into producing the media object, or reviews that the media object has received from reputable sources. Some wikis strictly adhere to this ethos of documentation; others—like the *Lost* wiki Lostpedia[74] or the *Supernatural* wiki[75]—allow editors to also include content about fan-theories and fanfiction. The *Adventure Time* Wiki leans more towards the former category, and while fans are allowed to speculate in dedicated "Trivia" sections, most articles are focused on documentation rather than extracanonical guesswork.

During my interviews with those in the fandom, time and time again I was reminded of the *Adventure Time* Wiki's importance. Fanfic writers used the site to cross-reference character interactions, reviewers used it to quickly look up facts about characters or episodes, and fanartists used its thousands of images as inspiration for new pieces. Some fans simply enjoyed reading articles to learn more about the Land of Ooo, and still others actively contributed to the site, ensuring that it was up to-date and relatively reliable. And the importance of the site was not just stressed by fans; Open Mike Eagle and John Moe, for instance, once mentioned on an episode of their *Adventure Time*–focused podcast *Conversation Parade* how invaluable the site was when it came time to record an episode. It seems that, whether people admit it or not, the *Adventure Time* Wiki has often been the first-stop-shop for anyone interested in learning more about the show.

But it would be a mistake to see the wiki as just a sterile information repository; instead, as evinced by the many users who contribute to it, the site is very much a community, with its own rules, customs, and systems of communication. The wiki admin "Creampuff," to whom I spoke while working on this section, emphasized this aspect of the site, telling me:

> Ever since I joined fandom, I've wanted to make the wiki as much of a community as I could. When I first joined, there were so many different people to chat with . . . The wiki was a magical place for me because it was the first time I could just talk with other people who loved *Adventure Time*, and I've wanted to keep it that way, to spread that magic to everybody who stops by. . . . There are some users who aren't the kindest, but me and my 4 trusted moderators have been making fun activities, and we are essentially always trying to get more people to join.[76]

To further this sense of playful community, Creampuff and the site's other admins helped organize the Who Would Win Tournament (a bracket-style competition to determine the series' most formidable character), the Golden Stakes Awards (a digital "awards show" to highlight the series' best episodes), and the Music Hole Awards (which functioned as the fandom's answer to the Grammy Awards by celebrating the show's music).[77] These competitions encouraged active participation and dialogue between members, helping to strengthen the site and its users' collective identity.

As of August 2021, the *Adventure Time* Wiki comprises 4,084 unique pages, which have been collectively created over the last decade by 5,452 Fandom editors.[78] The wiki also serves as a repository for thousands of images, including screenshots from episodes, background art pieces, production drawings of characters and props, and rough doodles made by the show's writers, producers, and storyboard artists. For anyone interested in learning more about the show and its world, the wiki is an invaluable resource.

Twitter

No discussion of online fandom in the 2010s can go without discussing the role played by Twitter. Founded in 2006 by Jack Dorsey, Noah Glass, Biz Stone, and Evan Williams, the site allows users (whose online handles are indexed by the presence of a @ sign, e.g., @AdventureTime) to send 280-character messages (called "tweets") out to their followers. Followers in turn can "like" these tweets or "retweet" them, the latter of which being a way to broadcast an original message to a larger audience. Messages can be made up entirely of text, or contain URLs, images, videos, emoticons, or "hashtags" (which function as keywords and are denoted by the presence of a # sign, e.g., #AdventureTime). Because it enables real-time dialogue, millions of users log into Twitter every day, using it as a means to discuss everything from breaking news to idle gossip.

According to Fanlore, "The 280-character limit makes it so that most fans use Twitter for more casual conversation that they feel don't belong on their main Tumblr or journal."[79] Some *Adventure Time* fans therefore use the site less as a vehicle for discussion and more as a channel through which to celebrate the show via the circulation of what Henry Jenkins, Sam Ford, and Joshua Green call "spreadable media." This includes content like memes, screencaps, and fanart. Popular accounts that focused on the circulation of this sort of material included @hallofegress's "*Adventure Time* Moments" and @Adventre Time's "*Adventure Time* Fans"—both of which boasted well over ten thousand followers.

Still other fans used the site to interact directly with the writers, storyboard artists, directors, and voice actors responsible for the show that they loved. In fact, when *Adventure Time* was in production, it was not uncommon to see fans tweeting questions or comments to the writers and producers, who in turn were often willing to discuss aspects of production with fans.[80] Other writers were known for tweeting out promotional illustrations for episodes that were slated to air.[81]

When *Adventure Time*'s initial seasons aired, Twitter was of course a popular site, but it was far from the main "hub" of the show's fandom. This began to change in the years following the series finale. For whatever reason, Twitter caught the eye of a considerable number of (largely Gen Z) fans, who began to use the site to connect and communicate with one another. Soon, ad hoc connections between individual users evolved into a large, decentralized community of users that became known as "*Adventure Time* Twitter" (or "attwt" for short). This constellation of fans spent considerable effort tweeting at one another, sharing fanart and discussing the finer technicalities of the show. Many of these users also expressed their love for the show by selecting a still of their favorite character as their profile picture. I was a part of the fandom during the height of this Twitter Renaissance (in fact, the edition of this book that you are now reading was inspired at least in part by suggestions from my *Adventure Time* Twitter followers), and while this activity was nowhere near the halcyon days of 2012 Tumblr, the rapid ascendency of attwt proved that the *Adventure Time* fandom was far from dead.

Formspring

Like Twitter, Formspring was a social media avenue through which fans communicated with the show's writers and producers. Formspring's premise was rather straightforward: users could create accounts and follow others. They could then anonymously ask other users specific questions, and the receiving users could answer those inquiries at their leisure. Because it provided them with an easy way to answer questions about the show, many members of the *Adventure Time* crew made use of the site, and by 2011, over a half dozen of the show's creative minds had created accounts of their own.[82] This turn of events delighted many fans who were interested in behind-the-scenes details, especially those who were ardent editors of the *Adventure Time* Wiki, and thanks to their diligence in particular, many Formspring answers became footnoted citations on the growing wiki.

In early 2013, Formspring began to have troubles with hosting, and by March, the site officially announced that it would be closing down within a month. At the eleventh hour, however, new investors swooped in and saved the site, which soon thereafter was rechristened "Spring.me." This iteration of the site continued to function for several more years until mid-2015, when it was fully absorbed (with almost no warning) by Twoo, a social media dating site. Unfortunately, this merger resulted in the loss of the former Formspring/Spring.me content, leading almost all of the *Adventure Time* crew to abandon the world of online question-and-answer sites. The lone exception was Adam Muto, who continued to answer fan questions long after the show's end via Ask.fm (a site that functioned in the same way as Formspring, although it embraced a different aesthetic).

Reddit

Another key to the *Adventure Time* fandom's online growth was Reddit. Founded in 2005 by two entrepreneurs named Steve Huffman and Alexis Ohanian,[83] Reddit is perhaps best described as a content aggregator, ranking content based on user approval or disapproval. If users want to show appreciation for a post or a comment, they can click on a small upward-facing arrow next to the content in question. This is known as "upvoting," and content that is heavily upvoted will eventually rise to the top of the site. Conversely, if users dislike a post or a comment, they can also click a small downward-facing arrow, which "downvotes" the content in question.[84] Posts that are heavily downvoted sink to the bottom, and in some cases are "buried" (that is, hidden from view).[85] According to a late 2019 press release, the site averages around 430 million users per month; altogether, these users have contributed almost 200 million unique posts, and have made just under 2 billion total comments.[86]

Reddit itself is divided into smaller communities, called "subreddits." These subsets of the larger Reddit universe are focused on specific topics and are denoted in text by affixing the prefix "/r/-" to the topic on which the subreddit is focused; the subreddit devoted entirely to *Adventure Time* is therefore perhaps unsurprisingly called /r/adventuretime. Created on October 11, 2010, /r/adventuretime grew at an astonishing speed, and by the end of 2012, it had racked up nearly fifty thousand users, catapulting it into the top 200 most-visited subreddits. In mid-2013—at the acme of *Adventure Time*'s popularity—/r/adventuretime became the 133rd most-subscribed subreddit, with just over one hundred thousand active users.[87]

The *Adventure Time* subreddit allows users to submit various types of posts, such as links, images, and text-based discussions. Of the three, links and images are by far the most popular[88] (likely due to their broad visual appeal), and while there are numerous text-only posts that discuss fan theories, these threads are often written for—and thus read by—a smaller, more fervent portion of the fandom. According to the *Adventure Time* fan Mordecai626:

> Reddit . . . was flooded with pictures of fans doing cosplays, tattoos, drawings, etc. It was difficult to discuss the show on there as much because there were so many other posts about other material. Though, the occasional text posts and episode discussion threads did provide people with a place to argue different perspectives and takes on the show.[89]

The YouTuber UncivilizedElk told me something similar. However, contra Mordecai626, UncivilizedElk argued that the rarity and tone of discussion posts made them easier (rather than harder) to locate:

> As far as discourse goes, every now and then there would be some good conversations on Reddit about the deeper aspects of the show. . . . Reddit of course had a bunch of fanart/silly/shitpost type stuff, but it was easier to notice when somebody wanted to dive deep and give super detailed thoughts.[90]

For many fans, the fact that the subreddit was composed largely of "silly" content like fanart or memes was not at all an issue—this was a site dedicated to a cartoon, after all. But for others, the limited discussion was frustrating; to ameliorate this issue, some users migrated to other sites, such as the Land of Ooo forums, where active discussions about plot developments or character motivations were more the focus.

But regardless of any perceived deficiencies, /r/adventuretime was, at its prime, one of the most-subscribed subreddits focused on a television show, which almost certainly helped the show gain popularity with teenagers and young adults. Even today—several years after *Adventure Time*'s season-ten finale—/r/adventuretime is still active. In fact, as of August 2021, /r/adventuretime had 329,164 subscribers (ranking as the site's 1,473 most-subscribed subreddit), with an average of 39 new posts and 222 new comments being created per day.[91]

Tumblr

Tumblr is a microblogging platform that allows users to create accounts, upload content, and share that content with other users. Founded in 2007 by tech wiz David Karp, Tumblr was in many ways a spiritual successor to blogging site LiveJournal, which had served as a fandom stronghold for much of the early 2000s.[92] From the beginning, Tumblr set itself apart from other (micro)blogging platforms by not only allowing fans to post, tag, and "like" content, but also by enabling users to "reblog" (i.e., share, à la Twitter's "retweet" option) content. In a nutshell, the "reblog" action takes someone else's post and republishes it on another's "dashboard" (i.e., a user's homepage). This effectively "signal boosts" the original post, thereby giving it a wider audience.[93] According to the fan scholar Louisa Ellen Stein, the reblog feature "resonated with fan practices of return, recirculation, and transformative reworking,"[94] turning Tumblr into a new hotbed of fannish activity that "defined a great deal of the Internet's culture" from 2008–14.[95]

Given its conduciveness to fandom playfulness, Tumblr inevitably attracted legions of *Adventure Time* fans, many of whom settled right in by creating accounts, reblogging fanart, discussing the show's mythology, and arguing about the finer details of shipping, among many other things. During *Adventure Time*'s heyday, there were thousands of Tumblr blogs dedicated to the show, but perhaps the most important account was the "King of Ooo" blog,[96] which was run not by fans, but by crew members of *Adventure Time* itself. Through this account, the show's producers posted behind-the-scenes content, like background pieces, character models, storyboards, song demos, animatics, promotional images, and other assorted miscellanea. Thanks to this one site, fans were privy to the often-mysterious process of how an episode of a modern animated television program is made.

Tumblr is the outlet of social media with which I have the most direct experience, as for the last six I have used the site to regularly post *Adventure Time*-related content under the moniker "GunterFan1992." I created my account in early 2014, and used it mostly to post short thought-pieces about story arcs or characters. While my first few posts received hardly any attention, my readership began to expand once I—emulating the approach of one of my favorite websites, the *A.V. Club*—started posting reviews of episodes. This growth increased dramatically when I began reaching out to members of the show's production crew and arranging miniature interviews, which I subsequently published as shareable Tumblr posts (posts that, in many ways, were the seeds for this book). While I cannot speak for all of my followers, it is likely that these interviews were alluring to fans who were interested in questions like the "why" and "how" of writing and storyboarding.

Interest in my blog arguably peaked with the airing of the *Adventure Time* finale in September 2018, and many of my posts during that month were liked or reblogged by hundreds upon hundreds of readers. And while I assumed that my readership would dry up and disappear in the following months, I somehow managed to hold onto a loyal contingent of readers, who have continued to interact with me well into 2020. (In fact, many of the subjects analyzed in this section of the book were solicited at least partially from my Tumblr posts.) Given all the excitement on the site about the *Distant Lands* specials and the upcoming *Fionna and Cake* limited series, it seems that Tumblr will likely remain a locus of fan activity for at least a few more years.

4chan

Now it is time to focus on a somewhat darker corner of the Internet: 4chan. The site is an anonymous message board that has gained a certain degree of infamy due to its association with groups like the activist "organization" Anonymous,[97] or the loosely affiliated "alt-right" movement.[98] A spin-off of the Japanese message board 2chan.net, 4chan allows users to create threads or make comments without having to create an account, thereby ensuring that all content is posted anonymously. To facilitate discussion, the site is divided into various "boards"—that is, themed forums dedicated to everything "from pornographic niches, to television, gaming, and cooking."[99] Included among the more popular boards are /pol/ (a forum for "politically incorrect" discussions), /b/ (a "random content" forum in which pretty much anything goes), and /co/ (a forum dedicated to discussion of comics, anime, manga, and cartoons).

It was on /co/ that most *Adventure Time* discussion took place, and during the show's first few seasons, many /co/ board members embraced the program eagerly, praising its fun characters, catchy music, and overall whimsical spirit. During this 4chan "golden age," it was not uncommon to find multiple *Adventure Time*–related threads open at once, or for episode-specific threads to reach the one-thousand-reply limit.[100] Sometimes, series artists, like Jesse Moynihan or Natasha Allegri, would log onto /co/ and chat directly with the board members themselves.

As the show wore on, however, /co/'s opinion began to change. The first wave of critics emerged early in Season 3, when Princess Bubblegum reverted back to her older form; many on /co/ found this reversion lazy and indefensible. Further ire was raised during Seasons 4 and 5, when some episodes began to focus on the newly introduced Flame Princess, which likewise corresponded with the show focusing more on Finn's passage through adolescence, leading to the exploration of heavy topics like love, loss, despair, and depression. This tonal shift bothered some /co/ members, who had originally started to watch the program for its light-hearted weirdness; some even began to bemoan that the show was drifting into pretentiousness. This growing frustration was further compounded when Rebecca Sugar left to create *Steven Universe*, encouraging some /co/ members to openly deride *Adventure Time* for "losing its soul." Paradoxically, others argued that Sugar's undeniable influence in Seasons 3, 4, and 5 "ruined" the program by steering it into "SJW"[101] territory.

/co/'s hyperbolic opinions about "nuAT"[102] only snowballed from there: Finn and Flame Princess breaking up was a misstep. Adam Muto was a bad showrunner. "Breezy" was an atrocious episode. Bubblegum was a Nazi. The Orgalorg plot went nowhere. *Stakes* ended right where it started . . . and on and on. But perhaps no other topic raised as much ire on 4chan as the show confirming Marceline and Bubblegum's romantic feelings for one another in the series finale; this anger was readily apparent in the days following the finale's airing when numerous posts on /co/ lambasted the show for this decision. While many board members argued that they were offended by the "obvious fan service,"[103] much of their rage seemed engendered by the fact that Finn did not end up in a romantic relationship with Princess Bubblegum, Marceline, or Flame Princess. To make this whole situation all the more colorful, many /co/ members expressed these frustrations while liberally mixing in slurs, off-color memes, and pornographic "Rule 34" content; 4chan, after all, has never been known for its tact or decorum.

Members of the *Adventure Time* fandom whom I interviewed for this book were often deeply ambivalent about 4chan, with many recognizing the site's place in the fandom while simultaneously distancing themselves from it due to its notorious nature. For instance, during a chat about fansites, one fan named "The Lich" told me:

> I was aware of 4chan's controversial history, and avoided it for a long time. I only visited it when there were whispers of [episode] leaks ... which did turn out to be true a few times, mostly during the season six era. The experience [on /co/] was intriguing, to put it in the most respectful way. It was a strange circus you could not look away from, that is for sure. I saw a large mix of fascinating analyses combined with trolling, strong dislike (especially in seasons five and six), and just flat out bizarre posts.... Regardless of [how] you feel about the site, there's no denying 4chan always gets attached to a piece of media and can find a way to have an impact.[104]

All things considered, 4chan is something of a mercurial enigma. While it almost certainly played a part in making *Adventure Time* popular with select viewers, by the time that the show had ended, the site had also become a strange bastion for *Adventure Time* hate.

The Land of Ooo Forums

For those who have long lurked online, the term "forum" will likely trigger a flood of memories and emotions. A specialized website on which fans digitally congregate to discuss some object of mutual interest, forums have long held a place in the history of fandom online. This is because they allow users to create "threads" (i.e., new pages for discussion), post messages to those threads, and message one another. While becoming less and less common in the social media era, fan forums are still an important aspect of the online fan experience, with Paul Booth (citing Henry Jenkins) arguing that "message boards and forums become knowledge communities that structure and organize the fans' knowledge about a particular text."[105] Given *Adventure Time*'s immense popularity in the mid-2010s, it may come as a surprise that only one fansite managed to really catch on: the Land of Ooo (LoO) forums.

This site was founded in the summer of 2010 by Tom Olson Jr. In time, it grew to a respectable size and was one of the go-to destinations for *Adventure Time*–related news, discussion, and idle speculation. Unlike a social media platform such as Twitter, Land of Ooo was highly organized, being divided into numerous subforums, each of which was dedicated to specific aspects of the show (e.g., there was a subforum for general *Adventure Time* news, one for episode-specific discussions, and another for character discussions). Additional threads were also focused on more ancillary topics, such as fanfiction, text-based role-plays, and television shows not related to *Adventure Time*. To invoke a cliché, LandOfOoo.com really had something for everyone, which led to it eventually boasting around seven thousand users who collectively contributed almost a quarter million posts to the site.

For many of the forum's members, watching an episode and then immediately logging in to chat about what they had just seen was something of a weekly ritual. Land of Ooo user Jake Suit, for instance, told me: "Back when the LoO was up and *Adventure Time* was still having weekly premiers was incredible. I'd watch the new episode Monday, and we'd discuss the episode and make predictions for next week's episode. Rinse and repeat month after month."[106] User The Lich, echoed this thought when he told me: "Discussing episodes as they aired was another fun aspect the forum allowed for, and [it] helped bond the fandom together."[107] While discussing the site's ability to facilitate conversation, the former forum member Fernando López noted that the Land of Ooo forums helped facilitate dialogue across space, as well as time and language: "Watching the show at the same time it premiered in the US and talking right on the forum was very enjoyable instead of waiting for CN LatAm's dubbed version."[108]

While fairly small as far as some fansites go, the Land of Ooo was nevertheless big enough to attract the attention of the show's production staff, and from time to time, crew members would even drop by. According to The Lich:

> My favorite memory of the forums [was] both times [storyboard artist] Jesse Moynihan visited—particularly when he visited the site's chat box one random day in April 2015. I was among several users in the chat at the time . . . and getting to have a consistent one-on-one conversation with a writer of the show was an extremely rare moment. . . . The fact that the forums attracted the attention of the *Adventure Time* crew at all is quite impressive, showing how special the forums were.[109]

Other members of the show's crew who were known to "lurk" on the site include character designer/storyboard artist Andy Ristaino and showrunner Adam Muto.[110]

Aside from Tumblr, Land of Ooo was the *Adventure Time*–focused website that I most often frequented. Sometime in 2013, I created my account (username: "GunterFan," about which I was often playfully teased, given that my profile picture was almost always of my true favorite character, Marceline), and within only a few days of posting, I found myself surrounded by some of the show's most ardent fans—many of whom I am now lucky enough to call my friends. While I remained on the forum until its very end, I was most active between 2013 and 2014, when *Adventure Time* was at the peak of its popularity. Looking back on this time, I cannot begin to count the hours I spent going from thread to thread, discussing new episodes, shooting messages to my online friends, or helping others compile spoilers for upcoming seasons.

During those years that I was most active, I remember feeling as if there was something special about the forums, but I could never quite express what that *je ne sais quoi* was. I realize now, upon reflection, that what I was feeling was the connective power of the site, which enabled hundreds of fans to congregate in one digital space and form a community centered on something we all loved. Former member Sophie told me something similar when she said:

> [Land of Ooo] was a safe haven where you could chat with like-minded individuals with a shared interest and no judgment—unless you disagreed with a ship, ha! It was fun to talk to others who actually know what you're talking about, as sometimes among young adults, it's hard to find people in real-life with a shared interest in a cartoon. On the forum you would encounter people of all ages and genders, from all over the world, who loved the show for what it was. Whether you were having a heated debate, laughing about a screen grab from the latest episode, or creating and discussing crazy theories with other [*Adventure Time*]-nerds, it was all a pleasure to read and be a part of.[111]

Sophie's comments touch upon a deeper truth. As social animals, we humans have a natural desire to fit into a group made up of people who understand and accept us for our interests. For those of us who frequented the Land of Ooo forums, the site in many ways provided us with that sort of warm feeling of community.

Unfortunately, all good things must also come to an end.

By late 2013, the cost of hosting the Land of Ooo forums was getting prohibitively expensive, and soon there was talk of shutting the forum down. Determined to save the site that so many loved, I, along with a few other forum users, organized a fundraiser in the winter of 2014, in which we raffled off character doodles made by members of the *Adventure Time* production crew. This ad hoc fundraiser was a short-term success and kept the website alive until that summer, when it temporarily went offline, necessitating a total reboot a few weeks later. A similar crash occurred again in 2017. Unfortunately, each of these crashes resulted in more and more users abandoning the site, turning it into a desolate shell of its former self. LandOfOoo.com went offline for good in 2017, and without a digital home, members of the forum scattered. While a few of the more seasoned members created a Discord channel to stay in touch, others disappeared into the wild mists of the internet.

It is sad that Land of Ooo forum never was able to fully return from the dead like some sort of digital Prismo, but given the important role it played in allowing *Adventure Time* fans to communicate with one another online, at least it can be remembered in a book chapter.

CONCLUSION

Over the last several pages, I have attempted to draw attention to the *Adventure Time* fandom, which, as of this book's publication, is an aspect of the show that has yet to be thoroughly engaged with in the scholarly literature. Having said that, I should note that this chapter is by no means a comprehensive survey, and each topic covered could likely be fleshed out into its own many-paged monograph (a book or article on *Adventure Time* cosplay, for instance, would be a fascinating piece of research). Instead of being some sort of complete treatment, I intend for this chapter to serve as an exploratory overview, and an opening for future researchers to further analyze the complex behaviors endemic to the community that is the *Adventure Time* fandom.

Conclusion

THE FUN WILL NEVER END

At 6 p.m. on September 3, 2018, my wife and I huddled around the television in our living room to catch the series finale of *Adventure Time*, "Come Along with Me." During the hour that followed, the two of us laughed, cried, and sat on the edge of our seats as we watched the ultimate adventure unfold before our very eyes.

I was quite heartbroken when the episode ended. It was not that I disliked the finale (on the contrary, I actually enjoyed it quite a bit); rather, I was upset because I realized that my favorite show—a show that had played a major role in my life—had finished its initial run.

Adventure Time was dead.

Or so I thought . . .

As I write this conclusion, *Adventure Time* has yet to disappear into the postfinale oblivion that awaits many television series after their initial run. On the contrary—Pendleton Ward's work has managed to somehow remain relevant in the wild, exciting world of contemporary animation. What is the show's secret to its continued success?

Perhaps it was the writing: *Adventure Time*, after all, was one of the first major cartoons of the twenty-first century that served up real emotional gut-punches alongside inane hilarity. This is not to say that animated programs of the past were incapable of poignancy—simply that *Adventure Time* had a tonal range that few shows could claim to rival. (How many other programs have managed to produce something as dark as "Simon & Marcy" in the same season as something carefree like "James Baxter the Horse"? And—perhaps more importantly—how many of those shows have done so while avoiding tonal dissonance?) Early in its run, *Adventure Time* directly contradicted the prevailing wisdom of the animation industry, proving that a cartoon could still be a hit comedy with kids and adults without sacrificing a sense of emotional affect. In this way, *Adventure Time* was a trailblazer, paving the way for other cartoons that deftly balance comedy with pathos, such as Rebecca Sugar's *Steven Universe* (2013–20), Raphael Bob-Waksberg and Lisa Hanawalt's *BoJack*

Horseman (2014–20), and ND Stevenson's *She-Ra and the Princesses of Power* (2018–20).

Maybe *Adventure Time* is still popular thanks to its unique aesthetic. Prior to the show's debut, most cartoons embraced the "thick-line" approach to animation which had been repopularized by Hanna-Barbera cartoons in the late 1990s. But then, in 2010, *Adventure Time* burst onto the scene, and overnight its modern-yet-nostalgic style—namely, its thin outlines, its liberal use of cel shading, and its penchant for "noodly" limbs that bend in seemingly impossible ways—became the "it" aesthetic. In no time, it seemed that all new cartoons were emulating the *Adventure Time* look. Some people have seen this widespread emulation as a sign that the 2010s were "lazy" or lacking in originality; on the contrary, I see it is a testament to *Adventure Time*'s artistic strength. The show's style was so refreshing that it caught the attention of animators and viewers alike, begetting an aesthetic realignment in the world of animation; not every cartoon changes the game so drastically.

Or maybe the show is still popular because it was always willing to try new things: From guest directors to complex miniseries, *Adventure Time* was ever inventive, refusing to cement itself as one thing. Instead, it chose to experiment with the cartoon medium, pushing it beyond its established limits in the name of limitless creativity. As such, it is hard to imagine a world where innovatively weird cartoons like *Midnight Gospel* (2020) or *Summer Camp Island* (2018–23) were greenlit, had *Adventure Time* not existed first.

In truth, there is probably no single answer as to why *Adventure Time* has remained evergreen. But after considering all the potential answers, one thing is clear: the show has impacted modern media in a variety of ways and because of this, I have no hesitancy in arguing that *Adventure Time* is not just a great work of modern animation, but of pop culture in general. And as with all pop culture masterpieces, there are innumerable aspects of the show that have yet to be teased out. There is no reason that *Adventure Time* cannot be like other works of pop culture past, such as Alfred Hitchcock's filmography, *The Lord of the Rings* trilogy, or the original *Buffy the Vampire Slayer* television series, all of which are media objects that, despite being released decades ago, still engender dozens of journal articles, monographs, and think pieces to this very day.

It can thus be said that this book is my attempt to breathe new life into the critical discussion of *Adventure Time*. In doing so, I hope to keep that promise that Pendleton Ward first made well over a decade ago when he, in front of an intimidating group of Frederator executives, pitched the series: "The fun will never end."

NOTES

INTRODUCTION: "C'MON, GRAB YOUR FRIENDS..."

All personal communications in this book were conducted via email, phone, or social media.

1. For a more in-depth take on this comparison, see Aaron Kerner and Julian Hoxter, *Theorizing Stupid Media: De-Naturalizing Story Structures in the Cinematic, Televisual, and Videogames* (London, UK: Palgrave Macmillan, 2019), 120–25.
2. James Poniewozik, "The 20 Best TV Dramas since *The Sopranos*," *New York Times*, 2019, https://www.nytimes.com/interactive/2019/arts/television/best-drama-series.html.
3. There is a popular belief that fans of *Adventure Time* are all habitual drug users. This is a major assumption. Taking drugs is by no means a prerequisite for one to "get" the show.
4. Cf. Poniewozik, "20 Best TV Dramas."
5. Mike Rugnetta, "Is Nostalgia the Reason for *Adventure Time*'s Amazing Awesomeness?" PBS Idea Channel, YouTube, 2012, https://www.youtube.com/watch?v=7MVvkqbXiws.
6. Jennifer Luxton quoted in Grzegorz Czemiel, "Speculative Cuteness: Adventures of Ideas in *Adventure Time*," *View: Theories and Practices of Visual Culture*, no. 19 (2017), http://pismowidok.org/index.php/one/article/view/509/1074.
7. Czemiel.
8. Hui-Ying Kerr, "What Is Kawaii—And Why Did the World Fall for the 'Cult of Cute'?" *The Conversation*, 2016, https://theconversation.com/what-is-kawaii-and-why-did-the-world-fall-for-the-cult-of-cute-67187.
9. Czemiel.
10. Czemiel.
11. Kerr, "What Is Kawaii."

1. TWO RAD BROS: FINN THE HUMAN AND JAKE THE DOG

1. Maria Cassano, "15 Things You Didn't Know about *Adventure Time* That Will Make the Show Even More Amazing," The Things, 2016, https://www.thethings.com/15-things-you-didnt-know-about-adventure-time-that-will-make-the-show-even-more-amazing/.
2. Chris McDonnell, *The Art of Ooo* (New York: Abrams, 2014), 18; Pendleton Ward, Rebecca Sugar, Tom Kenny, John DiMaggio, and Jeremy Shada, "*Adventure Time* Panel"

(Discussion panel presented at the San Diego Comic-Con, 2012), viewable at https://www.youtube.com/playlist?list=PL33C7EDB51EAD9885.

3. Tim Surette, "Inside the Brain of *Adventure Time* Creator Pendleton Ward," TV.com, 2011, accessed https://web.archive.org/web/20110211015822/http://www.tv.com/story/25069.html.

4. Robert Lloyd, "As *Adventure Time* Wraps, a Look Back at How the Series Broke Barriers and Changed the Genre," *Los Angeles Times*, 2018, http://www.latimes.com/entertainment/tv/la-ca-adventure-time-oral-history-20180823-htmlstory.html.

5. McDonnell, *The Art of Ooo*, 23.

6. nutsquasha, "Pen Pendleton Ward Talkin *Adventure Time* at Cartoon Network's Comic Con Panel 2009," YouTube, 2009, https://www.youtube.com/watch?v=FJd91ld9jJE.

7. Phil Rynda, personal communication, June 1, 2021.

8. Jeremy Shada, "*Adventure Time* Interview: Jeremy Shada Speaks to Brendon Connelly," Vimeo, 2014, https://vimeo.com/85525511.

9. Zach Blumenfeld, "The Animated Adolescence of *Adventure Time*'s Jeremy Shada," *Paste*, 2016, https://www.pastemagazine.com/articles/2016/03/the-animated-adolescence-of-adventure-times-jeremy.html.

10. Whitney Matheson, "A Chat with . . . *Adventure Time* Creator Pendleton Ward," *USA Today*, 2011, http://content.usatoday.com/communities/popcandy/post/2011/12/a-chat-with-adventure-time-creator-pendleton-ward/1; Zack Smith, "*Adventure Time* Creator Talks '80s," *USA Today*, 2012, http://www.usatoday.com/story/popcandy/2012/11/01/adventure-time-creator-talks-80s/1672583/; Neil Strauss, "*Adventure Time*: The Trippiest Show on Television," *Rolling Stone*, 2014, https://www.rollingstone.com/tv/tv-news/adventure-time-the-trippiest-show-on-television-84180/; Pendleton Ward, "Pendleton Ward Live" (Presentation at ArcadeCon, 2014), viewable at https://www.youtube.com/watch?v=2kBnMoMTYcA.

11. Ward, "Pendleton Ward Live."

12. Adam Muto, Kent Osborne, and Pendleton Ward, "How an Idea Becomes *Adventure Time*," *Adventure Time*: The Complete Third Season, DVD (Los Angeles: Cartoon Network, 2014).

13. "Interview with *Adventure Time*'s Jeremy Shada (Finn the Human)," Skwigly, 2016, https://www.skwigly.co.uk/interview-jeremy-shada/.

14. "The Comet" (Season 6, Episode 43).

15. This name is fitting, given that "Minerva" was the Roman goddess of protection and the patron of doctors.

16. Patrick McHale, personal communication, January 23, 2019.

17. Pendleton Ward, "The Lich" commentary track, *Adventure Time*: The Complete Fourth Season, DVD (Los Angeles: Cartoon Network, 2014).

18. Jack Pendarvis, personal communication, August 9, 2019.

19. Tom Herpich, "The Lich" commentary track, *Adventure Time*: The Complete Fourth Season, DVD (Los Angeles: Cartoon Network, 2014).

20. Pendarvis, personal communication, August 9, 2019.

21. A portmanteau combining "Ooo" and "universe." I will use it throughout this book as a shorthand for "the fictional universe in which *Adventure Time* takes place."

22. Jesse Moynihan, "'May I Come In?' + 'Take Her Back' Episode Discussion Thread" [comment], Reddit, 2016, https://www.reddit.com/comments/3tdh3b/_/cx62rkz.

23. Jesse Moynihan, "Clarity and the Comet," 2015, http://jessemoynihan.com/?p=3023.

24. To quote Jake. "Dark Purple" (Season 6, Episode 29).

25. Moynihan, "'May I Come In?'"

26. Dan Tabor and Pendleton Ward, "A Chat with Pendleton Ward, Creator of *Adventure Time*," *Geekadelphia*, 2012, http://www.geekadelphia.com/2012/07/10/a-chat-with-pendleton-ward-creator-of-adventure-time-interview/.

27. Tabor and Ward.

28. "Jake Suit" (Season 5, Episode 27).

29. Pendleton Ward, "Bulldog," Formspring, 2010, archived at http://archive.is/IpRWw.

30. Alexander Ulloa and Ian Albinson, "*Adventure Time* (2010)," Art of the Title, 2010, https://www.artofthetitle.com/title/adventure-time/.

31. Pendleton Ward, interview by Tim Surette, 2011. (Transcript provided by Surette.)

32. Pendleton Ward, "*Adventure Time* Pitch Bible," 2008, https://www.scribd.com/document/3122798/Adventure-Time-series-presentation#from_embed.

33. Christopher Vogler, *The Writer's Journey*, 3rd ed. (Studio City, CA: Michael Wiese Production, 2007), 39.

34. Vogler.

35. John Moe, Open Mike Eagle, and John DiMaggio, "Finn, Jake, and the Necessity of Manuals," podcast audio, *Conversation Parade* 19:27. 2015, https://www.stitcher.com/podcast/american-public-media/conversation-parade-an-adventure-time-podcast/e/39560885.

36. Charlie Jane Anders, "*Futurama*'s John DiMaggio Explains Why *Adventure Time* Baffled Him," Gizmodo, 2013, https://io9.gizmodo.com/futuramas-john-dimaggio-explains-why-adventure-time-ba-510553095.

37. Moe, Eagle, and DiMaggio, "Finn, Jake, and the Necessity of Manuals."

38. Named after series storyline writer Julia Pott's "imaginary high school boyfriend." Jack Pendarvis, "I also don't think . . ." Twitter, 2018, https://twitter.com/JackPendarvis/status/975474997799129093.

39. Steve Wolfhard, "Jake the Dad . . ." [thread], Twitter, 2013, https://twitter.com/wolfhard/status/288518314878193664.

40. Wolfhard.

41. Wolfhard.

42. Wolfhard.

43. Wolfhard.

44. Steve Wolfhard, "Another pup: Gibbon!" Instagram, 2018, https://www.instagram.com/p/BnHCR83hvBw/?taken-by=wolfhard%7CSteve.

45. See https://tvtropes.org/pmwiki/pmwiki.php/Main/OvernightAgeUp.

2. SUGAR AND SPICE: PRINCESS BUBBLEGUM AND MARCELINE THE VAMPIRE QUEEN

1. Lloyd, "Series Broke Barriers."

2. Cassano, "15 Things You Didn't Know"; Pendleton Ward Jesse Moynihan, Andy Ristaino, Steve Wolfhard, Ryan North, Michael DeForge, and Bob Flynn, "*Adventure Time* Panel" (Discussion panel presented at the Toronto Comic Arts Festival, May 5, 2012), viewable at https://www.youtube.com/playlist?list=PLA4147EA1DCA15F5A.

3. Robertryan Cory, "Old AT Preliminary Design 1," Flickr, 2012, https://www.flickr.com/photos/robertryancory/7695153422/in/photolist-cVzW8Q-afBX43-cHZF21.

4. "Paige Moss," Behind the Voice Actors, accessed June 14, 2019, https://www.behindthevoiceactors.com/Paige-Moss/.

5. Phil Rynda, "Yeah . . ." Formspring, 2010, http://www.formspring.me/philrynda/q/1165246010 (site discontinued).

6. Hynden Walch, personal communication, April 16, 2021.

7. Walch.

8. Bridget Blodgett and Anastasia Salter, "The Doctors Who Waited," in *Women in STEM on Television*, edited by Ashley Lynn Carlson (Jefferson, NC: McFarland & Company, 2018), 22.

9. Or, rather, Glob.

10. Cf. Rob Latham, "Mad Scientist," in *Horror Literature through History*, edited by Matt Cardin (Santa Barbara, CA: ABC-CLIO, 2017), 584.

11. "Wizards Only, Fools" (Season 5, Episode 26).

12. "Come Along with Me" (Season 10, Episode 13–16).

13. Marceline is never addressed by this full name in the series, but it has been used in the official Boom! Comics, the *Epic Tales* series of books, and by many in the fandom.

14. McHale, personal communication, January 23, 2019.

15. Ulloa and Albinson, "*Adventure Time* (2010)."

16. Pendleton Ward Jesse Moynihan, Andy Ristaino, Steve Wolfhard, Ryan North, Michael DeForge, and Bob Flynn, "*Adventure Time* Panel" (Discussion panel presented at the Toronto Comic Arts Festival, May 5, 2012), viewable at https://www.youtube.com/playlist?list=PLA4147EA1DCA15F5A.

17. Adam Muto, "It Came from the Nightosphere" commentary track, *Adventure Time: The Complete Second Season*, DVD (Los Angeles: Cartoon Network), 2013.

18. Pendleton Ward, "How did you come up with the name Marceline?" Vyou, 2010, http://vyou.com/pendletonward/150003/How-did-you-come-up-with-the-name-Marceline-Its-kinda-weird-sounding (Site discontinued).

19. Rynda, personal communication, June 1, 2021.

20. Rynda.

21. Phil Rynda, personal communication, June 28, 2021.

22. John Moe, Open Mike Eagle, and Olivia Olson, "Fionna and Cake, Marceline, and Addiction," podcast audio, *Conversation Parade* 41:50, 2015, https://www.apmpodcasts.org/conversation-parade/2015/08/fionna-and-cake-marceline-and-addiction/?autoplay=true; Florida Supercon, "*Adventure Time* Panel on Friday at Magic City Comic Con 2015," YouTube, 2015, https://www.youtube.com/watch?v=-TBRgddRGUs.

23. Olivia Olson, "The Mary Sue Exclusive Interview: Olivia Olson, Voice of Marceline the Vampire Queen," Mary Sue, 2013, https://www.themarysue.com/olivia-olson-interview/; Lloyd, "Series Broke Barriers."

24. Lloyd; Olson.

25. René A. Guzman, "Another Piece of Fiona and Cake," *San Antonio Express-News*, 2013, 2F.

26. "Henchman" (Season 1, Episode 22).

27. E.g., Andrew Boylan, "Children of the Night," in *Growing Up with Vampires*, edited by Simon Bacon and Katarzyna Bronk (Jefferson, SC: McFarland and Company, 2018), 25.

28. Vogler, *Writer's Journey*, 59.

29. Clarissa Pinkola Estés, *Women Who Run with the Wolves* (New York: Ballantine, 1992), 10.

30. E.g., Ward, "*Adventure Time* Pitch Bible," 20.

31. McKenzie Atwood, Adam Muto, Ian Jones-Quartey, Ben Levin, and Matt Burnett, "'Rebecca Sugar' with Adam Muto, Ian Jones-Quartey, and Ben Levin & Matt Burnett (Vol. 3/Ep. 9)," podcast audio, *Steven Universe Podcast* 58:22, 2018, http://podbay.fm/show/1261418557/e/1544079600?autostart=1.

32. Pendleton Ward, "Feel good . . ." Formspring, 2010, archived at http://archive.is/69GsK.

33. "Marceline the Vampire Queen" (Season 7, Episode 6).

34. Judith L. Herman, *Trauma and Recovery* (New York: Basic, 2015), 176–87.

35. Herman, 196.

36. Herman, 203.

37. Herman, 2.

38. "The Dark Cloud" (Season 7, Episode 13).

39. Olivia Olson and Adam Muto, "Making *Adventure Time Distant Lands: Obsidian* with Marceline | BAFTA Kids," YouTube, 2021, https://www.youtube.com/watch?v=8zDeUlofgZQ&t=122s.

40. In this section, I use the umbrella term "queer" to describe all relationships and orientations that are not considered heteronormative.

41. The major exceptions being: Simon Bacon, "'A Dream within a Dream,'" in *New Queer Horror Film and TV*, edited by Darren Elliot-Smith and John Edgar Browning (Cardiff, UK: University of Wales Press, 2020), 105–19; Mage Hadley, "From Censorship To 'Obsidian,'" in *Analyzing "Adventure Time": Critical Essays on Cartoon Network's World of Ooo*, edited by Paul Thomas (Jefferson, NC: McFarland, forthcoming).

42. Sarra Sedghi and Adam Muto, "Adam Muto Thinks an *Adventure Time* Reboot Is Just a Matter of Time," The Dot and Line, 2018, https://dotandline.net/adam-muto-adventure-time-interview-ce3981dcb3da.

43. Ward, "*Adventure Time* Pitch Bible."

44. Charlie Jane Anders, "Pendleton Ward Explains How He's Keeping *Adventure Time* Weird," Gizmodo, 2012, https://io9.gizmodo.com/5890128/pendleton-ward-explains-how-hes-keeping-adventure-time-weird.

45. Rebecca Sugar, personal communication, email, February 22, 2020.

46. Sugar.

47. Dan Rickmers, "'What Was Missing' Recap," YouTube, 2011, archived at https://www.youtube.com/watch?v=4G55ZV91TY8.

48. Fred Seibert, "Well, I Screwed Up," Frederator, 2011, archived on May 31, 2020 at https://tinyurl.com/ybf3jc3y.

49. Kjerstin Johnson, "*Adventure Time* Gay Subtext: 'Spicy' or Adorbz?" *Bitch*, 2011, accessed https://web.archive.org/web/20150309022518/http://bitchmagazine.org/post/what-the-math.

50. Zack Smith, "*Adventure Time* Creator Pen Ward Talks before Season Finale," Newsarama, 2012, archived at https://web.archive.org/web/20130527140217/https://www.newsarama.com/9077-adventure-time-creator-pen-ward-talks-before-season-finale.html.

51. Adam Muto, "I don't mind . . ." Formspring, 2011, archived at http://www.webcitation.org/6FGgPUQLY.

52. Initially, fans online referred to the pairing as "Sugarless Gum"—a phrase that obliquely referenced the lyrics of "I'm Just Your Problem." This label was soon eclipsed by the more intuitive "Bubbline."

53. Connie Wu, "*Adventure Time* Fans Rejoice! Olivia Olson Confirms Marceline and Princess Bubblegum Dated," Pride.com, 2014, https://www.pride.com/geek/2014/08/15/adventure-time-fans-rejoice-olivia-olson-confirms-marceline-and-princess-bubblegum.

54. Olivia Olson, "I like to make things up at panels. Ya'll [*sic*] take my stories way too seriously . . ." Twitter, August 8, 2014, archived at http://archive.is/QcNvU#selection-733.0-733.78.

55. Tara Strong, Greg Cipes, Olivia Olson, and Jessica DiCicco, "We Ship Bubblegum & Marceline from *Adventure Time* with the Cast and Cosplayers," *The Ship-it Show*, 2020, https://www.youtube.com/watch?v=6_n-b9LPXmo.

56. "Come Along with Me" (Season 10, Episodes 13–16).

57. Andy Swift, "*Adventure Time* EP Talks Bubblegum and Marceline's Series Finale Moment: 'These's Enough to Draw a Conclusion,'" TV Line, 2018, https://tvline.com/2018/09/03/adventure-time-series-finale-bubblegum-marceline-kiss-bubbline-confirmed/.

58. Swift.

59. Eric Kohn, "*Adventure Time* Finale Review," IndieWire, 2018, https://www.indiewire.com/2018/08/adventure-time-finale-review-come-along-with-me-1201996663/.

60. Bridget Blodgett and Anastasia Salter. "What Was Missing." In *Queerbaiting and Fandom*, edited by J. Brennan (Iowa City: University of Iowa Press, 2019), 142–55.

61. Hanna K. Nyström, "AT Distant Lands Obsidian," August 2021, https://www.instagram.com/p/CSP_tkoDLaV/ [quote in comments].

62. Sugar, personal communication.

63. Sugar.

64. Cartoon Network, "First time at #Pride?" Twitter, 2022, https://twitter.com/cartoonnetwork/status/1535313382152314881.

3. "BEST FRIENDS [AND FOES] IN THE WORLD": THE ENSEMBLE CHARACTERS

1. Sean Edgar and Patrick McHale, *The Art of "Over the Garden Wall"* (Milwaukie, OR: Dark Horse, 2017), 13–14; Patrick McHale, "@whoiam989 i had a robot . . . ," Twitter, September 7, 2011, archived at http://archive.is/9KRJz.

2. Patrick McHale, personal communication, July 2, 2021.

3. At the 2011 Comic-Con panel, Ward claimed that BMO was inspired by the "Apple II," although it is likely that he meant the Macintosh Classic II, which more closely resembles BMO's design. Rob Sorcher, Pendleton Ward, Kent Osborne, Jeremy Shada, Hynden Walch, Olivia Olson, John DiMaggio, and Matt Groening, "*Adventure Time* Panel" (Discussion panel presented at the San Diego Comic-Con, 2011), viewable at https://www.youtube.com/watch?v=SP0DNS8WBY4.

4. Amanda Pillon and Niki Yang, "The Voice of *Adventure Time*'s BMO and Lady Rainicorn Told Us How She Feels about the Show Ending," Sweety High, 2017, https://www.sweetyhigh.com/read/niki-yang-adventure-time-interview-040317.

5. Niki Yang, personal communication, April 20, 2021

6. Niki Yang, personal communication, February 11, 2020.

7. Pillon and Yang, "Niki Yang Interview."

8. Adam Muto, "The latter . . ." Formspring, 2013, archived at http://archive.today/Wj19V.

9. ShotGaming, "*Adventure Time* Interview with Pendleton Ward, Creator of Adventure Time!" YouTube, 2011, https://www.youtube.com/watch?v=JbOUl7giO_0.

10. Steve Wolfhard, personal communication, January 18, 2022.

11. Sugar, personal communication, February 22, 2020.

12. Wolfhard, personal communication, January 18, 2022.

13. Christopher J. Olson and CarrieLynn D. Reinhard, "A Computer Boy or a Computer Girl?" in *Heroes, Heroines, and Everything in Between* (Lanham, MD: Lexington Books, 2017), 183.

14. Olson and Reinhard, 188.

15. Olson and Reinhard, 179.

16. For a longer discussion on this, see Olson and Reinhard, 179–80.

17. Olson and Reinhard, 180.

18. See also: Emma A. Jane, "'Gunter's a Woman?!,'" *Journal of Children and Media* 9, no. 2 (2015): 231–47. https://doi.org/10.1080/17482798.2015.1024002.

19. Ward, "Pendleton Ward Live"; Adam Muto, "My favorite changes . . ." ask.fm, 2015, https://ask.fm/MrMuto/answers/132306656456.

20. Yang, personal communication, February 11, 2020.

21. Pendleton Ward, "Irradiated Stardust," 2010, Formspring, http://www.formspring.me/buenothebear/q/867949958 (site discontinued).

22. Patrick McHale, personal communication, August 29, 2019.

23. Pendleton Ward, Tom Kenny, and Jeremy Shada, "*Adventure Time* Roundtable Interview" (Roundtable at the New York Comic-Con, 2011a), viewable at https://www.youtube.com/watch?v=E7MyjoyB1ro.

24. Pendleton Ward, Phil Rynda, Steve Wolfhard, Andy Ristaino, Michael DeForge, and Bob Flynn, "*Adventure Time* Panel" (Discussion panel presented at the Toronto Comic Arts Festival, May 7, 2012), viewable at https://www.youtube.com/watch?v=aXKFDF-seMg.

25. "Skyhooks II" (Season 9, Episode 9).

26. See https://tvtropes.org/pmwiki/pmwiki.php/Main/WorldHealingWave.

27. See Tom Herpich and Steve Wolfhard, "'Apple Wedding' Final Storyboard," Scribd, 2014, https://www.scribd.com/document/199789252/AT-148-Apple-Wedding-final-storyboard.

28. Gaayathri Nair, "'*Adventure Time*': Why Lumpy Space Princess is Important," Bitch Flicks, 2014, http://www.btchflcks.com/2014/06/adventure-time-why-lumpy-space-princess-is-important.html#.XTkSYy2ZPjA.

29. Characters continue to call her "Flame Princess" even after she ascends the Fire Kingdom throne.

30. This appellation is derived from the ancient Greek term *phoibos*, meaning "bright, pure one," and in a slightly different form (i.e., "Phoebus") was used as an epithet for the

Greco-Roman deity Apollo, who was popularly believed to be the god of the sun. It would make sense that the flame elemental would have a name associated with the hottest bit of fire in the Solar System.

31. "Earth & Water" (Season 5, Episode 32).

32. Pendleton Ward, Jeremy Shada, Maria Bamford, Kent Osborne, Cole Sanchez, Ian Jones-Quartey, and Andy Ristaino ("*Adventure Time* Panel," panel at WonderCon, 2012), viewable at https://www.youtube.com/watch?v=6sEY85ReoIA.

33. Adam Muto, "Incendium" commentary track, *Adventure Time*: The Complete Third Season, DVD (Los Angeles: Cartoon Network, 2014).

34. McDonnell, *The Art of Ooo*, 133; Rebecca Sugar, "Incendium" commentary track, *Adventure Time*: The Complete Third Season, DVD (Los Angeles: Cartoon Network, 2014).

35. Sugar.

36. "Incendium," commentary by Adam Muto.

37. John Moe, Open Mike Eagle, and Jessica DiCicco, "Finn's Swords and Flame Princess," podcast audio, *Conversation Parade* 36:12, 2015, https://www.stitcher.com/podcast/american-public-media/conversation-parade-an-adventure-time-podcast/e/39731492.

38. Rebecca Sugar, "Hot to the Touch" commentary track, *Adventure Time*: The Complete Fourth Season, DVD (Los Angeles: Cartoon Network, 2014).

39. Moe, Eagle, and DiCicco, "Finn's Swords and Flame Princess."

40. Mike Gencarelli and Jessica DiCicco, "Jessica DiCicco Talks about Voicing Flame Princess on *Adventure Time* and Directing Kovas' Music Video for 'Ice Cream,'" Media Mikes, 2013, https://mediamikes.com/2013/03/jessica-dicicco-talks-about-voicing-flame-princess-on-adventure-time-and-directing-kovas-music-video-for-ice-cream/.

41. Jessica DiCicco, personal communication, May 14, 2021.

42. Gencarelli and DiCicco, "Voicing Flame Princess."

43. "Hot to the Touch" (Season 4, Episode 1).

44. "Ignition Point" (Season 4, Episode 22).

45. DiCicco, personal communication, May 14, 2021.

46. DiCicco.

47. "Princess Potluck" (Season 5, Episode 18).

48. Lloyd, "Series Broke Barriers."

49. "John Kassir," Behind the Voice Actors, accessed June 14, 2019, https://www.behindthevoiceactors.com/John-Kassir/.

50. Tim McKeon, personal communication, December 16, 2020.

51. "Tom Kenny Reflects on 20 Years of *SpongeBob* at C2E2," Culturess, 2018, https://culturess.com/2018/04/11/shadowhunters-season-3-episode-4-recap-review-thy-soul-instructed/.

52. Britt Hayes, "*Adventure Time* Interview: Creator Pendleton Ward and Star Tom Kenny," ScreenCrush, 2012, https://screencrush.com/adventure-time-interview/?utm_source=tsmclip&utm_medium=referral.

53. Hayes.

54. Tom Kenny, "Interview: Tom Kenny on the Hilarious Creepiness of *Adventure Time*'s Ice King," MTV, 2011, http://www.mtv.com/news/2623036/interview-tom-kenny-on-the-hilarious-creepiness-of-adventure-times-ice-king/.

55. Kenny.

56. Cory, "Old AT Preliminary Design 1."

57. Eric Thurm, "Why Ice King Is *Adventure Time*'s Best Character," *Vulture*, 2018, https://www.vulture.com/2018/09/adventure-time-ice-king-appreciation.html.

58. McHale, personal communication, August 29, 2019.

59. Matt Fowler, "*Adventure Time* Creator: It's Awesome If We Give People Nightmares," IGN, 2012, https://www.ign.com/articles/2012/03/05/adventure-time-creator-its-awesome-if-we-give-people-nightmares.

60. McHale, personal communication, August 29, 2019.

61. Pendleton Ward and Adam Muto, "Holly Jolly Secrets" commentary track, *Adventure Time*: The Complete Third Season, DVD (Los Angeles: Cartoon Network, 2014).

62. Paul Thomas, "Tom Herpich Interview," Tumblr, 2015, https://gunterfan1992.tumblr.com/post/127672988829/tom-herpich-interview.

63. See also: "Mind Over Pop Culture: *Adventure Time* 'I Remember You,'" Mental Health America, 2013, http://www.mentalhealthamerica.net/blog/mind-over-pop-culture-adventure-time-i-remember-you.

64. Neda Ulaby and Lev Grossman, "An 'Adventure' for Kids and Maybe for Their Parents, Too," National Public Radio, 2013, https://www.npr.org/series/pop-culture-happy-hour/2013/06/17/192385255/an-adventure-for-kids-and-maybe-for-their-parents-too?sc=tw&cc=share.

65. "Distant Bands: The Music of *Adventure Time*," *Adventure Time*: The Complete Fourth Season, DVD (Los Angeles: Cartoon Network, 2014).

66. Ghostshrimp and Kent Osborne, "Episode 080: *Adventure Time* Interview Part One: Kent Osborne," podcast audio, *Ghostshrimp and Friends* 2:22:00, 2020, https://soundcloud.com/ghostshrimp/episode-080-adventure-time-interview-part-two-kent-osborne.

67. Jesse Moynihan, "You Made Me," 2012, https://web.archive.org/web/20130714070417/http://jessemoynihan.com/?p=1712; Jesse Moynihan, Michael DeForge, Sam Alden, and Scott Roberts, "*Adventure Time* Artists Panel" (Discussion panel presented at the DePaul Visiting Artists Series, 2014), viewable at https://www.youtube.com/watch?v=PpLx6WzihoQ.

68. Jesse Moynihan claimed in 2013 on his Formspring that the character's name was originally "Lemonsnatch." "Originally . . ." Formspring, 2013, archived at http://archive.is/AZ0gd. Elsewhere, however, he has claimed that the original name was "Lemonsour." Moynihan et al., "*Adventure Time* Artists Panel."

69. Moynihan, "You Made Me."

70. Moynihan.

71. Tom Herpich, "You Made Me" commentary track, *Adventure Time*: The Complete Fourth Season, DVD (Los Angeles: Cartoon Network, 2014).

72. Benjamin Van Den Broeck and Justin Roiland, "Interview with Justin Roiland: Voice of Lemongrab," Blogger, 2012, http://nebulamedia.blogspot.com/2012/10/interview-with-justin-roiland-voice-of.html.

73. McDonnell, *The Art of Ooo*, 157; Van Den Broeck and Roiland.

74. Van Den Broeck and Roiland.

75. John Moe, Open Mike Eagle, and Jesse Moynihan, "The Best of C-Listers and Lemongrab Evolution," podcast audio, *Conversation Parade* 51:05, 2015, https://www.apmpodcasts.org/conversation-parade/2015/07/best-c-listers-lemongrab-evolution/?autoplay=true.

76. Moynihan, "You Made Me."

77. "Bonnie & Neddy" (Season 7, Episode 1).

78. *Webster's Unabridged Dictionary*, 2nd ed., s.v. "Lich"; Adam Muto, "No," Formspring, 2011, http://www.formspring.me/MrMuto/q/2221449707 (site discontinued).

79. Gary Gygax and Robert Kuntz, *Dungeons & Dragons: Supplement I: Greyhawk* (Lake Geneva, WI: TSR Rules, 1975), 35.

80. A "Big Bad" is a main enemy in a series (see https://fanlore.org/wiki/Big-Bad). The term was first used by the writers and fans of *Buffy the Vampire Slayer* to describe the primary villains of each season. Only a few enemies in Adventure Time can be considered bona fide Big Bads, namely: The Lich, Uncle Gumbald, and GOLB.

81. Ward, "*Adventure Time* Pitch Bible," 25.

82. Edgar and McHale, *The Art of "Over the Garden Wall,"* 14; Rebecca Sugar, "Mortal Folly" commentary track. *Adventure Time*: The Complete Second Season, DVD (Los Angeles: Cartoon Network, 2013).

83. Patrick McHale, personal communication, July 2, 2021.

84. See https://adventuretime.fandom.com/wiki/The_Lich_(character)/Gallery.

85. Phil Rynda, "Thanks!" Formspring, 2010, http://www.formspring.me/philrynda/q/1165244228 (site discontinued).

86. Sugar, "Mortal Folly" commentary track.

87. OmegaTsunami, "How Ron Got into *Adventure Time* C2E2 2013," YouTube, 2013, https://www.youtube.com/watch?v=bQviOcNDPek.

88. None of this is stated in the show per se, although most fans accept it as implied canon.

89. As evidenced by: Andy Ristaino, "Originally . . ." Formspring, 2011, archived at http://archive.today/8MnqH.

90. Implied by the events in "Finn the Human"/"Jake the Dog" (Season 5, Episodes 1–2).

91. Specifically Ezekiel 37:7–10.

92. "Escape from the Citadel" (Season 6, Episode 2).

93. "Whispers" (Season 9, Episode 14).

94. Bhagavad Gita, 11:32.

95. To borrow a phrase from Sequoia Stone's essay "'And we will happen again and again': *Adventure Time* and the Sisyphean Struggle," in *Analyzing "Adventure Time": Critical Essays on Cartoon Network's World of Ooo*, edited by Paul Thomas (Jefferson, NC: McFarland, forthcoming).

4. THE "C-LISTERS": OTHER CHARACTERS OF NOTE

1. Betty's last name is a reference to Stanislov Grof, a medical doctor and transpersonal psychologist. Jesse Moynihan, "Betty's last name . . ." Twitter, 2014, archived at https://archive.is/vXUUy#selection-749.0-749.48.

2. Bill Graham, "Comic-Con: *Adventure Time* Panel Features Live Radio Play with Audio; A Brief Look at New Flame Princess Episode," Collider, 2012, http://collider.com/comic-con-adventure-time-recap/.

3. Adam Muto and Kent Osborne, "*Adventure Time* (2014): Adam Muto & Kent Osborne Interview," HappyCool, 2014, https://www.youtube.com/watch?v=mYhjZHc9_ms.

4. Billy was originally named "Hogarth." Niki Yang, Kent Osborne, and Adam Muto, "'Finn Meets His Hero' Storyboard," Scribd, 2009, https://www.scribd.com/document/28992310/Finn-Meets-His-Hero-Storyboard.

5. "Billy's Bucket List" (Season 5, Episode 52).

6. Lou Ferrigno, personal communication, April 19, 2021.

7. "Finn," Adventure Time Wiki, accessed 2019, https://adventuretime.fandom.com/wiki/Finn.

8. A direct reference to *Sir Gawain and the Green Knight*. Jack Pendarvis, personal communication, August 7, 2019.

9. Pun intended.

10. Ditto.

11. Pendarvis, personal communication, August 7, 2019.

12. This name is pronounced differently across the series. Variations include "Gun**th**er," "G**oo**nter," and "Gunter." The last of these has been used throughout this book for consistency.

13. Tom Herpich, personal communication, January 23, 2019.

14. Andy Ristaino, personal communication, May 19, 2020.

15. Jesse Moynihan, "Adv Time—Flute Spell," 2016, http://jessemoynihan.com/?p=3452 (subscription required).

16. Jenny Slate, "*Adventure Time . . .*," Twitter, 2012, https://twitter.com/jennyslate/status/187406537126457345?lang=en.

17. Jack Pendarvis, "@PaulThomas1992 Well, he's the King of Ooo . . . ," October 31, 2015, https://twitter.com/JackPendarvis/status/660558187276468225.

18. The exception to this is the eighth-season episode "Lady Rainicorn of the Crystal Dimension."

19. Bert Youn, "@jaypds. . . ." Twitter, June 26, 2011, https://twitter.com/goodliverstore/status/85145729823289345. Note, the translation used in this book was provided by Vickie Doll.

20. Pillon and Yang, "The Voice of *Adventure Time*'s BMO."

21. Niki Yang, "Interview with *Adventure Time*'s Niki Yang," ToonBarn, 2014, archived at https://web.archive.org/web/20141025231250/http://www.toonbarn.com/cartoon-network/toonbarn-interviews-adventure-times-niki-yang/.

22. Cassano, "15 Things You Didn't Know."

23. Yang, "Interview with *Adventure Time*'s Niki Yang."

24. Jesse Moynihan, "My #1 is Magic Man," Formspring, 2012, archived at http://archive.is/w49Ld.

25. Ward et al., "*Adventure Time* Panel" (TCAF, May 5, 2012).

26. Jesse Moynihan, "Adventure Time Ghost," 2012, http://jessemoynihan.com/?p=1461; Jesse Moynihan, "Adventure Time Update," 2012, http://jessemoynihan.com/?p=1676.

27. Moynihan, "*Adventure Time* Update."

28. Moe, Eagle, and Moynihan, "The Best of C-Listers and Lemongrab Evolution."

29. Moe, Eagle, and Moynihan.

30. Jesse Moynihan, "U Forgot Ur Floaties," 2015, http://jessemoynihan.com/?p=2438.

31. Andy Milonakis, "I am Andy Milonakis—AMA" [comment], Reddit, 2013, https://www.reddit.com/comments/1l7udi/_/cbwl216/.

32. Steve Wolfhard, "*Adventure Time* 1000+," Tumblr, 2018, http://wolfhard.tumblr.com/post/177979408531/going-to-do-a-bit-of-an-adventure-time-dump.

33. Wolfhard was inspired to make Shermy a cat because of Finn's assertion in "Mortal Recoil" that he "is an agile cat." Wolfhard, *Adventure Time* 1000+."

34. Pendleton Ward, "Susan Strong" commentary track, *Adventure Time*: The Complete Second Season, DVD (Los Angeles: Cartoon Network, 2013).

35. Adam Muto and Rebecca Sugar, "Susan Strong" commentary track, *Adventure Time*: The Complete Second Season, DVD (Los Angeles: Cartoon Network, 2013).

36. McHale, personal communication, August 29, 2019.

37. Muto and Sugar, "Susan Strong," commentary.

38. Muto and Sugar.

39. Chris McDonnell, *Steven Universe: Art & Origins* (New York: Henry N. Abrams, 2017), 48.

40. Dennis Tardan, "S04–10 A Conversation with Polly Lou Livingston," podcast audio, *Conversations with Dennis Tardan* 26:27, 2013, http://www.blogtalkradio.com/dennistardan/2013/01/20/s04-10-a-conversation-with-polly-lou-livingston.

41. William J. Sibley, "Polly Lou Livingston," *San Antonio Current*, 2009. https://www.sacurrent.com/sanantonio/polly-lou-livingston/Content?oid=2286195

42. Tardan, "S04–10 a Conversation with Polly Lou Livingston."

43. Polly Luo Livingston, "I am Polly Lou Livingston, voice actress of Tree Trunks on Adventure Time. AMA!" Reddit, 2013, https://www.reddit.com/comments/36jjc1/.

44. Livingston.

45. "Jake the Dog" (Season 5, Episode 2). This is a direct reference to the 1902 short story "The Monkey's Paw," by British author W. W. Jacobs.

46. James R. Duncan, *Owls of the World* (Buffalo, NY: Firefly Books, 2003), 89–105.

47. McDonnell, *The Art of Ooo*, 114–15.

48. Jesse Moynihan, "*Adventure Time #3*," 2011, http://jessemoynihan.com/?p=1119.

49. Moynihan, "*Adventure Time #3*."

50. Ezekiel 1:5–6.

51. Genesis 3:24; J. C. J. Metford, *Dictionary of Christian Lore and Legend* (London, UK: Thames and Hudson, 1983), 66.

52. Pendleton Ward, "Sons of Mars" commentary track, *Adventure Time*: The Complete Fourth Season, DVD (Los Angeles: Cartoon Network, 2014).

53. Frederator uploaded a copy of the "Glorriors" storyboard onto Flickr, but this version was a postrevision copy that did not include the scenes featuring Abe Lincoln. Ian Jones Quartey, personal communication, January 31, 2022.

54. Doug TenNapel, "Dick Masterson of 'The Dick Show' on Culture, Faith & Politics!" YouTube, 2018, https://www.youtube.com/watch?v=L4xQPnm7r9s.

55. Ward, "Sons of Mars" commentary.

56. As suggested in "Puhoy" (Season 5, Episode 16). GOLB first appears in this episode after Finn "dies" but before he returns back to Ooo, ignorant of the pillow universe. The implication is that GOLB may have erased the pillow universe from existence, explaining Finn's amnesia.

57. Who in turn writes fanfiction about "Janet the Fox" and "Lynn the Person." Talk about turtles all the way down.

58. See https://tvtropes.org/pmwiki/pmwiki.php/Main/RuleSixtyThree.

59. See https://fanlore.org/wiki/Genderswap.

60. Ann-Derrick Gaillot, "Internet Crush: *Adventure Time*'s Natasha Allegri," *Bitch*, 2011, https://www.bitchmedia.org/post/internet-crush-natasha-allegri.

61. Guzman, "Fiona and Cake"; Pendleton Ward, "Fionna and Cake" commentary track, *Adventure Time*: The Complete Second Season, DVD (Los Angeles: Cartoon Network, 2014).

62. Rebecca Sugar, "Fionna and Cake" commentary track, *Adventure Time*: The Complete Second Season, DVD (Los Angeles: Cartoon Network, 2014).

63. Guzman, "Fiona and Cake"; Chris Sims, "*Adventure Time*'s Gender-Swapped Episode and the Art of Natasha Allegri," Comics Alliance, 2011, http://comicsalliance.com/adventure-times-fionna-cake/.

64. "Monday Cable Ratings: 'Monday Night Football' Wins Night, 'WWE Raw,' 'Teen Moms II,' 'Pawn Stars,' 'Catfish,' 'Real Housewives' & More," TV by the Numbers, 2012, https://tvbythenumbers.zap2it.com/sdsdskdh279882992z1/monday-cable-ratings-monday-night-football-wins-night-wwe-raw-teen-moms-ii-pawn-stars-catfish-real-housewives-more/157261/.

65. Guzman, "Fiona and Cake."

5. BEHIND THE EASEL: HOW AN EPISODE WAS MADE

1. Adam Muto, announcement at the "Series Finale Screening Event," August 27, 2018.

2. Adam Muto, et al., "Farewell Tour," DVD (Los Angeles: Cartoon Network, 2019).

3. On a related note, Herpich told me in an interview: "To create everything from scratch makes the whole thing that much more engaging to work on. It's sort of an irony of this job—for me anyways—that I usually want everything to be really difficult, because then it's interesting, and therefore feels easier, whereas easy simple stuff is boring so it feels like hard work." Thomas, "Tom Herpich Interview."

4. Ben Blacker, "Pendleton Ward's Exquisite Corpse," BenBlackerWrites, 2012, https://benblackerwrites.wordpress.com/2012/11/27/pendleton-wards-exquisite-corpse/.

5. Graham, "Comic-Con."

6. Martin Gero, Pendleton Ward, and Kent Osborne, "#65: Pendleton Ward, Martin Gero, and Kent Osborne," podcast audio, *Nerdist Writers Panel* 1:37:06, 2012, https://archive.nerdist.com/nerdist-writers-panel-65-pendleton-ward-martin-gero-and-kent-osborne/; Ward et al., "*Adventure Time* Panel" (TCAF, May 5).

7. McDonnell, *The Art of Ooo*, 260; Indie Memphis Film Festival, "Indie Talks: Bringing *Adventure Time* to Life by Kent Osborne," YouTube, 2014, https://www.youtube.com/watch?v=TPyAniGrhJc.

8. Pendleton Ward, Tom Kenny, and Jeremy Shada, "*Adventure Time* Roundtable Interview" (Roundtable at the New York Comic-Con, 2011b), viewable at https://www.youtube.com/watch?v=UwgDDJIXLMo.

9. Ward et al.

10. Noel Murray, "*Adventure Time* Creator Pendleton Ward," *A.V. Club*, 2012, https://tv.avclub.com/adventure-time-creator-pendleton-ward-1798230723.

11. Gero, Ward, and Osborne, "#65: Pendleton Ward, Martin Gero, and Kent Osborne."

12. Rich Goldstein, "This Is How an Episode of Cartoon Network's *Adventure Time* Is Made," *Daily Beast*, 2013, https://www.thedailybeast.com/this-is-how-an-episode-of-cartoon-networks-adventure-time-is-made.

13. Polly Guo, personal communication, October 30, 2018.

14. "Showrunner" is a unique term denoting an "executive producer . . . whose vision reigns supreme . . . The showrunner is responsible for all creative aspects of the show as well as its day-to-day management." Eve Light Honthaner, *The Complete Film Production Handbook*, 4th ed. (Burlington, MA: Focal, 2013), 395.

15. Guo, personal communication, October 30, 2018.

16. Sandra Lee, personal communication, May 3, 2019.

17. Tom Herpich, personal communication, September 16, 2018.

18. During the show's earliest seasons, storyboard artists were given four weeks exactly to turn in their storyboards, but as the show grew more popular, Cartoon Network agreed to give the artists an additional week. Jesse Moynihan and Dominick Rabrun, "Jesse Moynihan (*Forming, Adventure Time*) | DSC Interview," Dom's Sketch Cast, 2013, https://www.youtube.com/watch?v=nyl5k4sMu80.

19. Herpich, personal communication, September 16, 2018.

20. Laura Knetzger, personal communication, September 13, 2018.

21. Knetzger.

22. Biff [pseud.], Danimator [pseud.], and Andy Ristaino, "45—GIANT ROBOTS & Filling the Well with Andy Ristaino," podcast audio, *Geek Pile* 1:36:44, 2014, http://www.blogtalkradio.com/geekpile/2014/09/01/45-giant-robots-filling-the-well-with-andy-ristaino.

23. Pendleton Ward et al., "*Adventure Time* Roundtable Interview" (NYCC, 2011a).

24. Paul Thomas, "Ako Castuera Interview (2021)," Tumblr, 2022, https://bit.ly/ako-2021.

25. Corey Barnes, personal communication, April 23, 2021.

26. Elizabeth Ito, personal communication, May 4, 2021.

27. Ian Jones-Quartey, personal communication, February 1, 2022.

28. Biff [pseud.] et al., "45—Giant Robots & Filling the Well with Andy Ristaino."

29. Thomas, "Ako Castuera Interview (2021)."

30. Knetzger, personal communication, September 13, 2018.

31. Thomas, "Kris Mukai Interview."

32. Paul Thomas, "Kris Mukai Interview," Tumblr, 2015, http://gunterfan1992.tumblr.com/post/135747471089/kris-mukai-interview.

33. Lee, personal communication, May 3, 2019.

34. Shada, "Interview with Jeremy Shada."

35. McDonnell, *The Art of Ooo*, 132.

36. Barnes, personal communication, April 23, 2021; Joseph Game, personal communication, April 27, 2021; Justin Schultz, personal communication, April 29, 2021.

37. Harold Whitaker, John Halas, and Tom Sito, *Timing for Animation*, 40th Anniversary ed. (Amsterdam, Netherlands: Focal Press, 2021), 19.

38. Lee, personal communication, May 3, 2019.

39. Paul Thomas, "Derek Kirk Kim Interview," Tumblr, 2016, http://gunterfan1992.tumblr.com/post/150234549724/derek-kirk-kim-interview.

40. "On-model" drawings adhere closely to established character models, whereas off-model drawings "violate" these models by adjusting or exaggerating things like character height, limb proportions, facial features, and level of detail.

41. Paul Thomas, "Alex Campos Interview," Tumblr, 2015, http://gunterfan1992.tumblr.com/post/126428045701/alex-campos-interview; Game, personal communication, April 27, 2021.

42. Game, personal communication, April 27, 2021.
43. Derek Hunter, personal communication, February 26, 2019.
44. Hunter.
45. Hunter.
46. Game, personal communication, April 27, 2021.
47. McDonnell, *The Art of Ooo*, 350–51.
48. Tony White, *Animation from Pencils to Pixels* (New York: Focal, 2012), 199.
49. Tom Herpich, "Her Parents—1/24/11," Blogger, 2011, https://www.blogger.com/comment.g?blogID=3720677890630923366&postID=4551161569599174865 (comments).
50. Toon Boom, "Customer Productions," https://www.toonboom.com/company/customer-productions.
51. Phil Rynda, "*Adventure Time* is animated . . . ," Twitter, October 13, 2014, https://twitter.com/philrynda/status/521894394136256513; Game, personal communication, April 27, 2021.
52. McDonnell, *The Art of Ooo*, 350–51.
53. Lee, personal communication, May 3, 2019.
54. Lee.

6. THE FUN BEGINS: THE PILOT AND SEASON 1

1. Ramin Zahed, "And Now for Something Entirely Brilliant!" *Animation* 24, no. 1 (2010): 15.
2. Lloyd, "Series Broke Barriers."; McDonnell, *The Art of Ooo*, 15.
3. Sorcher et al., "*Adventure Time* Panel"; Nolan Feeney, "The Weird World of *Adventure Time* Comes Full Circle," *Time*, March 29, 2013, https://entertainment.time.com/2013/03/29/the-weird-world-of-adventure-time-comes-full-circle/.
4. Bart Carroll and Pendleton Ward, "Pendleton Ward Interview," Wizards of the Coast, 2011, https://dnd.wizards.com/articles/interviews/pendleton-ward-interview?x=dnd/4spot/20110408.
5. René A. Guzman, "Cartoonist Lets His Creative Process Lead his Characters," *San Antonio Express-News*, 2010, 01C.
6. See https://www.csssaf.org/alumni/.
7. Patrick McHale, personal communication, January 20, 2019.
8. McHale, personal communication, August 25, 2019.
9. Strauss, "*Adventure Time*."
10. Lloyd, "Series Broke Barriers."
11. Eric Homan, personal communication, March 23, 2021.
12. Lloyd, "Series Broke Barriers"; McDonnell, *The Art of Ooo*, 23.
13. Fred Seibert and Dominick Rabrun, "Fred Seibert Discusses the First Time He Met Pendleton Ward (Creator of *Adventure Time*)," Dom's Sketch Cast, 2013, https://www.youtube.com/watch?v=EKVyCleWIVk.
14. Fred Seibert, personal communication, March 31, 2021.
15. Ed Liu and Pendleton Ward, "Toonzone Interview: Pendleton Ward, Creator *Adventure Time*," ToonZone, 2011, https://www.toonzone.net/toonzone-interviews-pendleton-ward-creator-of-adventure-time/.

16. Andrew Farago, "Random Thoughts from Frederator Cartoonists," Animation World Network, 2009, https://web.archive.org/web/20120626040621/http://www.awn.com:80/articles/people/random-thoughts-frederator-cartoonists/page/3%2C1.

17. Farago.

18. McDonnell, *The Art of Ooo*, 23; Fred Seibert, "From Another Era, It Seems Like," Frederator, 2012, accessed http://archive.is/zsNUd.

19. McDonnell; Seibert.

20. Fred Seibert, *Best of Original Cartoons Produced by Fred Seibert (1981–2018)*, edited by Pancho Nakasheff, 5th ed. (New York: FredFilms, 2020), 44.

21. Zahed, "Something Entirely Brilliant," 14.

22. Seibert, personal communication, March 31, 2021.

23. Liu and Ward, "Toonzone Interview."

24. Seibert, personal communication, March 31, 2021.

25. Eric Homan, "'The Enchiridion' Storyboards," Frederator, 2010, archived at https://web.archive.org/web/20120426192911/http://archives.frederatorblogs.com/adventure_time/2010/04/22/the-enchiridion-storyboards/.

26. Homan, personal communication, March 23, 2021.

27. Homan, "'The Enchiridion' Storyboards."

28. Homan, "'The Enchiridion' Storyboards."

29. Seibert, personal communication, March 31, 2021.

30. Homan, personal communication, March 23, 2021.

31. McHale, personal communication, August 25, 2019.

32. Seibert, personal communication, March 31, 2021.

33. McHale, personal communication, August 25, 2019.

34. Seibert, personal communication, March 31, 2021.

35. McHale, personal communication, August 25, 2019.

36. Ghostshrimp and Kent Osborne, "Episode 079: *Adventure Time* Interview Part One: Ghostshrimp," podcast audio, *Ghostshrimp and Friends* 1:46:24, 2020, https://soundcloud.com/ghostshrimp/episode-079-adventure-time-interview-part-one-ghostshrimp.

37. Ghostshrimp and Osborne, "Episode 079"; Ghostshrimp and Osborne, "Episode 080."

38. Ulloa and Albinson, "*Adventure Time* (2010)."

39. Barnes, personal communication, April 23, 2021.

40. McHale, personal communication, August 25, 2019.

41. McHale.

42. McDonnell, *The Art of Ooo*, 35, 40–41.

43. Ghostshrimp, "Episode 050: *Adventure Time* Redux," podcast audio, *Ghostshrimp and Friends* 1:54:32, 2018, https://soundcloud.com/ghostshrimp/episode-050-adventure-time-redux.

44. Ghostshrimp; Ghostshrimp, "Episode 010: I Am a Total Fuck Up," podcast audio, *Ghostshrimp and Friends* 1:36:04, 2017, https://soundcloud.com/ghostshrimp/episode-010-i-am-a-total-fuck-up.

45. Ghostshrimp, "Episode 050."

46. Rynda, personal communication, June 1, 2021.

47. Ghostshrimp and Phil Rynda, "Episode 051: *Adventure Time* Memories Continued with Phil Rynda," podcast audio, *Ghostshrimp and Friends* 2:00:23, 2018, https://soundcloud.com/ghostshrimp/episode-051-adventure-time-memories-continued-with-phil-rynda.

48. Ghostshrimp and Rynda.

49. In the animation industry, "turn-arounds" are designs showing what a character looks like from different angles.

50. Ghostshrimp and Rynda, "Episode 051."

51. Rynda, personal communication, June 1, 2021.

52. Ghostshrimp and Rynda, "Episode 051."

53. Phil Rynda, "Phil Rynda Responses," Formspring, 2012, archived at https://archive.is/zsLg6#selection-3263.0-63.34.

54. Gero, Ward, and Osborne, "#65: Pendleton Ward, Martin Gero, and Kent Osborne."

55. Sandra Lee, personal communication, April 16, 2019.

56. Nate Kan, "From Storyboarder to Soldier—Bert Youn's Atypical Journey as an Animator," Maekan, 2018, https://www.maekan.com/article/from-storyboarder-to-soldier-bert-youns-atypical-journey-as-an-animator.

57. Mike Gencarelli and Niki Yang, "Niki Yang Talks about Voicing Beemo and Lady Rainicorn on *Adventure Time*," Media Mikes, 2013, https://mediamikes.com/2013/03/niki-yang-talks-about-voicing-beemo-and-lady-rainicorn-on-adventure-time/.

58. Gencarelli and Yang.

59. Gencarelli and Yang.

60. Yang, personal communication, February 11, 2020.

61. Ito, personal communication, May 4, 2021.

62. Ito.

63. Paul Fraser, "CalArts Alumni, Faculty Nominated for 40th Annual Annie Awards," California Institute of the Arts, 2012, http://blog.calarts.edu/2012/12/06/calartians-nominated-for-40th-annual-annie-awards/.

64. Cole Sanchez, "Masterclass: Cole Sanchez" (Presentation at Comic-Con Paris, 2016), viewable at https://www.youtube.com/watch?v=KVg9y7Vohc8.

65. See https://www.emmys.com/shows/spongebob-squarepants.

66. Ghostshrimp and Osborne, "Episode 080."

67. Ghostshrimp & Osborne.

68. Seibert, personal communication, March 31, 2021.

69. Eric Homan, "Get 'Evicted!' Tonight," Frederator, 2010, accessed https://web.archive.org/web/20141006194257/http://adventuretime.frederator.com/post/725318032/get-evicted-tonight; Eric Homan, "'Business Time' Sneak Preview Tonight," Frederator, 2010, accessed https://web.archive.org/web/20160303195301/http://adventuretime.frederator.com/post/449703459/business-time-sneak-preview-tonight.

70. Robert Lloyd, "*Adventure Time with Finn & Jake* Enters a Wild New World," *Los Angeles Times*, 2010, https://www.latimes.com/archives/la-xpm-2010-apr-05-la-et-finn-jake5-2010apr05-story.html.

71. Robert Seidman, "Monday Cable: Pawning & Picking Good for History; 'Damages' & 'Nurse Jackie' Damaged," TV by the Numbers, 2010, http://tvbythenumbers.zap2it.com/2010/04/06/monday-cable-pawning-damages-em-nurse-jackie-damaged/47625/.

72. Of note, this model would become the norm for most of the show's initial ten-season run, although it was later supplanted by the "bomb" model of episode delivery, as described later in this chapter.

73. A short sequence of Tree Trunks wandering in the Crystal Dimension was tacked on to the episode's ending to make it less horrific. Nevertheless, this "amended" ending is still a bit of a non sequitur.

7. FROM CULT FAVORITE TO MAINSTREAM HIT: SEASONS 2–5

1. Although McHale would step down as creative director at the end of Season 2, he would remain on as a storyline writer until midway through the show's fifth season.
2. He would return to storyboard during the show's third, fourth, and sixth seasons.
3. See, for instance: Mihaela Mihailova, "Drawn (to) Independence: Female Showrunners in Contemporary American TV Animation," *Feminist Media Studies* 19, no. 7 (2019): 1009–25, https://doi.org/10.1080/14680777.2019.1667065.
4. "Rising Stars of Animation," *Animation* 27, no. 9 (2013): 22.
5. "Rising Stars of Animation."
6. McDonnell, *Steven Universe*, 18.
7. Kwame Opam, "Sugar on Animation."
8. Sugar, personal communication, February 21, 2020.
9. Joe Bursely, "Sugar's Universe"; McDonnell, *Steven Universe*, 18.
10. See https://www.emmys.com/shows/adventure-time.
11. Cameron Esposito and Rebecca Sugar, "Rebecca Sugar," Podcast audio, *Queery* 1:07:42, 2017, https://www.earwolf.com/episode/rebecca-sugar/.
12. Rynda, "Phil Rynda Responses."
13. Tom Herpich, "*Adventure Time*," Blogger, 2009, http://herpich.blogspot.com/2009/02/adventure-time.html.
14. Ghostshrimp and Rynda, "Episode 051."
15. Herpich, personal communication, September 16, 2018.
16. Herpich.
17. Herpich.
18. "Heat Signature" (Season 2, Episode 26).
19. "Too Young" (Season 3, Episode 5).
20. Thomas, "Tom Herpich Interview."
21. E.g., Thomas, "Alex Campos Interview."
22. Thomas, "Tom Herpich Interview."
23. Thomas, "Ako Castuera Interview (2021)."
24. Jesse Moynihan, "Post 642," Land of Ooo, 2013, archived at https://web.archive.org/web/20141205181127/http://landofooo.com/community/topic/3590-jesse-moynihan/page-33.
25. Paul Thomas, "Ako Castuera Interview," Tumblr, 2016, http://gunterfan1992.tumblr.com/post/140123981299/ako-castuera-interview; Ghostshrimp, and Ako Castuera, "Episode 053: More *Adventure Time* Homies with Ako Castuera," podcast audio, *Ghostshrimp and Friends* 1:32:05, 2018, https://soundcloud.com/ghostshrimp/episode-053-more-adventure-time-homies-with-ako-castuera.
26. Ghostshrimp and Castuera, "Episode 053."
27. Jesse Moynihan, "About Jesse Moynihan," http://jessemoynihan.com/?page_id=2.

28. Moynihan, "Forming Hiatus"; Gero, Ward, and Osborne, "#65: Pendleton Ward, Martin Gero, and Kent Osborne."

29. Jesse Moynihan, "*Adventure Time* Airing," 2010, http://jessemoynihan.com/?p=1018.

30. Duncan Trussell and Jesse Moynihan, "Episode 220: Jesse Moynihan," podcast audio, *Duncan Trussell Family Hour* 1:29:14, 2016.

31. Moe, Eagle, and Moynihan, "The Best of C-Listers and Lemongrab Evolution."

32. This being a leetspeak abbreviation for the phrase "too deep for you," implying that Moynihan's spiritual and philosophical musings were superficially complex or pretentious.

33. David M. Ewalt, "It's *Adventure Time*! Pendleton Ward Talks about His Cartoon," *Forbes*, 2011, https://www.forbes.com/sites/davidewalt/2011/11/15/its-adventure-time-pendleton-ward-talks-about-his-hit-cartoon/#38f37ffe5c69; John H. Maher and Patrick McHale, "Exclusive: A Q&A with Patrick McHale," The Dot and Line, 2016, https://dotandline.net/patrick-mchale-over-the-garden-wall-interview-292f5661cc23.

34. Pendleton Ward, "Dream of Love" commentary track, *Adventure Time*: The Complete Fourth Season, DVD (Los Angeles, CA: Cartoon Network, 2014).

35. Castuera remained on as a regular storyboard artist until the conclusion of the show's fifth season. Afterwards, she contributed to a few freelance storyboards (including, three episodes of the *Stakes* miniseries), before working as a storyboard revisionist during the show's final few seasons.

36. The "Mortal Folly"/"Mortal Recoil" two-parter was intended to cap off the season, but due to production delays, "Heat Signature" aired as the finale. Tom Herpich, "Heat Signature—4/25/11," Blogger, 2011, https://www.blogger.com/comment.g?blogID=3720677890630923366&postID=6995612668048196117.

37. Cartoon Network, "Cartoon Network's 'Adventure Time,' 'Regular Show' and 'Mad' to Return for Additional Seasons," news release, 2010, http://archives.frederatorblogs.com/adventure_time/2010/11/30/the-secrets-out-adventure-time-gets-thirds-season/.

38. Sugar, personal communication, February 21, 2020.

39. Ghostshrimp and Osborne, "Episode 080."

40. Ghostshrimp and Osborne.

41. Cartoon Network, "Neil Patrick Harris Leads Cartoon Network's *Adventure Time* to Best Ratings in Its 3-Season History," press release, TV by the Numbers, 2011, http://tvbythenumbers.zap2it.com/network-press-releases/neil-patrick-harris-leads-cartoon-networks-adventure-time-to-best-ratings-in-its-3-season-history/.

42. Mike LeChevallier, "Review: *Adventure Time*: Season Three," *Slant*, 2011, https://www.slantmagazine.com/tv/adventure-time-season-three/.

43. Will Pfeifer, "Time for Adventure! Wonderfully Weird Series Fun for Kids, Grown-Ups Arrives on DVD," *Rockford Register Star*, September 24, 2011, Access World News.

44. Tom Herpich, "Conquest of Cuteness" commentary track, *Adventure Time*: The Complete Third Season, DVD (Los Angeles: Cartoon Network, 2014).

45. Anders, "Keeping *Adventure Time* Weird."

46. Anders.

47. Moynihan, "U Forgot Ur Floaties."

48. Anders, "Keeping *Adventure Time* Weird."

49. Kevin Ohannessian, "Pendleton Ward on Keeping *Adventure Time* Weird," Fast Company, 2012, https://www.fastcompany.com/1681874/pendleton-ward-on-keeping-adventure-time-weird.

50. To quote Rob Scorcher.
51. Anders, "Keeping *Adventure Time* Weird."
52. Ward et al., "*Adventure Time* Panel" (WonderCon, 2012).
53. Jesse Moynihan, "Adv Time—The Mountain," 2015, http://jessemoynihan.com/?p=2361.
54. Moynihan.
55. Ward, interview by Tim Surette, 2011.
56. Goldstein, "This Is How an Episode of Cartoon Network's *Adventure Time* Is Made."
57. Steve Wolfhard, personal communication, January 17, 2022.
58. Wolfhard.
59. Sugar identifies as a "non-binary woman."
60. Eric Kohn, "*Adventure Time* Writer Rebecca Sugar on *Steven Universe*, Being Cartoon Network's First Female Show Creator and Why Pop Art Is 'Offensive,'" IndieWire, 2013, https://www.indiewire.com/2013/11/adventure-time-writer-rebecca-sugar-on-steven-universe-being-cartoon-networks-first-female-show-creator-and-why-pop-art-is-offensive-33362/; McDonnell, *Steven Universe*, 13–24.
61. Kohn, "*Adventure Time* Writer Rebecca Sugar."
62. Ward, interview by Tim Surette, 2011.
63. Herpich, personal communication, January 23, 2019.
64. Adam Muto, "With Breezy . . ." [comment], Reddit, 2020, https://www.reddit.com/r/adventuretime/comments/hgdkqw/_/fw3enow/.
65. Patrick McHale, personal communication, July 2, 2021.
66. McHale.
67. Herpich, personal communication, January 23, 2019.
68. Jesse Moynihan, "Adv Time Cut Scene—Comment 6," 2017, http://jessemoynihan.com/?p=3431 (subscription required).
69. Jesse Moynihan, "'Something Big' Promo by Writer/Storyboard Artist Jesse Moynihan," King of Ooo (blog), Tumblr, 2014, http://kingofooo.tumblr.com/post/90413746144/something-big-promo-by-writerstoryboard.
70. Moe, Eagle, and Moynihan, "The Best of C-Listers."
71. Moe, et al.; Moynihan, "'Something Big' Promo."
72. Moynihan.
73. Moe, Eagle, and Moynihan, "The Best of C-Listers."
74. Herpich, personal communication, January 23, 2019.
75. Moe, Eagle, and Moynihan, "The Best of C-Listers."
76. Adam Muto, "Adam, Glory and Niki here—ask us anything!" Reddit, 2020, https://www.reddit.com/comments/hgdkqw/.
77. Strauss, "*Adventure Time*."
78. Maria Bustillos, "How *Adventure Time* Came to Be," The Awl, 2014, accessed https://popula.com/2018/09/03/the-literature-of-the-universe/, http://theholenearthecenteroftheworld.com/.
79. Ghostshrimp and Osborne, "Episode 080."
80. Ghostshrimp and Osborne.
81. Ghostshrimp and Osborne.
82. Ghostshrimp and Osborne.

83. Andy Ristaino, "Andy Ristaino"; Ghostshrimp and Andy Ristaino, "Episode 024: Guns, Money, And Drugs with Andy Ristiano," podcast audio, *Ghostshrimp and Friends* 1:38:24, 2018, https://soundcloud.com/ghostshrimp/episode-010-i-am-a-total-fuck-up.

84. Seo Kim, personal communication, July 26, 2021.

85. Chris Stokel-Walker, "Seo Kim: Cats, Comic, & Burbank," Tumblr, 2012, http://storyboard.tumblr.com/post/37259672615/seo-kim-cats-comics-burbank-she-said-it-with#seo-kim-cats-comics-burbank.

86. Payton Teffner, "The Return of Pendarvis: Jack Is Back," *Daily Mississippian*, 2014, https://thedmonline.com/the-return-of-pendarvis-jack-is-back/.

87. Jack Pendarvis, personal communication, April 30, 2019.

88. "Monday Cable Ratings."

89. Namely, Episodes 1–19 and 23 of Season 5.

90. Namely, Episodes 20–22, and 24–52 of Season 5.

91. Thomas, "Ako Castuera Interview (2021)."

92. E.g., Emily Guendelsberger, "Just Past 150 Episodes, *Adventure Time* Has Yet to Hit a Rut," *A.V. Club*, 2014, https://tv.avclub.com/just-past-150-episodes-adventure-time-has-yet-to-hit-a-1798179817.

93. E.g., Eric Kohn, "Why *Adventure Time*, Now in Its Fifth Season, Is More Groundbreaking Than You May Realize," IndieWire, 2012, https://www.indiewire.com/2012/11/why-adventure-time-now-in-its-fifth-season-is-more-groundbreaking-than-you-may-realize-43449/.

94. Emily Nussbaum, "Castles in the Air: The Gorgeous Existential Funk of *Adventure Time*," *New Yorker*, 2014, https://www.newyorker.com/magazine/2014/04/21/castles-in-the-air.

95. See https://adventuretime.fandom.com/wiki/Thanksgiving_Day_Parade.

8. COMING OF AGE IN OOO: SEASONS 6 AND BEYOND

1. Jesse Moynihan, "Wizards Only, Fools!" [comment], 2013, archived at https://web.archive.org/web/20131015131016/http://jessemoynihan.com/?p=2013.

2. Tom Herpich and Skyler Page, "'The Lich' Storyboard," Scribd, 2012, https://www.scribd.com/document/112716702/The-Lich-Storyboard.

3. Charlie Jane Anders, "Why *Adventure Time* Is Finally Breaking Its Status Quo Once and for All," Gizmodo, 2014, https://io9.gizmodo.com/why-adventure-time-is-finally-breaking-its-status-quo-0-1564741572.

4. According to Wolfhard, "Tom and I both worked really hard on this one . . . I was proud to get to board Finn getting his arm cut off and the aftermath. . . . Also, one of biggest laughs that I had gotten during an episode pitch was when I have Tree Trunks start to tell Mr. Pig that she wants a divorce, especially since I had just pitched an episode about them getting married."

5. Muto and Osborne, "*Adventure Time* (2014)."

6. Alden would later be hired on as a permanent storyboard artist starting in Season 7.

7. According to Herpich: "'Walnuts & Rain' was the first time I'd done both on the same episode. As nice as it is working with a partner, there's a level of spontaneity and immersion

in the writing process that's impossible to get to if you're sharing control over the episode. So yeah, it was exciting to be firing on a couple more cylinders than usual, juggling more balls, etc. Plus I'd had that story brewing in my head for so long before working on it that I was really confident that it would 'work,' which is definitely not always the case going into a new board. So that took some pressure off, too." Thomas, "Tom Herpich Interview."

8. For "Outstanding Short Form Animated Program" and "Outstanding Individual Achievement in Animation," respectively.

9. According to Wolfhard: "I was working on that headcanon [long before] the Orgalorg stories were being boarded, because my original [episode] idea involved a comet. [It was] inspired by the French *Donjon* comics. Those comics take place over three distinct eras. So, in correlation, *Adventure Time* would have the Mushroom Wars, current "Finn time," and the 1000+ future. I also thought that [the episode] worked with the thesis of the show—that there are no real endings, that life doesn't have endings. Things keep growing and changing. Characters die, but that's not the end of the story." Personal communication, January 18, 2022.

10. Eric Thurm, et al., "The Best TV Shows of 2014 (Part 1)," *A.V. Club*, 2014, https://tv.avclub.com/the-best-tv-shows-of-2014-part-1-1798275359.

11. Henry W. Grady College of Journalism and Mass Communication at the University of Georgia, "*Adventure Time* (Cartoon Network)," Peabody Awards, 2015, http://www.peabodyawards.com/award-profile/adventure-time/.

12. To quote Nussbaum, "Castles in the Air."

13. Jesse Moynihan, "Smuggle Brothers Final Board," 2017, http://jessemoynihan.com/?p=4053 (comments).

14. Eric Kohn, "*Adventure Time* Is Slowly Going off the Air, And Everyone's Moving On," IndieWire, 2017, https://www.indiewire.com/2017/02/adventure-time-ending-cartoon-network-1201785332/.

15. Nielsen ratings are reliably sourced here: https://en.wikipedia.org/wiki/List_of_Adventure_Time_episodes.

16. For the record, Season 6 had only two Ice King episodes, one major Marceline episode, one major Flame Princess episode, and no BMO-centric episodes.

17. Jesse Moynihan, "Adv Time 2 Part Finnale," 2015, archived at https://web.archive.org/web/20160315182437/http://jessemoynihan.com/?p=2452&cpage=1#comments.

18. Thomas, "Tom Herpich Interview."

19. Frank Allegra, "New Season of *Adventure Time* Gets Airdate and First Look at New York Comic Con," Polygon, 2015, https://www.polygon.com/2015/10/9/9489615/adventure-time-season-seven-airdate-comic-con.

20. Jeremy Dickson, "From the Mag: Maximizing Miniseries," Kidscreen, 2015, accessed September 7, 2018, http://kidscreen.com/2015/09/14/from-the-mag-maximizing-miniseries/.

21. Todd DuBois, "NYCC 2015: Roundtable Interviews for the *Adventure Time* Miniseries and Season 7," Toonzone, 2015, https://www.toonzone.net/nycc-2015-roundtable-interviews-adventure-time-miniseries-season-7.

22. Patrick McHale, personal communication, August 31, 2019.

23. Allegra, "New Season of *Adventure Time*"; McHale.

24. Allegra.

25. As revealed by the miniseries' storyboards.

26. During Seasons 5 and 6, Marceline starred in only seven episodes (out of a total of 95): "Five More Short Graybles," "Bad Little Boy," "Simon & Marcy," "Sky Witch," "Red Starved," "Betty," and "Princess Day."

27. Storyboard artist Jesse Moynihan once admitted that he found Marceline to be among the hardest characters to write. Paul Thomas, "Jesse Moynihan Interview," Tumblr, 2015, https://gunterfan1992.tumblr.com/post/125847184210/jesse-moynihan-interview. Moynihan's long-serving storyboard partner Ako Castuera likewise noted in an interview that she was not "a big vampire person." John Moe, Open Mike Eagle, and Ako Castuera, "Stakes, Eating, Patterns, and Eurydice," podcast audio, *Conversation Parade* 28:54, 2015, https://www.apmpodcasts.org/conversation-parade/2015/11/stakes-eating-patterns-and-eurydice/.

28. Herpich, personal communication, July 2, 2019.

29. Eric Thurm, "Rebecca Sugar's Cartoon Worlds Have the Best Music on TV," Pitchfork, 2015, https://pitchfork.com/thepitch/963-rebecca-sugars-cartoon-worlds-have-the-best-music-on-tv/.

30. "Cartoon Network Unveils Upfront Slate For 2015–2016," Deadline, 2015, https://deadline.com/2015/02/cartoon-network-upfront-powerpuff-girls-adventure-time-1201376480/.

31. The first Cartoon Network promo, for instance, prominently featured scenes from "Everything Stays" (the only episode in the miniseries made up mostly of flashbacks) and promised that viewers would "discover Marceline's vampire-hunting past."

32. Geo Neo, "Hanna K, 2014," Illustrator's Lounge, https://illustratorslounge.com/editorial/hanna-k/.

33. Paul Thomas, "Hanna K. Nyström Interview," Tumblr, 2017, https://gunterfan1992.tumblr.com/post/158352078174/hannak.

34. Thomas.

35. Moynihan et al., "*Adventure Time* Artists Panel"

36. Sam Alden, personal communication, August 22, 2019.

37. Bustillos, "How *Adventure Time* Came to Be."

38. Ashly Burch, "Ashly Burch." https://www.ashlyburch.com/.

39. John Moe, Open Mike Eagle, and Ashly Burch, "Bonnie & Neddy, Varmints, and Ashly Burch," podcast audio, *Conversation Parade* 29:12, 2015, https://radiopublic.com/conversation-parade-an-adventure-6vQdQW/ep/s1!96bef.

40. Moe et al.

41. Moynihan, "Thoughts on leaving *Adventure Time*."

42. Moynihan.

43. Moynihan.

44. Jack Pendarvis, "I'm going back to work tomorrow and I'm very happy!" Twitter, 2015, https://twitter.com/JackPendarvis/status/630586705976754176.

45. Tom Herpich, "It's been a long while . . . ," Tumblr, 2016, http://herpich.tumblr.com/post/153190942114/its-been-a-long-while-about-5-months-but.

46. Kohn, "Going off the Air."

47. In an interview, McHale noted that the "island wasn't necessarily [his own] idea," but that he was the one who was working to "[connect] all the dots" and "make all the loose pieces fit together." Personal communication, June 8, 2020.

48. Ghostshrimp and Osborne, "Episode 080."

49. Kohn, "Going off the Air."

50. Pendarvis, personal communication, April 30, 2019.

51. Ghostshrimp and Osborne, "Episode 080."

52. Adam Muto, "*Adventure Time | Elements* | Behind the Scenes (Legendado/Spoilers)," YouTube, 2017, https://www.youtube.com/watch?v=ZG4_VBRTx0Q.

53. Lloyd, "Series Broke Barriers"; Mercedes Milligan, "DePaul U Brings Phil Tippett, Julia Pott, Pritt Parn to Fxf Conference," *Animation Magazine*, 2019, https://www.animationmagazine.net/events/depaul-u-brings-phil-tippett-juia-pott-pritt-parn-to-fxf-conference/; "*Summer Camp Island* Takeover | Julia Pott | Cartoon Network This Week," YouTube, 2018, https://www.youtube.com/watch?v=iCSiWXTOLQU.

54. "New Show Creators Panel | San Diego Comic-Con 2018 | Cartoon Network," YouTube, 2018, https://www.youtube.com/watch?v=oJo4RsrfXR4.

55. Lloyd, "Series Broke Barriers."

56. "*Summer Camp Island* Takeover."

57. Eric Thurm, "'*Adventure Time*' as Talent Incubator," *New York Times*, 2018, Late Edition, C6.

58. Jack Pendarvis, "Waaaaahhhhhhhh!" Blogspot, 2016, https://jackpendarvis.blogspot.com/2016/11/waaaaahhhhhhhh.html.

59. Kent Osborne (@kentisawesome), "#AdventureTimeSeason9," Twitter, July 21, 2016, 10:45 a.m., https://twitter.com/kentisawesome/status/756183428920283136. Note, at the time of this announcement, the writers were under the impression they were working on the ninth, rather than tenth season.

60. Lloyd, "Series Broke Barriers."

61. Andy Swift, "*Adventure Time* EP Previews 'Satisfying' Series Finale Surprises," TV Line, 2018, https://tvline.com/2018/09/02/adventure-time-series-finale-preview-interview-season-10-ending/.

62. Lee, personal communication, May 3, 2019.

63. Ghostshrimp and Kent Osborne, "Episode 049: *Adventure Time* Finale Reactions with Kent Osborne," podcast audio, *Ghostshrimp and Friends* 1:20:47, 2018, https://soundcloud.com/ghostshrimp/episode-049-adventure-time-finale-reactions-with-kent-osborne.

64. Herpich, personal communication, September 16, 2018.

65. Ghostshrimp and Osborne, "Episode 049."

66. Lloyd, "Series Broke Barriers."

67. Ghostshrimp and Osborne, "Episode 049." Tom Herpich revealed that he might recycle some of these ideas in the future. Personal communication, September 16, 2018.

68. "Interview with *Adventure Time* Head Writer Kent Osborne," Skwigly, 2016, http://www.skwigly.co.uk/kent-osborne/; Kohn, "Going off the Air."

69. Kohn, "*Adventure Time* Finale Review."

70. Kohn, "Going off the Air."

71. Steve Hulett, "The Streaming Horse Race," Blogger, 2019, http://tombcartoonmonkeyskeleton.blogspot.com/2019/07/the-streaming-horse-race.html.

72. Comic-Con International, "HBO Max and Cartoon Network Studios: *Adventure Time: Distant Lands* | Comic-Con@Home 2020," YouTube, 2020, https://www.youtube.com/watch?v=W1gfCWo4dKw.

73. Muto, "Adam, Glory and Niki here."

74. Muto.

75. Although possibly related to the AT&T and Time Warner merger finalized in mid-2018.
76. Comic-Con International, "*Adventure Time: Distant Lands.*"
77. Comic-Con International.
78. Comic-Con International.

9. GOOD JUBIES: THE GUEST-ANIMATED EPISODES

1. Jacky Ke Jiang, personal communication, December 13, 2018.
2. Jiang.
3. Jiang.
4. Jiang.
5. Jiang.
6. David OReilly, personal communication, January 15, 2020; Daniel Rourke, "Datamoshing the Land of Ooo: A Conversation with David OReilly," Rhizome, 2013, http://rhizome.org/editorial/2013/apr/25/datamoshing-land-ooo-conversation-david-oreilly/.
7. OReilly.
8. G. A. Duarte, *Fractal Narrative* (Bielefeld, Germany: Transcript Verlag, 2014), 294. For more, see William Brown and Meetali Kutty, "Datamoshing and the Emergence of Digital Complexity from Digital Chaos," *Convergence* 18, no. 2 (2012): 168.
9. Rourke, "Datamoshing the Land of Ooo."
10. IndieCade, "Indiecade Festival 2014: 'A Conversation with Pendleton Ward and David Oreilly,'" YouTube, 2016, https://www.youtube.com/watch?v=NObcW1bzdIk.
11. OReilly seems to take a certain pleasure in knowing that this disturbing scene was funded by Cartoon Network Studios. IndieCade.
12. IndieCade.
13. OReilly, personal communication, January 15, 2020.
14. Carrie Battan, "Listen to a New Flying Lotus Song, Recorded for Cartoon Network's *Adventure Time* Series," *Pitchfork*, 2013, https://pitchfork.com/news/50206-listen-to-a-new-flying-lotus-song-recorded-for-cartoon-networks-adventure-time-series/; Rourke, "Datamoshing the Land of Ooo."
15. OReilly, personal communication, January 15, 2020.
16. IndieCade, "Indiecade Festival 2014."
17. James Baxter, personal communication, March 18, 2021.
18. Adam Muto, "James Baxter the Horse," Formspring, 2013, archived at https://archive.is/NnqPd.
19. Baxter, personal communication, March 18, 2021.
20. McDonnell, *The Art of Ooo*, 299
21. Baxter, personal communication, March 18, 2021.
22. Baxter.
23. Baxter.
24. Baxter.
25. See https://tvtropes.org/pmwiki/pmwiki.php/Creator/MasaakiYuasa.
26. Michelle Xin, personal communication, July 1, 2019.

27. Masaaki Yuasa and Eunyoung Choi, "*Adventure Time* 'Food Chain' Director Masaaki Yuasa and Eunyoung Choi Interview," *Anime! Anime!*, 2015, https://animeanime.jp/article/2015/01/01/21440.html (Translated from Japanese by Rosalyn Lucas).

28. Masaaki Yuasa, Eunyoung Choi, and Chris Prynoski, "112—Masaaki Yuasa," The Tongue & Pencil, 2019, https://www.youtube.com/watch?v=J8KExt8uipM.

29. In Japanese, サイエンスSARU.

30. Yuasa and Choi, "*Adventure Time* 'Food Chain' Director."; Masaaki Yuasa and Eunyoung Choi, "About," Science SARU, 2019, https://www.sciencesaru.com/about.

31. Yuasa and Choi, "*Adventure Time* 'Food Chain' Director."

32. *Anime! Anime!* staff.

33. Kent Osborne and Jessica DiCicco, "Our Interview with *Adventure Time*'s Head of Story and the Voice of Flame Princess!" Mary Sue, 2014, https://www.themarysue.com/adventure-time-nycc-interview/.

34. Yuasa, Choi, and Prynoski, "112—Masaaki Yuasa."

35. Zack Smith, "Pre-SDCC 2014: *Regular Show*'s Minty Lewis Gives Us an 'Eileen Day' at KaBOOM!" Newsarama, 2014, https://www.newsarama.com/21637-pre-sdcc-2014-regular-shows-minty-lewis-gives-us-an-eileen-day-at-kaboom.html.

36. Smith.

37. Yuasa, Choi, and Prynoski, "112—Masaaki Yuasa."

38. For an example, see the comments on Amid Amidi, "How Masaaki Yuasa Used Flash to Create His *Adventure Time* Episode," Cartoon Brew, 2015, https://www.cartoonbrew.com/flash/how-masaaki-yuasa-used-flash-to-create-his-adventure-time-episode-107691.html.

39. Amidi.

40. Oliver Sava, "Adventure Time: 'Food Chain,'" *A.V. Club*, 2014, https://tv.avclub.com/adventure-time-food-chain-1798180705.

41. Amid Amidi, "David Ferguson's Animated Shorts," Cartoon Brew, 2009, https://www.cartoonbrew.com/animators/david-fergusons-animated-shorts-13363.html.

42. Terry Anderson and David Ferguson, "David 'Swatpaz' Ferguson," podcast audio, *Drawn Out Podcast* 27:02, 2015, http://www.drawnoutpodcast.com/david-swatpaz-ferguson/.

43. Anderson and Ferguson.

44. Anderson and Ferguson.

45. Anderson and Ferguson.

46. Anderson and Ferguson.

47. Muto, "Adam, Glory and Niki here."

48. Oliver Sava, "*Adventure Time*'s Kirsten Lepore on the Joys and Pains of Stop Motion Animation," *A.V. Club*, 2016, https://tv.avclub.com/adventure-time-s-kirsten-lepore-on-the-joys-and-pains-0-1798243340.

49. Kirsten Lepore, personal communication, October 10, 2018.

50. Sava, "Joys and Pains."

51. Lepore, personal communication, October 10, 2018.

52. Lepore.

53. Lepore.

54. Kirsten Lepore, et al., "Good Jubies: The Making of 'Bad Jubies,'" DVD (Los Angeles: Cartoon Network, 2017).

55. Lepore, personal communication, October 10, 2018.
56. Lepore, et al., "Good Jubies."
57. Lepore, personal communication, October 10, 2018.
58. Disasterpeace, personal communication, November 12, 2018.
59. Disasterpeace.
60. MassArt Alumni, "Alex and Lindsay: Best Fwends," Massachusetts College of Art and Design, n.d., https://www.alumni.massart.edu/s/1432/17/interior.aspx?sid=1432&gid=1&calcid=2901&calpgid=1051&pgid=256&ecid=1977&crid=0.
61. Lauren Morse, Jessica Doll, Lindsay Small-Butera, and Alex Small-Butera, "'Baman Piderman' Creators, Alex & Lindsay Small-Butera (Part 2)," podcast audio, *DIY Animation Show* 37:09, 2016, https://soundcloud.com/diyashow/baman-piderman-creators-alex-lindsay-small-butera-part-2-diy-animation-show-2.
62. Morse et al.
63. Lindsay Small-Butera, personal communication, August 22, 2019.
64. Small-Butera.
65. Lindsay Small-Butera, "Hello!" Tumblr, 2016, http://smallbutera.tumblr.com/post/146564096972/hello-as-you-might-have-seen-we-animated.
66. Small-Butera, "Hello!"
67. Morse et al., "'Baman Piderman' Creators, Alex & Lindsay Small-Butera (Part 2)."
68. Lindsay Small-Butera (@SmallBuStudio), "Being excited over the Annies has had me looking back over our 2017 work fondly" [thread], Twitter, 2018, https://twitter.com/SmallBuStudio/status/960211313527083009.
69. Lindsay Small-Butera, "We're very humbled . . ." Tumblr, 2017, http://smallbutera.tumblr.com/post/156779020507/were-very-humbled-to-announce-that-this-year-alex.
70. Small-Butera, "Being excited over the Annies . . ."
71. Small-Butera, personal communication, August 22, 2019.
72. Small-Butera, "Being excited over the Annies . . ."
73. Lydia Winters, personal communication, June 3, 2021.
74. Tom Stone and Adam Muto, "*Adventure Time* Minecraft Episode," Minecraft.net, 2018, https://minecraft.net/en-us/article/adventure-time-minecraft-episode.
75. Stone and Muto.
76. Winters, personal communication, June 3, 2021.
77. Stone and Muto, "*Adventure Time* Minecraft Episode."
78. Joe Sparrow, "Late last year . . ." Tumblr, 2018, http://joe-sparrow.tumblr.com/tagged/Adventure-Time.
79. Winters, personal communication, June 3, 2021.
80. Winters.
81. Laura Polson and Paul Kalina, "*The Simpsons* Opening Sequence Created by Australians Ivan Dixon and Paul Robertson," *Sydney Morning Herald*, 2015, https://www.smh.com.au/entertainment/tv-and-radio/the-simpsons-opening-sequence-created-by-australians-ivan-dixon-and-paul-robertson-20150512-ggyxj9.html.
82. Stone and Muto, "*Adventure Time* Minecraft Episode."
83. Beat Staff, "SDCC 18: Saying Goodbye to *Adventure Time*," Comics Beat, 2018, https://www.comicsbeat.com/sdcc18-saying-goodbye-to-adventure-time/.

84. Don Hertzfeldt, personal communication, April 28, 2021.
85. Adam Muto, "Beat Boards by AT creator Pendleton Ward," Tumblr, 2021, https://kingofooo.tumblr.com/post/655990108627124224/beat-boards-by-at-creator-pendleton-ward-in-2013.
86. Time Out New York, "Symphonie Fantastique: Inside Basil Twist's Psychedelic Underwater Puppet Show," YouTube, 2018, https://www.youtube.com/watch?v=fgkU2Vm3qOE.
87. Basil Twist, personal communication, August 9, 2021.
88. Muto, "Beat Boards."
89. Twist, personal communication, August 9, 2021.

10. THE INSTITUTE OF SO UND: THE MUSIC OF *ADVENTURE TIME*

1. Emma Garland, "We Spoke to the Musical Masterminds behind *Adventure Time*," Noisey, 2015, https://noisey.vice.com/en_us/article/rpygqb/we-spoke-to-the-musical-masterminds-behind-adventure-time.
2. Casey James Basichis, personal communication, February 3, 2020.
3. Garland, "Musical Masterminds."
4. Basichis, personal communication, February 3, 2020.
5. Tim Kiefer, "Tim Kiefer Interview"; Eric Homan, "Manlorette Party Song," Frederator, 2010, archived at http://archives.frederatorblogs.com/adventure_time/2010/09/30/manlerette-party-song/.
6. Tim Kiefer, personal communication, October 17, 2019.
7. Kiefer.
8. Kiefer, "Tim Kiefer Interview."
9. Kiefer.
10. Basichis, personal communication, February 3, 2020.
11. Garland, "Musical Masterminds."
12. Tim Kiefer, "Wondercon—*Adventure Time*—Tim Kiefer Interview," JeanBookNerd, 2018, http://www.jeanbooknerd.com/2018/05/adventure-time-tim-kiefer-interview.html.
13. Casey James Basichis, "Behind the Music on Cartoon Network's *Adventure Time*," MPEG video (Los Angeles: Cartoon Network, 2013).
14. Basichis.
15. Basichis, personal communication, February 3, 2020.
16. Casey James Basichis, personal communication, July 29, 2020.
17. "Sonic Sounds," interview with Casey James Basichis and Tim Kiefer.
18. Kiefer's love of these genres can perhaps best be heard in the episode "Shh!" which features a remix of the song "No Wonder I" by LAKE in the juke/footwork style.
19. "Skweee" is a type of Scandinavian electronica that Kiefer colorfully describes as "weird guys with a lot of synths and a good sense of humor." Bleeding Cool, "Saying Goodbye to *Adventure Time* at WonderCon 2018 with Tim Kiefer," YouTube, 2018, https://www.youtube.com/watch?v=fyYDnJF7urw.
20. Bleeding Cool, "Saying Goodbye to *Adventure Time*."
21. Bleeding Cool.
22. See https://soundcloud.com/staypuft.
23. Kiefer, "Tim Kiefer Interview."

24. "Sonic Sounds," interview with Casey James Basichis and Tim Kiefer.
25. McDonnell, *The Art of Ooo*, 274–75.
26. Garland, "Musical Masterminds"; McDonnell, *The Art of Ooo*, 274–75.
27. Kiefer, personal communication, October 17, 2019.
28. McDonnell, *The Art of Ooo*, 274–75.
29. Kiefer, personal communication, October 17, 2019.
30. "Distant Bands."
31. Dom's Sketch Cast, "Fred Seibert."
32. "Distant Bands."
33. "Distant Bands."
34. "Distant Bands."
35. Basichis, personal communication, February 3, 2020.
36. Sean Jimenez and Bert Youn, "'Evicted!' Storyboard," Scribd, 2009, https://www.scribd.com/document/11659237/Evicted-Storyboard.
37. Patrick McHale, "Oh Marceline," Tumblr, 2016, https://oldsidelinghill.tumblr.com/post/150797635706/im-not-sure-if-this-has-been-posted-already-but.
38. "Distant Bands."
39. Basichis, personal communication, February 3, 2020; "Distant Bands."
40. McHale, personal communication, January 20, 2019.
41. "Distant Bands."
42. Basichis, personal communication, February 3, 2020.
43. Tracy Brown, "The *Adventure Time* Songs That Make You Cry," *Los Angeles Times*, 2018.
44. Ward et al., "*Adventure Time* Panel" (TCAF, May 5).
45. Brown, "*Adventure Time* Songs."
46. Rebecca Sugar, "The Song from 'Nightosphere,'" Posterous, 2010, archived at https://web.archive.org/web/20120315061023/http://rebeccasugar.posterous.com/the-song-from-nightosphere.
47. "Distant Bands."
48. Eric Homan, "Rebecca Sugar's First Board (Nightosphere)," Frederator, 2010, http://archives.frederatorblogs.com/adventure_time/2010/10/11/rebecca-sugars-first-board-nightosphere/.
49. Basichis, personal communication, February 3, 2020.
50. Eric Homan, "A Kettle of 'Fry Songs,'" Frederator, 2010, archived at http://archives.frederatorblogs.com/adventure_time/2010/12/13/a-kettle-of-fry-songs/.
51. Rebecca Sugar, "Susan Strong Song—The Demo Track," Posterous, 2011, archived at https://web.archive.org/web/20120102085044/http://rebeccasugar.posterous.com/susan-strong-song-the-demo-track; "Susan Strong," commentary by Pendleton Ward.
52. Kent Osborne, "Video Makers" commentary track, *Adventure Time*: The Complete Second Season, DVD (Los Angeles: Cartoon Network, 2013).
53. Yang, personal communication, February 11, 2020.
54. Rebecca Sugar, "Memory of a Memory" commentary track, *Adventure Time*: The Complete Third Season, DVD (Los Angeles, CA: Cartoon Network, 2014).
55. Tom Herpich, "Memory of a Memory" commentary track, *Adventure Time*: The Complete Third Season, DVD (Los Angeles, CA: Cartoon Network, 2014).

56. Pendleton Ward, "Memory of a Memory" commentary track, *Adventure Time*: The Complete Third Season, DVD (Los Angeles, CA: Cartoon Network, 2014).

57. See https://www.youtube.com/watch?v=1CjM3NLjXnE.

58. Adam Muto, "Fionna and Cake" commentary track, *Adventure Time*: The Complete Second Season, DVD (Los Angeles: Cartoon Network, 2014).

59. Rebecca Sugar, "Here is the demo for 'Oh Fionna.'" Tumblr, 2011, https://rebeccasugar.tumblr.com/post/9867585093/here-is-the-demo-for-oh-fionna-which-neil.

60. Rebecca Sugar, "What Was Missing" commentary track, *Adventure Time*: The Complete Second Season, DVD (Los Angeles: Cartoon Network, 2013).

61. Sugar.

62. "Marceline's Closet" (Season 3, Episode 21).

63. Jesse Moynihan, "*Adventure Time*: Marceline's Closet," 2011, http://jessemoynihan.com/?p=1417.

64. Moynihan.

65. Ward, "Pendleton Ward Live."

66. Moynihan, "Adventure Time: Marceline's Closet."

67. "Distant Bands."

68. Olivia Olson, "*Adventure Time* 10th Anniversary Livestream," Twitch.tv, 2020 (official stream deleted).

69. Olson.

70. Beat Staff, "Saying Goodbye."

71. McHale, personal communication, January 20, 2019.

72. "Distant Bands."

73. Jesse Moynihan, "Video Chat Critique Reward Tier," 2015, http://jessemoynihan.com/?p=3091#comment-2397079527 (comments).

74. Rebecca Sugar, "Daddy's Little Monster" commentary track, *Adventure Time*: The Complete Fourth Season, DVD (Los Angeles: Cartoon Network, 2014).

75. Patrick McHale, "@PaulThomas1992 mostly i was just trying to do something like 'i can show you the world.' . . ." Twitter, 2014, https://twitter.com/Patrick_McHale/status/505825107835883520.

76. "Distant Bands."

77. "Distant Bands."

78. "Distant Bands."

79. Rebecca Sugar, "I Remember You" commentary track, *Adventure Time*: The Complete Fourth Season, DVD (Los Angeles: Cartoon Network, 2014).

80. Rebecca Sugar, "Good Little Girl Demo!" Tumblr, 2013, https://rebeccasugar.tumblr.com/post/43467059818/good-little-girl-the-demo-and-chords-thanks-to.

81. Guzman, "Fiona [*sic*] and Cake."

82. Ghostshrimp and Osborne, "Episode 080."

83. Rob Sugar, "Well, she didn't make a demo of that . . ." [comment], YouTube, 2013, https://www.youtube.com/watch?v=0RVABjYg4V0&lc=Ugw1iUCLwyDiEUd-RsB4AaABAg.

84. Adam Muto, "Originally . . ." Formspring, 2013, archived at http://archive.today/9rY4M.

85. TV Equals, "Adventure Time Season 7 Interview: Jeremy Shada, John DiMaggio, Olivia Olson, Tom Kenny & Adam Muto," YouTube, 2015, https://www.youtube.com/watch?v=k4IF-PE5PfM.

86. Muto, "Originally . . ."

87. Gary Portnoy, personal communication, February 5, 2020.

88. Andy Ristaino, personal communication, March 2, 2020.

89. Andy Ristaino, "As I've said before . . ." Tumblr, 2013, https://skronked.tumblr.com/post/64747914557/as-ive-said-before-it-was-amazing-to-get-to.

90. Ristaino.

91. Ristaino, "As I've said before . . ."; Andy Ristaino, "this is a very early version . . ." Tumblr, 2014, https://skronked.tumblr.com/post/104386406727/this-is-a-very-early-version-of-the-song-i-wrote.

92. Ristaino, personal communication, March 2, 2020.

93. Herpich, personal communication, January 23, 2019.

94. Leslie Wolfhard and Steve Wolfhard, "Baby's Building a Tower into Space," King of Ooo (blog), Tumblr, 2014, https://kingofooo.tumblr.com/post/84942160809/babys-building-a-tower-into-space-demo-from-the.

95. Justin Moynihan, personal communication, January 9, 2020.

96. Moynihan.

97. Jesse Moynihan, "I wanted this episode . . ." Tumblr, 2014, archived at https://archive.ph/JDoth.

98. Moynihan.

99. Justin Moynihan, "With Breezy . . ." [comment], Reddit, 2014, https://www.reddit.com/comments/2cir3a/_/cjfwxrs/.

100. Moynihan, personal communication, January 9, 2020.

101. Soichi Terada, personal communication, June 13, 2019.

102. Mike Sunda, "Soichi Terada Arrives Fashionably Late to the Global House-Music Scene," *Japan Times*, 2015, https://www.japantimes.co.jp/culture/2015/12/06/music/terada-arrives-fashionably-late-house-scene/.

103. Terada, personal communication, June 13, 2019.

104. Ristaino, personal communication, March 2, 2020.

105. Ristaino, "this is a very early version . . ."

106. Ristaino.

107. Andy Ristaino, "here's my demo . . ." Tumblr, 2014, https://skronked.tumblr.com/post/104384501112/heres-my-demo-of-the-song-a-kingdom-from-a.

108. Tim Kiefer, "A Kingdom from a Spark," Tumblr, 2019, https://thenightkitchen.com/post/185111431089/i-had-a-blast-making-this-medieval-chant-y-track.

109. DiCicco, personal communication, May 14, 2021.

110. Jesse Moynihan, "Marceline Song," 2014, http://jessemoynihan.com/?p=2335.

111. Moynihan, "Marceline Song."

112. Hanna K. Nyström, "Rebecca Sugar—Everything Stays," Tumblr, 2015, archived at https://web.archive.org/web/20151121101321/http://hannakdraws.tumblr.com/post/133588762987/rebeccasugar-the-original-demo-for-everything.

113. Jimmy Aquino, Emily Edwards, and Rebecca Sugar, "Episode 679: MoCCA Mirth w/ Rebecca Sugar!" podcast audio, *Comic News Insider* 1:28:16, 2016, https://www.comicnewsinsider.com/2016/04/episode-679-mocca-mirth-w-rebecca-sugar-.html.

114. Aquino, et al.

115. Aquino, et al.

116. Aquino, et al.

117. Kiefer, personal communication, October 17, 2019.

118. Kim, personal communication, July 26, 2021.

119. Yang, personal communication, February 11, 2020.

120. Paul Thomas, "Andres Salaff Interview," Tumblr, 2022, https://gunterfan1992.tumblr.com/post/682708997573394432/andres-salaff-interview.

121. Guo, personal communication, October 30, 2018.

122. Guo.

123. Guo.

124. Guo.

125. Guo.

126. Evil was recording under the moniker "Babeo Baggins" when the episode aired.

127. Evil, "I just wanna slow dance with you . . ." Tumblr, 2017, archived at https://genius.com/18186904.

128. Evil [stage name], personal communication, February 5, 2020.

129. Polly Guo, personal communication, May 22, 2019.

130. Evil, "Babeo's Big Feel Better Cartoon List!" Tumblr, 2016, https://babeobaggins.tumblr.com/post/154775325797/babeos-big-feel-better-cartoon-list.

131. Evil, personal communication, February 5, 2020.

132. See https://www.youtube.com/watch?v=DjYch8-WG0M.

133. Evil, personal communication, February 5, 2020.

134. Mey Rude, "Bubbline Is Canon: 7 Gayest Moments from Adventure Time's Cutest Relationship," *them.*, 2018, https://www.them.us/story/bubbline-is-canon-adventure-time.

135. Evil, personal communication, February 5, 2020.

136. Atwood et al., "Rebecca Sugar."

137. Sugar, personal communication, February 21, 2020.

138. Kiefer, personal communication, October 17, 2019.

139. See https://genius.com/15537393.

140. Who would later play in LAKE with Eriksson.

141. A story artist who has worked on a number of lauded projects, including *Spider-Man: Into the Spiderverse* (2018).

142. The creator of Cartoon Network's *Regular Show* (2010–17).

143. Ashley Eriksson, personal communication, May 15, 2019.

144. Eriksson.

145. Robin Murray, "Next Wave #884: Zuzu," *Clash*, 2019, https://www.clashmusic.com/next-wave/next-wave-884-zuzu.

146. Zuzu, personal communication, June 2, 2021.

147. Zuzu.

148. Zuzu.

149. Zuzu.

150. Karen Havey, personal communication, November 11, 2020.

151. Havey.

152. Zuzu, personal communication, June 1, 2021.

153. Havey, personal communication, November 11, 2020.

154. Amanda Jones, personal communication, June 24, 2021.

155. Jones.

156. Jones.

11. THE ANCILLARY ADVENTURES OF FINN AND JAKE: COMICS, VIDEO GAMES, AND MORE

1. Tom Spurgeon, "CR Holiday Interview #20—Shannon Watters," Comics Reporter, 2013, https://www.comicsreporter.com/index.php/cr_holiday_interview_20_shannon_watters/.
2. Jared Shurin, "'Hey guys, it's me again, stuck in a hole.'–An Interview with Ryan North," Pornokitsch, 2016, https://www.pornokitsch.com/2016/12/me-again-interview-ryan-north-romeo.html.
3. Chris Sims, "Ryan North Talks *Adventure Time* Comic: 'The Zombies Represent Friendship,'" Comics Alliance, 2011, https://comicsalliance.com/ryan-north-adventure-time-interview/.
4. Sims.
5. Jimi Jaxon, "Ryan North—Writer of the *Adventure Time* Comic Series," Disco Droppings, 2011, https://discodroppings.com/2011/12/21/ryan-north-writer-of-the-adventure-time-comic-series/.
6. Mark Medley, "North Exposure," *Globe and Mail*, 2016, https://www.theglobeandmail.com/arts/books-and-media/choose-your-own-profile-ryan-north/article30328294/.
7. Shelli Paroline, personal communication, July 8, 2021.
8. Dana Forsythe, "These 2 Boston Area Artists Fell in Love through Comics, Made a Mark on *Adventure Time* Series," wbur, 2018, https://www.wbur.org/artery/2018/10/17/boston-comics-adventure-time-braden-lamb-shelli-paroline.
9. Braden Lamb, "Ryan, help me out," Tumblr, 2014, https://bradenlamb.tumblr.com/post/106642549439/ryan-help-me-out-how-do-braden-and-shelli-split.
10. Braden Lamb, personal communication, July 8, 2021.
11. Caleb Goellner, "*Adventure Time* #25: Artists Shelli Paroline and Braden Lamb Talk Two Years of Teamwork [Interview]," Comics Alliance, 2014, https://comicsalliance.com/adventure-time-25-shelli-paroline-braden-lamb-interview/.
12. Sims, "Ryan North Talks *Adventure Time* Comic."
13. Lamb, personal communication, July 8, 2021.
14. Shannon O'Leary, "How Cartoon Network Became a Haven for Some of the Best Independent Comic Book Creators Working Today," *Publishers Weekly*, 2012, https://www.publishersweekly.com/pw/by-topic/industry-news/comics/article/51954-how-cartoon-network-became-a-haven-for-some-of-the-best-independent-comic-book-creators-working-today.html.
15. Chris Sims, "Finn, Jake and Marceline Hack the Planet in *Adventure Time* #13 [Review]," Comics Alliance, 2012, https://comicsalliance.com/adventure-time-13-review-boom-studios/.
16. https://en.wikipedia.org/wiki/List_of_awards_and_nominations_received_by_Adventure_Time
17. Lamb, personal communication, July 8, 2021.
18. Christopher Hastings, personal communication, June 23, 2021.
19. Hastings.
20. Hastings.
21. Hastings.
22. Hastings.

23. Hastings.

24. Hastings.

25. Lamb, personal communication, July 8, 2021.

26. Darryn Bonthuys, "*Adventure Time*'s Pendelton [*sic*] Ward Is Keen on a Game Adaptation," Critical Hit, 2011, https://www.criticalhit.net/gaming/adventure-times-pendelton-ward-is-keen-on-a-game-adaptation/.

27. J. Fletcher, "WayForward Working on *Adventure Time* DS Game," Engadget, 2012, https://www.engadget.com/2012-03-23-wayforward-working-on-adventure-time-ds-game.html.

28. James Montagna, personal communication, August 2, 2021.

29. Brian Crecente, "*Adventure Time* Creator's Love of Video Games and Animation Are Hopelessly Entwined," Polygon, 2012, https://www.polygon.com/gaming/2012/8/28/3272199/adventure-times-pendleton-ward-video-game.

30. Montagna, personal communication, August 2, 2021.

31. Crecente, "*Adventure Time* Creator's Love of Video Games."

32. Montagna, personal communication, August 2, 2021.

33. Montagna.

34. Montagna.

35. Crecente, "*Adventure Time* Creator's Love of Video Games."

36. Z., "GeekDad Talks *Adventure Time* with WayForward Technologies," *Wired*, 2012, https://www.wired.com/2012/11/adventure-time-wayforward/.

37. Z.

38. Additionally, Montagna revealed: "Pen was inspired by the Japan-exclusive PlayStation game *Pepsiman* at the time, so he had this awesome idea that there could be live action FMV clips of him at the end of the game, being boisterous and congratulating players for beating the game, similar to the kind of videos found in *Pepsiman*. We were looking into the technical constraints of doing this on Nintendo DS and Nintendo 3DS, but ultimately the decision to crosspollinate Pen himself into the *Adventure Time* world was nixed . . . Despite this, we did manage to sneak something in. If you input Up, Up, Down, Down, Left, Right, Left Right, B, A on the title screen of the Nintendo 3DS version of the game, you'll reach a screen that has an audio clip of Pen singing a little song about the 'secret screen' and some ultra low-res pixel art that he himself made." Personal communication, August 2, 2021.

39. For a cumulative analysis of the gamer's reviews, see https://www.metacritic.com/game/3ds/adventure-time-hey-ice-king!-whyd-you-steal-our-garbage!.

40. Tomm Hulett, personal communication, June 15, 2021.

41. Gabriella Tata, "Transforming *Adventure Time* into a dungeon crawler: our WayForward interview," Shack News, 2013, https://www.shacknews.com/article/81499/transforming-adventure-time-into-a-dungeon-crawler-our-wayforward-interview.

42. Hulett, personal communication, June 15, 2021.

43. Hulett.

44. Tata, "Transforming *Adventure Time*."

45. Hulett, personal communication, June 15, 2021.

46. Hulett.

47. Tomm Hulett, personal communication, October 6, 2021.

48. Tata, "Transforming *Adventure Time*."

49. Tata.

50. Keza MacDonald, "*Adventure Time: Explore the Dungeon Because I DON'T KNOW!* Review," IGN, 2013, https://www.ign.com/articles/2013/12/06/adventure-time-explore-the-dungeon-because-i-dont-know-review.

51. Carolyn Petit. "*Adventure Time: Explore the Dungeon Because I DON'T KNOW!* Review," GameSpot, 2013, https://www.gamespot.com/reviews/adventure-time-explore-the-dungeon-because-i-don-t/1900-6415587/.

52. James Higginbotham, "PN Interview—*Adventure Time: Secret of the Nameless Kingdom*," Pure Nintendo, 2014, https://purenintendo.com/pn-interivew-adventure-time-secret-of-the-nameless-kingdom/.

53. Hulett, personal communication, June 15, 2021.

54. Hulett.

55. Hulett.

56. Dave Ellis, personal communication, June 13, 2021.

57. Ellis.

58. Ravi Sinha, "*Adventure Time Finn & Jake Investigations* Interview: Getting Weird with Vicious Cycle," Gaming Bolt, 2015, https://gamingbolt.com/adventure-time-finn-jake-investigations-interview-getting-weird-with-vicious-cycle.

59. Ellis, personal communication, June 13, 2021.

60. Ellis.

61. Ellis.

62. Fandom, "How to Make an *Adventure Time* Game," YouTube, 2018, https://www.youtube.com/watch?v=G1CSNleOqIg.

63. Kieron Verbrugge, "*Adventure Time: Pirates of the Enchiridion*'s Devs Are Passionate about Doing the Franchise Justice," Well-Played, 2018, https://www.well-played.com.au/adventure-time-pirates-of-the-enchiridions-devs-are-passionate-about-doing-the-franchise-justice/.

64. Fandom, "How to Make an *Adventure Time* Game."

65. Verbrugge, "*Adventure Time*."

66. Jason Stettner, "*Adventure Time Pirates of the Enchiridion* Interview," Gamer Headquarters, 2018, archived at https://archive.is/znNIV.

67. Stettner.

68. Allegra Frank, "*Adventure Time* Creator Working on Movie, but Nothing Official Yet," Polygon, October 9, 2015, https://www.polygon.com/2015/10/9/9489817/adventure-time-movie-pendleton-ward.

12. UTTER FINNDEMONIUM! THE INS AND OUTS OF THE *ADVENTURE TIME* FANDOM

1. Neil Cicierega, "I think every . . ." Twitter, 2019, https://twitter.com/neilcic/status/1126267499182469120.

2. Francesca Coppa, "A Brief History of Media Fandom," in *Fan Fiction and Fan Communities in the Age of the Internet*, edited by Karen Hellekson and Kristina Busse (Jefferson, NC: McFarland, 2006), 41 (emphasis mine).

3. Francesca Coppa, "Writing Bodies in Space," in *The Fan Fiction Studies Reader*, edited by Karen Hellekson and Kristina Busse (Iowa City: University of Iowa Press, 2014), 219.

4. Henry Jenkins, *Textual Poachers: Television Fans and Participatory Culture* (New York: Routledge, 1992), 162–63.

5. Biggerboot [pseud.], personal communication, February 11, 2020.

6. Instragram handle: @adventure.soph.

7. Sophie [pseud.], personal communication, February 18, 2020.

8. Jenkins, *Textual Poachers*, 162.

9. Juliette Grace Harrisson, "Shipping in Plato's Symposium," *Transformative Works and Cultures*, no. 21 (2016), https://journal.transformativeworks.org/index.php/twc/article/view/690/576.

10. See https://tvtropes.org/pmwiki/pmwiki.php/BrokenBase/WesternAnimation.

11. See https://www.fanfiction.net/s/7005076/1/The-Last-Human/.

12. See https://www.fanfiction.net/s/9016987/1/Change-Everlasting/.

13. See https://www.fanfiction.net/s/10765042/1/A-Love-Like-War/.

14. Jenkins, *Textual Poachers*, 171.

15. Gale [pseud.], personal communication, February 10, 2019.

16. myqueenmarceline [pseud.], personal communication, July 7, 2019.

17. myqueenmarceline.

18. Ann K. McClellan, *Sherlock's World: Fan Fiction and the Reimagining of BBC's Sherlock* (Iowa City: University of Iowa Press, 2018), 142.

19. Camille Bacon-Smith, *Enterprising Women: Television Fandom and the Creation of Popular Myth* (Philadelphia: University of Pennsylvania Press, 1992), 44–45.

20. Karen Hellekson and Kristina Busse, eds., *Fan Fiction and Fan Communities in the Age of the Internet: New Essays* (Jefferson, NC: McFarland, 2006), 55.

21. See https://www.fanfiction.net/cartoon/Adventure-Time-with-Finn-and-Jake/.

22. See https://archiveofourown.org/tags/Adventure%20Time/works/.

23. For more on this topic, see https://fanlore.org/wiki/Fanfiction/.

24. https://fanlore.org/wiki/Adventure_Time.

25. Sophie, personal communication, February 18, 2020.

26. Emphasis on amateur.

27. Jagm [pseud.], personal communication, January 29, 2020.

28. Cf. Jessica Seymour, "Racebending and Prosumer Fanart Practices in Harry Potter Fandom," in *A Companion to Media Fandom and Fan Studies*, edited by Paul Booth (Hoboken, NJ: Wiley Blackwell, 2018), section "Fan/art Studies; Harry Potter and Beyond."

29. Robin Brenner, *Understanding Manga and Anime* (Westport, CT: Libraries Unlimited, 2007), 204.

30. Robin Brenner, "Teen Literature and Fan Culture," *Young Adult Library Services* 11, no. 4 (2013): 33.

31. Loycos [pseud.], personal communication, May 22, 2021.

32. Otto, personal communication, May 23, 2021.

33. To use Jenkins's terms. See Jenkins, *Textual Poachers*; Henry Jenkins, "*Star Trek* Rerun, Reread, Rewritten: Fan Writing as Textual Poaching," *Critical Studies in Mass Communication* 5, no. 2 (1988): 85–107.

34. https://www.deviantart.com/.

35. See https://www.deviantart.com/search?q=adventuretime.

36. For more on this topic, see https://fanlore.org/wiki/Fanart/.

37. Paul Booth, *Playing Fans: Negotiating Fandom and Media in the Digital Age* (Iowa City: University of Iowa Press, 2015), 162.

38. Lamerichs, *Productive Fandom*, 202.

39. Theresa M. Winge, *Costuming Cosplay: Dressing the Imagination* (London, UK: Bloomsbury Visual Arts, 2019), 2–3.

40. Booth, *Playing Fans*, 163.

41. Nicolle Lamerichs, *Productive Fandom: Intermediality and Affective Reception in Fan Cultures* (Amsterdam, Netherlands: Amsterdam University Press, 2018), 237; Nicolle Lamerichs, "Stranger than Fiction: Fan Identity in Cosplay," *Transformative Works and Cultures*, no. 7 (2011), https://doi.org/10.3983/twc.2011.0246.

42. Lamerichs, *Productive Fandom*, 237; Lamerichs, "Stranger Than Fiction."

43. Lamerichs, *Productive Fandom*, 203.

44. These are somewhat blanket statements. Fanart can have materiality (e.g., paint on canvas). Likewise, cosplay can also be digital (e.g., Booth, *Playing Fans*, 150–72).

45. Sophie, personal communication, February 18, 2020.

46. Novalee Cosplay [pseud.], personal communication, July 28, 2019.

47. Olson, "Interview: Olivia Olson."

48. For two early discussions, see Bacon-Smith, *Enterprising Women*, 175–78; Jenkins, *Textual Poachers*, 228–54.

49. For a comprehensive overview of fancams, see https://fanlore.org/wiki/Fancam.

50. For an interesting discussion of this evolution, see Bareerah Sayed, "Remember when they were just called AMVs/MMVs and not goddamn fancams" [thread], Twitter, 2020, https://twitter.com/S_Bareerah/status/1264004838943227913.

51. Foeyia [pseud.], personal communication, May 27, 2021.

52. Foeyia.

53. Bee [pseud.], personal communication, May 27, 2021.

54. Jason Mittell, *Complex TV: The Poetics of Contemporary Television Storytelling* (New York: NYU Press, 2015), 314.

55. Mittell, 316.

56. OOM-32, "Are the Simon and marcy comic series good?" [comment], Reddit, 2019, https://www.reddit.com/comments/dky1qs/_/f4kqct4. This epithet echoes Jason Mittell's claim that fan documentation is alluring because it offers one "mastery" over a media object's fictional world. Mittell, 314.

57. See http://atchronology.com/.

58. Jagm, personal communication, January 29, 2020.

59. See https://www.youtube.com/watch?v=oiLdWXLXDeA.

60. Jenkins, *Textual Poachers*, 86.

61. For more on this topic, see https://fanlore.org/wiki/Review/.

62. Myself included.

63. Jenkins, *Textual Poachers*, 97.

64. Headcanon is the fannish term for "a private and personal mini-story created by a fan for their favorite series, usually focusing on beloved characters. A key element of [headcanon] is that it . . . fills in the gaps, but doesn't contradict the established storyline." Emily

Lauer and Balaka Basu, *The Harry Potter Generation: Essays on Growing Up with the Series* (Jefferson, NC: McFarland, 2019), 114.

65. Uncivilized Elk [pseud.], personal communication, March 23, 2019.
66. Uncivilized Elk.
67. Eric Stone, personal communication, January 18, 2020.
68. Stone.
69. See https://adventuretime.fandom.com.
70. Despite similar features, Fandom and Wikipedia.org are separate organizations.
71. For more on Fandom/Wikia, see https://fanlore.org/wiki/Wikia.
72. Tavis Lam, personal communication, June 25, 2019.
73. Jason Mittell, "Wikis and Participatory Fandom," in *The Participatory Cultures Handbook*, edited by Aaron Delwiche and Jennifer Jacobs Henderson (New York: Routledge, 2013), 38, 40. The ban on original content is not universal, however; see Mittell, 41.
74. Jason Mittell, "Sites of Participation: Wiki Fandom and the Case of Lostpedia," *Transformative Works and Cultures*, no. 3 (2009), https://doi.org/10.3983/twc.2009.0118. https://journal.transformativeworks.org/index.php/twc/article/view/118/117.
75. See http://supernaturalwiki.com/Category:Fandom.
76. Creampuff [pseud.], personal communication, May 23, 2021.
77. See https://adventuretime.fandom.com/wiki/User_blog:Creampuff_the_Baked_Good/2021_Music_Hole_Awards.
78. See https://adventuretime.fandom.com/wiki/Special:Statistics and https://adventuretime.fandom.com/wiki/Special:ListUsers.
79. See https://fanlore.org/wiki/Twitter.
80. For a related discussion, see Annemarie Navar-Gill, "From Strategic Retweets to Group Hangs: Writers' Room Twitter Accounts and the Productive Ecosystem of TV Social Media Fans," *Television & New Media* 19, no. 5 (2018): 415–30.
81. Promotional illustrations (often referred to as "episode promos," or simply "promos") were drawings mocked up, usually by storyboard artists, to promote an upcoming episode, thereby allowing them to "personally connect with fans" while also "reinforc[ing] the sense of authorship that storyboard artists enjoy on board-drive shows." McDonnell, *The Art of Ooo*, 346. Rebecca Sugar popularized this practice when she uploaded to her Posterous account a drawing that promoted "It Came from the Nightosphere" on October 7, 2010.
82. Including Natasha Allegri, Ian Jones-Quartey, Jesse Moynihan, Adam Muto, Andy Ristaino, Phil Rynda, David C. Smith, and Pendleton Ward.
83. Katie Elson Anderson, "Ask Me Anything: What Is Reddit?" *Library Hi Tech News* 32, no. 5 (2015): 9, https://doi.org/doi:10.1108/LHTN-03-2015-0018.
84. Anderson, 8.
85. Alex Leavitt and John J. Robinson, "Upvote My News: The Practices of Peer Information Aggregation for Breaking News on Reddit.Com," *Proceedings of the ACM on Human-Computer Interaction* 1, no. CSCW (2017): 5.
86. Janko Roettgers, "Reddit Ends 2019 with 430 Million Monthly Active Users," *Variety*, 2019, https://variety.com/2019/digital/news/reddit-430-million-mau-1203423360/.
87. See http://redditmetrics.com/r/adventuretime#disqus_thread.
88. See https://www.reddit.com/r/adventuretime/top/?t=all.
89. Mordecai626 [pseud.], personal communication, February 11, 2020.

90. Uncivilized Elk, personal communication, March 23, 2019.

91. See https://subredditstats.com/r/adventuretime/.

92. Dale Beran, *It Came from Something Awful* (New York: All Points Books, 2019), 177; Louisa Ellen Stein, "Tumblr Fan Aesthetics," in *The Routledge Companion to Media Fandom*, edited by Melissa A. Click and Suzanne Scott (New York: Routledge, 2017), 86–87.

93. Beran, *It Came from Something Awful*, 177–79; Melanie E. S. Kohnen, "Tumblr Pedagogies," in *A Companion to Media Fandom and Fan Studies*, edited by Paul Booth (Hoboken, NJ: Wiley Blackwell, 2018), 351–67.

94. Stein, "Tumblr Fan Aesthetics," 87.

95. Beran, *It Came from Something Awful*, 177.

96. Accessible at http://kingofooo.tumblr.com.

97. Cole Stryker, *Epic Win for Anonymous: How 4chan's Army Conquered the Web* (New York: Overlook, 2011).

98. Beran, *It Came from Something Awful*; Mike Wendling, *Alt-Right* (London, UK: Pluto, 2018).

99. Dillon Ludemann, "/pol/emics: Ambiguity, Scales, and Digital Discourse on 4chan," *Discourse, Context & Media* 24 (2018/08/01/ 2018): 92.

100. Mordecai626 [pseud.], personal communication, February 11, 2020.

101. "SJW" is short for "social justice warrior." It is a pejorative term for activists interested in promoting equity in regard to race, sex(uality), gender, and ability.

102. A slang abbreviation for "new *Adventure Time*," generally referring to episodes after Seasons 2 or 4 (depending on when the user of the term believed that the show "jumped the shark").

103. Despite the show having teased the ship for some time. See http://atchronology.com/bubbline.html.

104. The Lich [pseud.], personal communication, July 25, 2019.

105. Paul Booth, *Digital Fandom 2.0* (New York: Peter Lang, 2016), 114, 29.

106. Jake Suit [pseud.], personal communication, February 9, 2020.

107. The Lich, personal communication, July 25, 2019.

108. Fernando López, personal communication, February 9, 2020.

109. The Lich, personal communication, July 25, 2019.

110. Andy Ristaino, personal communication, February 17, 2014.

111. Sophie, personal communication, February 18, 2020.

INDEX

Abadeer, Hunson, 37, 41, 80, 128, 168, 195, 222
Abadeer, Marceline. *See* Marceline the Vampire Queen
Adobe Flash, 104, 183, 189
Adventures of Dr. McNinja. *See* Hastings, Christopher
Adventure Time: comic series, 232–39; movie, 139–41, 250; Wiki, 10, 259, 260, 263–64, 266
Adventure Time Reviewed, 262
Adventure Time video game adaptations: *Explore the Dungeon Because I Don't Know!*, 242–45; *Finn & Jake Investigations*, 246–48; *Hey Ice King! Why'd You Steal Our Garbage?!!*, 239–44; *Pirates of the Enchiridion*, 248–50; *The Secret of the Nameless Kingdom*, 244–46
Aeneid (Virgil), 163
Aladdin (1992), 207, 211
Alden, Sam, 71, 149, 156–58, 167–68
Allegri, Natasha, 46, 60, 92, 102, 207, 270
alternate universe. *See* fanfiction
alt-right, 269
Alzheimer's disease, 68
AMO, 55
Ampersand, Warren. *See* Jake the Dog
Annie Awards, 6, 110, 150, 183, 188
Anonymous, 269
AO3. *See* Archive of Our Own
Archie comics, 43
Archive of Our Own, 254
Archive.org, 10
Arrested Development, 27

Artemis, 80
Ask.fm, 10, 266
Atari, 174
AT Chronology, 255, 260
Autodesk Maya, 175

Ballard, Derek, 39, 149
Baman Piderman, 189, 191
Bamford, Maria, 81
Banker, Mark, 123
Basichis, Casey James, 199–202, 203–5, 209, 217
Baxter, James, 128, 178–80, 275
Bayeux Tapestry, 251
Beauty and the Beast (1991), 178
Billy the Hero, 74, 77–78
Bix Pix Entertainment, 186
Blade Mistress, 86, 206
BMO, 6, 20, 44, 53–58, 84, 134, 152, 163, 170–71, 174, 185–86, 191, 200, 237, 238, 249; and gender, 56–58; origin of, 55–56; voice of, 54, 82, 117, 206, 220. *See also* Yang, Niki
Bob's Burgers, 27–28
Bob-Waksberg, Raphael, 275
BoJack Horseman, 275
bomb scheduling, 151, 160, 167
Boom! Comics, 10, 232–38
Booth, Paul, 256–57, 271
Borderlands 2, 158
Breezy, 158
Brewster, Paget, 28
Bronwyn. *See* Jake the Dog

Bubblegum. *See* Princess Bubblegum
Bubbline, 43–51, 131, 167, 227, 229, 252
Bueno the Bear, 16–17, 199
Buffy the Vampire Slayer, 31, 77, 276
Bugs Bunny, 29
Burbank, 103, 116, 138, 157, 179, 184
Burch, Ashly, 156, 158, 163–64
Buscarino, Jackie, 88, 126
Butler, Judith, 57, 257

Cake the Cat. *See* Fionna and Cake universe
CalArts, 17, 64, 86, 106–11, 116–18, 127, 135, 174, 178, 185, 199
California Institute of the Arts. *See* CalArts
Campbell, Minerva, 21–22, 165
Camp Lazlo, 104
Campos, Alex, 103
Candy Elemental. *See* elemental magic
Candy Kingdom, 6, 15, 22, 30, 35, 69, 74, 81, 88, 166, 244, 249
Cannon, Kevin, 238
Canyon (character), 77
Capcom, 241
Carey, Mariah, 39
Cartoon Network, 6, 17–18, 26, 31–32, 47, 49, 51, 64, 89, 101, 111–20, 123, 130–35, 137, 139, 141, 151–70, 177–86, 189, 192, 195, 199, 202, 205, 219–26, 237–39, 242–50, 263
Cash, Nate, 135
Castuera, Ako, 77, 83, 101, 126–27, 146, 155, 156, 175
CBS, 3, 28
Charlie. *See* Jake the Dog
Choi, Eunyoung, 182
Choose Your Own Adventure book series, 234
Cicierega, Neil, 251
Clarence, 135, 189
Climax Studios, 248
Clockwork Orange, A (1962), 125
/co/. *See* 4chan
Comedy Central, 26, 81
Comic-Con, 17, 44, 77, 105, 118, 149, 170–72, 194, 234, 250–58
Contra 4, 242
Conversation Parade, 26, 264

Cory, Robertryan, 31, 65
Cosmic Owl, 89
cosplay, 40, 93, 147, 255–58, 267, 274
Crews, Kelly, 130
Criminal Minds, 28
Crowley, Aleister, 84, 153
Cthulhu, 80
Czemiel, Grzegorz, 8–9

Daly, Andrew, 81
Dawson, Delilah S., 238
Day, Felicia, 77
Dead Head Fred, 246
Death (character), 74, 77, 89, 90, 230
DeForge, Michael, 99
DeLisle, Grey, 91
del Toro, Guillermo, 72
DeviantArt, 256
Diablo, 242
DiCicco, Jessica, 61–63, 132, 218
DiMaggio, John, 25–26, 54, 110, 210
Dinosaur Comics. *See* North, Ryan
Disasterpiece. *See* Vreeland, Richard
Distant Lands specials. *See* production of Adventure Time
Dixon, Ivan, 193
Doug, 3
Dr. Gross, 161
Dr. Katz, Professional Therapist, 191
D3 Publisher, 241, 244
Dungeons & Dragons (D&D), 24, 72, 105–6, 112, 119, 235

Eagle, Open Mike, 71, 264
Earl of Lemongrab, 68–71, 84, 134, 136, 146
Eat Lead: The Return of Matt Hazard, 246
Eisner Awards, 235
elemental magic, 30, 34, 59, 60, 62, 66, 73, 165
Elements (*Adventure Time* miniseries), 162–66, 183, 222
Elise, 171
Ellis, Dave, 246–48
Emmy Award, 6, 62, 118, 124, 126, 139, 143, 149, 150, 151, 188, 190, 191, 229, 230
Enchiridion (*Adventure Time*), 47, 56, 136

Escher, M. C., 114
Evergreen, Urgence, 66, 73, 79
Evil (musician), 222–23
exquisite corpse, 98
External World, The (2010), 175, 177
Ezekiel (book and prophet), 74, 90
Ezzy, Hayden, 78, 161

Fairly OddParents, The, 102, 108
Falk, Graham, 137, 167
fanart, 254–56
fancams, 258–59
fan comics. *See* fanart
fan documentation, 259–61
fanfiction, 41, 91–92, 252–54
Ferguson, David, 149, 183–85
Fern, 78–79, 161, 165
Ferrer, Miguel, 89
Fez, 188
Finn the Human, 6–7, 10, 15–24, 37, 40, 43–44, 46, 48, 53, 55–56, 58–68, 70, 74–75, 77–82, 85–86, 88, 90, 111–12, 120–21, 126, 128–29, 131–41, 145–56, 160–77, 184, 186–90, 193, 237–38, 240–41, 244, 249, 252–59, 270; backstory, 18–24, 67, 148, 152; death and reincarnation of, 22–24, 146, 172, 236; and his relationship with Jake, 15–24, 29, 172, 206; and music, 204, 206–10, 214–18, 220–21, 224; origin of, 16–18, 108, 110; relationship with Princess Bubblegum, 18, 22–23, 30–31, 60, 79, 120, 129, 131, 146; voice of, 17–18, 110. *See also* Campbell, Minerva; Jake the Dog; Jermaine the Dog; Joshua the Dog; Margaret the Dog; Mertens, Martin
Fionna and Cake universe, 91–93, 127, 139, 145, 157, 166, 167, 173, 207, 212–13
Fionna the Human. *See* Fionna and Cake universe
fire elemental. *See* elemental magic; Flame Princess
Flame Princess, 6, 18–19, 35, 60–63, 132, 133, 146, 152, 160–61, 214, 218, 220, 253, 255, 270
Fleischer, Max, 102, 116
Flores, Madéleine, 149
Flying Lotus (Steven Ellison), 177
Football (persona). *See* BMO

Formspring, 10, 266
4chan, 150, 152, 213, 263, 269–71
Frederator, 17, 45–46, 108–13, 116–17, 119, 183, 203, 205, 260, 276
Futurama, 26

Game Boy, 53, 188
Game of Thrones, 69
Garfield and Friends, 3
Garfunkel and Oates, 150
Gauntlet, 242
Generation Z. *See* zoomers
Ghostshrimp, 114–15, 127, 142, 155, 213
Gilhwan, Kim, 28, 212–13
Glob, 80, 82, 89–90, 136
Glover, Donald, 92
god. *See* Glob
Goffman, Erving, 57
GOLB (character), 75–76, 83, 91, 167, 169
Goliad, 35
Gone Home, 135
Graham, Brandon, 99
grass curse. *See* Fern
Gravity Falls, 27
Gray, Rae, 28
graybles, 134–35, 137, 145
Green Knight. *See* Fern
Grob Gob Glob Grod. *See* Glob
Grof, Betty, 66, 76–77, 91, 164, 228
Grossman, Lev, 68
Gunter (the dinosaur), 66
Gunter (the penguin), 79–80
Guo, Polly, 99, 220–22

HALF SHY. *See* Havey, Karen
Han, Bonghui, 104
Hanawalt, Lisa, 175
Harris, Neil Patrick, 207
Harry Potter book series (1997–2007), 173
Harvey Awards, 236
Havey, Karen, 227–29
Hastings, Christopher, 236–39
Hellboy film series (2004–19), 72
Herpich, Tom, 22, 27, 45, 55, 68–71, 74, 84, 89, 98–104, 123, 125–28, 131, 133, 135, 138, 140, 145, 149, 153–55, 162, 167, 175, 207, 216

Hertzfeldt, Don, 194
Hey Arnold, 3
Hitchcock, Alfred, 38, 276
Home Movies, 191
Hulett, Tomm, 242–45
Hunchback of Notre Dame, The (1996), 178
Hunter, Derek, 103
Huntress Wizard, 80–81, 253

ice elemental. *See* elemental magic
Ice King, 4, 6, 7, 14, 31, 41, 64–68, 72, 79, 80, 84, 91, 122, 134, 152, 154–55, 164, 168, 176, 184, 210–12, 221, 235, 241, 254; backstory, 66–68, 76–77, 125, 131, 136–37, 145; origin of, 17, 64, 67, 108, 110; voice of, 64–65. *See also* Kenny, Tom
Ice Queen. *See* Fionna and Cake universe
in-between animation, 104, 116
Islands (*Adventure Time* miniseries), 20, 21, 162–67, 183, 191
It Follows (2014), 188
Ito, Elizabeth, 101, 116–18

Jackson, Marc Evan, 28
Jacobs, Gillian, 83
Jake Jr. *See* Jake the Dog
Jake the Dog, 6, 7, 10, 24–29, 30, 31, 34, 37, 40, 44, 48, 53, 55, 56, 58, 60, 64, 66–68, 74, 77, 78, 82, 84–91, 98, 99, 110–12, 120, 121, 126, 128–40, 145, 147, 149, 156, 161–77, 184–90, 201, 204–10, 215, 220, 222, 224, 232, 237, 238, 241, 244–49, 254, 263, 272; and his family, 26–28, 137, 145, 168; and his relationship with Finn, 15–24, 29, 172, 206; origin of, 17, 110–12; voice of, 25–26. *See also* DiMaggio, John
Jenkins, Henry, 252, 261, 265, 271
Jennings, Nick, 103, 114
Jermaine the Dog, 20, 26
Jesus Christ, 90
Jiang, Jacky Ke, 174–75
Jimenez, Sean, 116
Jodorowsky, Alexandro, 89, 153
Jones, Amanda, 230–31
Joshua the Dog, 20, 26, 27, 143, 168, 207, 246
Journey, 174

KaBOOM!. *See* Boom! Comics
Kara. *See* Strong, Susan
Kassir, John, 64
kawaii culture, 9
Kenny, Tom, 64–65, 82, 169–70, 214
Kerr, Hui-Ying, 9
key poses, 104, 179
Kick-Heart (2013), 182
Kiefer, Tim, 10, 104, 199–202, 209, 217, 218, 220, 224
Kim, Derek Kirk, 102
Kim, Seo, 143–44, 167, 189, 220
Kim Kil Whan. *See* Jake the Dog
Kim Possible, 104
King of Mars. *See* Lincoln, Abraham (character)
King of Ooo, 35–36, 81
King of Ooo blog. *See* Tumblr
Knetzger, Laura, 100–101
Konami, 242
K-pop, 258–59

Lady Rainicorn, 27, 54, 82
Lamb, Braden, 234–39
Lamerichs, Nicolle, 256–57
Land of Ooo, 6–7, 21, 26, 34, 56, 59, 115, 123, 129, 132, 134, 135, 146, 163–64, 215
Land of Ooo forums, 271–74
Lee, Roy, 250
Lee, Sandra, 103–4, 116
Legend of Zelda, The, 31, 65, 241–42, 244–46, 248
Lego Movie, The (2014), 250
Leichliter, Larry, 102, 114, 115
Leong, Sloane, 99, 149
Lepore, Kirsten, 185–89
Lewis, Jerry, 144
Lewis, Minty, 182
Lich, 6, 29, 71–75, 77–78, 89, 129, 136, 145, 153, 165, 234
Life Is Strange, 158
Lilo & Stitch: The Series, 104
Lincoln, Abraham (character), 4, 52, 90–91, 110, 112, 136
Little, Steve, 84, 123, 211
Little Mermaid, The (1989), 140

Little Orbit, 246–47
Livingston, Polly Lou, 86–87
LOO.com. *See* Land of Ooo forums
Lord Monochromicorn. *See* Fionna and Cake universe
Lord of the Rings, The (2001–3), 276
Louie, 151
Love Actually (2003), 39
Lovecraft, H. P., 80
LSP. *See* Lumpy Space Princess
Lumpy Space Prince. *See* Fionna and Cake universe
Lumpy Space Princess, 6, 28, 47, 58–60, 92, 120, 150, 164, 186

Machiavelli, 52
Macintosh Classic II, 53
Macy's Day Parade, 6, 147
Magic Man, 76, 82–84, 90, 135–36, 153
Marceline the Vampire Queen, 4, 6, 7, 37–52, 92, 98, 122, 145, 152, 160, 186, 191, 249, 258, 272; backstory, 40–43, 45, 67–68, 128–29, 131, 136–37, 154–56; and Ice King, 41, 67–68, 136–37; relationship with Princess Bubblegum, 30–31, 43–52, 125, 170–71, 207–8, 221–23, 227, 229, 252–53, 259, 270; songs sung by, 124–25, 201–2, 205, 207–9, 211–12, 214, 218–23, 226–31; voice of, 38–39, 47. *See also* Abadeer, Hunson; Bubbline; Elise; Olson, Olivia
Margaret the Dog, 20, 26, 168
Margles, 83
Mars, 4, 80, 83, 90, 135–36
Marshall Lee. *See* Fionna and Cake universe
Marvelous Misadventures of Flapjack, The, 18, 86, 111, 114, 115, 118
"Mathematical!" series, 45–46
Matrix, The (1999–2021), 56
McCormick, Joey, 238
McCreery, Conor, 238
McGinty, Ian, 237–39
McHale, Patrick, 21–22, 53, 58, 67, 72, 86, 107–8, 111–18, 123, 127–28, 130, 140, 144, 154–55, 168, 193, 204, 210–11, 225
McKay, Chris, 250
McKeon, Tim, 64

McLaurin, Luther, 116
Meatballs (1979), 25
Melamed, Fred, 87
Mertens, Martin, 19–22, 85, 148, 152
millennials, 9
Milonakis, Andy, 84
Mind Game (2004), 181
Minecraft, 192–94
Mintz, Dan, 28
Mirzaian, Armen, 116
Moe, John, 158, 264
Mojang, 192–93
Monlongo, Jorge, 238
Montagna, James, 239–41, 243
Moss, Paige, 31
Moynihan, Jesse, 23, 69–71, 77, 80–81, 83–84, 89, 98–100, 123, 126–27, 131, 133, 135, 140, 146, 149, 151, 153–59, 209–10, 216, 219, 270, 272
Moynihan, Justin, 216–17
Mukai, Kris, 101
Murphy, Phil, 237
Murray, Bill, 25
Mushroom War, 7, 41, 68, 74, 76, 131, 137, 162, 218
music of *Adventure Time*, 199–231; individual songs, 202–30; soundtrack composers, 104, 199–202, 230–31. *See also* Basichis, Casey James; Evil (musician); Harvey, Karen; Jones, Amanda; Kiefer, Tim; Sugar, Rebecca; Zuzu
Muto, Adam, 4–5, 58, 60, 138, 141, 166, 250, 266; artistic partnership with Rebecca Sugar, 45–46, 55, 86, 93, 124, 208, 213, 219–21; and *Distant Lands*, 170–73; in early seasons, 110–18, 123–24, 128, 135, 205; mythology (fiction), 4, 51, 79, 83, 85, 90, 120, 127, 129, 131–32, 137, 146, 149, 152, 161, 163, 268; as showrunner, 49, 99, 103, 141–44, 146, 149, 154–57, 162–63, 167, 184–94, 222–30, 270, 272; time at CalArts, 107–10

Nanjiani, Kumail, 89
Neely, Brad, 79
NEPTR, 134, 220
Ngai, Sianne, 8
Nickelodeon, 3, 17, 31, 64, 105, 108, 110–11, 114, 116, 240

Nicktoons Network, 17, 31, 110–11, 263
9/11 terrorist attacks, 36
Nintendo Game Boy, 53, 240–42, 247–49
noir films, 56
North, Ryan, 233–36, 237–39
North East School of the Arts, 106
Nyström, Hanna K., 49, 51, 155, 156–57, 158, 167–68, 171, 193, 219

off-model animation, 103, 127
Olson, Martin, 38, 41, 128
Olson, Olivia, 38–39, 41, 43, 47, 51, 128, 166, 202, 205–6, 209, 214, 258
OReilly, David, 137, 175–78
Orgalorg, 80, 140, 270. *See also* Gunter
Osborne, Kent, 69, 77, 98–99, 102, 118–19, 123, 128, 130–31, 133, 137, 142–44, 149, 157–58, 163–64, 166, 169, 186, 206, 213
outlining. *See* production of *Adventure Time*
Outright Games, 249
Over the Garden Wall, 154

Page, Skyler, 22, 135
Paroline, Shelli, 234–39
Partridge, Lyle, 155
PATRIOT Act, 36
PBS Idea Channel, 8
Peabody Award, 6, 97, 150–51
Pearson, Luke, 99, 155
Pendarvis, Jack, 22, 79, 81, 144, 163–64, 171
Pen the Human. *See* Finn the Human
Peppermint Butler, 48, 84–85, 172–73
performativity, 57, 257
Perlman, Ron, 72–73
Petrikov, Simon. *See* Ice King
Phineas and Ferb, 38, 151
Picard, Jean-Luc, 18
Ping Pong, 181
pitch bible, 25, 37, 40, 43, 72
Pott, Julia, 164, 194
Powerpuff Girls, The, 113, 170
Prince Gumball. *See* Fionna and Cake universe
Princess Bubblegum, 4, 6, 7, 15, 17, 30–37, 43–52, 64, 74, 81, 91, 98, 108, 110–11, 122, 156, 158, 176–77, 211, 215, 217, 220, 258, 270; backstory, 31, 35–37, 45, 161, 166–69, 244; family, creations, and subjects of, 68–71, 82, 84, 87–88; relationship with Finn, 18, 22–23, 30–31, 60, 79, 120, 129, 131, 146; relationship with Marceline, 30–31, 43–52, 125, 170–71, 207–8, 221–23, 227, 229, 252–53, 259, 270; and scientism, 33–35; voice of, 31–33. *See also* Bubbline; Earl of Lemongrab; Uncle Gumbald
Princess Diana, 59
Princess Peach, 31
Princess Zelda, 31
Prismo, 74, 88–89, 274
production of *Adventure Time*, 97–173; *Distant Lands* specials, 170–73; final season, 166–67; original Season 7, 153–59; original Season 8, 161–64; pilot, 108–11; production process, 97–104; reordering of seasons, 159, 165; Season 1, 111–20; Season 2, 123–28; Season 3, 130–31; Season 4, 133–35; Season 5, 137–44; Season 6, 148–49
Psycho (1960), 38

/r/adventuretime. *See* Reddit
Rainicorn. *See* Lady Rainicorn
Random! Cartoons, 108, 111
Reddit, 266–68
Rejected (2000), 194
Ren & Stimpy Show, The, 104
Richardson, Kevin Michael, 186
Rick and Morty, 70
Ristaino, Andy, 80, 100–101, 123, 143–44, 156, 214–15, 218, 272
Robertson, Paul, 193
Roiland, Justin, 70
Root, Stephen, 20
Rough Draft Studios, 104
Rugnetta, Mike, 8
Rugrats, 3, 116
"Rule 34," 270
"Rule 63," 92
"Rumble Jaw," 170–71. *See also* production of *Adventure Time: Distant Lands* specials
Rynda, Phil, 17, 31, 38, 72, 102, 115–16, 124, 125, 174

SAEROM, 28, 103–4
Salaff, Andres, 31, 220–21
Samurai Jack, 170
Science SARU, 182–83, 217
Schaal, Kristen, 27, 28
School of Visual Arts, 115, 123–24, 125, 208
Sennwald, Aleks, 156–58, 167, 168
Serafinowicz, Peter, 92
Shada, Jeremy, 16–18, 207, 210
Shada, Zack, 16–18, 110
Shantae, 239
Shawkat, Alia, 27
She-Ra and the Princesses of Power, 276
Shermy and Beth, 56, 85
shipping, 43–52, 252–53, 268
Shoko. *See* Finn the Human
Silent Hill, 242
Simpsons, The, 76, 104–5, 134, 193
Slate, Jenny, 81
slime elemental. *See* elemental magic
Small-Butera, Lindsay and Alex, 189–91
Snyder, Tom, 191
songs. *See* music
Sparrow, Joe, 193
Spirit, Stallion of the Cimarron (2002), 178
SpongeBob SquarePants, 240
Squigglevision, 191
Stakes (*Adventure Time* miniseries), 36, 41–42, 48, 81, 154–57, 160–62, 164, 166, 183, 214, 219–20, 260, 270
Star Trek: The Next Generation, 18, 145; *First Contact*, 55
Sterling, Zachary, 237, 239
Stevenson, ND, 276
Steven Universe, 44, 86, 123, 139, 213, 270, 275
Stewart, Patrick, 18
storyboard process. *See* production of *Adventure Time*
St. Pim, Patience, 163
Street Fighter II, 241
Strong, Susan, 20–21, 85–86, 126, 132, 161, 163, 206

Sugar, Rebecca, 40, 44–45, 50–51, 55, 60–61, 67–68, 77, 86, 93, 100, 123–25, 130–31, 136, 139, 145, 155–56, 229, 270, 275; as songwriter, 201, 205–8, 210–13, 215, 219–20, 223–25
sword and sorcery genre, 78
Syvertsson, Anna, 193

Tales from the Crypt, 64
Tamaki, Jillian, 99, 149
Tamaki, Mariko, 238–39
Teenage Mutant Ninja Turtles, 170
Teen Titans, 32
Temple University, 127
TenNapel, Doug, 90–91
Terminator (character), 56
THQ, 240
Tolkien, J. R. R., 106
Toon Boom Harmony, 104
transhumanism, 55, 162
Trump, Donald, 166
Tumblr, 4, 194, 268–69
T.V. *See* Jake the Dog
TV Tropes, 181
Twist, Basil, 194–95
Twitter, 265–66

UncivilizedElk, 261–62, 267
Uncle Gumbald, 31, 79, 87–88, 166–69

van Orman, Thurop, 118, 123
Vicious Cycle Software, 246
Viola. *See* Jake the Dog
Vreeland, Richard, 188

Walch, Hynden, 31–33, 51, 89, 211
Walsh, M. Emmet, 89
Ward, Bettie, 31, 87, 105
Ward, Pendleton, 5, 15–18, 22–25, 31, 37–39, 43, 46, 55, 58–59, 64, 70, 72, 78, 82–87, 91–103, 105–18, 123–28, 130–40, 156–58, 170, 175, 177, 186, 193, 195, 233, 239, 240–44, 250, 255, 276; as a voice actor, 59–60, 120; early life, 105–6; early production of *Adventure Time*, 108–18; friendships, 86, 107–8, 116–18, 127–28, 141–42, 199; and music, 200–225;

retirement, 141–43; time at CalArts, 16–17, 64, 86, 106–11, 116–18, 127, 178–79
Watters, Shannon, 232, 234
Wayforward, 239–45
Whitney, Leopard, 236, 238
wiki. See *Adventure Time* Wiki
Williams, Merriwether, 114
Wolfhard, Steve, 27–28, 55–56, 71, 81, 85, 137–39, 145, 149, 153, 167, 216
Won, Dongkun, 104

Xayaphone, Somvilay, 86, 123, 127–28, 135, 144, 146, 167, 189

X-Files, The, 252
Xin, Michelle, 181–82

Yang, Niki, 54, 58, 82, 116–17, 206, 220
Yellow Submarine (the Beatles), 26
Youn, Bert, 82, 116–17, 127, 135
YouTube, 62, 64, 110, 115, 194, 206, 211, 213–14, 223, 233, 258, 260–61, 267
Yuasa, Masaaki, 149, 180–83, 217

Zeus, 91
zoomers, 9
Zuzu, 226–27, 229

ABOUT THE AUTHOR

Paul A. Thomas is a library specialist at the University of Kansas who holds a PhD in library and information management from Emporia State University. He is the author of *Inside Wikipedia* (Rowman & Littlefield, 2022) and *I Wanna Wrock!* (McFarland, 2018). Currently, he is preparing an edited volume about *Adventure Time* for McFarland.

www.ingramcontent.com/pod-product-compliance
Lightning Source LLC
Chambersburg PA
CBHW022050160426
43198CB00008B/177